THE USES OF SCRIPT AND PRINT,
1300–1700

This volume builds upon the growing interest in the connections between culture and communication in medieval and early modern Europe. Focusing on the example of England, it critically reconsiders the scholarly paradigm of the shift from script to print, tracing commonplaces about the enlightening power of print to their origins in Reformation polemic. Exploring how the pen and the press were used in the spheres of religion, law, scholarship and politics, the essays examine the possibilities and the limitations of these media as vehicles of information and meaning. They discuss scribal activity both before and after the advent of printing, illuminating its role in recording and transmitting controversial, literary, antiquarian and utilitarian texts. They also investigate script and print in relation to the spoken word, emphasising the constant interaction and symbiosis of the oral, written and typographical. As a whole, the collection seeks to promote dialogue between scholars on either side of the traditional disciplinary divide; to refine the boundaries between the cultures of speech, manuscript and print; and to reassess the historiographical fissures which they have come to represent.

JULIA CRICK and ALEXANDRA WALSHAM are Senior Lecturers in History, University of Exeter.

THE USES OF SCRIPT AND PRINT, 1300–1700

EDITED BY

JULIA CRICK AND ALEXANDRA WALSHAM

University of Exeter

CAMBRIDGE
UNIVERSITY PRESS

PUBLISHED BY THE PRESS SYNDICATE OF THE UNIVERSITY OF CAMBRIDGE
The Pitt Building, Trumpington Street, Cambridge, United Kingdom

CAMBRIDGE UNIVERSITY PRESS
The Edinburgh Building, Cambridge, CB2 2RU, UK
40 West 20th Street, New York, NY 10011–4211, USA
477 Williamstown Road, Port Melbourne, VIC 3207, Australia
Ruiz de Alarcón 13, 28014 Madrid, Spain
Dock House, The Waterfront, Cape Town 8001, South Africa

http://www.cambridge.org

First published 2004

Printed in the United Kingdom at the University Press, Cambridge

Typeface Adobe Garamond 11/12.5 pt.   *System* LATEX 2ε   [TB]

A catalogue record for this book is available from the British Library

ISBN 0 521 81063 9 hardback

Contents

v

Illustrations

Figures

Notes on contributors

MARGARET ASTON is an independent scholar who has published on Lollardy, literacy and images, as well as on topics relating to Reformation iconography and iconoclasm. She was president of the Ecclesiastical History Society in 2000–1, when the theme was 'The Church and the Book'. Her publications include *The Fifteenth Century: The Prospect of Europe* (1968), *Lollards and Reformers: Images and Literacy in Late Medieval Religion* (1984), *England's Iconoclasts* (1988), and *The King's Bedpost* (1993).

JONATHAN BARRY is Senior Lecturer in History and Head of the School of Historical, Political and Sociological Studies at the University of Exeter. He has written extensively on provincial culture in early modern England, especially on Bristol and the south west, and on the politics of print culture. He is currently preparing books on religion in Bristol and witchcraft and demonology in the south west, as well as editing various collections.

ANDREW BUTCHER is Director of the Canterbury Centre for Medieval and Tudor Studies, University of Kent. His teaching and research interests are in pre-modern English cultural history, literatures, and in anthropology, and especially in urban societies. He is co-author of the *Age of Saturn: literature and history in the Canterbury Tales* (1992). His current research and forthcoming publications include work on inheritance and cultural transmission, identity and ethnicity, the visual and material culture of the urban house, and scribal practice and the writing of urban culture.

JAMES G. CLARK is Lecturer in History at the University of Bristol. His research focuses on the English Benedictines, their life and learning in the later Middle Ages. He has written on monastic books, education, and chronicle writing and on the process of the Dissolution itself. He has edited *The Religious Orders in Pre-Reformation England* (2002) and his book, *Monastic Learning in Late Medieval England* is forthcoming.

JULIA CRICK is Senior Lecturer in History at the University of Exeter. Her publications include *The Historia Regum Britannie of Geoffrey of Monmouth III: Summary Catalogue of the Manuscripts* (1989) and *The Historia Regum Britannie of Geoffrey of Monmouth IV: Dissemination and Reception in the Later Middle Ages* (1991), as well as a number of essays on pre-Conquest England, palaeography and the transmission of texts in the later Middle Ages. Her edition of the charters of St Alban's Abbey for the British Academy is forthcoming.

DAVID D'AVRAY is Professor of History at University College London. He is currently working on marriage symbolism's influence on medieval social practice, and on the rationalities of the medieval papacy. His most recent book is *Medieval Marriage Sermons. Mass Communication in a Culture without Print* (2001).

THOMAS S. FREEMAN is Research Editor for the British Academy John Foxe Project and is affiliated with the University of Sheffield. In addition to publishing many essays on Foxe and the *Actes and Monuments*, he has co-edited with Susan Doran *The Myth of Elizabeth* (2003).

ANN HUGHES is Professor of Early Modern History at the University of Keele and the author of *Politics, Society and Civil War Warwickshire 1620–1660* (1987) and *The Causes of the English Civil War* (2nd edition, 1998) as well as many articles and essays on politics and religion in mid-seventeenth-century England. She is completing a book length study of Thomas Edwards's *Gangraena*.

SCOTT MANDELBROTE is Fellow and Director of Studies in History at Peterhouse, Cambridge, and a Fellow of All Souls College, Oxford. He has written *Footprints of the Lion: Isaac Newton at Work* (2001) and (with Jim Bennett) *The Garden, the Ark, the Tower, the Temple: Biblical Metaphors of Knowledge in Early Modern Europe* (1998).

CHRISTOPHER MARSH is Reader in History at Queen's University Belfast. His publications include *The Family of Love in English Society 1550–1630* (1994) and *Popular Religion in Sixteenth-Century England* (1998). He is currently working on the history of popular music in England during the early modern period.

ANTHONY MUSSON is Senior Lecturer in the School of Law at the University of Exeter and Visiting Senior Research Fellow of the Institute of Advanced Legal Studies. His most recent book is *Medieval Law in*

Context: The Growth of Legal Consciousness from Magna Carta to the Peasants' Revolt (2001).

FELICITY RIDDY is Professor of English in the Centre for Medieval Studies at the University of York. She has published extensively on late medieval English literature, including a monograph on Malory, and has edited Middle Scots poetry. Her current research project is on privately-owned urban manuscripts, 1300–1476.

ALEXANDRA WALSHAM is Senior Lecturer in History at the University of Exeter. She is the author of *Church Papists: Catholicism, Conformity and Confessional Polemic in Early Modern England* (1993) and *Providence in Early Modern England* (1999). Her current projects include a survey of tolerance and intolerance in England between 1500 and 1700 and a study of the post-Reformation history of holy wells and healing springs.

Acknowledgements

This volume of essays grew out of a conference on 'The Uses of Script and Print 1300–1700' held at the University of Exeter in April 2000. The editors are grateful to all those who attended, offered papers and participated in the lively discussions which followed the sessions and to those who have expressed interest in this project at various stages. Special thanks are due to Margaret Aston for so readily agreeing to our invitation to write the epilogue to this collection and to our contributors for responding constructively to editorial suggestions and for tolerating delays. Our colleagues at Exeter have offered much encouragement, and we should particularly like to acknowledge the support of Jonathan Barry, Michael Duffy and Sarah Hamilton and the secretarial assistance rendered by Debbie Freeman.

For permission to reproduce items in their collections, we record our gratitude to the British Library, London, and the Bodleian Library, Oxford. The cover illustration is used by permission of the Abbess of Syon Abbey, South Brent, Devon, and courtesy of the University of Exeter Library (Special Collections), where the Syon Abbey library is deposited. We thank Jessica Gardner, Special Collections Librarian at the University of Exeter, for her help in this regard.

At Cambridge University Press, we owe much to William Davies, who offered wise advice and encouragement prior to our formal approach to the Syndics and who has been a model of patience in the intervening years.

Julia Crick and Alexandra Walsham

Abbreviations

BL	British Library, London
Bodl. Lib.	Bodleian Library, Oxford
CHBB 3	L. Hellinga and J. B. Trapp (eds.), *The Cambridge History of the Book in Britain*, vol. III, *1400–1557* (Cambridge, 1999)
CHBB 4	J. Barnard and D. F. McKenzie, with M. Bell (eds.), *The Cambridge History of the Book in Britain*, vol. IV, *1557–1695* (Cambridge, 2002)
CSP Dom.	*Calendar of State Papers Domestic*
CUL	Cambridge University Library
EETS	Early English Text Society
EHR	*English Historical Review*
ESTC	R. C. Alston (ed.), *The Eighteenth Century Short Title Catalogue (ESTC): The British Library Collections* (1993)
HMC	Historical Manuscripts Commission
HJ	*Historical Journal*
JBS	*Journal of British Studies*
JEH	*Journal of Ecclesiastical History*
L&P	J. Gairdner and R. H. Brodie (eds.), *Letters and Papers, Foreign and Domestic, of the Reign of Henry VIII* (1862–1932)
NS	new series
OED	Oxford English Dictionary
OS	old series, original series
P&P	*Past & Present*
PMLA	*Publications of the Modern Language Association of America*
PRO	Public Record Office, London
SCH	Studies in Church History
SP	State Papers
STC	A. W. Pollard and G. R. Redgrave, *A Short-Title Catalogue of Books Printed in England, Scotland, and Ireland and of*

The place of publication is London unless otherwise stated.

Introduction: Script, print, and history

Alexandra Walsham and Julia Crick

When, in 1793, the fugitive French philosophe the Marquis de Condorcet traced his *Outline of an Historical View of the Progress of the Human Mind* through ten ages of history, he placed print in the seventh age, preceded by darkness. For him, the invention of printing marked a critical point in the process by which Western European society escaped the yoke of priestly dogmatism and monkish tyranny and launched from intellectual blindness into the age of Enlightenment.[1] In presenting medieval scribal culture as a symbol of clerical hypocrisy, corruption and dominance, and in linking the advent of the press with the triumph of reason and civilisation over ignorance and barbarity, Condorcet was reproducing a motif over 200 years old. In 1740 Prosper Marchand had likewise heralded printing as 'un riche Présent du Ciel', a conceit given graphic expression in the frontispiece to his book, which depicted the press descending from the heavens and being presented by Minerva and Mercury to Germany, and thence to the nations of Holland, England, Italy and France (Illustration 1).[2] But the myth of print as a providential instrument had its taproot in Reformation polemic. It was a trope which found its most classic articulation in John Foxe's *Actes and Monuments*. For Foxe, as for Martin Luther before him, printing was a 'divine' and 'miraculous' art, a special gift from God which had dispelled the mists of idolatry and superstition and 'heaped upon that proud kingdome', the papacy, 'a double confusion'.[3] The theme was constantly echoed in the following century: by George Hakewill in 1627, who celebrated the role of this 'new kinde of writing' in redeeming books out of their 'bondage' in the libraries of the monasteries, and in 1662 by an anonymous apologist for the printing industry itself, who declared that

---

[1] Marquis de Condorcet, *Outlines of an Historical View of the Progress of the Human Mind* (1795; first publ. in French 1793), esp. pp. 178–85.

[2] Prosper Marchand, *Histoire de l'origine et des premiers progrès de l'imprimerie* (The Hague, 1740), p. 1 and frontispiece.

[3] John Foxe, *Actes and Monuments*, 2 vols. (1583), vol. II, p. 707.

Illustration 1 The press descending from the heavens. Prosper Marchand, *Histoire de l'origine et des premiers progrès de l'imprimerie* (The Hague, 1740), frontispiece.

the pen compared with the press was 'but as a Rush-candle to a Torch' and boasted that by this means 'the Church of Rome hath received such a wound, as she will never be able to cure: for upon its discovery, such a light hath broken forth, that many Kingdoms and Countries that formerly had no other glimpse but what proceeded from her Dark Lanthorn, have hence received so great Illumination, that they finde just occasion to forsake her'.[4]

The concept of a printing revolution, as retrospectively created by early modern writers, has exerted enduring and powerful influence over subsequent historians. In her famous book, *The Printing Press as an Agent of Change* (1979), Elizabeth Eisenstein saw the invention of the mechanical press as the mainspring of a major cultural metamorphosis, as a development which, by bringing standardisation, permanence, and the possibility of mass dissemination, not only facilitated and transformed the Renaissance, Reformation and the Scientific Revolution in turn, but even altered 'the nature of the causal nexus itself'. In surveying the late medieval culture of scribal copying, she emphasised the inherent instability and infidelity of manuscript transmission and portrayed the handwritten text as an early and easy casualty of the introduction of the new technology.[5] For Eisenstein and the generation of scholarship she represented, the boundary between 'script' and 'print' demarcated the barrier between the medieval and early modern eras.

Medievalists stand in uneasy relation to this divide. While acknowledging that printing belongs to the complex of events which have been used to define the Middle Ages from their inception, some have fiercely resisted such cultural partitions, rejecting a 'crude binarism that locates modernity ("us") on one side and premodernity ("them") on the other'.[6]

---

[4] George Hakewill, *An Apologie of the Power and Providence of God in the Government of the World* (Oxford, 1627), book III, p. 257 and pp. 256–9 *passim*. Hakewill was echoing the words of Polydore Vergil, *A Brief Discourse Concerning Printing and Printers* (1662), pp. 22–3.

[5] E. L. Eisenstein, *The Printing Press as an Agent of Change: Communications and Cultural Transformations in Early Modern Europe*, 2 vols. in 1 (Cambridge, 1980 edn), p. 703. For her characterisation of medieval scribal culture, see pp. 10–14. Her work was influenced by M. McLuhan, *The Gutenberg Galaxy: The Making of Typographical Man* (Toronto, 1962). See also the optimistic assessment of the impact of printing in L. Febvre and H.-J. Martin, *The Coming of the Book: The Impact of Printing 1450–1800*, trans. D. Gerard (London and New York, 1976; first publ. Paris 1958).

[6] L. Patterson, 'On the Margin: Postmodernism, Ironic History and Medieval Studies', *Speculum* 65 (1990), 93. See also his 'Critical Historicism and Medieval Studies', in L. Patterson (ed.), *Literary Practice and Social Change in Britain, 1380–1530* (Oxford, 1990), p. 4; D. Aers, 'A Whisper in the Ear of Early Modernists; or, Reflections on Literary Critics Writing the History of the Subject', in D. Aers (ed.), *Culture and History 1350–1600: Essays on English Communities, Identities and Writing* (1992), p. 192; D. Wallace, *Chaucerian Polity: Absolutist Lineages and Associational Forms in England and Italy* (Stanford, 1997), pp. xiv–xvi.

Yet this inherited model of polarity and periodisation still shapes the con-
tours of much academic endeavour. The opposition between the two media
is institutionalised in libraries in which the 'Rare Books' and 'Manuscript'
rooms occupy separate spaces and are frequented by different sets of readers.
Its chronological dimension is perpetuated in the traditional disciplinary
distinction between 'medievalists' and 'early modernists' and reflected in
the lack of dialogue, even the degree of misunderstanding and distrust,
which can divide those working in these respective fields. For if the shift
'from script to print' has long set the agenda for specialists of the sixteenth
and seventeenth centuries, much medieval English historiography over the
past two decades has moved in semi-conscious parallel, respecting the advance traced by Michael Clanchy between 1066 and 1307, 'from memory
to written record'.[7]

In recent years, however, new research by both medievalists and early
modernists has begun to unsettle old assumptions about the nature and
development of communication in the period between 1300 and 1700. The
interfaces between literacy and orality and between the products of the
pen and the press have prompted a wealth of important and stimulating
studies.[8] In the process the ingrained contrast between 'script' and 'print'
has begun to blur and fade, giving way to an emphasis on their lingering co-existence, interaction and symbiosis both before and after 1500. To
change the metaphor, the division between the *terra cognita* of printing
and the obscure, unmapped world of scribal culture now seems to have
almost run its rhetorical course. Building on the burgeoning literature
which has grown up under the rubric of 'the history of the book', this
collection of essays seeks to promote discussion and collaboration between
scholars working on either side of this long-standing divide and to tran-
scend the constraints imposed by conventional periodisation, technical

[7] M. T. Clanchy, *From Memory to Written Record: England 1066–1307*, 2nd edn (Oxford, 1993). S. D.
White, in his review of the second edition, noted Clanchy's indebtedness to the script-print model:
Speculum 77 (1997), 131–3. This has earlier roots: H. J. Chaytor, *From Script to Print: An Introduction
to Medieval Literature* (Cambridge, 1945).
[8] Including G. P. Tyson and S. S. Wagonheim (eds.), *Print and Culture in the Renaissance: Essays on
the Advent of Printing in Europe* (Newark, 1986); A. Grafton and A. Blair (eds.), *The Transmission of
Culture in Early Modern Europe* (Philadelphia, 1990); S. Hindman (ed.), *Printing the Written Word:
The Social History of Books, c.1450–1520* (Ithaca and London, 1991); A. F. Marotti and M. D. Bristol,
Print, Manuscript, and Performance: The Changing Relations of the Media in Early Modern England
(Columbus, OH, 2000). Such themes have also been explored in several festschrifts, containing essays
which are largely bibliographical in character: e.g. R. Beadle and A. J. Piper (eds.), *New Science out
of Old Books: Studies in Manuscripts and Early Printed Books in Honour of A. I. Doyle* (Aldershot,
1995) and A. S. G. Edwards, V. Gillespie and R. Hanna (eds.), *The English Medieval Book: Studies
in Memory of Jeremy Griffiths* (2000). See also *CHBB 3 and 4*. Many of these studies perpetuate the
medieval/early modern division.

specialisation, and confessional historiography. It is concerned to refine the boundaries between the cultures of speech, manuscript and print in England and to investigate the origins and implications of the historical fissures which they have come to represent. It seeks to emphasise that writing and print have overlapping but also separate histories and associations and to demonstrate the ways in which the medium not only encloses but also often encodes and engenders the message. The purpose of this introduction is to provide a backdrop for the twelve essays and the epilogue that follow.

We begin with the observation that some of the most striking challenges to the older paradigm of the printing revolution have come from historians of print themselves. Against the earlier emphasis upon the immutability of print, the late D. F. McKenzie and others have drawn attention to its ephemerality, to the ways in which it facilitated the emergence of a topical literature which was inherently transient. Meanwhile, the work of Roger Chartier has cast doubt on the uniformity which authoritative printed texts are alleged to have been able to create by underlining the diverse and infinite ways in which such objects could be appropriated, used and interpreted by their consumers.[9] More recently, in *The Nature of the Book*, Adrian Johns has persuasively contested the assumption that fixity and fidelity were intrinsic qualities of the products of the mechanical press, arguing instead that these were features which had to be artificially grafted on to them. Printing did not possess preservative power *per se*; it did not protect texts from corruption or guarantee stability, truth or reliability any more than manuscript copying. On the contrary, it often led to the cumulative accretion of error, a point emphasised here in Scott Mandelbrote's discussion of seventeenth-century printed editions of Scripture. To combat this, mechanisms for creating the impression of definitive knowledge and credit had to be manufactured, among which we may number the footnote.[10]

This recognition of the contested and unstable character of printed materials is partly a function of fresh awareness of the role which entrepreneurial printers, compositors and stationers played in determining content, meaning and form. Far from transparent projections of an unmediated authorial

---

[9] D. F. McKenzie, 'Speech-Manuscript-Print', *The Library Chronicle of the University of Texas at Austin*, 20 (1990), 99–100. Roger Chartier has expounded this thesis in a variety of publications: see esp. his *The Cultural Uses of Print in Early Modern France*, trans. L. G. Cochrane (Princeton, 1987); 'General Introduction: Print Culture', in R. Chartier (ed.), *The Culture of Print: Power and the Uses of Print in Early Modern Europe* (Cambridge, 1989), pp. 1–10; 'Texts, Printing, Readings', in L. Hunt (ed.), *The New Cultural History* (Berkeley, 1989), pp. 154–75.

[10] A. Johns, *The Nature of the Book: Print and Knowledge in the Making* (Chicago and London, 1998), pp. 2–6, 30–6, 624–5, and *passim*. A. Grafton, *The Footnote: A Curious History* (1997).

voice, printed books need to be seen as the outcome of a complex negotiation between the commercial instincts of the businessmen who produced
them and the priorities of those who had initially written and composed
them. William Caxton, England's proto-typographer, is a case in point:
combining the functions of editor and publisher, he 'corrected' and altered the text of Chaucer's *Canterbury Tales* in ways which significantly
shaped it.[11] New research is likewise revealing how significantly figures like
John Day contributed to the making of key works like Foxe's 'Book of
Martyrs', while Ian Green's exhaustive survey of Protestant bestsellers provides further evidence of how the strategies employed by shrewd publishers
in their efforts to establish a niche in a rapidly expanding market subtly
distorted and diversified the messages of godly ministers and preachers.[12]
The piracy and plagiarism which were rife in the book trade presented a
chronic threat to the credibility of its products, so much so that as late as
1734 Jean Theophilus Desaguliers announced he would inscribe his name
in each copy of his *Course of Experimental Philosophy* in order to deter
unauthorised versions of this work. Ironically, the only way to ensure the
authenticity of a text was to abandon typography and return to the personal seal of approval which could be bestowed upon it by the more ancient
technology of the pen.[13]

Equally, historians are becoming increasingly conscious of the constraints
upon the printing industry in England. Compared with the highly decen-
tralised culture of print which was the pattern in most Continental countries, its English counterpart was overwhelmingly concentrated in London,
with minor offshoots in the university towns of Oxford and Cambridge.
Not until 1695 did the lifting of restrictions enable provincial presses to
be legally established. Traffic in printed materials, by contrast with scribal
products, thus travelled largely in one direction: from the capital outwards.
Moreover, as Andrew Pettegree has recently stressed, at least for the first century after the invention of printing, England must be regarded as occupying
'the outer ring of a two-speed Europe'. Despite – even, perhaps, because of –
the vast body of scholarship devoted to Caxton, it is not always recognised
that early English print culture was relatively modest in scope, held back
by a variety of structural and economic barriers. One measure of this is

[11] L. Hellinga, 'Manuscripts in the Hands of Printers', in J. B. Trapp (ed.), *Manuscripts in the Fifty Years after the Invention of Printing* (1983), pp. 3–11.
[12] E. Evenden and T. S. Freeman, 'John Foxe, John Day and the Printing of the "Book of Martyrs"', in R. Myers, M. Harris and G. Mandelbrote (eds.), *Lives in Print: Biography and the Book Trade from the Middle Ages to the Twenty-First Century* (2002), pp. 23–54; I. Green, *Print and Protestantism in Early Modern England* (Oxford, 2000), pp. 444, 590 and *passim*.
[13] Cited in Johns, *Nature of the Book*, p. 182.

its slender output of incunables – no more than 3% of the total of 10,000 for Europe as a whole.[14] Neither the monument to English bibliography which is the *STC*, nor the swift growth of the industry in the sixteenth and seventeenth centuries, should blind us to its limitations. The granting of a monopoly to the Stationers' Company in 1557, combined with repeated governmental efforts to regulate the press, placed considerable obstacles in the way of the development of the print trade. While debate continues about the scale and effectiveness of official censorship and internal licensing, it is clear that these mechanisms for control had an inhibiting effect upon printed publication.[15] Although intermittent and spasmodic in character, they certainly persuaded some to adopt silence as the path of discretion and safety. More significantly for the preoccupations of this volume, they also helped to ensure that manuscript retained its vitality as a medium of communication long after the arrival of print.

This has been the theme of a number of important studies by Harold Love, Arthur Marotti, Peter Beal, Henry Woudhuysen, and Margaret Ezell.[16] As these and other scholars have shown, unprinted texts occupied a fundamental place in sixteenth- and seventeenth-century English life. Script was absolutely central to the administrative and bureaucratic

[14] A. Pettegree, 'Printing and the Reformation: The English Exception', in P. Marshall and A. Ryrie (eds.), *The Beginnings of English Protestantism* (Cambridge, 2002), esp. pp. 157–65. For recent surveys of key aspects of the early printing industry, see the essays in the section 'Technique and Trade' in *CHBB 3*; D. F. McKenzie, 'Printing and Publishing 1557–1700: Constraints on the London Book Trades', in *CHBB 4*, pp. 553–67. For the book-trade in the provinces, see J. Barnard and M. Bell, 'The English Provinces', in *ibid.*, pp. 665–86. For the broader European context, see D. McKitterick, 'The Beginning of Printing', in C. Allmand (ed.), *The New Cambridge Medieval History*, vol. VII, *c.1415–c.1500* (Cambridge, 1998), pp. 287–98.

[15] For emphasis on the repressiveness of the censorship system, see A. Patterson, *Censorship and Interpretation: The Conditions of Reading and Writing in Early Modern England* (Madison, WI, 1984) and C. Hill, 'Censorship and English Literature', in *Collected Essays*, vol. I, *Writing and Revolution in Seventeenth Century England* (Brighton, 1985). For revisionist analyses see S. Lambert, 'State Control of the Press in Theory and Practice: The Role of the Stationers' Company before 1640', in R. Myers and M. Harris (eds.), *Censorship and the Control of Print in England and France, 1600–1910* (Winchester, 1992), pp. 1–32; A. B. Worden, 'Literature and Political Censorship in Early Modern England', in A. C. Duke and C. A. Tamse (eds.), *Too Mighty to be Free: Censorship in Britain and the Netherlands* (Zutphen, 1987), pp. 45–62; C. S. Clegg, *Press Censorship in Elizabethan England* (Cambridge, 1997) and *Press Censorship in Jacobean England* (Cambridge, 2001).

[16] H. Love, *Scribal Publication in Seventeenth-Century England* (Oxford, 1993); A. F. Marotti, *Manuscript, Print and the English Renaissance Lyric* (Ithaca and London, 1995); H. R. Woudhuysen, *Sir Philip Sidney and the Circulation of Manuscripts 1558–1640* (Oxford, 1996); P. Beal, *In Praise of Scribes: Manuscripts and their Makers in Seventeenth-Century England* (Oxford, 1998); P. Beal, *Index of English Literary Manuscripts*, I: *1450–1625*, 2 vols. (1980); II: *1625–1700*, 2 vols. (1987–93); M. J. M. Ezell, *Social Authorship and the Advent of Print* (Baltimore and London, 1999). See also M. Hobbs, *Early Seventeenth-Century Verse Miscellany Manuscripts* (Aldershot, 1992). It may be noted that literary scholars have so far dominated the rediscovery of post-print scribal culture. The enterprise has also left its mark in *English Manuscript Studies 1100–1700* (1989–). Scribal publication was also the abiding concern of the late and much lamented Jeremy Maule.

culture of the period, the basic instrument of record-keeping in the late
Tudor and Stuart state and Church and the chief means of issuing execu-
tive instructions, as it had been in Lancastrian England. More intimate and
flexible in character than the abstract and impersonal organ of print, it was
also the preferred method for reproducing and disseminating a wide range
of other texts. Poets like Sir Philip Sidney and Andrew Marvell scorned the
press, regarding resort to it as 'a lapse in gentlemanly taste and decorum'.
Some, like John Donne, who revered God himself as scrivener, felt obliged
to apologise for ever having 'descended' to it at all.[17] Script was the choice
of writers who sought to communicate with an exclusive circle of readers
or retain a reserved status for the knowledge they conveyed: it flattered patrons, concealed secrets, and surrounded religious revelations with an aura
of sacredness. The Bristol prophetess Grace Carrie, for instance, refrained
from printing a narrative of a vision she received in 1635 on the grounds
that it was 'very unfitt, that such divine & miracalous truth shuld be made
common in these times wherin so manie falasies and false printed papers
are set fourth'.[18] Gender and geography also played their part: women and
provincial writers without access to the patronage networks and presses of
the capital gravitated quite naturally towards the scribal medium.[19] And
often reluctance to communicate through the device of movable type may
have merely reflected unease and anxiety about the rapid pace of technological change.[20]

There was also a thriving trade in handwritten legal crib books and educational texts and, right up to the end of the seventeenth century, commercial
scriptoria played an active role in the circulation of 'separates' recounting
parliamentary affairs and overseas news. Offering more latitude for the expression of subversive, heterodox and unacceptable ideas, manuscript was
the natural medium for obscene verse and for critical political commentary. Flourishing in times of governmental repression, scribal publication
of such material tended to falter only during periods when the machinery
of censorship crumpled or collapsed.[21] It was also a trusty ally of religious
dissent: as Thomas Freeman's exploration of the epistolary activity of the

---

[17] P. Beal, 'John Donne and the Circulation of Manuscripts', in *CHBB 4*, p. 122. See also A. F. Marotti, *John Donne, Coterie Poet* (Madison, WI, 1986).

[18] Quoted by M. J. M. Ezell, *The Patriarch's Wife: Literary Evidence and the History of the Family* (Chapel Hill, NC, 1987), p. 65.

[19] See *ibid.* and Ezell, *Social Authorship*, esp. p. 18 and chs. 1, 5; *English Manuscript Studies 1100–1700*, vol. 9, *Writings by Early Modern Women*, ed. P. Beal and M. Ezell (2000).

[20] McKenzie, 'Speech-Manuscript-Print', p. 109.

[21] Woudhuysen, *Circulation of Manuscripts*, p. 391.

Marian martyrs shows below, it could be a powerful weapon in the hands of the persecuted and dispossessed.[22]

Crucially, these new studies have demonstrated that long after the introduction of the mechanised press scribal copying remained economically viable. It should not be assumed that typographical reproduction was necessarily more cost effective: the high initial investment required in typesetting made print uncompetitive in the case of small numbers of texts. Manuscripts, by contrast, could be produced to order, without the problem of disposing of unsold copies.[23] As Woudhuysen concludes, 'for at least two centuries the procreative pen and its many different and individual offspring complemented and at times rivalled the press's more uniform products'. Far from a 'curious anachronism', scribal copying remained a competitive technology for transmitting texts even after 1700.[24]

This discovery has encouraged scholars of early modern communication to approach the manuscript book with greater sophistication and sensitivity, to become more closely attuned to the fluidity and malleability of texts, to the ways in which the acts of creation and duplication are interwoven. As a consequence, historians of sixteenth- and seventeenth-century culture have begun to embrace and absorb assumptions and expectations which have long underpinned the study of medieval textuality. As in 'the medieval manuscript matrix' described by Stephen Nichols, the copying of texts is increasingly seen as 'an adventure in supplementation rather than faithful imitation', a dynamic, open-ended process in which consumers merge with producers and in which concepts like 'authorship' and 'originality' are rendered virtually meaningless.[25] The disciplinary frontline between historians of medieval and early modern culture is steadily withering away.

In questioning received wisdom about the occlusion of script by print and the relative roles and merits of the two media, furthermore, the work

[22] See also M. Greengrass, 'Informal Networks in Sixteenth-Century French Protestantism', in R. A. Mentzer and A. Spicer (eds.), *Society and Culture in the Huguenot World 1559–1685* (Cambridge, 2002) and Alexandra Walsham's essay, below.

[23] McKenzie, 'Speech-Manuscript-Print', p. 94; Love, *Scribal Publication*, pp. 126–34.

[24] Woudhuysen, *Circulation of Manuscripts*, p. 391; Beal, *In Praise of Scribes*, p. v; Ezell, *Social Authorship*, p. 12.

[25] S. G. Nichols, 'Introduction: Philology in a Manuscript Culture', *Speculum* 65 (1990), 1–10, at 8 and 3 respectively. See also E. H. Reiter, 'The Reader as Author of the User-Produced Manuscript: Reading and Rewriting Popular Latin Theology in the Late Middle Ages', *Viator* 27 (1996), 151–69; G. L. Bruns, 'The Originality of Texts in a Manuscript Culture', in his *Inventions: Writing, Textuality, and Understanding in Literary History* (New Haven, 1982), pp. 44–59; S. Reynolds, *Medieval Reading: Grammar, Rhetoric and the Classical Text* (Cambridge, 1996). For early modernists acknowledging these points, see Marotti, *Manuscript*, ch. 3; Woudhuysen, *Circulation of Manuscripts*, pp. 15–16; Beal, *In Praise of Scribes*, pp. 24–5; Ezell, *Social Authorship*, p. 40.

of early modernists converges with the insights which have emerged from accounts of scribal activity before 1500. As Michael Clanchy emphasised twenty years ago, we need to see the invention of printing not so much as the starting point of a new age as the culmination of a millennium, during which the displacement of the scroll by the codex in late antiquity was perhaps the most critical landmark. To speak of 'the coming of the book' in the 1450s is to ignore ten centuries of its long and complex history. To understand the success of the press we must investigate the social and intellectual soil from which it sprang.[26] The foundation of the European universities in the twelfth and thirteenth centuries placed new demands on the supply and even structure of books. Concentrations of scholars in need of texts were served by a book trade capable of large-scale production, detectable in the French capital as early as the last quarter of the twelfth century, and in Oxford a hundred years later. Richard and Mary Rouse have recently reconstructed in vivid detail the life of the scribal quarters of late medieval Paris, which revolved around dynasties of professional scribes supplemented by the casual labour of priests and students, who were loaned out corrected exemplars for copying in quires (*pecia*).[27] In England, before 1250 the city of St Albans sought to regulate the employment of scriveners and in late fourteenth-century York they formed a guild of their own.[28]

Meanwhile, as Malcolm Parkes has argued, the patterns of reasoning and interrogation of authorities integral to scholastic learning caused changes in the organisation and layout of texts, as well as the evolution of increasingly sophisticated systems of glossing and mechanisms of reference, including the use of running titles, indexes and tables of contents.[29] Nurtured in the circles of Italian humanist scholars and in the renewed religious orders of northwestern Europe, these technical developments promoted enhanced utility and clarity and facilitated increasing accessibility to the written word.

[26] M. Clanchy, 'Looking Back from the Invention of Printing', in D. P. Resnick (ed.), *Literacy in Historical Perspective* (Washington, 1983), pp. 7–22. For equation of the age of print with the 'coming of the book', see Febvre and Martin, *The Coming of the Book*; M. B. Stilwell, *The Beginning of the World of Books, 1450–1470* (New York, 1972); and H. Bekker-Nielson *et al.* (eds.), *From Script to Book: A Symposium* (Odense, 1986). See also D. Pearsall, 'Introduction', in J. Griffiths and D. Pearsall (eds.), *Book Production and Publishing in Britain 1375–1475* (Cambridge, 1989), pp. 1–10, and A. Grafton's criticism of Eisenstein in 'The Importance of Being Printed', *Journal of Interdisciplinary History* 11 (1980), 273–5.

[27] R. H. Rouse and M. A. Rouse, *Manuscripts and their Makers: Commercial Book Producers in Medieval Paris 1200–1500*, 2 vols. (Turnhout, 2000), vol. I, p. 26. M. B. Parkes, 'The Provision of Books', in J. I. Catto and R. Evans (eds.), *The History of the University of Oxford* (Oxford, 1992), vol. II, pp. 418–21.

[28] Chaytor, *From Script to Print*, p. 17, and ch. 2 *passim*.

[29] M. B. Parkes, 'The Influence of the Concepts of *Ordinatio* and *Compilatio* on the Development of the Book', in J. J. G. Alexander and M. T. Gibson (eds.), *Medieval Learning and Literature: Essays presented to Richard William Hunt* (Oxford, 1976), pp. 115–41.

Within this collection David d'Avray argues that the volume of medieval scribal production has been greatly underestimated. Questioning the commonplace that commercial scribes had effectively superseded the regular clergy, he points to the key role of the friars and emphasises the ability of script to operate as a mass medium. Certainly, the physical evidence of books attests speed of production. Since the twelfth century an entire hierarchy of cursive scripts had been developed to facilitate the rapid copying of sought after texts[30] and the replacement of parchment by paper gradually made book production faster and cheaper.[31] As the Rouses have remarked, the period witnessed the birth of a book which in certain respects had more in common with the products of the mechanical press than it did with its earlier manuscript precursors.[32]

In England, as elsewhere, there was an unprecedented explosion in the availability and ownership of books in the late fourteenth and fifteenth centuries, an expansion which both sustained and was sustained by the rise of a literate laity. This boom owed much to the growing desire of laypeople to acquire their own copies of devotional works like primers and to the increasing tendency for university students and parish priests to transcribe key Latin texts for their personal use. However, the literate ambitions of private individuals ranged beyond the acquisition of immediately utilitarian texts into the preparation and collection of domestic commonplace books and 'household miscellanies' containing verse, religious prose, and a variety of other items.[33] These trends inspired amateur manuscript production on a scale which surely contributed to the textual instability taken by Eisenstein as typical of late medieval scribal culture. Individuals and institutions also had easy recourse to the services of professional scribes employed by workshops and stationers. In 1448–9, for example, twenty new processionals were purchased from a stationer to equip the newly founded All Souls College in Oxford[34] and the same century saw the routine commercial production

---

[30] M. B. Parkes, *English Cursive Book Hands 1250–1500* (1969), pp. xiii–xxv.

[31] But see the caveats of N. Barker, 'The Trade and Manufacture of Paper before 1800', in S. Cavaciocchi (ed.), *Produzione e commercio della carta e del libro secc. xiii–xviii* (Prato, 1992), p. 214.

[32] M. A. Rouse and R. H. Rouse, 'Backgrounds to Print: Aspects of the Manuscript Book in Northern Europe of the Fifteenth Century', in their *Authentic Witnesses: Approaches to Medieval Texts and Manuscripts* (Notre Dame, 1991), p. 451 and pp. 449–66 *passim*. See more generally C. Bühler, *The Fifteenth Century Book: The Scribes, the Printers, the Decorators* (Philadelphia, 1960); P. Saenger, 'Colard Mansion and the Evolution of the Printed Book', *The Library Quarterly*, 45 (1975), 405–18; B. Bischoff, *Latin Palaeography: Antiquity and the Middle Ages*, trans. D. Ó Cróinín and D. Ganz (Cambridge, 1990), pp. 224–9, 235–8.

[33] J. Boffey and J. J. Thompson, 'Anthologies and Miscellanies: Production and Choice of Texts', in Griffiths and Pearsall (eds.), *Book Production*, pp. 279–315. See also M. Vale, 'Manuscripts and Books', in Allmand (ed.), *New Cambridge Medieval History*, vol. vii, pp. 278–86.

[34] A. Wathey, 'The Production of Books of Liturgical Polyphony', in Griffiths and Pearsall (eds.), *Book Production*, p. 150.

of books of poetry in London alongside continuing provincial production in religious houses and elsewhere.[35]

Collectively, these observations underline the artificiality of drawing hard and fast boundaries between script and print. Instead we need to see the intermixture and hybridity of these two media as a keynote of the culture of communication in this period. Scholars and antiquarians owned texts printed from manuscript and manuscripts transcribed from printed texts. Aesthetics sometimes intervened. Forty-eight of fifty-eight surviving volumes in the library of the wealthy Flemish bibliophile Raphael de Marcatellis (1437–1508), for instance, were copied in part from print: extravagantly bound texts inscribed on white vellum in Gothic bookhand, their luxurious physical appearance disguised their typographical origins.[36] Such habits persisted. A mid-seventeenth-century English manuscript miscellany associated with Christ Church, Oxford, now preserved in the Bodleian Library contains transcriptions of two Wynkyn de Worde pamphlets which seek to recreate the impression of the printed text, complete with title-page, woodcuts, colophon and printer's device (Illustrations 2 and 3).[37]

It must also be recognised that for a long time print was simply regarded as a surrogate for manuscript. The aim of the producers of the earliest printed books was to reproduce the features of medieval literate culture as exactly as possible. Thus Gutenberg's famous 42-line bible was printed in a Gothic font (mimicking the formal book hand employed in the transcription sacred texts) and a psalter produced in 1457 involved three colours of ink and included mechanically generated calligraphic ornamentation.[38] Early sixteenth-century printed books of hours likewise sought to resemble precisely their illuminated manuscript cousins: they were less expensive replicas of texts readers regarded above all as holy objects (Illustration 4). Bureaucratic documents such as indulgence certificates and legal contracts, by contrast, simulated medieval chancery hands[39] and both incunables and

---

[35] A. S. G. Edwards and D. Pearsall, 'Manuscripts of the Major English Poetic Texts', in Griffiths and Pearsall (eds.), *Book Production*, pp. 258, 267.

[36] A. Derolez, 'The Copying of Printed Books for Humanistic Bibliophiles in the Fifteenth Century', in H. Bekker-Nielsen *et al.*, *From Script to Print: A Symposium* (Odense, 1986), pp. 144–6, and 140–60 *passim*. See also Bühler, *Fifteenth-Century Book*, pp. 34–9; C. E. Lutz, 'Manuscripts Copied from Printed Books', *Yale University Library Gazette*, 49 (1974–5), 261–7; M. D. Reeve, 'Manuscripts Copied from Printed Books', in Trapp (ed.), *Manuscripts*, pp. 12–20.

[37] For other examples, see Marotti, *Manuscript*, pp. 326–30.

[38] See N. F. Blake, 'From Manuscript to Print', in Griffiths and Pearsall (eds.), *Book Production*, pp. 404–7; Rouse and Rouse, *Manuscripts*, vol. 1, p. 328; McKitterick, 'Beginning of Printing', pp. 294–6.

[39] See Clanchy, 'Looking Back', pp. 12–13; R. Hirsch, 'Scribal Tradition and Innovation in Early Printed Books', in his *The Printed Word: Its Impact and Diffusion* (1978).

Illustration 2 Manuscript transcription of printed pamphlet in a mid-seventeenth-century
verse miscellany probably associated with Christ Church, Oxford: 'Here begynneth a lyttel
propre Jeste Called cryste crosse me spede. a.b.c.' (*STC* 14546.5, Wynkyn de Worde
[c.1534?]), title-page. (Bodleian Library, MS Eng. Poet. e. 97, p. 207.)

Illustration 3 Manuscript transcription of printed pamphlet in a mid-seventeenth-century verse miscellany probably associated with Christ Church, Oxford: 'Here begynneth a lyttel propre Jeste Called cryste crosse me spede. a.b.c.' (*STC* 14546.5, Wynkyn de Worde [c.1534?]), colophon. (Bodleian Library, MS Eng. Poet. e. 97, p. 211.)

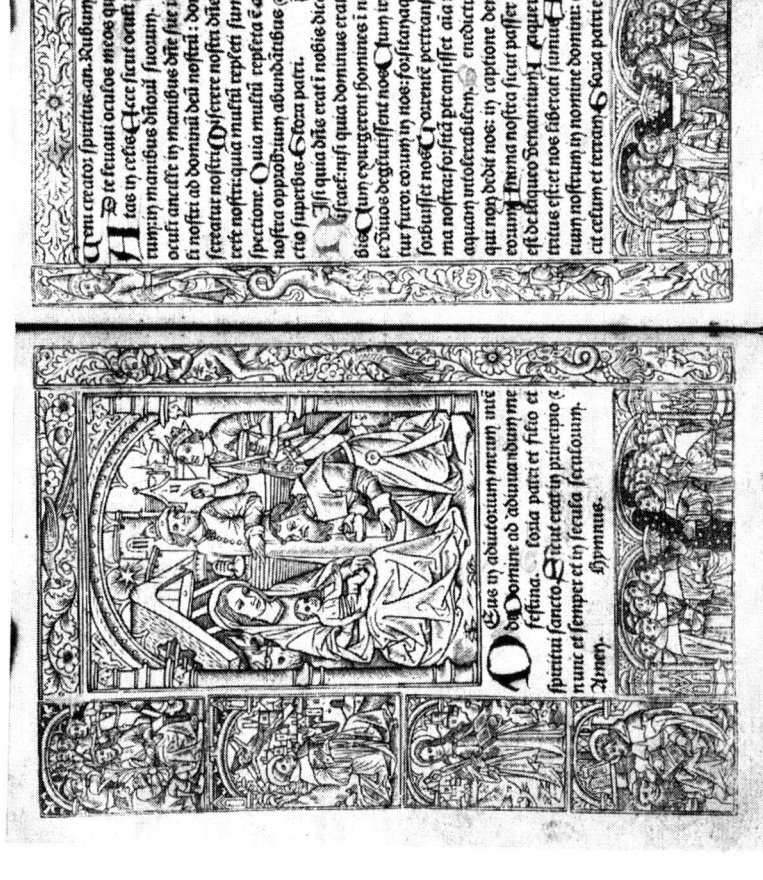

Illustration 4 Page from an incunable book of hours (Salisbury use) showing the Adoration of the Magi, imitating an illuminated manuscript written in Burgundian cursive. The initials have been inserted in red and blue ink by hand. *Hore beate Marie v[ir]gi[ni]s secundu[m] usum Sarum* ([Paris: I. Philippe for] Thielman Kerver, 1497), *STC* 1585, sigs. e 2v–e 3r.

marriage charters sometimes left the printers unfinished, with the expecta-tion that initials, decoration and even text would be added by hand.[40]

As these examples suggest, neither script nor print can be taken as an un-differentiated whole: different registers within them had always conveyed different messages and carried different values. The highly abbreviated cur-sive of scholastic Latin communicated distinctly from the outsize textura of a liturgical manuscript, just as printing in black letter reached a wider audience than Roman type. The shift in the seventeenth century from the former to the latter may be seen as one symptom of the growing prestige of print. Even so, a residual sense of the superior intimacy and presence intrinsic to manuscript persisted, not least in the device of entitling books *An epistle* and *A copy of a letter*. It is also perhaps evident in the character-istic impulse of owners to personalise printed texts by filling their margins with annotations, a practice which might be seen as a transmutation of the medieval art of glossing.[41]

It may also be remarked that in some respects the new technology re-inforced older ways of thinking by ensuring they were more uniformly diffused. The *Golden Legend* is one staple of the age before print to which the press gave a new lease of life. John Foxe himself extolled the role of print in preserving and rejuvenating texts which had been buried in the darkness of the past, insisting that God had sent this 'excellent art' 'to revive agayne the lost lyght of knowledge to these blynde tymes, by renuing of holsome and auncient writers: whose doinges and teachinges otherwise had lyen in oblivion . . .'.[42] His own massive tome, which prints many manuscript 'monuments' to the trials and sufferings of proto-Protestant sects, is a tes-tament to this process, as is the frequent reproduction in the Reformation era of the fifteenth-century Lollard text *Wycliffes Wycket*.[43] In this volume Julia Crick shows how Anglo-Saxon charters (not a few of them forgeries) gained a new readership in the era of print.

---

[40] E. König, 'The Influence of the Invention of Printing on the Development of German Illumination', in Trapp (ed.), *Manuscripts*, p. 85. R. Chartier, 'From Ritual to the Hearth: Marriage Charters in Seventeenth-Century Lyons', in Chartier (ed.), *The Culture of Print*, p. 187.

[41] See P. Saenger and M. Heinlen, 'Incunable Description and its Implications for the Analysis of Fifteenth-Century Reading Habits', in Hindman (ed.), *Printing the Written Word*, pp. 225–58. For later examples, see J. Morrill, 'William Dowsing, the Bureaucratic Puritan', in J. Morrill, P. Slack, and D. Woolf (eds.), *Public Duty and Private Conscience in Seventeenth-Century England* (Oxford, 1993), esp. pp. 182–7; W. H. Sherman, *John Dee: The Politics of Reading and Writing in the English Renaissance* (Amherst, MA, 1995), esp. ch. 4.

[42] J. Foxe (ed.), *The Whole Workes of W. Tyndall, John Frith, and Doct. Barnes, three Worthy Martyrs* (1573), sig. A2r.

[43] A text known only from surviving printed editions. See A. Hudson, '"No Newe Thyng": The Printing of Medieval Texts in the Early Reformation Period', in her *Lollards and their Books* (London and Ronceverte, 1985), pp. 227–48.

The part played by print in reviving and propagating the products of scribal culture neatly parallels the manner in which it served to nourish and reinvigorate unwritten tradition. As Adam Fox and others have demonstrated, at least in the short term typography (and indeed chirography) popularised long cherished beliefs that had hitherto been confined to the sphere of speech. Fox argues that the development of print and the spread of writing in the sixteenth and seventeenth centuries led to a tremendous enriching of the verbal and vernacular repertoire and to a renewal of many traditions hitherto confined to the realm of the spoken word. It preserved legends, rhymes, and pieces of proverbial wisdom on paper and in the guise of the broadsheet rescued many songs from near extinction. Old stories and romances of Robin Hood, King Arthur, Bevis of Southampton, and Guy of Warwick – some of which had flowed out of literate culture themselves – were likewise revitalised.[44]

This brings us to a further theme which can be traced through the pages of this collection, and that is that script and print must be explored in relation to speech. To echo Keith Thomas, for all their imperialistic potential, they never displaced the spoken word. The relationship between these three media was one of mutual infusion and reciprocal interaction, symbiosis and dynamic continuum. Sight and sound, hearing and seeing, were equally important in the creation of meaning. Oral communication remained central to the day-to-day workings of English society, in the form of speeches delivered in parliament, pleadings in law courts, teaching in schools, and preaching and catechising in church.[45] As Isaac Barrow declared in 1678, 'tis the force of this little machine', the tongue, 'that turneth all the humane world about'.[46] Contemporaries privileged speech as the paradigm of authentic language use: godly ministers reluctantly consigned their sermons to print, speaking disparagingly of the 'dead letter' of the text in the absence of the 'lively' organ of the voice.[47] Michael Clanchy's

---

[44] A. Fox, *Oral and Literate Culture in England 1500–1700* (Oxford, 2000), esp. pp. 8–10, 50, 410–11. See also P. R. Coss, 'Aspects of Cultural Diffusion in Medieval England: The Early Romances, Local Society and Robin Hood', *P&P* 108 (1985), 35–79.

[45] K. Thomas, 'The Meaning of Literacy in Early Modern England', in Gerd Baumann (ed.), *The Written Word: Literacy in Transition* (Oxford, 1986), p. 113 and pp. 97–131 *passim*; Fox, *Oral and Literate Culture*; B. R. Smith, *The Acoustic World of Early Modern England: Attending to the O-Factor* (Chicago, 1999); A. Fox and D. Woolf (eds.), *The Spoken Word: Oral Culture in Britain, 1500–1850* (Manchester, 2002).

[46] Quoted in Love, 'Oral and Scribal Texts', p. 100.

[47] See D. R. Woolf, 'Speech, Text and Time: The Sense of Hearing and the Sense of the Past in Renaissance England', *Albion* 18 (1986), esp. 173–6; and the examples cited in A. Walsham, *Providence in Early Modern England* (Oxford, 1999), p. 54. Playwrights expressed similar anxieties: McKenzie, 'Speech-Manuscript-Print', p. 90.

analysis of how oral habits of thought lingered on in the presence of writing applies to the period between 1300 and 1700 no less than to the two centuries which preceded it.

Literacy of all kinds was closely intertwined with aurality. If fifteenth-century elites engaged in recreational reading aloud of Chaucer and other English poetic and prose works, sixteenth-century Protestants manifested a similar instinct for 'the social experience of literature', placing the recitation of sermons, bibles and devotional treatises at the very heart of household devotion.[48] In chapter 9 Christopher Marsh reminds us that we must attune our ears to the sound of print: detached from the melodies and tunes to which they were sung, half the message of early modern ballads is lost. Furthermore, material texts of all types must also be recognised as an adjunct of the 'art of memory': many functioned primarily as an aid to remembering information filed away inside their readers' minds.[49]

The oral performance of written texts was a powerful factor in defining communities. The tendency to align written culture with privacy and individualism belies the way in which, either verbally rehearsed or silently perused, books forged links between scattered individuals and groups of people. They cemented bonds between members of religious sects from the Cathars in the thirteenth century through to the Quakers in the seventeenth and in the form of the liturgy provided a focal point for communal worship within the established Church.[50] Within late medieval urban contexts, as Andrew Butcher suggests in chapter 8 in a foretaste of a fuller study in preparation, the scribal rituals of bureaucracy helped to synthesise and sustain a sense of corporate identity. Borrowing insights from linguistic anthropology, he argues that the macaronic records generated by the clerks of Hythe and other Kentish towns gave oral and ceremonial expression to civic custom, tradition and consciousness in a manner which questions any sharp distinction between 'pragmatic' and 'literary' texts. In the latter half of our period, the circulation of printed pamphlets and handwritten separates around networks of readers like that linked with the Cheshire gentleman William Davenport fostered a shared set of political assumptions and values, while the reading practices of Samuel Hartlib and his circle indicate

[48] J. Coleman, *Public Reading and the Reading Public in Late Medieval England and France* (Cambridge, 1996), p. xiv. For puritan household devotion, see, e.g., D. M. Meads (ed.), *Diary of Lady Margaret Hoby 1599–1605* (1930).
[49] F. Yates, *The Art of Memory* (1966); M. J. Carruthers, *The Book of Memory: A Study of Memory in Medieval Culture* (Cambridge, 1990).
[50] For the concept of 'textual communities', see B. Stock, *The Implications of Literacy: Written Language and Models of Interpretation in the Eleventh and Twelfth Centuries* (Princeton, 1983), esp. pt II.

define 'publish'

the ways in which texts both in manuscript and print helped to engender a republic of letters.[51]

Such evidence highlights another conceptual problem inherent in the historiography of print culture: how we define the word 'publication'. Too often publication has been treated as synonymous with printing, without thought for how texts reached the reading public in highly literate and sophisticated scribal cultures such as Augustan Rome or fifth-century Africa, not to say Western Europe before 1500, where it was often equated with the act of presenting a work to a patron.[52] In the light of recent work, the parameters of the term are expanding. Harold Love has used it to describe 'a movement from a private realm of creativity to a public realm of consumption', a formulation which explicitly avoids equating the process with a transition from script to print.[53] Here, in her investigation of the dissemination of the fourteenth-century mystic Julian of Norwich's *A Revelation of Love* Felicity Riddy argues that in medieval England the term 'publication' related not to writing but speech. In utilising it, therefore, we must accommodate not only the duplication of books by scribal copying but also the posting of placards on church doors and in market-places, the oral proclamation of news, the singing and scattering of vernacular libels and scurrilous rhymes. At critical junctures such as the Peasants' Revolt of 1381, the Reformation in the 1530s, the years prior to the outbreak of the Civil War in 1642, and the Exclusion Crisis in the late 1670s, the whole range of such 'texts' played their part in the making of public opinion.[54]

Historians have often linked the development of what Jürgen Habermas, writing of the eighteenth century, called 'the public sphere', with the advent of print culture itself and a recent study by David Zaret rather reinforces the tendency to see the new technology as 'democracy's

---

[51] See Love, *Scribal Publication*, pp. 179–84; J. S. Morrill, 'William Davenport and the "Silent Majority" of Early Stuart England', *Journal of the Chester Archaeological Society*, 18 (1975), 115–29; M. Greengrass, 'Samuel Hartlib and Scribal Communication', *Acta Comeniana*, 12 (1997), 47–62.

[52] See R. K. Root, 'Publication before Printing', *PMLA*, 28 (1913), 417–31; H. S. Bennett, 'The Production and Dissemination of Vernacular Manuscripts in the Fifteenth Century', *The Library*, 5th ser., 1 (1946–7), 167–78; Chaytor, *From Script to Print*, ch. 6; B. Guenée, *Histoire et culture historique dans l'Occident médiéval* (Paris, 1980), pp. 248–99, esp. 285–95.

[53] Love, *Scribal Publication*, p. 36.

[54] See key studies by S. Justice, *Writing and Rebellion: England in 1381* (Berkeley and London, 1994); E. H. Shagan, *Popular Politics and the English Reformation* (Cambridge, 2002); R. Cust, 'News and Politics in Early Seventeenth-Century England', *P&P*, 112 (1986), 60–90; D. Freist, *Governed by Opinion: Politics, Religion and the Dynamics of Communication in Stuart London 1637–1645* (London and New York, 1997); A. Bellany, *The Politics of Court Scandal in Early Modern England: News Culture and the Overbury Affair, 1603–1660* (Cambridge, 2002); T. Harris, *London Crowds in the Reign of Charles*, vol. II, *Propaganda and Politics from the Restoration to the Exclusion Crisis* (Cambridge, 1987).

handmaiden'.[55] But this may be to accord printing exaggerated importance, to be beguiled by the high rate of survival of the artefacts to which it gave rise, and to ignore the fact that it remained closely interwoven with oral and written forms of controversy and discussion. Jonathan Barry's essay on late seventeenth-century Bristol rejects any simple linkage between political debate and consciousness and the proliferation of print and Ann Hughes' examination of Thomas Edwards' *Gangraena* likewise emphasises that in Civil War London the use of print as a polemic weapon continued to be embedded in relationships based on personal ties and face-to-face encounters. Both also remind us that 'authority' was not an intrinsic feature of the typographical medium, but rather a quality dependent upon particular local circumstances and contexts. Print did not necessarily guarantee the 'credit' of information or news: indeed it was frequently accused of disseminating fictions and falsehoods. As an early sixteenth-century Italian critic of the new technology declared, '*Est virgo hec penna, meretrix est stampificata*' ('The pen is a virgin, the printing press a whore').[56]

There is a danger, however, of muddying the waters of historiographical tradition too much, of emphasising continuity at the expense of a due appreciation of change. It cannot be denied that dramatic as well as gradual shifts were taking place in the culture of communications in the four centuries under investigation and it is important to retain an awareness of the impact of the new art of mechanical printing. Print spread texts in a different way from manuscript: it multiplied them not consecutively but simultaneously, in consequence widening the social milieu within which they circulated, both horizontally and vertically. The anxieties which surrounded the publication of translations of the Bible, among some early Protestants as well as medieval and Tridentine Catholics, attest the recognition that the press had the capacity to lift sacred knowledge and scriptural exegesis out of the hands of the clerical elite and, to create, as never before, a priesthood of all believers.[57] Print probably accelerated the development of

---

[55] J. Habermas, *Structural Transformation of the Public Sphere* (Cambridge, MA, 1962); D. Zaret, *Origins of Democratic Culture: Printing, Petitions and the Public Sphere in Early-Modern England* (Princeton, 2000), p. 254.

[56] Quoted in R. Chartier, 'The Practical Impact of Writing', in R. Chartier (ed.), *A History of Private Life*, vol. III, *Passions of the Renaissance* (Cambridge, MA and London, 1989), p. 123. See also D. Woolf, 'News, History and the Construction of the Present in Early Modern England', in B. Dooley and S. Baron (eds.), *The Politics of Information in Early Modern Europe* (London and New York, 2001), esp. pp. 100–4.

[57] See J.-F. Gilmont, 'Protestant Reformations and Reading' and D. Julia, 'Reading and the Counter-Reformation', in G. Cavallo and R. Chartier (eds.), *A History of Reading in the West* (Cambridge, 1999), pp. 219–23 and 243–50 respectively; B. Scribner, 'Heterodoxy, Literacy and Print in the Early German Reformation', in P. Biller and A. Hudson (eds.), *Heresy and Literacy 1000–1500* (Cambridge, 1994), pp. 255–78; A. Walsham, 'Unclasping the Book? Post-Reformation English Catholicism and the Vernacular Bible', *JBS*, 42 (2003), 141–66.

silent reading, a practice with roots in medieval monasticism, as well as fostering the emergence of new, less intensive habits of perusal in which texts were rapidly skimmed for relevant facts rather than examined in minute detail repeatedly.[58]

The rise of the vernacular and the slow but sure eclipse of Latin in literary and scholarly texts and administrative documents is a closely linked set of developments which quickened with the arrival of print and was in turn stimulated by it. The same may be said about the expansion of literacy, especially reading literacy: this too may be considered both a cause and an effect of the growth of the printing industry. The ability to write, by comparison, may have been less widely diffused, though Juliet Fleming has recently assembled fascinating evidence to the effect that graffiti on walls, furniture, pots and clothes was commonly practised in chronically paper-short early modern English society.[59]

We also need to register the growing authority accorded to the written and printed word. Wisdom transmitted by word of mouth was increasingly dismissed as untrustworthy and vulgar and the phrase 'old wives' tales' became a gendered byword for the unreliability of oral tradition. Historians and antiquaries crystallised and fossilised custom in writing and tended to relegate oral sources to the status of second-class evidence.[60] The same process may be observed in the sphere of the law: in chapter 5 Anthony Musson traces the process by which medieval judicial precedent was enshrined in text and explores its repercussions in the realm of legal practice. More generally, techniques of memorisation may be said to have gradually declined, as individuals relied on material books rather than 'aural texts' contained in their heads. Typography, like alphabetic writing before it, effected a significant mental shift from ear to eye, and sound to space.[61] And, over time, at least in popular perception, printing did come to carry a

---

[58] P. Saenger, 'Silent Reading: Its Impact on Late Medieval Script and Society', *Viator*, 13 (1982), 367–414, and his *Space between Words: The Origins of Silent Reading* (Stanford, 1997). On 'intensive' and 'extensive' reading, see Cavallo and Chartier (eds.), *History of Reading*, pp. 23–5. See also J. Raven, H. Small and N. Tadmor (eds.), *The Practice and Representation of Reading in England* (Cambridge, 1996).

[59] J. B. Trapp, 'Literacy, Books and Readers', in *CHBB 3*, pp, 31–43; D. Cressy, *Literacy and the Social Order: Reading and Writing in Tudor and Stuart England* (Cambridge, 1980); N. Wheale, *Writing and Society: Literacy, Print and Politics in Britain, 1590–1660* (1999); J. Fleming, *Graffiti and the Writing Arts of Early Modern England* (2001).

[60] See D. R. Woolf, 'The "Common Voice": History, Folklore and Oral Tradition in Early Modern England', *P&P*, 120 (1988), 26–52; A. Fox, 'Remembering the Past in Early Modern England: Oral and Written Tradition' and A. Wood, 'Custom and the Social Organisation of Writing in Early Modern England', *TRHS*, 6th ser., 9 (1999), 233–56, 257–69.

[61] Love, 'Oral and Scribal Texts', p. 102. Such shifts have been explored by W. Ong in his *Orality and Literacy* (1982) and many other books. On shifts in legal culture, note R. J. Ross, 'The Memorial Culture of Early Modern English Lawyers: Memory as Keyword, Shelter and Identity, 1560–1640', *Yale Journal of Law and the Humanities*, 10 (1998), 229–326.

kind of imprimatur. As the poet John Clare commented in the early nineteenth century: 'All counterfiets (*sic*) as from truths sacred mint/ Are readily believed if once put down in print'.[62]

The use of the press had one further fundamental effect: it dramatically altered the meaning of choosing to communicate in the scribal medium. Script ceased to be a purely utilitarian mode and imbued certain types of text with a distinctly political colouring. Handwritten works became surrounded by 'an aura of forbidden knowledge' and 'an air of privileged secrecy which made them more carefully attended to . . . and likewise more trusted than the output of the state supervised print media'.[63] To publish one's opinions in print, by contrast, implied a claim to orthodoxy and a bid to be part of the mainstream: hence the efforts of Calvinist licensers in the 1630s to 'massage' puritan texts to make them 'speak with a Laudian accent' and render them acceptable in a changing theological climate.[64] While the authors of printed books had to adopt strategies of allegory, irony and oblique reference to evade the attention of the censor, those who produced scribal texts could afford to be more direct and openly critical since they were not subject to the same degree of regulation.[65] In these and other ways, printing arguably contributed to the growth of authorial accountability and to what Joseph Loewenstein describes as the rise of the 'bibliographical ego'.[66] It helped create a new sense of the private ownership of words from which the concept of plagiarism was eventually precipitated in its modern form.

Finally we must return to the issue of how far the Reformation was implicated in and associated with these processes. Undoubtedly Protestantism generated some pressure towards the acquisition of literacy and in favour of the long-term triumph of the English language over Latin. Early Lutheran rhetoric resonated with the slogan 'everyman his own bible reader' and pietist and puritan devotion placed special emphasis on the personal encounter of true believers with God's word. The liberation of Scripture from imprisonment in an archaic and alien tongue likewise became a rallying cry of the early reformers and, despite the liberal influence of Erasmian

---

[62] 'St Martin's Eve', in E. Robinson and D. Powell (eds.), *John Clare* (Oxford, 1984), p. 178.

[63] Love, 'Oral and Scribal Texts', pp. 107, 109, 111.

[64] A. Milton, 'Licensing, Censorship and Religious Orthodoxy in Early Stuart England', *HJ*, 41 (1998), 625–51, at p. 647.

[65] Patterson, *Censorship and Interpretation*; Love, 'Oral and Scribal Texts', p. 118.

[66] J. Loewenstein, 'The Script in the Marketplace', *Representations*, 12 (1985), 101–14. See also his *The Author's Due: Printing and the Prehistory of Copyright* (Chicago, 2002); his 'Wither and Professional Work', in Marotti and Bristol (eds.), *Print, Manuscript, and Performance*, pp. 103–23; and Ezell, *Social Authorship*, ch. 6.

humanists, the issue became one of the shibboleths separating Wittenberg, Geneva and Canterbury from the militant Catholicism embodied in the decrees of the Council of Trent.[67] The heroic labours of William Tyndale in this behalf have ensured his immortalisation in popular English history as a national hero.

Nor can the significant impact which Protestantism had on the medieval culture of script be ignored. For Protestant polemicists, manuscript was an emblem of the scholastic corruption and clerical obscurantism which the Reformation had been launched to expose and overthrow. The world of scribal copying and learning, at least in the dominant form in which it was practised in the monasteries, was terminally disrupted by the Henrician Dissolution in the 1530s, an event which not only assisted the secularisation of the writing profession but also led to the iconoclastic destruction of thousands of texts. Treasured works by Duns Scotus, for instance, were 'faste nailede up upon postes in all comon howses of easment'. As a result the canon of authority and the community of scholarship which stretched back into the late antique past through the medium of Latin and the manuscript book was irrevocably severed. Although many texts were saved through the efforts of scholars like John Bale, as James Carley has emphasised, their endeavours at collection and preservation were often selective, influenced by a desire to remove the most egregious papists from the roll of illustrious writers.[68] This also explains why Lollard writings feature so prominently in lists like the *Index Britanniae Scriptorum*: Protestant historians and bibliographers had a vested interest in rescuing works which could be used to vindicate their claim to be part of an unbroken brotherhood of believers persecuted by the papacy throughout the Middle Ages.[69]

For similar reasons, the reformers also developed a distinct bias against verbal transmission. The doctrine of *sola scriptura* entailed a massive assault on Catholic reverence for the authority of ecclesiastical 'traditions' which had never been inscribed in Holy Writ, one side-effect of which was repeated reflection on the fallibility and fickleness of speech as a medium. In seeking to dissociate itself from the evils of the Church of Rome Protestantism aligned itself with the written word and forged an

---

[67] R. Gawthrop and G. Strauss, 'Protestantism and Literacy in Early Modern Germany', *P&P*, 104 (1984), 31–55, acknowledges but qualifies these links. On bible translation, see n. 57 above.

[68] J. P. Carley, 'Monastic Collections and their Dispersal', in *CHBB 4*, pp. 339–47, at p. 340. See also J. P. Carley and C. G. C. Tite (eds.), *Books and Collectors 1200–1700: Essays Presented to Andrew Watson* (1997), pt III.

[69] R. Rex, *The Lollards* (Basingstoke, 2002), p. 78.

enduring link in English culture between oral communication and popish 'superstition'.[70]

At the same time, it is important to recognise the extent to which such associations are components of a powerful confessional myth, legacies of a paradigm devised to justify a major historical rupture, and one which, as we have seen, still exerts more than residual influence over scholarly thinking. Recent research, though, has done much to modify and complicate these interconnections. We are now more aware of the vital role which the spoken word played in diffusing Reformation ideas, in the guise of informal discussion, reading aloud of pamphlets and tracts, singing of ballads and psalms, catechising, and, above all, preaching.[71] Evidence is emerging, too, of the ways in which Protestantism eventually engendered a kind of folklore of its own, a body of providential anecdotes, martyrological stories, and legends of the reformers which, when in turn recorded in writing and print, bore the tell-tale marks of oral transmission.[72] Some Protestants accorded an almost sacramental quality to speech, insisting time and again upon on its superior capacity as an instrument of revelation and as a vessel for conveying the saving knowledge of the Gospel. Printed sermons were often perceived to be a poor substitute for the animated, incarnate Word which was the inspired preacher in his pulpit. The early seventeenth-century London puritan minister, Thomas Taylor, for instance, was revered as 'a walking Bible'.[73] This is not to deny that many eagerly embraced the press as a means of amplifying the voice and of preserving, as if on a gramophone record or compact disk, the words of eminent ministers who had departed this world. Any polarisation of preaching and printing runs the risk of overlooking the extent to which contemporaries saw speech and writing as a continuum.[74]

The related view that post-Reformation Roman Catholicism exhibited a deep-seated distrust of the new medium and resisted its advance is also being slowly eroded. It has been easy to overlook how far humanist priorities were conducive to the exploitation of the new technology in view of their eclipse in the 1540s. It is also often forgotten that, even after the backlash marked by

[70] See A. Walsham, 'Reformed Folklore? Cautionary Tales and Oral Tradition in Early Modern England', in Fox and Woolf (eds.), *The Spoken Word*, pp. 173–80.

[71] R. W. Scribner, 'Oral Culture and the Diffusion of Reformation Ideas', repr. in his *Popular Culture and Popular Movements in Reformation Germany* (London and Ronceverte, 1987), pp. 47–69; P. Collinson, *The Birthpangs of Protestant England* (1988), ch. 4; T. Watt, *Cheap Print and Popular Piety, 1550–1640* (Cambridge, 1991), pt I; I. Green, *The Christian's ABC: Catechisms and Catechizing in England c.1530–1740* (Oxford, 1996); on sermons, A. Hunt, 'The Art of Hearing: Preachers and their Audiences 1590–1640', Ph.D. thesis, University of Cambridge (2000).

[72] R. W. Scribner, 'Incombustible Luther? The Image of the Reformer in Early Modern Germany', *P&P*, 110 (1986), 38–68; Walsham, 'Reformed Folklore?', pp. 180–88.

[73] Thomas Taylor, *The Works . . . Published according to his Manuscripts* (1653), sig. B3v.

[74] Eisenstein, *Printing Press*, p. 374.

the assembly at Trent, the Church's attempt to exert control over heretical and immoral books through institutions like the Inquisition and Index went hand in hand with its sponsorship of edifying devotional tracts and learned works of orthodox theology. Tridentine clergymen too lauded print as a valuable pastoral and evangelical tool: the Jesuit Alfonso Pisa, for instance, proclaimed in 1582 that 'one book is worth more to us than a thousand sermons. One Father can only address a few listeners in one college for an hour, whereas a printed book can reach readers of all types in a hundred different places for ever.' Like their Protestant counterparts, however, they sometimes found reason to rue the unruly forces which this invention had unleashed. Catholics made especially imaginative use of the press in contexts of persecution. It was against such a backdrop that the leaders of the English mission to England made publication, scribal and typographical, one of the priorities of their campaign to reclaim the nation to the Roman fold.[75] Indeed, as Alexandra Walsham argues here, on both sides of the denominational divide the experience of persecution and proscription may have been crucial in stimulating enthusiasm for the printed (and written) book as a substitute for vocal proselytising and personal guidance.

Our understanding of the relationship between the late medieval Church and the medium of printing is also beginning to change. As the notion of a reactionary institution in chronic decline and decay gives way to a vision of its vitality and adaptability to new conditions, historians such as Eamon Duffy are highlighting the ways in which fifteenth-century bishops and clergy harnessed the press as an agent of episcopal administration and didactic instruction. In the half century before the Reformation, thousands of printed primers circulated in England, along with hundreds of indulgences and images of pity.[76] In his essay in this volume, James Clark traces printing into the monasteries, the very seat of error which this 'divine art' was deemed to have been instrumental in sweeping away. His study of early provincial presses housed in several Benedictine communities further calls into question the old pairings of Protestantism and print, monasticism and a moribund manuscript culture. So too do the activities of the Brigittine monks of Syon Abbey, who were pioneers in the provision of devotional and catechetical texts addressed to the laity like Richard Whitford's *Werke*

[75] Alfonso Pisa, 'De excudendis adversus haereticos libris', in L. Lukács (ed.), *Monumenta Paedagogica Societatis Iesu, Nova*, 7 vols. (Rome, 1965–1992), vol. VII, p. 556. We owe this reference and the translation to Trevor Johnson. D. Julia, 'Reading and the Counter-Reformation', esp. pp. 251–67; A. Walsham, '"Domme Preachers"? Post-Reformation English Catholicism and the Culture of Print', *P&P*, 168 (2000), 72–123.

[76] E. Duffy, *The Stripping of the Altars: Traditional Religion in England 1400–1580* (New Haven and London, 1992), esp. ch. 2.

for Housholders ([1531?]).[77] As elsewhere in Europe, reformed branches of religious orders like the Carthusians and Augustinians were among the most
active early purchasers of the products of commercial presses. It is possible
to argue that mechanical printing owed much of its initial success to the
fact that the monastery was its market. By the 1530s, printed books were
beginning to take the place of older, tattered manuscripts in the collections
of some such establishments.[78] This is the context in which the Benedictine
abbot of Sponheim, Johannes Trithemius, wrote his *De laude scriptorum
[In Praise of Scribes]*, an eloquent call to his fellow monks to continue the
ancient and sacred vocation of scribal copying and earn the reward of eter-
nal glory as 'heralds of God'. Often interpreted as a nostalgic backward
glance to an age which had passed, this tract was the work of a man who
seems to have recognised the capacity of the press to reach a large audience,
publishing thirteen works before 1500. An emblem of the co-existence and
interweaving of the two media, this classic encomium of manuscript was
itself printed in Mainz in 1494.[79]

    In choosing as our title *The Uses of Script and Print 1300–1700* we stake
no claims to comprehensiveness or uniformity of coverage or approach.
As editors we have not imposed any particular set of agendas and there
are healthy differences of emphasis, areas of interpretative divergence no
less than consensus. The essays in this volume represent a set of individual
studies in a range of social, cultural and intellectual milieux which collectively demonstrate that the traditional narrative of a transition 'from script
to print' sits uneasily with the evidence and blur the inherited boundaries
between medieval and early modern history. By bringing together scholars
whose interests and expertise lie in the two centuries on either side of the
conventional divide of the year 1500, and by deliberately juxtaposing the
fruits of training in different traditions of scholarship, it is hoped that this
collection will contribute fresh insights about patterns of continuity and
change in the relationship between the spoken, written and printed word
over this period as a whole.

[77] J. T. Rhodes, 'Syon Abbey and its Religious Publications in the Sixteenth Century', *JEH*, 44 (1993),
11–25; V. Gillespie, 'The Book and the Brotherhood: Reflections on the Lost Library of Syon Abbey',
in Edwards *et al.* (eds.), *English Medieval Book*, pp. 185–208.

[78] Rouse and Rouse, 'Backgrounds to Print', esp. p. 464; Carley, 'Monastic Collections', p. 347. For
more cautious assessments, see D. N. Bell, 'Monastic Libraries: 1400–1557', in *CHBB* 3, pp. 229–54;
A. I. Doyle, 'Publication by Members of the Religious Orders', in Griffiths and Pearsall (eds.), *Book
Production*, pp. 109–24. See also Eisenstein, *Printing Press*, pp. 14–16.

[79] Johannes Trithemius, *In Praise of Scribes: De Laude Scriptorum*, ed. K. Arnold, trans. R. Behrendt
(Lawrence, KA, 1974), p. 35 and *passim*.

PART I

Script, print and late medieval religion

2

'Publication' before print: the case of Julian of Norwich

Felicity Riddy

The question this essay tries to answer is a very simple one: before the introduction of printing into England, how did authors publish their works?[1] Printing made it possible to produce several hundred copies of a work simultaneously, and this entailed a heavy financial outlay that had to be recouped through sales. Publication meant offering these mass-produced copies for sale to unknown readers, adapting the marketing methods that were already well-established in other kinds of trade.[2] The printer's interest in the dissemination of a book must usually have been much more urgent than the author's, who was anyway often dead. In the manuscript era, on the other hand, the production system, in which books – or parts of books – were copied one at a time on commission by the purchaser, created a different relationship between reader, book artisan and author. It was the customer's decision whether or not a book was made, and customers also often supplied copies of texts. In these circumstances it is harder to see how and by whom demand was created and fostered, and how, indeed, the author fits in at all.

Although the manuscript era is frequently regarded as one in which books travelled along the routes mapped out by personal contacts, nevertheless late-medieval authors often imagined their texts reaching an audience of strangers: 'yonge, fresshe folkes, he or she', 'simple men and women of gode wille', 'synful wrecchys'.[3] Authorial fantasies of communication did not,

[1] Late-medieval publication is discussed in H. S. Bennett, 'The Production and Dissemination of Vernacular Manuscripts in the Fifteenth Century', *The Library*, 5th ser., 1 (1946–7), 167–78; P. J. Lucas in *From Author to Audience: John Capgrave and Medieval Publication* (Dublin, 1997); A. I. Doyle, 'Publication by Members of the Religious Orders', in J. Griffiths and D. Pearsall (eds.), *Book Production and Publishing in Britain 1375–1475* (Cambridge, 1989), pp. 109–24.

[2] For recent discussion and references, see L. Hellinga, 'Printing', and C. P. Christianson, 'The Rise of London's Book Trade', in *CHBB* 3, pp. 65–104 and pp. 128–47 respectively.

[3] *Troilus and Criseyde*, v. 1835; all Chaucer quotations are from Larry D. Benson (ed.), *The Riverside Chaucer* (Oxford, 1988); J. Wogan-Browne, N. Watson, A. Taylor and R. Evans (eds.), *The Idea of the Vernacular. An Anthology of Middle English Literary Theory 1280–1520* (Exeter, 1999), p. 240; S. B. Meech and H. E. Allen (eds.), *The Book of Margery Kempe*, EETS, OS 212 (Oxford, 1940), p. 1.

however, necessarily correspond with readerly desire for the written word, and it is on the latter rather than the former that my discussion focuses. There is general agreement that, in the century before printing – from the late fourteenth century to the late fifteenth – the lay reading public in England expanded rapidly, fed by new kinds of writing in English, secular and religious. The mysterious processes by which writers reached this public are the subject of this essay.

In the first section of what follows I discuss the ways in which medieval 'publication' has been treated hitherto (and nervous inverted commas are a hallmark of the subject). The second section offers an alternative approach via the interaction between speech and writing. Finally, I discuss the specific example of the 'publication' of Julian of Norwich's *A Revelation of Love*, which seems to present the problem in its starkest form: how did the work of a woman immured in a Norwich anchorhold for at least twenty years come into being and get into circulation?

I

Modern discussions of how new works were published in England in the late Middle Ages have identified four main modes of 'publication'. The first two can be categorised as 'authorial': the presentation by the author of a copy to a patron, and the public reading by an author of a new work to an audience. The third, which relates only to religious writings, might be called 'official' and consists of the licensing of a work by an ecclesiastical authority. The fourth is 'commercial', and relates to the role of metropolitan book-producers in the dissemination of texts. Of these modes, the first has received the most attention since Robert K. Root first raised the question, nearly a century ago, of how medieval writers secured an audience.[4] Root drew largely on Italian sources, particularly Petrarch and Boccaccio. The latter seems to have seen 'publication' as a matter of presenting a copy of a new book to a well-placed friend: he writes, for example, to the dedicatee of his *De claris mulieribus* that he has been trying to think whom to send it to, 'that it might not languish in idleness on my hands'. He asks her to 'give it the courage to go forth to the public (*procedendi in publicum*); sent out (*emissus*) under your auspices it will go free . . . from the insults of the malicious'. He does much the same with *De casibus virorum illustrium*, asking an influential friend to receive it and read it 'and finally send it forth

[4] R. K. Root, 'Publication before Printing', *PMLA*, 28 (1913), 417–31.

Root = Present a copy to someone important and they will disseminate it

to the public (*emittas in publicum*) under your name'.[5] Root sees the formal presentation and 'release' of a text as the final stage in a publication process that began with the author settling down to write. He argues that these examples suggest that the dedicatee or patron 'was apparently under some obligation to further its "publication"': the idiom *emittere in publicum*, which Boccaccio uses of the patronal activity in both instances, seems to imply not merely passive reception but some kind of activity.[6] It is, moreover, an act of patronage available equally to men and women.

No doubt this practice is, as Root implies, a form of gift exchange. Nevertheless, the attribution of a quasi-entrepreneurial role to the dedicatee seems intrinsically unlikely: it is surely implausible to assume that busy and influential people would have felt obliged to encourage the circulation of an unsolicited piece of writing. It seems more likely that the reciprocal obligations of gift exchange had to do with rewards and favours that were comparatively easy to grant to the author. Only rarely can they have included actively furthering the dissemination of the book in the way Root imagines. It is anyway important to distinguish between kinds of literary patronage. In England the commoner kind seems to have been when a work was specifically ordered by a patron for his or her own purposes, and here we might think of Gower (apparently) writing the *Confessio Amantis* at the request of Richard II, or Sir Thomas Berkeley's commissioning of translations from John Trevisa, or the saints' lives composed by Osbern Bokenham for aristocratic women, or the many commissions that Lydgate received from royal, aristocratic, ecclesiastical and urban sources.[7] The riskier kind was when an author presented a copy speculatively to an influential person, as in the cases that Boccaccio seems to be describing. Here we might think of John Capgrave's presentation of copies of his works to two bishops, a duke and two kings, or of William Worcestre, who notes ruefully in 1472 that he presented his translation of Cicero's *De Senectute* to William Waynflete, 'but I got no reward from the Bishop'.[8] Hoccleve's 'Dialogue' contains a discussion with a Friend about what kind of poem the poet should compose

---

[5] *Ibid.*, 419.   [6] *Ibid.*
[7] For Berkeley, see R. Hanna III, 'Sir Thomas Berkeley and His Patronage', *Speculum*, 64 (1989), 878–916 and F. Somerset, *Clerical Discourses and Lay Audience in Late Medieval England* (Cambridge, 1998), pp. 62–100. Hanna argues that Berkeley encouraged the circulation of Trevisa's translations in London. This is close to but not identical with Boccaccio's relation with his patrons: Trevisa did not present his translations speculatively. For Osbern Bokenham, see *Legendys of Holy Wummen*, ed. M. S. Serjeantson, EETS, OS 206 (1936), pp. xx–xxi. For Lydgate, see A. E. Hartung (ed.), *A Manual of the Writings in Middle English 1050–1500* (New Haven, 1980), vol. VI, pp. 1809–1920.
[8] See Lucas, *Author to Audience*, p. 72, and p. 274, quoted from William Worcestre, *Itineraries*, ed. J. H. Harvey (Oxford, 1969), pp. 252–3.

much patronage was actually due to a bestsellering commercial for Humphrey, duke of Gloucester. The poet is advised by the Friend to write something in praise of women, to make up for wronging them in an earlier work, and so he decides to translate 'The Tale of Jereslaus' Wife'. The duke, says the Friend, takes pleasure in the company of ladies, and 'this book wole he shewen hem perchance', which looks like the Boccaccian trope of the poet-as-disseminator, though 'perchance' acknowledges the precariousness of this as a 'publication' strategy.[9]

Gifts of books seem to have been more complicated than Root allows for. Worcestre's comment shows that even the unsolicited presentation of a work may not have been primarily in order to have it disseminated, but in the hope of receiving payment. Capgrave's dedication to Humphrey, duke of Gloucester in the presentation copy of his commentary on Exodus contains a strong hint about reward: 'For princes and writers have always been mutually bound to each other by a special friendship, so that writers were supported by the authority [*auctoritas*] and monetary gifts [*impensae*] of the former while books were laid up by the labour and sweat of the latter.'[10] Gloucester seems to have remained impervious, however; the book went into his collection and was not disseminated, and Capgrave did not try him again. At around the same time, in 1439, John Lydgate received the first known payment to an English writer for a piece of writing: a handsome sum from John Whethamstede, abbot of St Albans, who had commissioned him to compose the life of the abbey's founder and paid him more than enough to cover his costs.[11] In 1456 John Hardyng gave an unsolicited copy of his *Chronicle* to Henry VI, with a reminder in the preface that Henry had failed to honour a long-standing commitment to reward him for acquiring documents relating to the English claim to the throne of Scotland. It seems to have worked, because Hardyng received a pension. There is no evidence, though, that this version of the *Chronicle* – which survives in the presentation copy only – was subsequently disseminated, and indeed it looks as if the whole point of making the gift was to create an occasion for airing an old grievance.[12] A much larger reward was at stake, after all, than Hardyng could have hoped to earn from the Chronicle alone,

---

[9] See Thomas Hoccleve, 'Dialogue', ll. 616–714, in J. A. Burrow (ed.), *Thomas Hoccleve's Complaint and Dialogue*, EETS OS 313 (Oxford, 1999). I am grateful to Linne Mooney for reminding me of this passage.

[10] Lucas, *Author to Audience*, p. 289; Lucas's translation. The manuscript is Bodl. Lib., MS Duke Humfrey b.1.

[11] D. Pearsall, *John Lydgate (1371–1449): A Bio-bibliography*, English Literary Studies Monograph Series 71 (Victoria, BC, 1997), pp. 35 and 59.

[12] BL, MS Lansdowne 204. See my 'Hardyng's *Chronicle* and the Wars of the Roses', *Arthurian Literature XII* (1993), 91–108.

if we regard the £3. 6s. 8d that Whethamstede gave to Lydgate as a going rate.

English manuscript illuminations showing books being presented seem to represent a range of symbolic relationships, as the Lydgate manuscripts show. For example, the depiction, in a manuscript of his *Fall of Princes*, of Boccaccio giving a book to another man, who is either Lydgate himself or possibly his immediate source, the French translator Laurent de Premierfait, seems to represent the process of translation as a gift made by one author to another.[13] It is an illustration, that is, of textual relationships, not of relations between men. Another Lydgate manuscript depicts a monk kneeling among a group of other monks and presenting a book to the child Henry VI; this manuscript was made to commemorate the visit of Henry to the abbey at Bury St Edmunds, and the illumination records the abbey's gift to him of the work by its currently fashionable in-house author.[14] It is not, therefore, an authorial presentation picture but a record of a gift-giving. And, of course, illustrations of an author giving a book to a donor do not occur only in presentation copies: several manuscripts of Lydgate's *Troy Book*, made long after the poem was originally composed, replicate the author-as-donor scene from their exemplars.[15] Perhaps in these cases we should read the author-as-donor scene as a means of attaching the 'name' or '*auctoritas*' of the recipient permanently to the text. The ideas of the author as originator and the recipient as guarantor together perform something like the function that Boccaccio envisaged for his *De claris mulieribus*: 'under your auspices it will go free from the insults of the malicious', only here the auspices are textual and not actual.

Something similar may be going on within dedications. The Lydgatian *Nightingale* is dedicated to the duchess of Buckingham: she is asked in the proem to 'asygne a place' for it among her books until an occasion presents itself for a household reading, when 'hyr ladyly goodnesse/ Luste for to cal unto hir highe presence/ Such of hyre peple that are in lustynesse/ Fresschly encoragyt, as galantus in prime tens,/ Desyrous for to here the amerouse sentensce/ Of the nyghtyngale' (8–13).[16] This does not necessarily allude to a real-life event; rather it attaches to the poem a definition of an ideal audience – or an ideal mode of reading – in order to secure the poem the most favourable reception possible: aristocratic, refined, eager, interested in

[13] San Marino, Huntington Library, MS HM 266; K. L. Scott, *Later Gothic Manuscripts, 1390–1490*, 2 vols. (1996), vol. I, pl. 306, vol. II, pp. 229–33.

[14] BL, MS Harley 2278, fo. 6; Scott, *Later Gothic Manuscripts*, vol. I, pl. 311, vol. II, pp. 225–9.

[15] Scott, *Later Gothic Manuscripts*, vol. II, p. 261.

[16] See Wogan-Browne *et al.* (eds.), *Idea of the Vernacular*, p. 188.

love and open to the nightingale's moral teaching on it. Precisely because the poet is not present, he seeks to control the way it is to be understood, and so every reading, aloud or silent, rehearses anew this imagined scenario as a preliminary to the poem itself. What all this seems to suggest is that Root may have read Boccaccio and Petrarch too literally; their dedications are prologues to what follows as much as they are records of real-life relationships and obligations.

The second of the 'authorial' modes of 'publication' assumed for the pre print era is that of the author reading a work aloud to an audience, presumably before somehow 'releasing' it in written form for the first time. This mode seems to be assumed most often in relation to Chaucer: the debates over the dating of *The Book of the Duchess* and *The Parliament of Fowls*, for example, often involve identifying specific occasions for which these poems might have been written – a memorial to the duchess of Lancaster or Richard II's wedding negotiations – and imply that they were performed at such events.[17] And of course the well-known frontispiece illumination in Cambridge, Corpus Christi College MS 61 of *Troilus and Criseyde*, dated around 1415, in which Chaucer is depicted reciting to an assembly of courtiers, has been used to lend credence to the idea – for which there is no documentary evidence – that he published his poems in this way.[18] The current consensus on the *Troilus* frontispiece is that it arises from and represents the poem's compelling closeness to speech, a 'myth of reading' rather than a depiction of a real event.[19] The practice of communal reading persisted, however, in late medieval England, even where the audience was literate: the performance of a written text could create temporary social cohesion.[20] It seems plausible to assume, therefore, that Chaucer's poems, and the work of certain other modern authors, were part of this performance culture and that English writers may sometimes have read their compositions aloud, as Froissart famously describes himself

---

[17] See A. Minnis, with V. J. Scattergood and J. J. Smith, *Oxford Guides to Chaucer: The Shorter Poems* (Oxford, 1995), pp. 73–80 and 256–61.

[18] 'Every one knows . . . that Chaucer read his poetry aloud to assembled audiences at the court, as indeed we see him doing in the beautiful Corpus Christi College, Cambridge manuscript of the *Troilus*': A. C. Baugh, 'Chaucer the Man', in B. Rowland (ed.), *Companion to Chaucer Studies* (Toronto, New York and London, 1969), p. 13.

[19] The phrase is Lee Patterson's in 'Chaucer's Audience: Discussion', *Chaucer Review*, 18 (1983), 175. See D. Pearsall, 'The *Troilus* frontispiece and Chaucer's Audience', *Yearbook of English Studies*, 7 (1977), 68–74, and B. Windeatt, *Oxford Guides to Chaucer: Troilus and Criseyde* (Oxford, 1992), pp. 12–19.

[20] J. Coleman, *Public Reading and the Reading Public in Late Medieval England and France* (Cambridge, 1996). Coleman's work challenges some of the arguments of P. Saenger, 'Silent Reading: Its Impact on Medieval Script and Society', *Viator*, 13 (1982), 367–414.

as doing at the court of the count of Foix.[21] Only on very rare occasions, though, can this kind of authorial reading – if indeed it took place – be understood as publication of a new work in anything like its modern sense.

The 'official' mode of 'publication' has been invoked most commonly with reference to Nicholas Love's early fifteenth-century translation of *The Mirror of the Blessed Life of Jesus Christ*, which is essentially a gospel harmony. In 1409, responding to the spread of Lollardy, Archbishop Arundel issued a set of draconian Constitutions which included an article forbidding unauthorised translation of the Bible on pain of excommunication.[22] Love, who was prior of the Carthusian house of Mountgrace, quickly sought official approval for his *Mirror*, and many of the manuscripts include Arundel's 'Memorandum of Approbation', issued around 1410. This records that the archbishop 'pronounced and commanded by his own metropolitan authority that it be placed in the public domain, as being orthodox, for the edification of the faithful and the confutation of heretics or Lollards'.[23] Scholars frequently equate Arundel's *imprimatur* with 'publication', despite the fact that there is evidence that manuscripts containing versions of the *Mirror* were already in circulation before it was shown to him.[24] Malcolm Parkes takes the plausible view that Love submitted his work to Arundel primarily because he knew that 'contaminated' versions, beyond his control, were already being read and he wished to exonerate himself, although at the same time the licence may also have 'stimulated a demand for copies'.[25] Capgrave possibly hoped to achieve the same effect when

---

[21] See Jean Froissart, *Chroniques*, ed. S. Luce *et al.*, Société de l'histoire de France, 15 vols. (Paris, 1869–75), vol. XI, p. 85. J. A. Burrow points out that in *Troilus and Criseyde*, v. 1797 ('And red wherso thow be, or elles songe'), 'Chaucer's reference to the "singing" [is] presumably [to] oral perfomance'; see his 'Scribal Mismetring', in A. J. Minnis (ed.), *Middle English Poetry: Texts and Traditions* (Woodbridge, 2001), p. 169.

[22] See N. Watson, 'Censorship and Cultural Change in Late-Medieval England: Vernacular Theology, the Oxford Translation Debate, and Arundel's Constitutions of 1409', *Speculum*, 70 (1995), 822–64, esp. 825–30.

[23] M. G. Sargent (ed.), *Nicholas Love's Mirror of the Blessed Life of Jesus Christ: A Critical Edition Based on Cambridge University Library Additional MSS 6578 and 6686* (New York, 1992), pp. xlv and 7. The Latin is: 'necnon & auctoritate sua metropolitica, vt pote catholicum, puplice communicandum fore decreuit & mandauit, ad fidelium edificacionem, & hereticorum siue lollardorum confutacionem'. I am grateful to my colleague Dr J. W. Binns for supplying the translation, which differs from Sargent's: 'and further decreed and commanded by his metropolitan authority that it rather be published universally' (p. xlv).

[24] A. I. Doyle, 'Reflections on Some Manuscripts of Nicholas Love's *Myrrour of the Blessed Lyf of Jesu Christ*', *Leeds Studies in English*, NS 14 (1983), 82–93.

[25] M. B. Parkes, 'Punctuation in Copies of Nicholas Love's *Mirror of the Blessed Life of Jesus Christ*' in S. Oguro, R. Beadle and M. Sargent (eds.), *Nicholas Love: Waseda 1995* (Woodbridge, 1997), p. 56.

he dedicated his commentary on Acts to the bishop of Ely in 1458: 'so that, in this way, the book, going forth from your Lordship marked either by the asterisk [of approval] or the obelus [of disapproval], may go down to others more safely, validated by such great authority.'[26] Neither of the surviving copies carries Bishop Gray's *imprimatur*, however, so there is no evidence here either of episcopal licensing as a straightforward mode of 'publication'.

The possibility of 'commercial publication' has been raised in relation to the production of manuscripts by professional lay scribes and the commercialisation of the book industry. Laura Hubbard Loomis's argument that the Auchinleck manuscript (National Library of Scotland, Advocates' MS 19.2.1) was produced in the 1330s in a London 'bookshop' in which writers and scribes worked together 'in the entirely realistic business of manufacturing romance for sale' used to be extremely influential.[27] Eleanor Hammond, who first identified the London scribe named after her, assumed that the prolific Hammond scribe was employed in a '*scriptorium* or a publishing business' in the 1460s and 1470s.[28] Both of these hypotheses, however, have now been largely superseded by a slightly different model, in which London scribes are located in their own working households, often collaborating, as craftsmen frequently did, with other self-employed book-artisans living nearby – parchmeners, limners, bookbinders – to produce books on demand.[29] Such arrangements were, of course, commercial in that the craftsmen were paid for their work, and the same people must also often have traded in second-hand books. They seem to have been book-makers and booksellers, though, rather than being in the business of launching new texts.

A somewhat different kind of medieval publishing venture is sometimes associated with the London manuscript-producer, John Shirley, in the 1430s and 1440s. Shirley, a secretary in the household of Richard Beauchamp,

---

[26] Lucas, *Author to Audience*, pp. 15–16. The fact that Pecock's books had been burned for heresy the year before, may have made some readers nervous.

[27] L. Hubbard Loomis, 'The Auchinleck Manuscript and a Possible London Bookshop of 1330–1340', *PMLA*, 57 (1942), 626.

[28] E. P. Hammond, 'A Scribe of Chaucer', *Modern Philology*, 27 (1929–30), 29.

[29] See C. P. Christianson, 'A Community of Book Artisans in Chaucer's London', *Viator*, 20 (1989), 207–18, and 'Evidence for the Study of London's Late Medieval Manuscript-Book Trade' in Griffiths and Pearsall (eds.), *Book Production*, pp. 87–108. Linne Mooney's recent suggestion that the Hammond scribe worked with two other scribes in a stationer's shop, writing texts to order, is essentially a variant of this model. She is careful not to claim that this was anything other than a bespoke business: that is, she rejects the older model of speculative 'publication'. See L. R. Mooney, 'Scribes and Booklets of Trinity College, Cambridge, Manuscripts R.3.19 and R.3.21', in A. J. Minnis (ed.), *Middle English Poetry: Texts and Traditions* (Woodbridge, 2001), pp. 241–66, at p. 265.

earl of Warwick, settled in London in his late fifties where he set about assembling and copying texts, including poems by Chaucer, Gower and especially Lydgate. Three anthologies in his own hand survive, and parts of others.[30] At first sight he looks different from the model I have just described in that he procured his own material, though of course many professional scribes must have done this too. Sometimes a client must have brought with her no more than an idea of the kind of text she wanted; knowledge of and access to the traffic in texts may well have been the mark of a successful stationer. It is not at all clear, though, why Shirley produced his anthologies or for whom. Part of the difficulty in locating him in the London book-trade is that he was an esquire who learned his skills in an aristocratic household rather than by apprenticeship to a craftsman. His social status does not preclude the possibility that he used those skills to earn a living after leaving Beauchamp's employ; nevertheless, the present state of our knowledge means that he cannot be used to prove anything certain about medieval publishing.

These four modes of 'publication' identified by modern scholarship all seem, on closer inspection, to be too limited, ambiguous or opaque to provide an answer to the question with which I began. It seems likely that there is no single answer anyway. Nevertheless, by paying attention to the 'public' in 'publication', it is possible to add another dimension to the problem.

II

Let us return to Root's examples. Boccaccio's anxiety that *De claris mulieribus* might otherwise 'languish in idleness on my hands', his desire that his works should go forth 'under the auspices' or the 'name' of an influential person, and the hope that this might afford protection from 'the insults of the malicious' have English parallels. I have already suggested that the dedication and the author-as-patron scene are means of attaching a 'name' to a piece of writing. Reginald Pecock shared Boccaccio's concern that books should not be idle: 'it is not ynou3 that . . . bokis be writen and made and leid up or rest in the hondis of clerkis'.[31] This sounds very like Boccaccio's languishing book, seen from the perspective of a churchman

---

[30] J. Boffey and J. J. Thompson, 'Anthologies and Miscellanies: Production and Choice of Texts', in Griffiths and Pearsall (eds.), *Book Production*, pp. 270–316, esp. pp. 284–87; M. Connolly, *John Shirley: Book Production and the Noble Household in Fifteenth-Century England* (Aldershot, 1998).

[31] J. L. Morison (ed.), *Reginald Pecock's Book of Faith* (Glasgow, 1909), p. 16; quoted by V. Gillespie, 'Vernacular Books of Religion', in Griffiths and Pearsall (eds.), *Book Production*, p. 335.

with a passionate commitment to the idea of a devout lay readership. Pecock goes on to say that 'tho bokis musten be distributid and delid abrood to manye'; 'abrood' is the risky sphere where the text will be exposed to critique, as he found to his cost in relation to his own writings.[32] More than a century earlier, Richard Rolle had written in his preface to *The English Psalter* that his commentary followed 'haly doctourys, for it may come in some envyous man that . . . wil say that I wist noght what I sayd, and swa doe harme til hym and tyl othere'.[33] A generation later, the author of *The Cloud of Unknowing* expressed his hope that his work would not fall into the hands of 'Fleschely janglers, opyn preisers and blamers of himself or of any other, tithing tellers, rouners and tutilers of tales and alle maner of pinchers'.[34] Boccaccio's phrases, *emittere/procedere in publicum* are not unlike Arundel's idiom, *commendo publice*, in the licence for Love's *Mirror*. We can gather what *in publicum* is like: risky, competitive, divisive, heady. But what exactly does *in publicum* mean? Perhaps to answer that question we need a framework of ideas relating to public and private, and to stop thinking of the manuscript era as one in which books belonged to the intimate sphere.

Harold Love, in his study of scribal publication in seventeenth-century England (where of course the simultaneous availability of two different modes of production – script or print – alters the whole issue), regards the public/private divide as fundamental:

The root sense . . . of publication [is] as a movement from a private realm of creativity to a public realm of consumption. The problem is to determine whether any given text – in our case a text transmitted through handwritten copies – has made this transition. We will need to recognise both a 'strong' sense in which the text must be shown to have become publicly available and a more inclusive 'weak' sense in which it is enough to show that the text has ceased to be a private possession.[35]

Love contrasts private creativity and public consumption, aligning these with private possession and public availability. The private and public 'realms' do not seem to be spatial here; this not a contrast between the home and the street. Rather, the pairing seems to distinguish the individual or personal from the collective or general. A somewhat similar approach is taken by the doyen of English medieval palaeographers, Ian Doyle, in an article on publication by members of religious orders in the manuscript era:

---

[32] Pecock's books were burned for heresy in 1457.
[33] Wogan-Browne *et al.* (eds.), *Idea of the Vernacular*, p. 246.   [34] *Ibid.*, p. 231.
[35] H. Love, *Scribal Publication in Seventeenth-Century England* (Oxford, 1993), p. 36.

Publication . . . must comprise, at least, communication (not necessarily by the author) of a piece to another person or persons, with leave (perhaps tacit) or motivation to pass it on to others; which *may* be preceded or followed by the growth of knowledge of its existence and interest, rousing a desire for further copies, consequent reproduction and gradual dissemination to a greater or lesser extent.[36]

Here too, publication seems to be a matter of access or availability that is not so much spatial as modal: a text is communicated to other people in a way that opens it to further copying and transmission. This too is a world of consumers – note Doyle's use of the word 'desire' – but consumers who seem to form an orderly reproductive chain, like that described by a Carthusian of Mountgrace in the manuscript of the *Revelation of the Hundred Paternosters*: 'I sent to a devoute preest of my knowlegge a copy of the Reuelacion . . . which ye sende me. And the same preeste sent dyuers copies to certeyn of his Frendes, of whom ther was a good husbond man harde of the grete vartu and grace of the forsaid prayers he vsed it dayly as deuoutly as he coude.'[37] Doyle's careful qualification that the person who initially hands over the piece may not be the author suggests that he may have in mind Chaucer's *Canterbury Tales*, on the manuscripts of which he has done seminal work. On Chaucer's death in 1400 the poet's papers must have been very quickly made available for copying by his executors, and the earliest surviving manuscripts of the (unfinished) *Canterbury Tales* were all professionally produced as separate commissions in London.[38] Doyle and Parkes have shown that the commissioners of copies competed with one another to employ the highly-skilled craftsmen involved.[39] In Harold Love's terms, the author's copy or copies of the *Canterbury Tales* ceased to be a private possession and became publicly available in the sense that anyone who could afford to and was able to secure a copyist could have a copy made. It looks, from the quality of the early manuscripts, as if the poem was caught up in turn-of-the-century consumerism, when increased personal

---

[36] A. I. Doyle, 'Publication by Members of the Religious Orders' in Griffiths and Pearsall (eds.), *Book Production*, p. 110; author's italics.

[37] See V. A. Gillespie, 'Cura Pastoralis in Deserto', in M. G. Sargent (ed.), *De Cella in Seculum: Religious and Secular Life and Devotion in Late Medieval England* (Cambridge, 1989), pp. 161–81, at pp. 176–7; he quotes from F. Wormald, 'The Revelation of a Hundred Pater Nosters', *Laudate*, 14 (1936), 81.

[38] For debate about whether any surviving manuscripts were produced during Chaucer's lifetime, see K. L. Scott, 'An Hours and Psalter by Two Ellesmere Illuminators', in M. Stevens and D. Woodward (eds.), *The Ellesmere Manuscript: Essays in Interpretation* (San Marino and Tokyo, 1996), pp. 87–119, and *Later Gothic Manuscripts*, vol. ii, p. 140; N. F. Blake, 'Geoffrey Chaucer and the Manuscripts of the *Canterbury Tales*', *Journal of the Early Book Society*, 1 (1997), 1–24.

[39] A. I. Doyle and M. B. Parkes, 'The Production of Copies of the *Canterbury Tales* and the *Confessio Amantis* in the Early Fifteenth Century', in M. B. Parkes and A. G. Watson (eds.), *Medieval Scribes, Manuscripts, and Libraries: Essays Presented to N. R. Ker* (1978), pp. 163–210.

wealth encouraged extravagant spending on luxury goods.[40] One of these is the illuminated vellum manuscript bound in pink leather containing the last work of London's most fashionable poet, which we call the Ellesmere manuscript.[41] Seen in this context, Doyle's orderly reproductive chain begins to look more like a commercial free-for-all.

Doyle also says that the handing over of the piece '*may* be preceded or followed by the growth of knowledge of its existence and interest, rousing a desire for further copies'. Here the issue is not public availability but public knowledge: people of course need to know that a text exists before they can order copies of it. Although Doyle regards knowledge as contingent – note how he stresses *may* – I believe that it is necessary. Another approach to the problem of 'publication' might be via a publicness that is not a realm of consumption but of talk. When the text moves from the private to the public sphere, it is not just available for copying now where previously it had not been, but people know this; in fact, this is what constitutes its publicness. And people presumably can only know about it because it is a topic of general discussion. The good husbandman 'harde' of the *Revelation of the Hundred Paternosters* before he read it; the author of *Speculum Devotorum* almost gave up writing his life of Christ when he 'herde telle' that Nicholas Love had already done it.[42] One of the most inaccessible areas for us in studying the past is the space of talk. We privilege written texts and documents because we have to, but this should not allow us to ignore the existence of a public sphere of discussion, debate, news, gossip and rumour, in which things were generally spoken of and generally known, a discursive rather than a spatial publicness. This, I suggest, is where medieval 'publication' took place, not as an event but as a process. This seems to be the risky realm of reputation and critique that Boccaccio envisaged, and in which word must have spread that the *Canterbury Tales* was available for copying. It is the realm that Chaucer himself had identified in the *House of Fame* as the restless wicker house of Rumour, 'fild ful of tydynges,/ Other loude or of whisprynges;/ And over all the houses angles/ Ys ful of rounynges and of jangles'.[43] It is the realm of critical talk that Chaucer's fellow-Londoner, Thomas Usk, invokes in the Prologue to his *Testament of Love*: 'Certes, I wote wel there shal be made

[40] See R. H. Britnell, *The Commercialisation of English Society 1000–1500*, 2nd edn (Manchester and New York, 1996), p. 171 and references in n. 95; D. Keene, 'Shops and Shopping in Medieval London', in L. Grant (ed.), *Medieval Art, Architecture and Archaeology in London* (1990), pp. 29–46.
[41] A. G. Cains, 'The Bindings of the Ellesmere Chaucer', in S. Lerer (ed.), *Readings from the Margins: Textual Studies, Chaucer, and Medieval Literature* (San Marino, CA, 1996), pp. 127–57.
[42] Wogan-Browne *et al.*, *Idea of the Vernacular*, p. 74.   [43] 'The House of Fame', ll. 1957–60.

more scorne and jape of me, that I, so unworthely clothed altogyder in the cloudy cloude of unconnynge, wyl putten me in prees to speke of love.'[44] And it is the disparaging realm against which Hoccleve's Friend warns him in the 'Dialogue': the poet describes how he read his account of his mental breakdown to his Friend, who asked uneasily: 'Hast thow maad this compleynte forth to go/ Among the peple?'[45] 'Forth to go among the peple' sounds like an Englishing of *procedere in publicum*, and the Friend goes on to warn Hoccleve of the folly of making his mental history a subject of malicious gossip.

Thinking in this way helps us to understand the range of meanings given to the Middle English word 'publisshen' which is closely related to speech; 'publisshen' means 'announce', 'proclaim', 'divulge' (as in divulge a secret), 'spread abroad' (as in gossip or news), 'propagate', 'publicise', 'become known'. It has the senses both of speaking and being spoken about, and is thus quite different from 'to issue or cause to be issued for sale to the public, copies of a book, music etc', which is one of the *OED* definitions. The first example of it (possibly) in the modern sense is in the era of print, from Thomas More's preface to *The Dialogue Concerning Heresies*: 'I am now driven . . . to this thirde busyness of publishynge and puttynge my boke in printe my selfe.'[46] The earlier sense of 'proclaim' is clear from *Mandeville's Travels*: 'For he þat wil pupplische ony thing to make it openly knowen, he wil make it to ben cryed and pronounced in the myddel place of a town'.[47] An example from *Piers Plowman* contrasts the verb 'publice[n]', meaning to make known, with 'prive' meaning secret, private, hidden: 'Thouȝ þow se yuel seye it noȝt first; be sory it nere amended;/ Thyng þat is pryue, publice þow it neuere.'[48] In the Towneley play of the Scourging, Jesus is said to have 'prechyd and puplyshed so playn/Cristen law', where 'puplyshed' means propagated.[49] Nicholas Love writes that the raising of Lazarus was 'publyshede and opunly knowen. In so miche þat gret multitude of Jerusalem . . . comen', where 'publyshede' means talked about.[50] 'Publisshen' can be more straightforwardly

[44] R. Allen Shoaf (ed.), *Thomas Usk, The Testament of Love* (Kalamazoo, MI, 1998), *Prologue*, ll. 67–9. I am grateful to Isabel Davis for this reference.

[45] Hoccleve, *Dialogue*, ll. 23–4, in Burrow (ed.), *Thomas Hoccleve's Complaint and Dialogue*.

[46] See *OED*, publish 4; T. McLawless, G. Marc'hadour and R. C. Marius (eds.), *A Dialogue Concerning Heresies*, Yale Edition of the Complete Works of Sir Thomas More (New Haven-London, 1981), vol. 6, p. 22.

[47] P. Hamelius (ed.), *Mandeville's Travels*, EETS, OS 153 (1919), p. 2.

[48] William Langland, *The Vision of Piers the Plowman*, ed. A. V. C. Schmidt (1995), XI.104–5.

[49] M. Stevens and A. C. Cawley (eds.), *The Towneley Plays*, 2 vols., EETS, supp. ser. 11 and 12 (Oxford, 1991), vol. 1, p. 27.

[50] Sargent (ed.), *Nicholas Love's Mirror*, p. 135.

pejorative: Chaucer says of Criseyde after her betrayal of Troilus: 'Hire name, allas, is publysshed so wide/ That for hire gilt it oughte ynough suffise.'[51] Here 'publysshed' seems to have the force of gossiped about, or spoken of disparagingly, and reminds us of the dangers of this risky sphere of general talk where reputations are made and broken. 'Publisshen' is also used of texts: Trevisa, in his translation of Higden's *Polychronicon* writes: 'To þis Marchus, Athanasius . . . wrete for seventy chapitres, þat were i-publesched in þe Synod Nicena'.[52] Here 'i-publesched' seems to mean 'made public' in the sense of 'read aloud': the Latin is *promulgatis*. Around 1464 Capgrave in his *Chronicle* says 'In this same ȝere Pope Jon pub-lisched that book which thei clepe "The Clementius"', which still permits the attested Middle English sense of publicised, made known.[53] Slightly earlier, Reginald Pecock in his *Donet* had written revealingly that St Gre-gory, 'not wiþstonding hise holy ententis and hise kunnyng, founde so much mysdiposid men forto lette and diffame and distroie his bokis . . . þat he wolde not þat eny of his bokis schulde be publischid bifore his deeþ'.[54] Here we can clearly see the riskiness of the public sphere, a zone in which the envious seek to vilify or suppress the views of others. Pecock is being self-protective, of course: his own works were publicly burned in 1457. He claims, in the same prologue, that his writings had been 'runne abrood and copied ayens my wil and myn entent', that he had been betrayed by friends to whom he had lent copies for their eyes only before he had had a chance to revise them, and that these copies had been passed on to other people. Whether or not he is telling the truth here, his words point to a distinction between distribution to the known reader and the subsequent transmission 'abrood' to a zone in which the text, and the discussion of it, have gone among strangers. Gregory is said not to have wanted any of his books to be 'publisched' before his death in this latter sense, rather than in the modern sense of 'being offered for sale'.

In the manuscript era the boundary between writing and talking is fre-quently blurred, and written texts often represent themselves as spoken. Writing, then as now, also came out of talk, however; it is the product of social exchange. The multifarious written texts that survive from the late Middle Ages did not float free but were always positioned, however ambiguously or loosely. Sermons, dream-visions, prayers, tales, chronicles, saints' lives, plays – even a revelation of love – arose from and responded to

[51] *Troilus and Criseyde*, v. 1095.
[52] C. Babington and J. R. Lumby, *Polychronicon Ranulphi Higden*, Rolls Series 41, 8 vols. (1865–86), vol. v, p. 147.
[53] F. C. Hingeston (ed.), *The Chronicle of England by John Capgrave*, Rolls Series 1 (1858), p. 183.
[54] E. V. Hitchcock (ed.), *The Donet by Reginald Peacock*, EETS, OS 156 (Oxford, 1921), p. 7.

the endless exchange of ideas that took place in the to-and-fro of sociability. 'Publication' is short for public conversation.

III

Where the author is a recluse, the issues around publicness seem particularly problematic. Julian of Norwich was a contemporary of Chaucer, though she outlived him, dying in her seventies around 1416. She spent certainly the last decades of her life, and perhaps longer, in a reclusorium attached to the wall of a Norwich parish church. The text that she wrote explains that at the age of thirty in 1373, during a grave illness, she had a series of visions that were initiated by the sight of the crucifix at the end of her bed beginning to bleed. The visions lasted for three days. The first account of these, known as the Short Version, was written ten or more years later. The writer continued to meditate on the meaning of her visions, however, and produced a longer, theologically much more daring and intellectually sophisticated revision sometime after 1393, which is known as the Long Version.[55] There are various titles, of which *A Revelation of Love* is one.[56] The Short Version survives in one manuscript in the British Library, of around 1450, which replicates a colophon dated 1413.[57] There is no surviving complete medieval copy of the Long Version, although there is a heavily excerpted text from about 1500.[58] The only complete manuscripts, on which all modern editions are based, date from the seventeenth century and were copied by English recusant nuns at Cambrai and Paris.[59] I have explored elsewhere what I call Julian's 'self-textualisation': the process, that is, whereby an intensely private experience took shape as a book.[60] 'Publication' was the next step.

Part at least of the interest of *A Revelation of Love* lies in the fact that, most unusually, the text describes the processes whereby it came into being *as a*

---

[55] See N. Watson, 'The Composition of Julian of Norwich's *Revelation of Love*', *Speculum*, 68 (1993), 637–84.

[56] E. Colledge, OSA and J. Walsh, SJ (eds.), *A Book of Showings to the Anchoress Julian of Norwich*, Studies and Texts 35, 2 vols. (Toronto, 1978); M. Glasscoe (ed.), *Julian of Norwich, A Revelation of Love* (Exeter, 1976; rev. 1993); G. R. Crampton (ed.), *The Shewings of Julian of Norwich* (Kalamazoo, 1994). All quotations are from the Colledge and Walsh edition.

[57] BL, Add. MS 37790; ed. in Colledge and Walsh (eds.), *A Book of Showings*; F. Beer (ed.), *Julian of Norwich's Revelations of Divine Love: The Shorter Version, ed. from BL Add. MS 37790*, Middle English Texts 8 (Heidelberg, 1978).

[58] H. Kempster, 'The Westminster Text of *A Revelation of Love*', *Mystics Quarterly*, 23 (1997), 177–245.

[59] Paris, Bibliothèque Nationale, MS fonds anglais 40 was probably copied in the first half of the seventeenth century; BL, MS Sloane 2499 is probably somewhat later.

[60] F. Riddy, 'Julian of Norwich and Self-Textualisation', in A. Hutchison (ed.), *Editing Women* (Toronto, 1998), pp. 101–24.

text, and these processes are presented as a movement from different kinds of privacy to publicness: from a bizarre insanity to a collected and rational meditation and, at the same time, from singularity to generality. Julian (the narrator is unnamed within the text) says that she came to understand what she had not realised at first: that the visions had not been given to her for her personal benefit. 'And thys shewyng', she writes, 'I toke syngularly to my selfe. But by alle the gracious comfort that folowyth, as ye shalle see, I was lernyd to take it to alle myn evyn cristen, alle in generalle and nothyng in specialle'.[61] Writing the book entailed remembering the original inchoate experience, finding meaning in it, organising it and shaping it into a text, designed for those fellow-Christians on whose behalf she believed the visions had been given to her. One of the manuscripts, which may represent the last stage in the process of making the text readerly, has an *imprimatur* of sorts, enjoining the reader to take counsel when reading it and not to pick out favourite bits like a heretic. Much of this is familiar enough; making manuscripts more user-friendly is a characteristic fifteenth-century development. Here, though, there is a specific impetus for this: it is not to be a book for the bookish but for the uneducated: 'I say nott this to them that be wyse, for thei wytt it wele. But I sey it to yow that be simple, for ease and comfort; for we be alle one in loue. . . . For yf I looke syngulery to my selfe I am ry3t nought; but in generall I am, I hope, in onehede of cheryte with alle my evyn cristen'.[62]

The belief that the visions were not intended for herself alone, but for all her fellow Christians, provides what Doyle calls 'the motivation to pass it on to others', which is where publication starts. This is a text that understands the rationale for its very existence as public. The distinction drawn between 'alle in generalle and nothyng in specialle' and between 'in generall' and 'singulery', is a distinction between private and public, not wholly different in kind from Harold Love's private creativity and public consumption. It is worth considering the distinction a little more closely. 'Special' and 'singulere' in Middle English, like 'propre', mean individual or particular. All three words are frequently contrasted with 'general' and 'commune', meaning pertaining to all, or serving the members of a community or organisation.[63] This private-public divide – special versus general, singular versus common – is not spatial: it does not have to do with accessibility versus inaccessibility, or with hidden versus disclosed;

[61] Vol. II, ch. 37, p. 442.   [62] Vol. II, ch. 9, p. 322.
[63] See *Middle English Dictionary*, ed. H. Kurath, S. M. Kuhn, and J. Reidy (Ann Arbor, MI, 1952–2001), special n., 3 (a); singulere, adj., 1 (a), 2 (a); propre, adj., 1 (a); general, adj. & n., 1 (a), 6 (a) and (c); commune, adj., 1 (a), 3 and 4.

it has to do with 'what is individual, or pertains only to an individual, versus what is collective'.[64] It is used frequently in relation to the common good; for example, in a proclamation of 1423 the Mayor and Aldermen of London forbade the merchants and victuallers to buy up goods before they reached the city's markets 'for their singler avauntage', at the expense of 'þe commune profit'.[65] Examples of this kind could be easily multiplied. This private-public distinction is a way of thinking about the human person in relation to his or her fellows, in which the collective is more highly valued than the individual. It is a mode of thinking that understands 'abrood' or '*in publicum*' or 'among the peple' as a discursive public sphere: not just as a realm of casual and destructive talk (though it is that too, of course), but as one in which individuals can identify common goods and participate in discussion of matters of common concern.

Somewhere behind this lie the modes of late medieval political thought about the common good that have recently been delineated in academic contexts.[66] The discursive public sphere is the arena where debate – about morality, about religion, about art, about politics, about books – must have been constantly engaged in. It is where Lollard ideas, for example, spread among different social groups; it is where people agreed about what kinds of behaviour should be stigmatised as wrongdoing and brought before the courts; it is where they argued about how towns should be governed, about the morality of fashion, about whether everyone would be saved.[67] Ideas in books must also have circulated in talk, and there must have been talk about books. The classic locales of the discursive public sphere of the eighteenth century are coffee houses, salons and clubs; in fourteenth- and fifteenth-century England – that intensely clubbable society – we should think of inns and taverns, of guildhalls, meeting-rooms in religious houses, of

---

[64] J. Weintraub, 'The Theory and Politics of the Public/Private Distinction', in J. Weintraub and K. Kumar (eds.), *Public and Private in Thought and Practice: Perspectives on a Grand Dichotomy* (Chicago and London, 1997), p. 5.

[65] R. W. Chambers and M. Daunt (eds.), *A Book of London English 1384–1425* (Oxford, 1931), pp. 102–3, from Guildhall, Letter-book K, fo. 11.

[66] M. T. Kempshall, *The Common Good in Late Medieval Political Thought* (Oxford, 1999).

[67] For Lollardy, see the 'Twelve Conclusions', posted on the doors of Westminster and St Paul's in 1395 'in oure langage', in order to be 'communed [communicated, told] to alle trewe Cristine men', in A. Hudson (ed.), *Selections from English Wycliffite Writings* (Cambridge, 1978), pp. 24–9, 150–1. For wrongdoing, see M. K. McIntosh, *Controlling Misbehaviour in England, 1370–1600* (Cambridge, 1998), pp. 23–45. For government, see my discussion of Norwich below. For fashion, see W. N. Francis (ed.), *The Book of Virtues and Vices*, EETS, OS 217 (1942), p. 43: 'maidenes and dameseles . . . þat ofte siþe aparailen hem more queyntely and gaily for to make nyse lokers to loke on hem, and weneþ not to do gret synne'. For salvation, see N. Watson, 'Visions of Inclusion: Universal Salvation and Vernacular Theology in Pre-Reformation England', *Journal of Medieval and Early Modern Studies*, 27 (1997), 145–87.

market-places and even homes. At the same time, we do not need to think
of this medieval public sphere as gendered, like the eighteenth-century
public sphere, given that these locales were open to both sexes.

Anchoresses certainly belonged to the realm of talk: the anchoress's window had been stigmatised as a site of idle gossip ever since Aelred of Rievaulx
waspishly observed that 'vnnethes [scarcely] now-a-dayes shaltow finde a
solitary recluse, that either tofore the windowe shal sitte an olde woman
fedynge hir with tales, or elles a new iangeler [gossip] and teller of tidynges
of that monke, or that clerke, or of widowes dissolucion, or of maidens
wantownes'.[68] More earnest conversations went on as well. In 1393–4 Anna
Palmer, a Northampton recluse, was accused of holding Lollard meetings
in her cell, and was charged with incontinence as well as Lollardy: she denied the incontinence.[69] We know from *The Book of Margery Kempe* that
its protagonist visited Julian in Norwich and that these two women writers
talked to each other over the space of three days.[70] Three fifteenth-century
anchoresses are listed as members of the York Corpus Christi gild which
was one of the most prestigious and popular religious gilds of the city.[71] Its
members included very large numbers of laypeople, many of them wealthy
merchants and their wives. One of these anchoresses might be the York
recluse who is mentioned in *The Book of Margery Kempe*. After being held
at Leicester on suspicion of heresy, 'the creatur' visited an anchoress who
had loved her before she went to Jerusalem, but the anchoress would not
receive her, 'for sche had herd telde so mech evyl telde of hir'.[72]

The differences between the surviving texts of *A Revelation of Love* can
be related to Julian's evolving sense of herself as an author under a divine
imperative to write 'for the profytte of many oder' or, in other terms, for
a common good.[73] These others were presumably, in the first instance at
least, her fellow-townspeople, the devout members of local religious gilds,
who may well have been the kind of people she grew up with and away
from.[74] The regulations of the Norwich St Katherine's gild state that at the

---

[68] This quotation is from the fifteenth-century translation of Aelred's *De Institutione Inclusarum* in
J. Ayton and A. Barratt (eds.), *Aelred of Rievaulx's De Institutione Inclusarum*, EETS OS 287 (Oxford,
1984), p. 1.

[69] See A. Warren, *Anchorites and their Patrons in Medieval England* (Berkeley, 1985), p. 81.

[70] Meech and Allen (eds.), *Margery Kempe*, p. 42.

[71] R. H. Skaife (ed.), *The Register of the Gild of Corpus Christi*, Surtees Society 57 (1972), pp. 15 and 17.

[72] Meech and Allen (eds.), *Margery Kempe*, p. 119.

[73] L. S. Johnson, 'The Trope of the Scribe and the Question of Literary Authority in the Works of
Julian of Norwich and Margery Kempe', *Speculum*, 66 (1991), 820–38, esp. 833.

[74] I disagree with Nicholas Watson's argument in 'Composition of Julian of Norwich's *Revelation of
Love*' (see n. 54 above) that the Short Text was written for a community of nuns. Its frequent references
to 'even-Christians' seem to me to indicate the wider audience that Watson allows only to the Long
Text.

funerals of dead members 'euery brother and sister yat is letterede shul seyn, for ye soule of ye dede, placebo and dirige . . . ande euery brother and sister yat bene nought letterede, shul seyn for ye soule of ye dede, xx. sythes, ye pater noster wᵗ Aue maria'.⁷⁵ Julian is addressing 'simple' people like these; in the preface to the Long Version she describes herself as 'a simple creature vnletturde'.⁷⁶ Her sense of 'onehede' with all her even-Christians extends more widely than this, however, because *A Revelation of Love* seems to be working out a theology of universal salvation. This a far bolder version of solidarity and inclusiveness even than that of the Norwich gild of St Christopher, whose ordinances include an unusually wide-ranging prayer on behalf of one's fellows that was to be said by the (male) members every time they met. Their prayer contains, though, a strikingly masculine and vertical conception of secular society compared with Julian's horizontal one. Male citizens and burgesses are placed as near to the top as they credibly can be, separated from their wives by franklins, true tillers and craftsmen; there are also conspicuous gaps around the lower rungs of society.⁷⁷ Moreover the St Christopher gild's rule about providing help for members who fall on hard times has the usual qualification: twelve pence a week will be available from donations by gild members to any gild brother or sister who 'falle in pouerte or myschef, *by auenture of ye werld*'.⁷⁸ Those members whose misfortunes are brought about by their own folly or dishonesty need not apply. It is instructive to read chapter 51 of Julian of Norwich's *A Revelation of Love* against this gild outlook. There Julian describes the fall of Adam, whom she represents as what the gild of St Christopher would call a true tiller. He quite literally falls into a mire as he runs to do his lord's bidding, and lies there groaning and helpless. His 'curtes lord', whom he cannot see, looks at him 'with grete ruth and pety' and says: 'Is it nott reson that I award hym his frey and his drede, his hurt and his mayme and alle his woo? And nott only this, but fallyth it nott to me to geve hym a ȝifte that be better to hym and more wurschypfull than his owne hele shuld haue bene? And ells me thyngkyth I dyd hym no grace.'⁷⁹ I am not simply suggesting that Julian has a better idea of what unself-interested love might look like than the members of the St Christopher gild, though she has. Nor am I simply suggesting that what for them are social issues are for her theological ones, though they are. Rather I want to suggest that we might see her book as positioned within the public sphere, not as occupying some quite separate discursive space. *A Revelation of Love* raises moral as well as theological issues about inclusiveness and love, and these issues are different but not

⁷⁵ T. Smith, *English Gilds*, EETS, OS 40 (1870), p. 20. ⁷⁶ Vol. ıı, ch. 2, p. 285.
⁷⁷ Smith, *English Gilds*, p. 22–3. ⁷⁸ *Ibid.*, p. 24. My italics. ⁷⁹ Vol. ıı, ch. 51, p. 518.

separate from the way Norwich citizens prayed or regulated their charity, or from debates that went on throughout Julian's adult life about how and by whom the town should be governed.

It seems that Norwich only slowly evolved in the course of the fourteenth and early fifteenth centuries a system of government, common elsewhere, whereby a small group of the most substantial citizens took over control of an authority that had earlier been vested in the 'commonalty' as a whole. From the 1370s on, this process created well-documented public dissension between different factions, all of whom claimed to be concerned with the common good.[80] It is not the nature of the debate, however, but the terms in which the factionalism was brought to an end that are relevant here. On February 14, 1415, an indenture was issued between the mayor, the sheriffs and the commonalty. The choice of St Valentine's day was deliberate, as the preamble stresses: 'on yᵉ day of Seint Valentyn martir . . . creatures thourgh loue of kynde as it [is] seide chesen her make'. The indenture goes on to speak of the 'holy preyer and mediacion of Seint Valentyn in whos day yᵉ Cite chaasce be loue . . . to . . . make pees unite and acord poore and ryche to ben oon in herte loue and charite neuermore fro this tyme forth to ben disseuered'.[81] 'Onehede of charite' is part of the contemporary discourse of urban social relations as well as of spiritual ones. And if there is an echo of Chaucer's *Parliament of Fowls* in the preamble, then perhaps his sophisticated and elusive juxtaposing of public and private kinds of love was also a subject of talk in early fifteenth-century Norwich.[82]

So how did Julian of Norwich 'publish' her contribution to this ongoing urban discussion of love? There is no dedicatee or patron. There was presumably no first public reading. We know, from a gossipy colophon, that the Short Version was in circulation before she died: 'Here es a visionn schewed be the goodenes of god to a deuoute womann, and hir name es Julyan, that is recluse atte Norwyche and ʒitt ys onn lyfe [is still alive], anno domini millesimo CCCC xiij°'.[83] The book, I suggest, like most books in the pre-print era, came out of the sea of talk and was cast back into it. The model of 'publication' proposed by Ian Doyle, which I quoted earlier, seems to work very well here: first, communication to another

---

[80] W. Hudson and J. C. Tingey, *The Records of the City of Norwich*, 2 vols. (Norwich, 1906–10); B. R. McCree, 'Religious Gilds and Civic Order: the Case of Norwich in the Late Middle Ages', *Speculum*, 67 (1992), 69–97.

[81] For the debate, see Hudson and Tingey, *Records of the City of Norwich*, vol. 1, pp. 64–93; for the indenture, see vol. 1, pp. 93–108, at 93–4.

[82] This is not wholly implausible. CUL, MS Gg.4.24, possibly dating from the second decade of the fifteenth century, is an East Anglian manuscript containing the *Parliament of Fowls*.

[83] Vol. 1, ch. 1, p. 201.

person; second, leave to pass it on; third, growth of knowledge of its existence; fourth, a desire for further copies; fifth, reproduction and dissemination. Julian spoke about love at the window of her cell, as *The Book of Margery Kempe* records her doing, and someone asked for a copy of the book. Its author's emphatic wish 'that it schulde be to euery ilke manne the same profytte that I desyrede to my selfe' must also have been a licence to pass it on.[84] Margery Kempe heard about her in Lynn, so by 1413 she had an established authorial identity, as the colophon to the Short Version manuscript confirms. And, finally, the variations between the surviving Long Version manuscripts suggest that Julian, or someone acting on her behalf, edited this version to make it increasingly accessible to readers, which implies 'a desire for further copies'.[85]

One way of explaining the fact that there are no surviving medieval manuscripts containing the Long Version in its entirety might be that it never reached a public at all. Appropriated by the clergy, it could, apparently like the sole manuscript of Margery Kempe's book, have been preserved in silence in a religious house until the Reformation and then come into recusant hands. Another explanation, though, is that it reached precisely the people for whom it was intended: unpretentious laypeople who read it in unbound booklets. The institutional copies survived the Reformation; the domestic copies, as evanescent as the talk on which they rested, were eventually discarded by uninterested heirs, or used to light the fire, or perhaps even read to bits.

---

[84] Vol. 1, ch. 6, p. 220.   [85] See Riddy, 'Julian of Norwich and Self-Textualisation'.

3

Printing, mass communication, and religious reformation: the Middle Ages and after[1]

David d'Avray

The modern literature on the impact of printing is voluminous and cannot be addressed systematically here.[2] Instead, this essay approaches the problem of script and print, from an unconventional point of departure: the book production which lay behind the popular preaching of the friars in the last three medieval centuries. The momentum of the argument leads on to a speculative and sceptical assessment of the causal relevance of the discovery of printing to the origins of the Reformation.

The books in question contained model sermons: material to help preachers with their 'live' preaching. Recently a Protestant pastor got into trouble for using material from an internet subscription service for his sermons. The equivalent of such borrowing was perfectly respectable in the Middle Ages (and after) so long as the ultimate audiences envisaged were lay congregations. The diffusion of stereotyped material from model sermon books and booklets by preachers to lay listeners all over Europe can fairly be described as a kind of mass communication. Huge numbers of manuscript volumes containing model sermons have survived from the later medieval centuries, and I will argue that the survivors are only a small proportion of the much larger number that once existed. The first part of the essay develops some rather technical textual arguments to demonstrate this. Arguments pointing in the opposite direction have been developed in a massive recent book,[3] and I examine this reasoning to see whether it

---

[1] I am grateful to Julia Walworth and to the editors of this volume, whose comments and criticisms greatly improved the original draft. I must apologise for borrowing freely from my *Medieval Marriage Sermons: Mass Communication in a Culture without Print* (Oxford, 2001), the excuse being that it might not normally come the way of early modernists, though some of the detailed data is quite relevant to this debate.

[2] See the introduction to this volume for some discussion of this literature.

[3] U. Neddermeyer, *Von der Handschrift zum gedruckten Buch. Schriftlichkeit und Leseinteresse im Mittelalter und in der frühen Neuzeit: quantitative und qualitative Aspekte*, Buchwissenschaftliche Beiträge aus dem Deutschen Bucharchiv München, 61 (Wiesbaden, 1998), 2 vols. (continuously paginated).

really neutralises my own, concluding that the loss rate of medieval sermon manuscripts really was colossal.

It thus becomes necessary to explain how so many could have been produced in the first place. It will be argued that two types of production operated side-by-side in the later medieval centuries. On the one hand, professional scribes copied manuscripts for money. That is the system commonly assumed by medievalists to have replaced monastic scriptoria.[4] Whether or not monastic scriptoria as conventionally pictured – a room in an abbey full of monks at their desks – really did lose their central role in book production, there is evidence that thousands of Dominicans and Franciscans were copying books for their own use and that of others. They probably did not work in scriptoria. Moreover friars moved from convent to convent quite freely (unlike Benedictine monks who were supposed to stay in the same monastery): so we should not expect identifiable local scribal schools. Nevertheless these friars could apparently work at a professional level, without being professionals. Their production must be added to that of scribes working for money.

If model sermons for preachers existed in enormous numbers, and could be used again and again, then printing's importance in popularising orthodox religion is relativised: but dissident ideas are a separate problem. There is no heretical equivalent to the book production of the Franciscan and Dominican orders. Nevertheless some religious dissident movements produced books on a significant scale. Furthermore they seem to have spread their ideas with astonishing speed by preaching. The capacity to spread unorthodox religious ideas and recruit followers existed before printing. It will be argued that the change which made the Reformation possible was not the invention of printing but the absence of state repression in the crucial formative stage of the religious revolt. Printing was important but not decisive.

After a century or so printing had transformed written communication, but it is easy to exaggerate the impact of its invention in the late fifteenth and earlier sixteenth centuries. The invention of printing is often compared to the creation of the internet, but there is a more useful *comparandum*:

---

[4] For the view that the Dominicans relied mainly on professional scribes, see M. Mulchahey, 'More Notes on the Education of the *Fratres communes* in the Dominican Order: Elias de Ferreriis of Salignac's *Libellus de doctrina fratrum*', in J. Brown and W. P. Stoneman (eds.), *A Distinct Voice: Medieval Studies in Honor of Leonard E. Boyle, O.P.* (Notre Dame, IN, 1997), pp. 328–69, at p. 338. The view that professional scribes took over from members of religious orders as the principal copyists of manuscripts after about 1200 is probably more widely diffused in the 'oral culture' of modern medieval specialists than it is in their printed productions.

the mechanical typewriter. Typewriters became universal in offices because they made writing quicker and so cheaper. Soon all official letters had to be typed, and authors could no longer expect publishers to read anything but a typescript. It was a revolution of sorts, but a superficial one; it did not change fundamental structures much. Let us try a thought-experiment. If a new technology is (to select a random low figure) 2% more efficient and economic, everyone will go over to it except traditionalists. On the surface everything looks different. Actually things are only different by a couple of percentage points.

The foregoing ideas may now be developed in greater detail. It may be useful to begin by stating them baldly as three theses:

(1) One can make 'qualitative calculations' about the loss rate of medieval manuscripts: the estimate currently holding the field probably needs to be revised quite drastically upwards.[5]

(2) Long before printing, from the thirteenth century on, the friars and their like built up a system for the mass communication of religious ideas: the same kind of men acted as scribes, copying model sermons, and as preachers, multiplying the impact of their content.

(3) The idea that printing made the Reformation possible is more wrong than right.[6]

I THE LOSS RATE

Here I must inflict a complex argument on the reader. I referred above to the *pecia* system of medieval universities.[7] This system is surprisingly well known at a superficial level. It is part of the repertoire of topics in courses in the 'History of the Book', and is much discussed by people who have never worked with *pecia* manuscripts. It facilitated the copying of manuscripts wanted in a university environment. The system was run by 'stationers', shops where books were hired as well as sold. So far as the *pecia* system was

---

[5] For previous estimates of the loss rate see Neddermeyer, *Von der Handschrift zum gedruckten Buch*, pp. 73–4.

[6] Here I follow others who have tried to get the impact of printing on the Reformation into proportion: notably R. W. Scribner, 'Oral Culture and the Diffusion of Reformation Ideas', repr. in his *Popular Culture and Popular Movements in Reformation Germany* (1987), pp. 49–69. For recent work on this problem, see J.-F. Gilmont, *The Reformation and the Book*, trans. K. Maag (Aldershot, 1998) and A. Walsham, '"Domme Preachers"? Post-Reformation Catholicism and the Culture of Print', *P&P*, 168 (2000), 72–123.

[7] The foundations of *pecia* studies were laid by J. Destrez, *La Pecia dans les manuscrits universitaires du XIIIᵉ et XIVᵉ siècle* (Paris, 1935); for an *aggiornamento* with many specific studies, L.-J. Bataillon, B. G. Guyot and R. H. Rouse, *La Production du livre universitaire au Moyen Âge: Exemplar et Pecia*, Actes du symposium tenu au Collegio San Bonaventura de Grottaferrata en mai 1983 (Paris, 1988).

concerned they were under the control of university authorities. In practice this seems to have amounted to little more than price regulation: there is little sign that university men supervised textual quality, which was often quite poor.

The idea was simple: an 'exemplar' in the form of loose quires was made available at a stationer's shop. Scribes could hire the exemplar to copy it. The price was fixed by the university. The hirer took out one quire at a time. The clever part was that a number of different scribes could hire and copy different quires at the same time. If a scribe returned his quire and found that the next one was out, he would estimate its length, leave an appropriate space, and take away the quire that followed the one already in use, which he could borrow on a later occasion to fill in the gap.

If a work was much in demand, two exemplars might be made available. That is not the only way in which a second *pecia* exemplar might come into existence: the original one might get damaged and be replaced. For *cognoscenti* of the *pecia* system one can reconstruct other complexities. For instance, if some but not all quires were damaged, the damaged ones might be replaced and if several quires together were replaced, the breaks between quires might be in new places.

Such technicalities have their own attraction to a scholar, but the *pecia* system does not quite deserve the prominence it has acquired. This prominence is due above all to the influential investigations of Jean Destrez, who travelled round Europe looking for manuscripts with the *pecia* indications that an experienced eye can detect. He found many such manuscripts. Even so, the ones he found were a modest proportion of the manuscripts he examined. There must have been *pecia* manuscripts which he examined but failed to recognise as such. Still, any notion that *pecia* production accounts for a large percentage of late medieval Latin manuscripts is a little absurd – scholars have been too captivated by the ingenuity of the system.

Nevertheless, a knowledge of the *pecia* system's technicalities can help with the problem addressed in this paper. The argument rests on a textual and codicological analysis of the transmission by the *pecia* system at Paris of two model sermon collections.[8] These are the series by the Dominican Pierre de Reims and the Franciscan collection known as *Legifer*.[9] They are works of the kind mentioned at the beginning of the paper: volumes

---

[8] For a fuller version of the argument in this section see my *Medieval Marriage Sermons*, pp. 17–19. For the nature and function of model sermon collections see e.g., D. d'Avray, *The Preaching of the Friars: Sermons diffused from Paris before 1300* (Oxford, 1985), ch. 2; see also *ibid.*, 'Appendix. Preaching and the *Pecia* System of the Paris University Stationers'.

[9] See *ibid.*, s.v. *Legifer*.

of written sermons, arranged according to the liturgical year, designed to provide materials for 'live' sermons, principally to audiences of ordinary laypeople. They would have been used by many different preachers, and again and again by the same preacher. Preachers could and would have adapted the material on particular occasions, and combined it with material from other preaching aids, such as collections of *exempla*, illustrative moral stories, but these sermon collections do tell us the common-places that would have recurred incessantly in different combinations in popular preaching. It must be remembered that charismatic or revivalist preaching would not have been the norm. These collections were designed for routine Sunday and Feastday preaching, where material had to be found year in, year out. Even before any arguments about the loss rate are developed, the large number of surviving copies is a fair guarantee that they were in demand and used.

Textual arguments suggest that many *pecia* copies must have been made of these collections. Hardly any have survived, but we can draw inferences from technicalities. First, *Legifer*. Two manuscripts with *pecia* indications are known. One (Troyes, Bibliothèque Municipale 1215) is an exemplar, which would have been kept by the stationer and hired out quire by quire. The other (Zurich, Zentralbibliothek Rh 181) is a *pecia* copy. We can tell this from small numbers in the margins, which mark the start of a new quire or piece of the exemplar. Note that in a *pecia* exemplar the numbers, if any, should be at the beginning of quires, whereas in a *pecia* copy they will normally be somewhere within the quire.[10] The surprise is this: the *pecia* copy was apparently not made from this exemplar. The numbers in the two manuscripts do not always correspond to the same points in the text. Furthermore the exemplar looks pristine, as if little used.[11] The best hypothesis to explain the complicated data would seem to be this: the exemplar originally produced for hire at the stationer's has been lost – it is not the Troyes manuscript. This original exemplar had been heavily used. Some quires had become so battered that they had to be re-made. Some of the quire divisions changed in the process. The Zurich manuscript was copied from the original exemplar but after these mutations. Eventually, it seemed worth making a second exemplar, which was not in the event much

---

[10] For the function of these numbers in *pecia* copies made by professional scribes, see J. Decorte, 'Les indications explicites et implicites de pièces dans les manuscrits médiévaux', in L.-J. Bataillon *et al.* (eds.), *La Production du livre universitaire*, pp. 275–84, at p. 276.

[11] This was pointed out to me many years ago by L.-J. Bataillon, who initiated me into the mysteries of *pecia* studies and introduced me to the *Nachlass* of Destrez, which is now kept at Le Saulchoir/Couvent Saint-Jacques in Paris.

used. Still, so far as the first exemplar is concerned the *pecia* venture had evidently been successful, producing many copies. Yet only one copy with *pecia* indications survives. The implication is a huge loss rate.

It is somewhat the same with the series of the Dominican Pierre de Reims. Here again we have a *pecia* exemplar, Assisi Biblioteca Comunale 452, discovered by Destrez.[12] No surviving *pecia* copies have been identified. Many surviving mansuscripts are closely related to the *exemplar* textually.[13] However, the Assisi manuscript contains errors from which the related manuscripts are free.[14] If they had been descended from *pecia* copies of the exemplar which is now Assisi 452, they would contain more of its errors. The best explanation,[15] is that the Assisi manuscript is a re-made exemplar, perhaps for another place. Like the Troyes manuscript of *Legifer*, it may not have been much used: if it had been, one would expect more manuscripts to carry its errors. Even so, the original exemplar was presumably used heavily. If not, why make a second exemplar?

Thus we have two similar cases: in each, the original lost *pecia* exemplar was copied at a lively rate; and in each case hardly any pecia copies have actually survived. The reasoning is complicated, but it converges on the conclusion that there was a remarkable loss rate.

Put this conclusion together with the earlier point that the *relative* importance of the *pecia* system in the transmission of manuscripts has been overrated, and the following chain of reasoning can be assembled:

... very few copies have survived from apparently successful *pecia* ventures. That is, the surviving *pecia* manuscripts are the tip of an iceberg. We have also noted that the few surviving *pecia* manuscripts are only a small proportion of the total number of surviving manuscripts. *Ergo*, if the *pecia* manuscripts are the tip of an iceberg, the other surviving manuscripts are the tip of a vastly larger iceberg.[16]

How could so many manuscripts go missing? Very easily, if they were heavily used. We have discussed the transmission of two model sermon collections. Model sermons were meant to be used again and again for different congregations. Possibly they were often carried around in the form of individual booklets or quires, *quaterni*.[17] The booklets might be thrown away when they got battered from use. On the whole, such booklets must

---

[12] Assisi Biblioteca Comunale 452 is now kept with the other Biblioteca Comunale manuscripts in the Sacro Convento Library at Assisi. For the history of the Assisi manuscripts see C. Cenci, *Bibliotheca Manuscripta ad Sacrum Conventum Assisiensem*, 2 vols. (Assisi, 1981).

[13] D'Avray, *Medieval Marriage Sermons*, pp. 90–1.   [14] *Ibid.*, pp. 93–4.

[15] Suggested to me by L. J. Bataillon.   [16] D'Avray, *Medieval Marriage Sermons*, p. 19.

[17] See *ibid.* p. 19, n. 55, and d'Avray, *Preaching of the Friars*, p. 2. See also the last sentence of Felicity Riddy's contribution to the present volume.

Talking about the survivability of books [handwritten annotation]

have had a slim chance of survival unless they were at some point bound together with others into a codex; and in fact there are relatively few medieval unbound *quaterni* around today. Who knows how many never made it into a bound book? Then, even proper codices could easily get lost, especially if used by Franciscan, Dominican, or secular priests, or by laypeople, whose books lacked the protection of a monastic library and users who stayed in one place. A book that could survive until the great secularisations of monastic libraries c.1800 is likely to be with us today. On the other hand any book owned by a private individual was vulnerable to time, whether the individual was lay or clerical. Friars' books were vulnerable too. A Franciscan or Dominican might take a tiny portable library of small format books as he moved from convent to convent. We do have some of these pocket books: breviaries, bibles, model sermon collections, confessional handbooks, and the like turn up relatively often in pocket formats.[18] Nevertheless, the *mouvementé* lifestyle of the friars who carried such books around makes it likely that the majority, the overwhelming majority, have gone missing. A moment's reflection on the conditions in which such books were used makes the conclusion of the foregoing textual and codicological reasoning eminently comprehensible. The discussion below of the library rules of the Franciscans and Dominicans points in just the same direction. This 'codicological haemorrhage' is not peculiar to the medieval period. How many modern paperbacks will survive the next half millennium?

The whole thrust of my argument points in a different direction from that of Uwe Neddermeyer, whose recent investigation[19] is much too important to be ignored. He argues for a low loss rate where manuscripts of the central Middle Ages are concerned; he even tries to estimate percentages. For some types of book he may well be right, but his arguments do not work well for the kind of books discussed above, mendicant preachers' portable books. Let it be said immediately that Neddermeyer's book is a monumental achievement. The criticisms below relate to one small part of the whole only.

Neddermeyer first estimates the percentage of manuscripts around at the end of the Middle Ages which made it through to our own time. He starts from the survival rate for incunables, on which he has some relatively hard data.[20] For manuscripts from the fourteenth and fifteenth centuries he

---

[18] D. d'Avray (with A. C. de la Mare), 'Portable *Vademecum* Books containing Franciscan and Dominican Texts', in A. C. de la Mare and B. C. Barker-Benfield (eds.), *Manuscripts at Oxford: An Exhibition in Memory of Richard William Hunt . . . on Themes Selected and Described by Some of his Friends* (Oxford, 1980), pp. 60–4.

[19] See above, n. 3. [20] Neddermeyer, *Von der Handschrift zum gedruckten Buch*, pp. 75–9.

estimates a somewhat higher survival rate, about 7%, than for incunables.[21] Thus one would multiply the number of surviving manuscripts by about fifteen to get the total in existence c.1500.[22] In my view there are no hard grounds for putting the survival rate of manuscripts which made it to 1500 higher than that of incunables from the same date. Some of the arguments Neddermeyer gives are very vulnerable, because they do not envisage the kind of books discussed above: friars' pocket books, functional, without pictures, often probably in loose quires, written in scripts illegible to many if not most early modern literate people. The fate of manuscript books or manuscript booklets might be more like that of small format incunables with relatively few pages. The survival rate of such incunables was much lower, according to Neddermeyer's own data and estimates: in the case of octavo volumes, very low indeed.[23] We have associated tiny pocket books with the friars. He surely tends to underestimate both the importance and the loss-rate of this kind of manuscript.

Neddermeyer thinks that manuscripts were more valuable as objects and so more likely to survive than incunables: but would someone have regarded a manuscript book as an especially valuable object in the late sixteenth or seventeenth century if it did not have illuminations and expensive decoration?[24] Neddermeyer argues that parchment is tougher and more valuable than paper.[25] True, but for that reason parchment books were cut up to be used in bindings in the early modern period.

Neddermeyer's 'multiplier' for estimating the number of manuscripts around c.1500 is seriously open to question, but it is not wild. A further question remains: how many manuscripts produced in earlier centuries never made it to 1500? How many thirteenth-century manuscripts got lost in the fourteenth century – and so on? Neddermeyer's answer deserves careful consideration, because the question is central and his argument is very clever. It is also compressed to the point of obscurity: few scholars will

---

[21] The arguments for and against a higher survival rate are set out *ibid.*, p. 80. As will be explained below, I partly disagree with Neddermeyer's conclusions.

[22] *Ibid.*, pp. 80–1. The calculation behind this figure seems to be as follows. Neddermeyer thinks that only about one out of every fifteen fourteenth- or fifteenth-century manuscripts in existence in 1500 made it through to our own times, and 7% is an approximation for one in fifteen, so one must multiply by fifteen to get the number in 1500. Thus if we had 100 manuscripts of the fourteenth or fifteenth centuries today, he would calculate that 1500 had been in existence in 1500.

[23] *Ibid.*, pp. 75–6. He suggests only up to 3% of octavo volumes survive.

[24] So I am not convinced by Neddermeyer's argument that the 'higher value [of manuscripts] (expensive initials, illuminations, etc.) have protected them, especially in the period before the invention of printing and then again at the latest from the seventeenth- and eighteenth-century on, *ibid.*, p. 80 (my translation).

[25] *Ibid.*

be able to take in at a first reading the argument of the crucial passage I am about to quote. The passage follows a table giving the relative numbers of surviving manuscripts listed in Sigrid Krämer's *Handschriftenerbe des deutschen Mittelalters* (1989–90):[26]

The number of eleventh-century manuscripts is only 25% more than that of tenth-century manuscripts. *Since one can hardly assume that more books were copied in the particularly turbulent tenth century than in the succeeding period, the losses which have to be added in can scarcely have been more than 10% to 15%.* If one applies this quota to later centuries, the result is still that accessions to Benedictine libraries declined significantly from the twelfth century to the fourteenth century. On these grounds I proceed, in the calculations which follow, from the assumption that in each of the centuries from the eleventh up to the fourteenth [so: to 1300] only 12.5% on average of the books in existence got lost. On the other hand the number of manuscripts of the eighth or ninth centuries destroyed in the dark centuries is probably somewhat higher. So we must at least double the number of manuscripts from this period which still survive, if we wish to draw a comparison with the number of manuscripts from the fourteenth or fifteenth centuries which are still preserved. [27]

If I understand the passage correctly the argument is this: if the loss rate during the medieval centuries had been high, the number of surviving manuscripts would go down dramatically as we move back in time from century to century. This is because the earlier manuscripts had to undergo a longer period of attrition. Assume that the rate of attrition in any given century is about the same for all manuscripts, whether they had been produced recently or long before. If the rate of attrition were substantially higher than Neddermeyer's 12.5%, let us say 50% per century, then only 6 or 7 out of 100 manuscripts in existence in 900 would make it to 1300, if the original number was halved at each century 'milestone'. To spell it out: 50 would make it to the year 1000; half that, 25, to 1100; about half

---

[26] S. Krämer, *Handschriftenerbe des deutschen Mittelalters*, Mittelalterliche Bibliothekskataloge Deutschlands und der Schweiz, Ergänzungsband 1, 3 vols. (Munich, 1989–90). Vol. III is a 'Handschriften-Register' compiled by Krämer and M. Bernhard.

[27] 'Die Zahl der Manuskripte des 11. Jahrhunderts liegt nur 25% über der des 10. Jahrhunderts. *Da kaum davon ausgegangen werden kann, daß in dem besonders unruhigem 10. Jahrhundert mehr Bücher geschrieben wurden als im folgenden Zeitraum, können die hinzuzurechnenden Verluste kaum über 10 bis 15% gelegen haben.* Wendet man diese Quote auch auf spätere Jahrhunderte an, ergibt sich daraus immer noch, daß die Akzession der Benediktinerbibliotheken vom 12. Jahrhundert zum 14. Jahrhundert hin deutlich zurückging. Bei den folgenden Berechnungen gehe ich aus diesen Gründen davon aus, daß vom 11. bis zum 14. Jahrhundert jeweils nur durchschnittlich 12.5% der vorhandenen Bücher verloren gingen. Dagegen wird die Zahl der in den dunklen Jahrhunderten zerstörten Manuskripte des 8./9. Jahrhunderts wohl etwas höher liegen. Man muß also aus dieser Zeit noch vorliegenden Handschriften mindestens verdoppeln, wenn man einen Vergleich mit den aus dem 14/15. Jahrhundert erhaltenen Exemplaren anstellt.' Neddermeyer, *Von der Handschrift zum gedruckten Buch*, p. 83 (my italics).

that, so 12 or 13, to 1200; about half that, so 6 or 7, to 1300. On the other hand, out of 100 manuscripts in existence in 1200, only half would be lost by 1300, leaving 50. Thus a graph showing the number of manuscripts, still surviving today, which were produced in each century, ought to show a very steep rise indeed if the loss rate was as high as 50% per century. Instead, the increase from one century to the next is quite modest. (In the case of Benedictine manuscripts, there is an actual decrease.) Ergo, the loss-rate must have been extremely low.

A crucial assumption seems to underlie the reasoning. It is that old books and more recent books had roughly the same chance of survival through any given block of time from the Carolingian period to c.1300. Neddermeyer's highly intelligent argument does not work well for the age of the friars. Books produced for them had a drastically lower likelihood of survival than books from earlier centuries which were safe in the libraries of Benedictine monasteries. The crucial assumption just mentioned is in fact unjustified. Figures for surviving manuscripts are thus biased, and disguise the increase in the total bookstock. As I shall argue in the next section, the friars were responsible for much of this increase, but their way of life was such that the books they used were not as likely to be preserved as the books in a Benedictine abbey. Benedictine books, like Benedictine monks, had *stabilitas loci*. A major subset of mendicant books did not. Thus the attrition rate of old Benedictine books from any century will have been much lower than the attrition rate of mendicant books from the thirteenth century on. This badly skews the argument from the survival rate: we should not after all expect a steep upward curve in the graph representing the number of manuscripts surviving from successive centuries.[28]

Some of the reasons for the vulnerability of mendicant books and booklets have already been discussed. A glance at their library systems provides more data pointing in the same direction. K. W. Humphreys' careful study of the book provisions of the friars explains why mendicant books were vulnerable.[29] For one thing, mendicant books could be sold.[30] Some might be bought by an abbey with a stable library, but others might go to a private individual – a wealthy student, a secular master, a parish priest – whose private library would eventually be dissipated. Moreover, many mendicant

---

[28] Neddermeyer is in fact aware of this type of reasoning, but applies it to the later Middle Ages rather than to the thirteenth century, arguing that parchment manuscripts were more likely to survive than paper ones. *Ibid.*, pp. 83–4. Against that assumption see G. Powitz, '*Libri inutiles* in mittelalterliche Bibliotheken. Bemerkungen über Alienatio, Palimpsestierung und makulierung', in *Scriptorium* 50 (1996), 288–304.

[29] K. W. Humphreys, *The Book Provisions of the Mediaeval Friars 1215–1400* (Amsterdam, 1964).

[30] *Ibid.*, pp. 30–1, 53.

books were not 'anchored' to any one library. Books could belong to provinces or in the Franciscan case also to custodies (subdivisions of Franciscan provinces) rather than to individual convents.[31] The Dominican provincial priors were supposed to 'keep a written list recording which books belong to the [provincial] community and to which brothers they are assigned'.[32] This sort of regulation seldom works properly.

Clearly it was hard to keep track of both provincial books and of conventual books out on loan. Humphreys quotes an order to the friars of the French Dominican province that 'brothers who have books granted to them for their use, whether by the provincial priors or by any of the convents, are bound to inform in writing the same priors of convents or their deputies (*vicariis*), and the provincial prior so far as the books of the province are concerned, within a month from receipt of this memorandum, about the aforesaid books, or otherwise they are *ipso facto* deprived of the use of these books.'[33] In other words, there was no record of who had what. Even modern libraries with immaculate records have trouble with readers who forget what they have out. Despite the rather pathetic sounding efforts to introduce some discipline into the borrowing system, it was a recipe for the loss of books, though from the point of view of the Dominicans' pastoral efficacy it was a perfectly sensible one. Franciscans too took out books. It is worth quoting Humphreys' summary of regulations, a prudent librarian's nightmare, about what to do when a Franciscan friar died. 'The books of a friar dying when away from his native convent were to be collected by the custodian or by the warden and sent back to the officers in charge of the custodies where the books had been first issued. The convent, custody or province which assigned the books was to have such books returned; other volumes, i.e. gifts, or the personal books of a friar were to go to the convent at which the friar had first been received. If it was impossible to discover who had originally assigned the books, they were to be sent to the province from which the friar first came. Any friar who had lent a book to another should ensure that it was returned to the custodian or warden at the death of the borrower.'[34] It is hard to imagine that this system worked like clockwork. Though books belonged to Franciscan custodies, Humphreys points out that there is no evidence that every custody had a library.[35] If books lacked a physical home it must have been difficult to keep track of them. Again, we know that books could be loaned to a Franciscan for life.[36] Friars could move around Europe a good deal in the course of their life, and books must have got lost in one way or another.

[31] *Ibid.*, pp. 27–8, 52, n. 51.   [32] *Ibid.*, p. 27 and n. 59.   [33] *Ibid.*, pp. 28–9, n. 68.
[34] *Ibid.*, p. 52.   [35] *Ibid.*, p. 57.   [36] *Ibid.*, p. 62.

A quire of sermons produced for the use of a Franciscan in the middle of the thirteenth century would face a hazardous existence. The chances that it would would still be in the order's possession by 1500 must surely have been much lower than the chances of a Benedictine book produced in 1000 making it through a period twice as long to the same date.

In another respect, however, the history of manuscript production does not differ so much between the 'Benedictine centuries' and the 'age of the friars' as has been supposed. So we must now turn to the question of manuscript production.

II THE FRIARS AND MASS COMMUNICATION

The loss rate can be explained, but how to explain the rate of production it implies? Arguably, the scribal activity of friars supplemented book production by professional scribes. This is not to deny that professional scribes were a massive new labour force in book production. The point here is to question a widespread assumption that professional scribes displaced or replaced members of religious orders as scribes.[37] So far as the older religious orders are concerned it is hard at present to say how much truth there is in this assumption. Where the Franciscans and Dominicans are concerned it cannot stand up to examination.

There is a good deal of direct evidence for scribal activity by friars: for instance, the book provisions of the Franciscans and Dominicans, read carefully, imply that a lot of copying was occurring, and we have chronicle evidence of scribal activity.[38] Here it is more interesting to concentrate on text-critical arguments from data which emerged in the course of preparing editions of mendicant model marriage sermons.

Some manuscripts have variants which are not errors, or trivial changes such as inversions. These variants look like the work of scribes in command of the subject-matter, confident enough to modify the text at will, almost at a whim – scribes acting in a small way as authors. Professional scribes copying for money are not likely to have taken such liberties with the text. If one hired a scribe to make a copy of an exemplar at the university stationers, one probably wanted the text of the exemplar, not the scribe's text. In the nature of the case it is not easy to prove this definitively from positive evidence: there is a risk of circular argument. Nevertheless commonsense considerations weigh strongly. With technical legal or theological treatises, where precise wording could be extremely important, scribal improvisation

---

[37] See above at n. 4.   [38] I summarise the data in my *Medieval Marriage Sermons*, pp. 25–8.

would greatly diminish the value of the copy. If the scribe did not follow the text as exactly as possible, he might misrepresent its message through imperfect understanding. In my experience *pecia* copies of sermons also follow the exemplar closely on the whole, human error apart. These scribes were the medieval equivalent of copy-typists. They were not paid to improvise. So when we do get free improvisation, the obvious explanation for these variants is that the scribes were users.[39] If they were copying primarily for themselves, rather than being paid to copy for others, it was up to them what they did with the text.[40] Usually, in my experience, their changes did not affect the core substance of the message very much. Nevertheless manuscripts copied by scribes with independent minds have much more individuality than the 'cloned' copies of printed books.

Far more evidence of the same kind could have been produced. Scribes evidently felt free to tinker with the text. Who then were these scribes? They clearly felt comfortable with preaching material. Probably they were the kind of men who also used the model sermons to help them preach (above all to the laity). If so, one may reasonably suppose that these author-scribes were friars, or educated pastorally active clerics of the same type, 'honorary friars', so to speak.

This free variation is not found only in untidy manuscripts which look like personal notebooks. One can find it in books which can hardly be distinguished from work of professional scribes. Cases in point are the script of various manuscripts of Pierre de Reims.[41] It is theoretically possible that these manuscripts were copied by professional scribes working for money from more rough and ready manuscripts written by friars, but even in that case the notebooks would not be 'end of the line' texts: they would have transmitted the text on to other manuscripts. In fact, however, there is no reason to doubt that many Franciscans and Dominicans could write as well

---

[39] For an illustration see the appendix on 'Scribal Independence'. In the critical apparatus to the texts edited in my *Medieval Marriage Sermons* the possible or probable cases of scribal independence are marked by sigla in heavy type.

[40] It should be noted that stable texts are also quite normal: the majority of manuscripts collated had an essentially identical text except in cases of scribal error, which is quite different from voluntary and intelligent variation. My distinction between professional scribes copying as exactly as possible in exchange for pay, and user scribes altering the text as they thought fit, is an ideal-type that may oversimplify. It is possible for example that vernacular texts might by commissioned by customers who did not worry too much whether the exemplar was followed exactly. The whole topic deserves further thought, especially with reference to genres other than those I have considered here.

[41] Lille, Bibliothèque Municipale, MS 107 (88); Milan, Biblioteca Ambrosiana, MS A. 4. Sup.; Paris, Bibliothèque Nationale, MS lat. 3578; Troyes, Bibliothèque Municipale, MS 303; Vatican City, Biblioteca Apostolica Vaticana, MS Borghes 343. I often worked from microfilm printout of the sermon to be edited only, so my observations apply to only that part of the manuscript in question.

as professional scribes.[42] The likely hypothesis is this: professional scribes paid to copy would try to keep to the text before them, whereas friars and the like might or might not. It would partly be a matter of temperament.

Thus not only professional scribes but also Franciscans and Dominicans were copying manuscripts on a large scale. The conclusions reached above about the number of manuscripts produced in the later Middle Ages become unsurprising. Sir Richard Southern guessed that there may have been c.28,000 Franciscans and 12,000 Dominicans in the early fourteenth century.[43] Not all were scribes, but we can now rule out the idea that it was odd or unusual for friars to copy manuscripts.

Then there is the final, oral stage of mass communication. A model sermon in a manuscript could be preached over and over again to different live audiences, each of which might contain many listeners. The preachers might adapt the content, perhaps in the same manner as some scribes did, no doubt often even more so. We can never know the precise content of any purely oral event.[44] When the same topoi recur again and again in written model sermons, however, we can be fairly sure that in one combination or another they were getting through to a mass audience. The large literature on this subject cannot be summarised more fully here.[45] Nevertheless, historians of the book, and students of literacy and orality, cannot afford to neglect its implications.

III PRINTING AND THE REFORMATION[46]

To show that there was mass communication before printing is one thing. To disprove the theory that printing made the Reformation possible is another. If we assume that the friars produced books and had them produced on a large scale: how could Luther have competed in the early days of the Reformation without a comparable labour force at his disposal? How could

---

[42] D'Avray, *Medieval Marriage Sermons*, p. 26.

[43] R. W. Southern, *Western Society and the Church in the Middle Ages* (Harmondsworth, 1970), p. 285.

[44] In relatively rare cases we have a *reportatio*. Even these were reconstructed from brief schematic notes. They were not, as a rule, stenographic reproductions of what had been said.

[45] See notably the following: L.-J. Bataillon, 'Approaches to the Study of Medieval Sermons', in his *La prédication au XIIIe siècle en France et Italie* (Aldershot, 1993), ch. 1; d'Avray, *Preaching of the Friars*, *passim*; N. Bériou, 'Latin and the Vernacular. Some Remarks about Sermons Delivered on Good Friday during the Thirteenth Century', in V. Mertens and H.-J. Schiewer (eds.), *Die deutsche Predigt im Mittelalter. Internationales Symposium am Fachbereich Germanistik der Freien Universität Berlin von 3.–6. Oktober 1989* (Tübingen, 1992), pp. 268–84. A good way of keeping up with the voluminous literature on medieval sermons is the newsletter, now a journal, *Medieval Sermon Studies*.

[46] Dr Maureen Jurkowski gave me a number of valuable references for this section and brought my analysis in line with recent scholarship (to which she is herself a central contributor) on Lollardy.

a dissident religious movement, in its early days, emulate the infrastructure of medieval preaching? He may have lacked the labour force but he did, however, have the printing press. So the preceding discussion seems to provide a new argument for the old idea that printing made the Reformation possible. But this new argument is not enough to save the assumption that printing was a *sine qua non* of the Reformation. Naturally the reformers used the latest technology. The question is, could they have managed without it? There is reason to think they could have succeeded quite well.

The history of medieval heresy shows that dissident ideas could be spread far and fast by preaching and proselytisation. The Cathar heresy seems to have been noticed first in the Rhineland in the 1140s,[47] and was well established in the Languedoc in the 1160s.[48] It probably became established in Western Europe in the aftermath of the first Crusade.[49] If so, it had made dramatic progress in the course of a few decades. The ultimate failure of Catharism probably had little to do with communication difficulties, and a lot to do with the power of persecution. As long as the power of the state was flung behind orthodoxy, heretical movements had little chance. Often the state worked with inquisitors, but even inquisitors were not needed for successful repression, as the following case from 1160s shows. It relates to some specifically English conditions, but nevertheless gives an idea of the kind of power the state could exercise even in the twelfth century.[50]

A small band of Cathar heretics was brought to England by a man named Gerard. According to the contemporary historian William of Newburgh, they were 'detected by certain men curious to explore to what strange sect they belonged, then seized and held in public custody. The king, however, being unwilling either to discharge them or to punish them without examination, ordered an episcopal synod to meet at Oxford.'[51] The doctrines they held match those of the Cathars: for example, they denied baptism, the Eucharist, and Marriage. The bishops had the accused 'publicly proclaimed heretics and handed them over to the king'.[52] They were branded, driven

[47] M. Lambert, *The Cathars* (Oxford, 1998), pp. 19–20.   [48] *Ibid.*, p. 42
[49] B. Hamilton, 'Wisdom from the East: The Reception by the Cathars of Eastern Dualist Texts', in P. Biller and A. Hudson (eds.), *Heresy and Literacy, 1000–1530* (Cambridge, 1994), pp. 38–60, esp. p. 45.
[50] For a modern account, see R. Bartlett, *England under the Norman and Angevin Kings 1075–1225* (Oxford, 2000), pp. 479–80; see also P. Biller, 'William of Newburgh and the Cathar Mission to England', in D. Wood (ed.), *Life and Thought in the Northern Church, c.1100–1700: Essays in Honour of Claire Cross*, SCH Subsidia 12 (Woodbridge, 1999), pp. 11–30.
[51] William of Newburgh, 'The History of England', bk 2, ch. 13, quoted from D. C. Douglas and G. W. Greenaway (eds.), *English Historical Documents*, vol. II, *1042–1189* (1953), no. 12, p. 330.
[52] *Ibid.*

out, rejected everywhere, and eventually died of exposure. The Assize of Clarendon of Henry II helps explain why they received so little sympathy: it included the following ordinance: 'The lord king forbids anyone in all England to receive in his land or in his soke or in a house under him any one of that sect of renegades who were branded and excommunicated at Oxford. And if anyone shall so receive them, he himself shall be at the mercy of the lord king, and the house in which they have dwelt shall be carried outside the village and burnt. And each sheriff shall swear an oath that he will observe this, and shall cause all his officers to swear this, and also the stewards of the barons and all knights and freeholders of the counties.'[53] Who knows what success they might have achieved without the crackdown by the king. William of Newburgh tells us that their leader 'had a smattering of learning', while 'the others were ignorant folk, unlettered and wholly un-cultivated, peasants of German race and tongue'.[54] Thus they had a literate focal point, even if most were unlearned: a reminder that general literacy was not needed for heretical groups to form. They had come a long way: a reminder of how easily heresy could travel if not stopped. The story of this group, up until the point when they were captured, would probably be quite typical of the way heresy was spread. In the nature of the case we will not usually know the details of how heretical ideas travelled, but the history of Catharism demonstrates beyond the shadow of a doubt the fact that it could travel. It penetrated the Balkans, Germany, Southern France, and briefly England, all without help from printing.

The movement was persecuted almost out of existence. Inquisition was a formidable force (though it never existed in England). The preaching of the friars was no doubt also a factor: powerful counter-propaganda. It must have helped that the friars aimed at the same sort of life of poverty and austerity as the Cathar leaders, the 'perfect'. This softened the previously striking contrast between worldly Catholic priests or bishops and the heretical hierarchy.

The Cathars might still have established themselves solidly with a little political protection: the sect could have become a real Church. Around 1200 they enjoyed some protection or at least toleration in the County of Toulouse, and seem to have become almost the dominant religion. The Albigensian crusade put an end to that. Afterwards, as is well known, secular authority and inquisition combined to persecute the Southern French Cathars out of existence. Otherwise, might not Catholicism have become the sect in that region, and Catharism the official church?

---

[53] Assize of Clarendon, 21, in *ibid.*, no. 24, p. 410.   [54] *Ibid.*, no. 12, p. 330.

The Waldensian heresy is perhaps a still more striking case. Beginning in Lyons in the twelfth century, it never received political protection yet spread throughout Europe and survives to this day.[55] The Waldensians' strength in the Alps has long been known.[56] What was not known until quite recently is that they were also present in astonishing numbers in Bohemia in the first half of the fourteenth century. Alexander Patschovsky showed that there was a mass persecution of heretics, above all Waldenses, who were clearly a powerful element among the German speaking population of the region.[57] Once again the inquisition and the secular arm worked together to crush a numerically very strong dissident religious movement.

Waldensianism spread across a vast geographical area and attracted a mass following without the help of the printing press, and, more remarkably, despite persecution. Persecution can explain why the Waldenses remained an underground movement throughout the Middle Ages. The problem is rather to explain how the Waldensians survived at all. The inquisition in fourteenth-century Bohemia was probably unusual in its intensity; in the Alpine regions the dissidents were no doubt harder to get at; even so their continued existence requires some explanation, as does the geographical range of their activities.

Brian Stock's notion of 'textual communities' is relevant here.[58] A text can influence even illiterates. Group leaders could explain texts to others who could not read them. That may have been how Gerard's group of Cathars worked. The way Waldensian textual communities worked has been quite well studied.[59] Patschovsky relates from Etienne de Bourbon the story of a cowherd 'who had acquired an astounding knowledge of the bible in a year, achieved, among other things, by committing to memory

[55] There is a massive literature on the Waldenses. For a straightforward introduction to their early development, see M. Lambert, *Medieval Heresy. Popular Movements from the Gregorian Reform to the Enlightenment* (Oxford, 1992 edn), chs. 5 and 8. For a series of illuminating papers, see P. Biller, *The Waldenses, 1170–1530* (Aldershot, 2001).

[56] Biller, *The Waldenses*, p. 159, for some recent literature on Waldenses in the Alps.

[57] A. Patschovsky (ed.), *Quellen zur böhmischen Inquisition im 14. Jahrhundert*, Monumenta Germaniae Historica Quellen zur Geistesgeschichte des Mittelalters XI (Weimar, 1979). Patschovsky argues convincingly (p. 24) that 'here we are not dealing with the persecution of a handful of people, or small marginal or splinter groups, but with formal mass persecutions, with an inquisition in the grand style making a lasting impact on the deep-rooted structures of the region' (my translation).

[58] B. Stock, *The Implications of Literacy: Written Language and Models of Interpretation in the Eleventh and Twelfth Centuries* (Princeton, 1983). On the relation between heresy and texts, see Biller and Hudson (eds.), *Heresy and Literacy*.

[59] See notably the contributions by A. Patschovsky, A. Brenon, P. Paravy, and G. Audisio to Biller and Hudson (eds.), *Heresy and Literacy*.

all the forty evangelical pericopes which he heard at the Sunday services in a Waldensian household'.[60]

It is the same with Lollardy in late medieval England. Anne Hudson's books and articles have surveyed magisterially the role of books in the diffusion of Wycliffite thought,[61] and the interaction of orality and literacy in Lollardy was illustrated long ago in a seminal article by Margaret Aston.[62] Thus William Wakeham of Devizes confessed 'that I with other heretics and Lollards was accustomed and used to hear in secret places, in nooks and corners, the reading of the Bible in English, and to this reading gave attendance by many years'.[63] James Brewster could not read himself, but he had reportedly 'been five times with William Sweeting in the fields keeping beasts, hearing him read many good things out of a certain book'; and others also heard Sweeting.[64] William Sweeting looks like the leader of a 'textual community'.[65] Actually, such 'textual communities' are not quite as different as they might appear from communities where everyone is supposed to read the Bible directly. In the latter case too the meaning can change at the reception end, as it merges with the contents and categories of a listener's mind; and preaching (with other forms of instruction) tends to guide interpretation by the individual bible reader.

One other mode of pre-print mass communication may be mentioned. Songs are a way in which ideas can extend their influence far beyond the boundaries of literacy, even while they are anchored in a written text. Propagandist songs seem to have been important in the movement which Wycliffe's ideas did much to inspire, Hussitism. A recent study has suggested that popular songs can be 'a form of witness, sign of solidarity, polemical device and expression of militarism. It may be argued successfully that Hussite popular songs fulfilled all four roles within a propagandist framework.'[66]

Could Lollardy and Hussitism have been more successful still? Space does not permit a discussion of how these two movements were ultimately

---

[60] A. Patschovsky, 'The Literacy of Waldensianism from Valdes to c.1400', in Biller and Hudson (eds.), *Heresy and Literacy*, pp. 112–36, at 132.

[61] See notably her *Lollards and their Books* (1985)

[62] M. Aston, 'Lollardy and Literacy', *History*, 62 (1977), 347–71.

[63] *Ibid.*, p. 353.   [64] *Ibid.*, pp. 353–4.

[65] See now A. Hope, 'The Lady and the Bailiff: Lollardy among the Gentry in Yorkist and Early Tudor England', in M. Aston and C. Richmond (eds.), *Lollardy and the Gentry in the Later Middle Ages* (Stroud, 1997), pp. 250–77.

[66] T. A. Fudge, *The Magnificent Ride. The First Reformation in Hussite Bohemia* (Aldershot 1998), p. 210; see also ch. 4 *passim*. I owe this reference to Dr Jurkowski.

checked. In both cases, however, I believe it could be shown that they achieved remarkable successes as long as they were tolerated by the state; and also that the down-turn in their fortunes had much to do with physical force.

Printing can distract attention from what was arguably the decisive variable: whether and how vigorously the movement was repressed, which in turn depended ultimately on the attitude of the ruler to the religious movement, since for force the Church depended on the support of the secular arm. Of course the state could not create religious movements. Nevertheless it could stifle them efficaciously. 'Medieval heresies' were breakaway movements which sooner or later came up against state opposition. That forced them underground. Otherwise they would doubtless be called Reformations. By contrast, Luther received political backing and protection. That gave his movement time to gather momentum. Without it, Lutheranism would presumably have its place in histories of medieval heresy. The problem was repression rather than communication. As we have seen dissident ideas could spread far and fast if given the chance, carried by dedicated missionaries, explained by preaching, crystallising around 'textual communities'.

With both heretical and orthodox religion, the combination of manuscript copying and oral dissemination should not be underestimated. As Bob Scribner has said in a Reformation history context: 'Orality was as important as the printed word in the formation of opinion, both collective and individual, manifest in the important role of the sermon in arousing evangelical fervour. Scribal culture was no less important . . . The handwritten pasquillade could, under local conditions, work as effectively as the printed broadsheet to focus views and precipitate political action.'[67] If scribal culture remained important in the age of the Reformation, it was surely much more important in the period before printing, precisely because it carried out functions which printing would take over.

A final analogy: the invention of printing can be compared with the invention of gunpowder. Over a long period of time printing transformed communication, just as gunpowder transformed war – not immediately in either case. One would laugh at the historian of warfare who thought that all fighting was hand-to-hand before guns were invented. Mendicant

---

[67] B. Scribner, 'Heterodoxy, Literacy and Print in the Early German Reformation', in Biller and Hudson (eds.), *Heresy and Literacy*, pp. 255–78 at 264.

books and even the books of heretics were the longbows of medieval communication.

Appendix: Scribal Independence

This appendix gives an illustration of how scribes acted as authors or editors, modifying the text they copied more or less freely in ways that made sense: i.e. we are not talking of scribal errors here. The data is abstracted from d'Avray, *Medieval Marriage Sermons*, pp. 106–7 and for the sake of brevity I use the sigla from the edition. The apparatus critici to the texts edited in that volume provide a plethora of further illustrations of intelligent scribal independence.

In some manuscripts the variations are so free that they cannot be contained within the confines of an apparatus criticus: manuscripts *An* and *M* in the edition of Pierre de Reims; *D* in the edition of Pierre de Saint-Benoît; and *A2* in the case of Guibert de Tournai. In all these cases sections had to be printed separately. There is no reason to think they represent authorial revisions, because they look like rather extreme cases of a common tendency to adapt the text. Because this tendency is so common, it is not credible that all the changes go back to revisions by an original author, even though the variations make sense: they are quite different from scribal errors. Examples make this clearer. Here I take one passage from Pierre de Reims. Really an examination of the apparatus is needed: the evidence is cumulative, as individual variations in isolation might be explained away as error or inadvertence, but not the overall pattern.

Pierre de Reims: Text

11/1/ Se*d* ne, quarto, in sua pulcritudine posset confidere, ut quasi propter speciositatem concupisceretur ab alio, etiam ipsam perdidit, quia 'egressus est a filia Syon omnis decor eius', Tren. i (6), et 'denigrata est super carbones facies eius', Tren. iiii (8). /2/ Hec est gratia interior que est decor anime, de qua, Ps. (144:14): 'Omnis gloria eius filie regis ab intus.'

Free Variants

11(all) *Cf.* **Lo**: 'Gratiam amisit', que est decor. Tren. 1 (6) 'Et egressus est a filia Syon omnis decor eius; facti sunt principes eius velud arietes non inuenientes pascua, et abierunt absque fortitudine ante faciem subsequentis.'

Ps. (44: 14): 'Omnis gloria eius filie regis ab (intus).' **11**/1/ ut quasi . . .
perdidit] ipsam amisit ***P1***   ut quasi . . . ab alio] *om.* ***V* 11**/2/ *(all)*] *om.*
P1   Hec est . . . anime] Hec est gratia, que est interior anime decor ***L***
Hec . . . interior] Et hoc est quia gratia interior exiuit ***T.***

It should be noted that skilful omission is one of the commonest kinds
of 'authorial' variant. Only a scribe in command of the content can omit
sentences or phrases without damaging the sense of a passage.

4

Print and pre-Reformation religion: the Benedictines and the press, c.1470–c.1550

James G. Clark

I

Printing has always been regarded by historians as an early modern phenomenon, a product of the Renaissance and a pre-requisite for Reformation that serves only to underline how much European society had changed by the turn of the fifteenth century.[1] Narrower still, in many of the most widely read textbooks, the early history of printing is presented almost solely as a sub-plot in the greater drama of the Protestant Reformation. The development of the press deserves attention in these narratives only on the grounds that it was an agent of religious change, an aid to Luther and Calvin and to those rulers who aimed to enforce a new confessional conformity on their subjects.[2] In this analysis printing and print culture emerge as the very antithesis of the medieval world, itself founded on a culture of manuscript books created by and (largely) for a clerical community committed to traditional, unreformed Catholicism.

Of course, there are ways in which the advent of printing does represent a break with the medieval past. Many of the earliest presses were established in urban centres such as Mainz, Strasbourg and Basle where there was

---

[1] The classic account of printing in this vein is E. L. Eisenstein, *The Printing Press as an Agent of Change: Communications and Cultural Transformations in Early Modern Europe*, 2 vols. (Cambridge, 1979), revised as the single-volume *The Printing Revolution in Early Modern Europe* (Cambridge, 1983). But even before Eisenstein's synthesis first appeared scholars tended to treat the coming of the press as marking a fundamental break with the medieval past. In their ground-breaking *L'Apparition du Livre* (Paris, 1958) Lucien Febvre and Henri Martin saw Gutenberg's invention as standing at the dawn of 'a new epoch'.

[2] E.g. *The New Cambridge Modern History* devotes a chapter to the development of printing only in the second volume, subtitled *The Reformation*, ed. G. R. Elton, 2nd edn (Cambridge, 1990). The same tunnel vision can also be found in many popular school and undergraduate texts such as G. R. Elton, *Reformation Europe, 1517–59* (1963) where passing reference is made to printing under the headings 'Luther and the Attack on Rome' (pp. 19, 33), also in H. G. Koenigsberger and G. L. Mosse, *Europe in the Sixteenth Century* (1968), where printing is discussed only in relation to the works of Luther and Calvin (pp. 306–7) and even recently in D. Nicholas, *The Transformation of Europe, 1300–1600* (1999), where printing is treated under 'the politics of religion' (pp. 213–4).

no pre-existing tradition of commercial book production.[3] Generally, the early printers were men of business who turned to printing after practising other trades; certainly the number of established scribes and stationers who embraced the *ars noua* was only very small.[4] Moreover, the clerical establishment does seem to have regarded the output of these first presses with more than a degree of scepticism. Famously, Johannes Trithemius, the reformist abbot of Sponheim, counselled members of his congregation that 'printing is no genuine friend of Holy Scripture' since it discouraged monks themselves from copying books, an ancient art which not only encouraged discipline and obedience in the cloister but also ensured that the sacred texts could pass complete and correct to future generations.[5] Such misgivings – even amongst those, like Trithemius, with humanist predilections – were serious enough to persuade Sixtus IV to issue licences for the censoring of books as early as 1479. Less than a decade later the first papal bull for the regulation of printing itself was published.[6]

Yet there is a danger in exaggerating the discontinuities that emerged in the European shift from manuscript to moveable metal types. In spite of the fears of the traditionalists like Trithemius, printing did not spell the end of the scribal art. Indeed the demand for manuscripts seems to have remained steady to the end of the fifteenth century, and recent studies have revealed a significant number of early imprints that served as the exemplar for a more select manuscript copy.[7] Moreover, there is a growing awareness that some of the oldest centres of scribal activity, the houses of the regular religious orders, and perhaps in particular the monasteries of the Benedictines, themselves played an important role in the promotion of printing in these early, pioneering decades. It has been suggested that

[3] The standard accounts of early European printing are now somewhat venerable; S. H. Steinberg, *Five Centuries of Printing*, rev. by J. Trevitt (1996); R. Hirsch, *Printing, Selling, Reading* (Wiesbaden, 1967); L. Febvre and H.-J. Martin, *The Coming of the Book: The Impact of Printing 1450–1800* (1976), pp. 45–56. For more recent studies see A. Kapr, *Johann Gutenberg* (1996); M. Davies, *The Gutenberg Bible* (1996); *CHBB 3*.

[4] S. Edmunds, 'From Schoeffer to Vérard: Concerning the Scribes who became Printers', in S. Hindman (ed.), *Printing the Written Word: the Social History of Books, c.1450–1520* (Ithaca and London, 1991), pp. 21–40.

[5] Johannes Trithemius, *De laude scriptorum*, ch. vii: 'Qui autem a scribendi studio cessat propter impressuram, verus amator scripturarum non est, quia presentia dumtaxat intuens nichil sollicitus est pro edificatione posterorum' (ed. K. Arnold (Lawrence, KA, 1974), pp. 64–5).

[6] R. Hirsch, 'Pre-Reformation Censorship of Printed Books', in his *The Printed Word: Its Impact and Diffusion* (1978), pp. 101–5.

[7] See, e.g., N. F. Blake, 'Manuscript to Print', in J. Griffiths and D. Pearsall (eds.), *Book Production and Publishing in Britain 1375–1475* (Cambridge, 1989), pp. 426–9; L. Houwen, 'Print into Manuscript: A Manuscript Copy of Part of the Boke of St Albans (1486)', in J. M. M. Hermands and K. van der Hoeck (ed.), *Boeken in de late Middeleeuwen: Verslag van de Groningse Codicologendagen 1992* (Groningen, 1994), pp. 41–52; J. B. Trapp, 'Illustrations of Petrarch's from Manuscript to Print and from Print to Manuscript', in M. Davis (ed.), *Incunabula: Studies in the Fifteenth-Century Printed Book Presented to Lotte Hellinga* (1999), pp. 507–47.

it was the particular needs of the monks of the Bursfeld congregation that guided Gutenberg, Füst and Schoeffer in planning the 42-line Bible and the Mainz Psalter, even down to the size, script and layout of these books.[8] Some of the most active and influential of the early German and Italian presses were actually established under the patronage of religious houses and operated within their precincts. It is well known, of course, that the first press in Italy, established by the Germans Pannartz and Sweynheim in 1465, was initially based at the monastery at Subiaco, outside Rome.[9] But there were other monastic presses elsewhere that flourished for longer periods. The first press at Augsburg was set up in 1472 in the Benedictine abbey of St Ulric and St Afra. The printer, Günther Zainer, had come from Strasbourg at the invitation of the abbot, Melchior von Stannheim. Over the next decade he produced not only the theological staples of use to the monastery but also a number of other landmark editions, including the lavish two-volume *Legenda aurea* (1472) and the first fully illustrated Bible (1475).[10] It appears the monks collaborated with him in this work, extending their own scriptorial activities to include the illumination and rubrication of the printed page. Probably in the majority of these cases the printing itself was handled by a professional, secular master, but there are some examples where monks did become directly involved in the technical process. At Strasbourg, Heinrich Eggestein is said to have taught the monks of the Carthusian monastery to operate the press for themselves. The Premonstratensians at Schüssenried also produced two printed books by their own hands in c.1478.[11] Monastic writers of this period – men such as Guillaume Briçonnet, the scholarly abbot of St Germain-des-Prés – were also amongst the first living authors to see their works into print. Even Abbot Trithemius himself overcame his natural objections to the new techonology sufficiently to see his little treatise through the press in 1494.[12]

There are good grounds for suggesting that the older monasteries played an equally important role in the development of printing in England. It has always been understood, of course, that the religious orders ceased to be involved in the production and publication of books by the middle of the fifteenth century. Except for some remarkable newcomers – such as the Brigittine monastery at Syon – it is generally assumed that monastic

---

[8] E. König, 'New Perspectives on the History of Mainz Printing: A Fresh Look at Illuminated Imprints', in Hindman (ed.), *Printing the Written Word*, pp. 143–73.

[9] Steinberg, *Five Centuries of Printing*, pp. 11–13, 18–19.

[10] *Ibid.*, pp. 23–4. See also Hirsch, *Printing, Selling and Reading*, p. 54.

[11] Steinberg, *Five Centuries of Printing*, p. 24; Hirsch, *Printing, Selling and Reading*, p. 55. See also M. Giesecke, *Der Buchdruck in der frühen Neuzeit: Eine historische Fallstudie* (Darmstadt, 1991).

[12] *De laude scriptorum* was first printed under Trithemius' supervision at the press of Peter von Friedberg at Mainz in 1494.

books and book-collections had fallen into neglect by this time as the tradition of claustral studies finally collapsed.[13] Even the most sanguine of monastic historians doubted whether English monks living in the shadow of the Dissolution 'either realised or wished to exploit the potentialities of [the] new tool'.[14] Indeed the history of early printing in England is usually presented as that of a commercial and more-or-less exclusively secular enterprise driven by the demands of an expanding lay (and largely vernacular) readership.[15] Although the work of the early presses beyond Westminster and London has attracted further attention in recent years, studies have tended to concentrate on only a handful of urban and university printers.[16]

However, this approach overlooks a significant body of evidence that suggests that the monastic order did develop a special interest in the new technology. In the first place a good many of the *incunabula* of English provenance that now survive show signs of monastic ownership. From the libraries of the greater Benedictine monasteries such as Christ Church Cathedral Priory, Canterbury, Durham Cathedral Priory, and St Swithun's Priory, Winchester as many as fifty or more early printed books have been identified.[17] Random survivals from the poorer, smaller houses would suggest that even these communities had their share of early editions.[18] Contemporary library catalogues and inventories, which offer a glimpse of the countless monastic books that have since been lost, reinforce this general impression that on the eve of the Dissolution the monasteries were well stocked with

[13] A. I. Doyle, 'Publication by Members of the Religious Orders', in Griffiths and Pearsall (eds.), *Book Production*, pp. 190–213; J. T. Rhodes, 'Syon Abbey and its Religious Publications in the Sixteenth Century', *JEH*, 44 (1993), 11–21; V. Gillespie, 'The Book and the Brotherhood: Reflections on the Lost Library of Syon Abbey', in A. S. G. Edwards, V. Gillespie and R. Hanna (eds.), *The English Medieval Book: Essays in Memory of Jeremy Griffiths* (2000), pp. 185–208. A new, annotated edition of the *registrum* of the Syon Library, by Vincent Gillespie, has been published in the *Corpus of British Medieval Library Catalogues*, vol. ix, 2001.

[14] D. Knowles, *The Religious Orders in England*, vol. iii, *The Tudor Age* (Cambridge, 1959), p. 26.

[15] For studies in this vein see H. S. Bennett, *English Books and Readers, 1475–1557* (Cambridge, 1969); N. F. Blake, *Caxton: England's First Printer* (1976).

[16] See, e.g., P. C. Christianson, 'An Early Tudor Stationers and the "Prynters of Bokes" ', *The Library*, 6th ser., 9 (1987), 259–62; P. C. Christianson, 'The Stationers of Paternoster Row, 1534–57', *Proceedings of the Bibliographical Society of America*, 87 (1993), 81–91; D. McKitterick, *A History of the Cambridge University Press*, vol. 1, *Printing and the Book Trade in Cambridge, 1534–68* (Cambridge, 1992).

[17] For the surviving printed books from these houses see N. R. Ker, *Medieval Libraries of Great Britain: A List of Surviving Books*, 2nd edn (1964), pp. 29–40, 199–201; N. R. Ker and A. G. Watson (eds.), *Medieval Libraries of Great Britain: Supplement to the Second Edition* (1987), pp. 10–12, 16–34. For Durham, see also A. I. Doyle 'The Printed Books of the Last Monks of Durham', *The Library*, 6th ser., 10 (1988), 206.

[18] See, e.g., the books surviving from Leominster, Ramsey and Thorney: Ker, *Medieval Libraries*, pp. 114, 153–4, 189.

a wide range of newly printed material. A catalogue of 147 books belonging to the Cluniac priory of Monk Bretton compiled some years after the surrender of the house is made up almost exclusively of printed editions, the majority dating from after 1520.[19] The personal account-book of Prior William More of Worcester (in office 1518–36) records the purchase of as many as sixty-nine printed editions from a variety of local and London dealers.[20] More was not the only early Tudor monk to acquire new books 'at source' in this way. In fact in the early decades of the sixteenth century several monasteries became directly involved in the production and publication of printed books. They offered their patronage to printers, provided them with manuscript exemplars, and worked with them in the preparation of some editions. Indeed it is often forgotten that as late as the 1530s – the last decade of monastic life in England – the only presses active outside London were those operating under the patronage of monasteries, at St Albans, and at St Augustine's Abbey, Canterbury.

II

In some respects it is not surprising to find evidence that the English monasteries responded enthusiastically to the advent of printing. Certainly much of their old monopoly on books and learning had been lost by the later Middle Ages with the expansion of the universities and secular schools and the rise in vernacular literacy. But there is no doubt that even in the second half of the fifteenth century many houses did remain closely involved to some degree in the insular book trade. Some of the larger, wealthier abbeys continued to produce books of their own, if not always at their own hands and not always in the context of a traditional *scriptorium*.[21] The scale of this work was sufficient at Canterbury, Reading and Westminster, to attract the services of skilled, professional scribes and illuminators, including Flemish

---

[19] The list is found on the opening leaves of the priory's early sixteenth-century cartulary, now BL, Add. MS 50755, fos. 4v–6r. See also M. C. Cross, 'A Medieval Yorkshire Library', *Northern History*, 25 (1989), 288; R. Sharpe *et al.* (eds.), *English Benedictine Libraries: The Shorter Catalogues*, Corpus of British Medieval Library Catalogues 5 (1996), B55. 1–147 (pp. 268–87).

[20] Sharpe *et al.* (eds.), *English Benedictine Libraries*, B118. 1–86 (pp. 662–74, esp. 664–74). For More's career see A. B. Emden, *A Biographical Register of the University of Oxford to AD 1500*, 3 vols. (Oxford, 1957–9) [hereafter *BRUO*], vol. II, pp. 1308–9.

[21] See, e.g., R. B. Dobson, *Durham Priory* (Cambridge, 1973), pp. 376–8; A. Gransden, 'Some Manuscripts from Cambridge from Bury St Edmunds', in A. Gransden (ed.), *Bury St Edmunds: Medieval Art, Architecture, Archaeology and Economy* (Leeds, 1998), pp. 239–44; R. M. Thomson, *A Descriptive Catalogue of the Medieval Manuscripts in Worcester Cathedral Library* (Cambridge, 2001), pp. xxv, xxxv–xxxvii; J. G. Clark, 'Thomas Walsingham Reconsidered: Books and Learning at Late Medieval St Albans', *Speculum*, 77 (2002), 841–3.

and German itinerants.[22] There is evidence that these greater abbeys also supported other book artisans in their precincts. Mirjam J. Foot has suggested that the beginnings of the English binding industry can be traced back to a network of monastic centres such as Canterbury, Durham, Jervaulx, Tavistock and Winchester that flourished in the decades after 1450.[23] It is very likely that some of the more intellectually active monastic communities also continued to play a small part in the 'publication' in manuscript of certain texts: on the evidence of surviving manuscript copies, for example, it is possible that at least one version of *The Travels of Sir John Mandeville* was of monastic origin.[24]

English monks continued to follow closely the rhythms of the book trade at the end of the fifteenth century, but, it seems, without a trace of the defensive nostalgia about manuscripts expressed by Abbot Trithemius. On the contrary, it appears the monks were amongst the very earliest buyers of printed books in England. It has been discovered that two vellum copies of Gutenberg's 42-line Bible had reached England before 1460, where both were richly illuminated: it is tempting to suggest that one or other of these was prepared for a monastic owner.[25] Certainly as early as the beginning of the 1470s, individual monks had begun to buy printed editions of favourite authors on a regular basis. The earliest examples come from Canterbury and Durham, many of whose monks studied at Oxford, and it was probably from the shops of the university stationers that these books were acquired. Before 1474 one Canterbury monk had bought a copy of the edition of Jerome printed by Pannartz and Sweynheim at Rome in 1468; by the end of the decade the same monk had also acquired Francesco Griffolini's edition of Chrysostom's Homilies on the Gospel of John printed in 1470.[26] By 1480 several Durham monks had made similar acquisitions. When he died in 1481, William Law was in possession of at least six printed books including a four-volume edition of Nicholas of Lyre, printed between 1474 and 1477.[27]

---

[22] A. Coates, *Medieval English Books: The Reading Abbey Collections from Foundation to Dispersal* (Oxford, 1999), pp. 110–12; R. A. B. Mynors, 'A Fifteenth-Century Scribe: T. Werken', *Transactions of the Cambridge Bibliographical Society*, 1:2 (1950), 97–104; M. B. Parkes, 'A Fifteenth-Century Scribe: Henry Mere', *Bodleian Library Record*, 6 (1961), 654–9.

[23] M. J. Foot, 'Bookbinding, 1400–1557', in *CHBB* 3, p. 116.

[24] One of the most important manuscripts of the English version of the *Travels*, BL, MS Egerton 1982, was in fact a St Albans' book. See also n. 65 below. For further discussion of the general issue see Doyle, 'Publication by Members of the Religious Orders', pp. 190–213.

[25] Davies, *The Gutenberg Bible*, pp. 53–6.

[26] Mynors, 'A Fifteenth-Century Scribe', 97–104. See also E. Armstrong, 'English Purchases of Printed Books from the Continent, 1465–1526', *EHR*, 94 (1979), 270.

[27] Doyle, 'Printed Books of the Monks of Durham', 206. For William Law see also Emden, *BRUO*, vol. II, pp. 1111–12.

Such prestige editions at this early date were the preserve of the greater monasteries. But already in the 1480s print was making an appearance even in smaller communities. In 1485, for instance, there was already a Strasbourg edition of Bartholomew Anglicus' *De proprietatibus rerum* at Tewkesbury Abbey.[28]

The earliest printers had confined themselves to the standard works of the best-known authors in the hope that churches, religious houses, schools and universities might be persuaded to buy them in bulk. By the turn of the fifteenth century, many of the larger monasteries in England do seem to have embarked on a process of re-stocking, substituting old manuscript copies of their most frequently used texts with new, printed editions. Books for worship such as breviaries, missals and psalters were bought in the editions of continental printers which were cheaper, easier for the choir monks to use on account of their size, and also no doubt more effective for the teaching of novices and juniors. The greater abbeys such as Abingdon and St Albans even went so far as to commission printed editions of their own.[29] Printed editions of the Rule of St Benedict, and the commentaries associated with it, now replaced the old and over-used manuscript versions which had, in any case, often been booklet copies lacking a permanent binding.[30] A wide range of printed schoolbooks were also bought to supplement, if not replace the somewhat haphazard collection of dictionaries, grammars, glossaries and 'readers' which had traditionally formed the basis of a monastic education. New authorities, as much as older books newly edited, proved popular in this context: copies of the *Hortus vocabulorum* (Westminster, 1500) and John Holt's *Lac puerorum* (London, 1505) were bought by the monks of Norwich before 1520.[31] It appears that the monks of St Albans bought several of Caxton's early works, including his English Boethius, the *Dictes and Sayings* and *Jason*, for use in the grammar school attached to the abbey; fragments of these texts have been recovered from the bindings of sixteenth-century books belonging to the school.[32]

Many monasteries also recognised that printing provided the solution to the perennial problem of supplying their students with the necessary textbooks when away from the home community at university. Since the thirteenth century every Benedictine house had been required to send one

[28] Ker, *Medieval Libraries*, p. 188.   [29] See below, pp. 86–7.

[30] For copies of the Rule in monastic libraries of the period see Sharpe *et al.* (eds.), *English Benedictine Libraries*, B55. 50, 125, B117. 32 (pp. 268–87, 667).

[31] *Ibid.*, B60. 22, 24 (p. 306).

[32] For these fragments see W. Blades (ed.), *The Boke of Saint Albans: by Dame Juliana Berners containing treatises on Hawking, Hunting and Cotearms* (1881), p. 19.

monk in every twenty to Oxford and Cambridge to study for a higher degree
in theology or canon law. While smaller houses may have evaded this injunction, the majority regularly supported two, three or even four of their number in academic studies for sometimes as much as a decade at a time.[33] The
monastic *studia* themselves were poorly equipped – the largest, Gloucester
College, at Oxford, had no common library at all – and it was the responsibility of each individual community to ensure their students were provided
with the necessary books.[34] By the turn of the fifteenth century, many of
those houses with a large complement of students had begun to buy multiple
copies of the standard textbooks in printed editions, works such as the postil
collections of Hugh of Saint-Cher and Nicholas of Lyre, and the Sentence
commentaries of Aquinas and Scotus.[35] The student monks were also encouraged to buy books for themselves out of their stipends. John Avington,
a Winchester monk student, bought more than six books while at Oxford
between c.1500–19, including editions of Scotus and John Lathbury's
popular commentary on Lamentations printed at the university in 1481.[36]
For the first time it was possible for individual students to access academic
texts on their own terms, without recourse to their home community and
its library. Before printing, it seems highly unlikely that a young student
monk like Thomas Marse, of St Mary's Abbey, York (at Gloucester College
in the early years of the sixteenth century) could have acquired his own copy
of Lyre's Bible commentaries in all four volumes.[37] Indeed it is tempting
to see this marked improvement in monastic book provision as one reason why there was sudden upsurge in the number of Benedictine scholars
completing degrees at the two universities between 1500 and 1540.[38]

It is worth noting that in England at least the monasteries began to re-
stock their manuscript libraries with printed books far earlier than many

---

[33] See R. B. Dobson, 'The Religious Orders, 1370–1540', in J. I. Catto and T. A. R. Evans (eds.), *The
History of the University of Oxford*, vol. ii, *Late Medieval Oxford* (Oxford, 1992), pp. 539–79.

[34] See M. B. Parkes, 'The Provision of Books', in Catto and Evans (eds.), *Late Medieval Oxford*,
pp. 446–55.

[35] Sharpe *et al.* (eds.), *English Benedictine Libraries*, B55. 2, 32, 60; B117. 11 (pp. 64, 262, 272, 276); Ker,
Medieval Libraries, pp. 19–20, 155, 199–201. For printed editions of Lyre and St Cher acquired at
Battle Abbey see M. Connolly, 'Books Connected with Battle Abbey before the Dissolution: Some
New Discoveries', *The Library*, 7th ser., 1 (2000), 122–3.

[36] For Avington, see J. Greatrex, *A Biographical Register of the English Cathedral Priories* [hereafter
BRECP] (Oxford, 1997), pp. 667–8.

[37] For Marse, see C. Cross, 'Monastic Learning and Libraries in Sixteenth-Century Yorkshire', in
J. Kirk (ed.), *Humanism and Reform: the Church in Europe, England and Scotland, 1400–1643*, SCH
Subsidia 8 (1991), p. 266.

[38] For the number of graduates recorded in this period see P. Cunich, 'Benedictine Monks at the
University of Oxford and the Dissolution of the Monasteries', in H. Wansborough and A. Marrett
Crosby (eds.), *The Benedictines in Oxford* (1997), p. 165.

comparable secular institutions. The university colleges at Oxford and Cambridge were slow to respond to the greater availability of academic texts in accurate and affordable printed editions. Several of their libraries – All Souls and Merton College at Oxford, King's College and Peterhouse at Cambridge – held as many manuscripts as the greatest monastic collections, but there are few signs of printed books being aqcuired in any number before the second decade of the sixteenth century.[39] The earliest record of printed books bought directly out of college funds is from Magdalen College, Oxford, and dates from between 1481 and 1485 but there is nothing like it elsewhere before 1500.[40] It was only after reformist scholars in both universities had begun to purge the colleges of their manuscripts after 1540 that the purchase of new, printed editions began in earnest.[41]

Even in England – where until the mid-sixteenth century the majority of printed books were imported – the spread of the new technology also brought a sharp fall in the price of books. For members of monastic communities this made personal acquisitions possible on a large scale for the first time. From the number and variety of surviving examples it is clear that by the end of the fifteenth century an increasing number of individual monks (and to a lesser degree, nuns) regularly bought printed books of their own. It remains unclear exactly how the monastic authorities responded to this behaviour. Before printing it was forbidden for a monk or nun to buy or otherwise take possession of books except under licence from their superior, and even the borrowing of a book was subject to a formal procedure.[42] Given that many religious were now in receipt of their own 'wages', however, and often spent long periods pursuing duties outside the cloister, such proscriptions must have become very difficult to enforce. It may also be the case that abbots, priors and episcopal visitors were positive about print

---

[39] For the Oxford libraries, see N. R. Ker, 'Oxford College Libraries Before 1500', in his *Books, Collectors and Libraries*, ed. A. G. Watson (1984), pp. 301–20; Parkes, 'The Provision of Books', pp. 407–83. For Cambridge, see K. Jensen, 'Textbooks in the Universities: The Evidence from the Books', in *CHBB 3*, pp. 354–79. See also P. D. Clarke (ed.), *The University and College Libraries of Cambridge*, Corpus of British Medieval Library Catalogues, vol. x (2002).

[40] See Oxford, Magdalen College, LCE/1, fos. 11v, 105v.

[41] See N. R. Ker, 'Oxford College Libraries in the Sixteenth Century', in his *Books, Collectors and Libraries*, ed. Watson, pp. 379–436; N. R. Ker, 'The Provision of Books', in J. J. McConica (ed.), *The History of the University of Oxford*, vol. iii, *The Collegiate University* (Oxford, 1986), pp. 441–519.

[42] The statutes of the General Chapters of 1277 and 1343 which were followed by all Benedictine houses in England ruled that no monk was to possess a book, even from the conventual library, except under licence from the abbot or prior. See W. A. Pantin, *Documents illustrating the activities of the General and Provincial Chapters of the English Black Monks, 1215–1540*, 3 vols., Camden Society, 3rd ser., 45, 47, 54 (1931–7), vol. i, p. 74 (1277); vol. ii, p. 51 (1343). Local constitutions usually included a similar injunction.

and the prospect it offered of a return to a purer form of monastic *lectio*. Probably the majority of monks made only occasional purchases, perhaps an accessible and accurate copy of an important textbook, a printed edition of the Rule – those including the commentary of Johannes de Turrecremata were especially popular – or some other meditation for private devotion. It became increasingly common for women religious to acquire a single, printed volume to commemorate their own profession. It was perhaps for this reason that Margaret Stanburne, a nun of St Mary's Stamford, was in possession of a well-preserved copy of the Rule in the translation of Richard Fox (pr. Richard Pynson, London, 1520: *STC* 1859) with no marks other than her own very proud *ex libris*.[43]

But there is no doubt that some religious now seized the opportunity to pursue their intellectual interests on a grander scale. By the beginning of the sixteenth century, in the larger, wealthier houses with a long-standing tradition of learning, it was not unusual not find monks in possession of several dozen printed books in their own name. The *ex libris* inscription of the Durham scholar monk, Thomas Swalwell, has been found in no fewer than thirty printed volumes and his marginal glosses have been identified in many others.[44] Swalwell's special interest was in theology and he turned to print in particular for reliable editions of the standard authorities, such as Augustine, Bernard of Clairvaux, and Scotus.[45] For other religious, however, it is likely that printing also represented an opportunity to acquire the recent or contemporary works which could not be found in their conventional (and manuscript-based) convent libraries. Print provided the best, and for some monks perhaps the only means of exploring the work of the Italian (and other) humanists. By the 1520s the printed works of (amongst others) Antoninus, Erasmus, and Marsilio Ficino, as well as scholarly editions of the Latin and Greek *auctores* were to be found in many Benedictine collections.[46] It is often forgotten that the humanist interests of the Evesham monk Robert Joseph and his circle (which flourished from c.1528–32) were fuelled for the most part by their reading of recently printed books.[47]

[43] The book is now Bodl. Lib., Arch. D. 15.

[44] Doyle, 'Printed Books of the Monks of Durham', 203–19; A. J. Piper, 'Dr Thomas Swalwell: Monk of Durham, Archivist and Bibliophile (d. 1539)', in J. P. Carley and C. G. C. Tite (eds.), *Books and Collectors: Essays Presented to Andrew Watson* (1997), pp. 71–100.

[45] These volumes are now Downside Abbey, 18274 (Bernard: pr. 1508); Durham Cathedral, Inc. 21b (Scotus: pr. 1481); Durham Cathedral, Inc. 45 (Augustine: pr. 1492).

[46] See, e.g., the range of authors found in print at Abingdon, Glastonbury, Reading and Worcester: Ker, *Medieval Libraries*, pp. 2–3, 90–1, 154–8, 205–15.

[47] See H. Aveling and W. A. Pantin (eds.), *The Letter Book of Robert Joseph, Monk of Evesham*, Oxford Historical Society, NS 19 (1967).

The greater opportunities for ownership and personal study which printing offered the professed religious may have also given rise to a new attitude
to books themselves. Monastic readers rarely left any traces of their own
presence on the folios, flyleaves and pastedowns of their manuscripts, save
for a handful of anonymous 'nota' marks, 'finger' pointers or underlines.
The only permissible expression of individuality was an *ex libris* inscription
in which the monk himself would be identified as the custodian of a book
which *de iure* belonged to the community itself; occasionally this was accompanied by the modest request, 'ora pro me'. With the coming of print,
however, monastic readers began to develop a more personal approach to
their books, treating them as any layperson might, as luxury objects in
which to indulge. Often they had them bound in the very best of contemporary leather bindings: the Durham monks of the turn of the fifteenth
century favoured the celebrated Oxford 'Rood and Hunt' binder for their
printed purchases.[48] William Edys, abbot of Burton-on-Trent (1518–30),
who amassed a personal library of more than a dozen early editions over
several decades, commissioned costly personalised leather bindings for his
books, each one bearing his name in *textura* capitals tooled into the front
board.[49] Increasingly, those monks who acquired printed books also believed them to be beyond the jurisdiction of their superiors or the community as a whole. They did not surrender them into the custody of the
common library as was customary, and in many cases willed them away
from the community at their death.[50] By the time of the Dissolution this
principle seems to have become widely accepted and many monks went
back into the world still retaining their collections of printed books whilst
their manuscripts and other written records became the property of the
crown.[51] Perhaps the most remarkable case is that of Philip Hawford, the
last abbot of Evesham, who, when he died in retirement on one of the former abbey estates in 1557, was in possession of no fewer than seventy-five

[48] Doyle, 'Printed Books of the Last Monks of Durham', 203–16.

[49] For the full list of books belonging to Edys see Ker, *Medieval Libraries*, pp. 15–16, 232. For his
distinctive bindings see especially Oxford, All Souls College, SR 62 a. 2 (Johannes Trithemius); SR
77 g. 13 (Henricus de Segusio); V. 2. 13 (Sermones). For his career see A. B. Emden, *A Biographical
Register of the University of Oxford, 1501–40* (Oxford, 1973) [*BRUO 1501–40*], p. 187.

[50] Such was the practice at Durham Priory where by the early sixteenth century many printed books
circulated independently from the conventual collection and were passed from one generation of
monks to another. See, e.g., the Basel edition of Jerome's *Letters* (1524: now Durham Cathedral, Inc.
15A) which passed through the hands of three different monks – William Bennet, William Wylom
and Nicholas Marley – in the dozen years before the Dissolution.

[51] E.g., according to the *ex libris* inscription an unnamed Brother Ryngstead, a monk of Bury St
Edmunds, retained an early edition of Aristotle (now BL, IB 40248) after the surrender of the house
in 1539; in the same way Humphrey Weobley of Worcester held on to his first edition of Erasmus'
Encomium Moriae (Antwerp, 1512: now Bodl. Lib., 8° M 127) on his return to the world.

printed books, the majority of them editions dating from before 1520, and therefore acquired during his monastic career.[52]

Personal libraries of this size bear witness to the close relationship some early Tudor monks must have enjoyed with booksellers and other professionals involved in the burgeoning book trade. Prior More of Worcester bought his books direct from the London markets.[53] From the evidence of their personal inventories, it would appear the Canterbury monks were regulars at the bookstalls in the capital and also at Oxford.[54] It is possible that some also established links with dealers, publishers and possibly even printers abroad. The large library of contemporary authors amassed by Richard Kidderminster, abbot of Winchcombe, for example, may have owed something to connections he had forged in France and the Low Countries. It is notable that in the early 1520s he was already very familiar with the work of Luther and his disciples: marginalia in his surviving books include references to several of their early treatises.[55]

III

The Benedictines were enthusiasts for the new medium from the first and as presses came to be established in England they also began to show an interest in the process of production itself. It has been suggested that even as early as 1477 one of the monks of Westminster assisted William Caxton in the preparation of his *Dictes and Sayings*; the manuscript on which the edition was based was apparently the work of a monastic scribe, one 'Haywarde'.[56]

Probably the earliest instance of direct monastic patronage occurred when Caxton himself had been in business for barely a decade. It is likely that the press that operated at St Albans intermittently between 1479 and 1486 was connected in some way with the monks of the abbey.[57] This was only the second provincial press in England and apart from the intermittent Oxford press of Theodoric Rood and Thomas Hunt it was the first

[52] E. A. Barnard, 'Philip Hawford, Pseudo Abbot of Evesham and Dean of Worcester: His Will and Inventory', *Transactions of the Worcestershire Archaeological Society*, NS 5 (1928), 52–69.
[53] Sharpe *et al.* (eds.), *English Benedictine Libraries*, B118. 1–86 (pp. 662–74, esp. 664–74).
[54] For these purchases see the inventories ed. by W. A. Pantin in his *Canterbury College, Oxford*, Oxford Historical Society, 4 vols., NS 6 (1946), vol. 1, pp. 80–96.
[55] For the full list of books known to have formed part of Kidderminster's collection see Ker, *Medieval Libraries*, pp. 198–9. The marginalia in his copy of Bede (Bodl. Lib., Douce MS 368) and the *Vitas patrum* (Bodl. Lib., Rawlinson Q. d. 12) is especially redolent of his contemporary concerns.
[56] Blake, 'Manuscript to Print', p. 414.
[57] For the St Albans press, see E. G. Duff, *The English Provincial Printers, Stationers and Bookbinders to 1557* (Cambridge, 1912), pp. 34–41; Blades (ed.), *The Boke of Saint Albans*, p. 19; L. Hellinga, 'Printing', *CHBB 3*, pp. 71–9.

to achieve any degree of longevity.[58] It was also the first press to be established using exclusively English expertise. The printer himself was almost certainly a native Englishman, and his founts had also been manufactured in England, some being borrowed from the Westminster master.[59] Like Theodoric Rood at Oxford, the St Albans printer probably was drawn to this provincial town with the prospect of tapping into the market for academic books that Caxton himself, concentrating on a variety of vernacular works, had not yet monopolised. St Albans was well placed, at the head of the main route northwards, and within relatively easy reach of the capital, and of Cambridge and Oxford, and with two grammar schools of its own. Of the eight books that were printed, four were standard academic textbooks, the Pseudo Albertus Magnus, *Liber de modis significandi* (1480: *STC* 268) Antonio Andrea's commentary on Aristotle's Logic (1483: *STC* 582), John Canon's commentary on Aristotle's Physics (1481: *STC* 14621), and the *Exempla sacre scripturae* (1481: *STC* 2993), and two were new studies of classical grammar and rhetoric by the Italian scholars Agostino Dato (1479: *STC* 6289) and Lorenzo Traversagni de Saona (1480: *STC* 24190). Only after a two-year hiatus (1483–5), did the printer produce vernacular texts, perhaps in a last desperate attempt to turn a profit, producing two final volumes, a collection of the chronicles of England (1485: *STC* 9995), and the famous *Bokys of Hawkyng and Huntyng and Cootarmuris* (1486: *STC* 3308).[60]

The identity of the St Albans printer still remains obscure. In his 1495 re-print of the *Chronicles of England* (*STC* 9996) Wynkyn de Worde famously described him as 'some time scholemaister of St Albones'.[61] It may be in fact that there were two printers. The two years which separate the printing of the Latin and English books and the obvious change of direction and intended market that this entailed would support the suggestion that there had in fact been a change of ownership. Whether two printers or one, whoever was behind this printing must have been well known to William Caxton. Not only did he employ the same fount as the Westminster printer for his two Latin grammars, but one of these texts, the *Noua rhetorica* of

---

[58] For the Rood and Hunt press, see E. G. Duff, *Early Printed Books* (1894), pp. 147–53.

[59] N. Barker, 'The St Albans Press: the First Punch Cutter in England and the First Native Type Founder', *Transactions of the Cambridge Bibliographical Society*, 7 (1979), 257–78.

[60] The vernacular texts have attracted greater attention than the academic titles. There have been several editions, the best of which is that edited by Blades (see above n. 32) and a partial facsimile, R. Hands (ed.), *English Hawking and Hunting in the Boke of St Albans* (Oxford, 1975). See also E. F. Jacob, 'The Boke of St Albans', in his *Essays in Later Medieval History* (Manchester, 1968), pp. 195–213.

[61] 'compyled in a book and also enprinted by our some time scholemaister of St Albones': *Chronicles of England*, prologue.

Traversagni, was a re-print of the edition produced by Caxton in 1478 (*STC* 24188.5). It is tempting to suggest that the printer(s) also had some connection with Cambridge. Traversagni himself was teaching at Cambridge between c.1472 and 1482, and what better reason to re-issue the printed text from a press not far from the university only two years after Caxton?[62]

Known to Caxton, and perhaps to the academic community in Cambridge, it is highly likely that the St Albans printer was also closely associated with the monks of the abbey. There is, of course, no evidence to suggest that the press was located within the grounds of the monastery. But in an old, entrenched monastic borough like St Albans, where the abbot and convent still dominated the economic and social life of the community, and where even the manorial court was still held within the abbey walls, it is scarcely credible that the monks knew nothing of the printer and his work.[63] Indeed it is unlikely that any press could have successfully operated in the town without the consent and co-operation of the monastic community. If the printer *were* the schoolmaster then he would have found himself *ex officio* under the jurisdiction of the abbot and convent. There were two grammar schools at St Albans in the fifteenth century: one was a small, elementary school attached to the almonry, the other and a larger institution located in the town itself but remaining under the supervision of the monastic almoner. The Master of this school was appointed by the abbot and convent and he was accommodated in a house on the monastery side of the precinct wall.[64]

It is worth noting that at the time the press was in operation at St Albans, or shortly thereafter, the monks themselves were in contact with William Caxton. Towards the end of his life it appears that Caxton gained access to the monastic library, and in April 1492 he borrowed a manuscript copy of the English *Mandeville* presumably to use as an exemplar for his printed edition.[65] The willingness of the monks to lend one of their books on this

---

[62] For Traversagni's sojourn at Cambridge, see E. Leedham-Green, 'University Libraries and Booksellers', in *CHBB 3*, p. 335.

[63] For the background to St Albans in this period, see V. H. Galbraith, *The Abbey of St Albans from 1300 to the Dissolution* (Oxford, 1911); L. F. R. Williams, *The Abbey of St Albans* (London, 1917); A. M. Levett, *Studies in Manorial History*, ed. H. M. Cam, M. Coate and L. S. Sutherland (Oxford, 1938).

[64] For a brief account of these schools see N. Orme, *English Schools in the Middle Ages* (1973), pp. 1–12, 120–1, 177–80. Their management, and the arrangement for the appointment and accommodation of the master are laid out in the fifteenth-century almoner's register, BL, Lansdowne MS 375, esp. fo. 3r–v.

[65] The manuscript is now BL, MS Egerton 1982. Caxton himself never completed an edition of Mandeville but the version published by Richard Pynson in 1496 (*The Boke of Iohn Maundvyle*, STC 17246) may have been derived from this manuscript. See also M. C. Seymour, 'The Early Editions of Mandeville's *Travels*', *The Library*, 5th ser., 19 (1964), 202–7.

occasion may reflect the fact that they had already become accustomed to assisting the St Albans printer(s) in this way.

It was perhaps the support of his monastic patrons that enabled the St Albans printer(s) to continue for as long as seven years. But like the Oxford printers before him, in due course it proved impossible to compete with the continental presses whose editions dominated the English market. The early protectionist legislation of the Yorkist and Early Tudor kings did not extend to dealers, wholesalers and others involved in the printed book trade. It was relatively easy therefore for the large, well-established printing-houses in France, Germany and Italy, and their armies of international agents, to overcome the meagre output of their few English competitors.[66] Indeed it was a measure of their confidence in this continuing monopoly that as late as 1494 a Venetian printer-publisher was prepared to fund an edition of the Sarum missal purely for export to England.[67]

There are grounds for suggesting that when the insular printing industry did begin to recover in the second quarter of the sixteenth century it was due in some part to the patronage of the older monastic order. Before the mid-1520s the only presses in operation outside London (and then only intermittently) were at Cambridge, Oxford and York. But in 1526 a press was established for the first time beyond the academic and ecclesiastical mainstream, in the south west of England, at the Benedictine abbey of Tavistock.[68] Little is known about the operation of the press, but it appears that it was situated within the monastery precincts and under the direction of the abbot and convent. There is no doubt that the printer himself, one Thomas Richard, was a monk.[69] He published only a single work, *The Boke of Confort* (*STC* 3200), a version of the English translation of Boethius' *Consolatio philosophiae* made by John Walton in c.1410.[70] But as the first to be printed in the region it seems to have found a ready audience. Indeed the edition was sponsored by a prominent local patron, Sir Robert Langdon, Commissioner of the Peace and Sheriff of Cornwall.[71] Richard not only brought printing out from the established centres of book-production, he

---

[66] Armstrong, 'English Purchases', 768–90; Hellinga, 'Printing', p. 68.

[67] *STC* 16167/68. See also Armstrong, 'English Purchases', 278.

[68] For a summary account of the Tavistock press see H. P. R. Finberg, *Tavistock Abbey. A Study in the Social and Economic History of Devon* (Cambridge, 1951), pp. 290–3. See also J. Ames, *Typographical Antiquities*, 3 vols. (1785–90), vol. III, p. 1440.

[69] Like many monks of his generation, Richard was an Oxford graduate. Little else is known of his career. See *BRUO 1501–40*, p. 484, where he is identified only as a monk of Totnes, a dependency of Tavistock.

[70] Walton's text as it circulated in manuscript has been edited as *Boethius, De Consolatione philosophiae*, trans. John Walton, ed. M. Science, EETS 170 (1927). For his career see *BRUO*, vol. III, p. 1975.

[71] For Langdon's tenure of these offices see *L&P*, IV (I), 137; XVIII, 1136; XII, 1795, 2002; VI, 6490.

also went some way towards establishing it as an acceptable channel for monastic scholarship. *The Boke of Confort* is to all intents and purposes a critical edition of Walton's little known translation, collated from a number of manuscript exemplars and incorporating a verse prologue and several new stanzas probably of Richard's own composition. It is possible that further editions were planned – a version of John Stanbridge's Long Accidence now in fragments has been attributed to the Tavistock press – but in 1528 Richard was appointed prior of Totnes and production probably ceased. In 1534 the abbot and convent returned to the press once only to publish a unique edition *The Confirmation of the Tynners Charter*, a summary of the statutes governing the tin mines on their estates.[72]

In the same period as the Tavistock press, the abbot and convent of Abingdon offered their patronage to John Scolar, one of the succession of troubled printers connected with Oxford.[73] Scolar had operated a press in the university town for at least two years between 1517 and 1518 but like his predecessors he struggled to sustain his business in the face of continuing continental competition and the university's own strict regulations.[74] He may have taken refuge in Abingdon early in the 1520s although his first and only printing for the monastic community was completed in 1528. This was an edition of the Latin breviary following the Abingdon usage (*STC* 15792), and given the complexity of the text and the need to consult correct exemplars it is probable that Scolar worked from within the monastery itself.

Both these experiments in printing were short-lived but during a decade when presses were struggling (and failing) to survive their very existence is significant. Moreover, it seems that by the beginning of the 1530s their example had been enough to persuade at least two of the larger, wealthier Benedictine houses – St Albans and St Augustine's, Canterbury – to embark on a more sustained programme of printed-book production.

The monks of St Albans Abbey were no strangers to print culture and even at the end of the 1520s there may have been a lingering tradition of their earlier involvement with the 'Schoolmaster Printer'. Theirs was also a self-consciously scholarly community, and even at this late date their students were prominent amongst the Benedictines at Oxford and Cambridge. The

---

[72] See Finberg, *Tavistock Abbey*, pp. 292–3.

[73] The Abingdon press has attracted no attention except for a short note by Joseph Ames. See his *Typographical Antiquities*, vol. III, p. 1439.

[74] For Scolar's Oxford career, see E. G. Duff, *A Century of the English Book Trade* (1948), p. 144. See also A. Coates, 'The Benedictine Monks and their Books in Oxford', in Wansborough and Marrett Crosby (eds.), *Benedictines in Oxford*, pp. 79–94.

establishment of their own press was thus a natural extension of their existing intellectual activities. The press itself appears to have located within the abbey precincts, although the printer, John Herford was a secular (and a Fleming) who had previously worked in London. Their first project was predictably utilitarian, the printing of the St Albans breviary (*STC* 15793.5). Completed in 1535, it met the needs not only of the monastery itself but the dozen other priories, hospitals and churches that were dependent on the abbey. With the completion of the breviary, however, Herford and his monastic patrons turned their attention to a series of literary and scholarly editions. The first of these was a revised and expanded version of John Lydgate's vernacular *Lyfe of Seint Albon* (*STC* 17025), illustrated with three specially commissioned woodcuts. In part the book was published as a public response to the claims made (in print) by a convent of German monks that they possessed the true relics of England's protomartyr.[75] But there is no doubt that it was also intended to raise the profile of the abbey and its patron saint at a time when all such shrines were under threat of destruction by Thomas Cromwell and his agents. Funded from the personal resources of Abbot Robert Catton, this political dimension was made explicit by the inclusion of a dedication addressed to King Henry and his new queen, Anne.

By the mid-1530s Herford had begun a close collaboration with a single monk, Richard Boreman alias Stevenage, the prior, and from 1538, the abbot of the monastery. Boreman was a graduate theologian and like the Tavistock printer Thomas Richard he seems to have regarded the abbey press as vehicle for his own scholarship. He worked closely with Herford on at least five books between 1536 and the surrender of the abbey in December 1539. Of these, three now survive only in fragments: a version of the popular schoolbook *An Introduction for to Lerne to Reken with the Pen* (*STC* 14117.7(A3)), and two theological dialogues, *An Epistle Agaynste the Enemies of Poor People* and *A Godlye Disputation between Justus and Peccator and Senex and Iuvenis*. Boreman's most important work, however, was the *Confutacyon of the Fyrst Parte of Frythes Boke* (*STC* 12557) an assault on the early Protestant John Frith and a reasoned defence of eucharistic theology. The *Confutacyon* was attributed on the title page to John Gwynneth, a secular priest resident at St Albans, but given that Gwynneth himself later claimed it was published without his permission, it is likely that Boreman was responsible for at least a part of the text. By 1536 St Albans was regarded with great suspicion by

---

[75] For the background to this controversy see John Lydgate, *Saint Alban and Saint Amphibalus*, ed. G. F. Reinecke, Garland Medieval texts 11 (New York and London, 1985).

Cromwell and his agents, and the monastic community itself was under investigation for harbouring those who opposed the Break with Rome, the Royal Supremacy, and the assault on the religious orders.[76] In this climate it is possible that Boreman saw the publication of the *Confutacyon* as means of re-presenting his community not as the supporters of sedition but rather as the resolute defenders of orthodoxy.

The beginning of a programme of printing under the patronage of St Augustine's, Canterbury is less well-documented but it does seem to have occurred in a similar atmosphere of growing political tensions. Probably a press was first established at Canterbury in 1533 on a site adjacent to the precincts of St Augustine's abbey.[77] The printer, John Mychell, was a professional who, like John Herford, had previously worked in London.[78] In origin, however, he may have been a Canterbury man: there is a John Mychell who appears in a list of the abbey's employees dating from 1520.[79] There is little doubt that Mychell established his press in the hope of attracting the abbey's patronage and at least three of the books he published before 1536 were produced in collaboration with the monks.

Like Herford at St Albans, it appears that Mychell worked closely with one monk, Robert Saltwood, whose name is connected with each one of the books that were printed during this period. Saltwood was a senior member of the monastic community, a graduate theologian and Warden of the Chapel of St Mary.[80] He was also a member of the circle of scholars surrounding the abbot of St Augustine's, John Essex, and the Canterbury schoolmaster, John Twyne, who were bound together by common interests in history, literature and the New Learning.[81] In fact Saltwood's first project with Mychell was a joint collaboration with Twyne. This was an English

---

[76] For the composition of the *Confutacyon* and the St Albans monks' struggles with Cromwell and the Crown see also my 'Reformation and Reaction at St Albans Abbey, 1530–58', *EHR*, 115 (2000), 297–328.

[77] For the fragmentary evidence of this first press see M. Zell, 'An Early Press at Canterbury?', *The Library*, 5th ser., 32 (1977), 155–6; J. C. Whitebrook, 'E. Campion, Bookseller and John Mychell, Printer', *Notes and Queries* 153 (1927), 255–9. See also Ames, *Typographical Antiquities*, vol. III, pp. 1452–4.

[78] For the single title, *The Life of St Gregory's Mother* (*STC* 1235.3) which may have been printed by Mychell in London, see *STC*, vol. III, p. 69.

[79] Canterbury Cathedral Archives, MS Lit. B. 2, fo. 58r.

[80] For Saltwood's career see *BRUO 1501–40*, p. 503.

[81] For summary accounts of the careers of both Essex and Twyne see *BRUO 1501–40*, pp. 193, 582–3. John Twyne recalled his membership of this circle in his *De rebus Albionicis Britiannicisatque Anglicis commentariorum* (1590). See also Knowles, *Religious Orders*, vol. III, p. 95. For Twyne's intellectual interests see A. B. Ferguson, 'John Twyne: A Tudor Humanist and the Problem of Legend', *JBS*, 9 (1969), 24–44; A. G. Watson, 'John Twyne of Canterbury (d. 1581) as a Collector of Medieval Manuscripts: a Preliminary Investigation', *The Library*, 6th ser., 8 (1986), 133–51.

translation of the Old French romance, the *Hystory and Questyons of Kynge Boccus and Sydracke* (*STC* 31860) published in 1534. Saltwood funded the book, standing 'cost and charge' as the colophon expresses it, whilst Twyne provided the preface and probably the greater part of the translation. It is, however, a curious, hybrid text, combining the legend (in verse) of Boccus and Sydracke with a series of more than 300 questions of both a moral and practical nature; 'Is it better to haue hate of woman or love?', 'Wherof comyth fattnesse in amannys body?'. These questions, several of which reflect distinctly monastic preoccupations with diet, discipline and the sinful nature of women, may have been contributed by Saltwood.

Mychell's next publication was a collaboration with Saltwood alone. The *Comparyson Bytwene iiii Byrdes, the Larke, the Nyghtyngale, ye Thrushe & the Cuckoo* (*STC* 21647) which appeared in 1536 was Saltwood's original composition. It was a pastoral fantasy, in self-conscious imitation of Classical models, but in uneven English verse. A traveller weighed down by worldly cares enters an enchanted forest where he experiences a dream-vision in which the four song-birds of the title dispute over who should be elected *Cantor* of the forest. Each bird with its distinctive song is presented as a metaphor for the virtues and vices of human society, and for the different estates of man in the contemporary world: the nightingale is virtue and 'the flowre of Chivalry', the larke is both beauty and gentility, the thrush pride and 'the dangerus recourse of marchandyse', and the cuckoo a symbol of simplicity, the honest labourer who 'druggeth the plough, playne as a packstafe be it frost or snow'. Clearly Saltwood intended the *Comparyson* to advertise his credentials as a scholar and imitator of Classical literature, perhaps especially for the entertainment of other members of the Essex-Twyne circle. But it is worth noting that he also expresses some slight apprehension of the gathering political storm, closing the poem with an appeal that 'Our prynce in his lovyng make his byrdes to report in armony from the breth of God defence them of the lake that the devyl blastyh owt spytefully'.

It would not have been wholly surprising if Saltwood had intended to use his association with Mychell to pass some public comment, however carefully veiled, on the troubles of the later 1530s. Like St Albans Abbey, by 1536 St Augustine's was already attracting a reputation for its outspoken criticism of the Crown. In that year, a senior monk, William Winchelsea, had been examined by Cromwell following allegations that he had spoken openly against the king's marriage, the Royal Supremacy and the many other religious changes. It is interesting to note that amongst the members of the community who offered themselves as character witnesses in support of

Wincheslea were both Robert Saltwood and John Mychell, who is described in the submissions as then resident in the abbey.[82]

It is very likely that the St Augustine's monks commissioned John Mychell to print one further book for them before the end of the 1530s. In his catalogue of English books compiled in 1595, the London bookseller Andrew Maunsell recorded the title of one which no longer survives, *A Goodly Narration how Augustine Raysed two deed at Longcompton* printed, according to Maunsell's notes, at 'Canterberie at St Austens'.[83] This must have been a printed edition of John Lydgate's verse *Legend of St Austin at Compton*, which recounts the miracles performed by St Augustine of Canterbury at Long Compton, a village on the outskirts of the city.[84] Like their counterparts at St Albans, it appears that St Augustine's monks were moved, perhaps at the instigation of Robert Saltwood, to make use of the press to publicise their patron saint and the potency of his shrine.

IV

Long before the printing press became the servant of religious radicals in the 1520s, it had already come to occupy an honoured position at the very heart of the clerical establishment. It is true, of course, that in the early years after Gutenberg's first experiments some Church leaders remained unconvinced of the usefulness of the new technology. Europe's primary centres of learning, the universities, were also slow to recognise the potential of the printed book as a supplement, if not an alternative to their collections of manuscripts. But in making these qualifications historians must not be too quick to pass over the early enthusiasm for printing and print culture that came from perhaps the most surprising quarter of the establishment, the regular religious orders. The Benedictine Order in particular showed early and sustained interest in the printing press and before the middle of the sixteenth century many houses across Europe had taken to printing for themselves. The reformed congregations of the Black Monks in Germany played an important role as patrons of the early printing pioneers of Gutenberg's generation. There is nothing to compare with this in fifteenth-century England, where insular printing started late and developed in the provinces only slowly. But there is nonetheless a case to be made that in a similar way the Benedictines here came to play a central part in the reception of

---

[82] The case papers are now PRO, SP 1/88, fos. 19r–20v (*L&P*, VII, 1608).

[83] F. B. Williams, 'The Lost Books of Tudor England', *The Library*, 5th ser., 33 (1978), 10.

[84] For the full text see H. McCracken (ed.), *The Minor Poems of John Lydgate*, EETS, extra ser., 107 (1911), pp. 193–206.

print culture. From as early as 1470 the Black Monks emerged as amongst the most important buyers – and possibly importers – of printed books. Their scholars were also amongst the first to make extensive use of printed texts at the universities, and to make a place for them in their personal collections and their own college libraries. In fact the ownership and use of printed books spread through every level of the monastic community. By the beginning of the sixteenth century it was possible to find one or two contemporary imprints passing through the hands of even the most humble cloister monk. Such is the evidence from the male communities, but there is no doubt that in the larger, wealthier houses Benedictine nuns were also exposed to print to some degree. A number of the older monasteries also became involved in the work of the printers themselves. Early efforts to offer patronage at St Albans, Abingdon and Tavistock were short-lived but they did succeed in taking the technology outside the clerical and commercial mainstream. Perhaps they also convinced the order as a whole of the benefits to be gained from a close relationship with the press. The programme of printing initiated at St Albans and St Augustine's, Canterbury, soon after 1530 seemed in some way to promise a new era for monastic scholarship, one in which the monasteries might revive their former public profile. If so it was cut short by the events of 1536–9, but the very fact that these presses had prospered at all at a time when printing in provincial England was moribund should be seen as significant.

The emergence of a print culture brought important changes to life in the Benedictine cloister. There is no doubt that book ownership, and therefore property ownership in general, became more widespread. It was now possible, and indeed probable, that individual monks would pursue their intellectual and spiritual interests independent of their brethren. In doing so, the presence of printed books guaranteed them a greater exposure to contemporary academic currents than had ever been possible in the manuscript age. But it would be wrong to present print as a destructive force in the monastic context. The ownership of books and other property and the 'privatisation' of monastic occupations had been noticeable trends in English communities long before the coming of the press and they were at least in part the fruits of their own self-conscious reform programme. At any rate, the availability of standard, uniform texts made possible through printing probably did more to improve monastic observance than it did to impede it. Moreover, it is clear that the sheer number and variety of books that now entered the cloister helped to stimulate a revival in learning and teaching: it is possible that the growing number of graduates in the order in the early sixteenth century was a direct consequence of this. It would be wrong to take this too far; there is no evidence that their interaction with print culture enabled the English Benedictines to effect an intellectual and spiritual revival comparable with the monks of the Bursfeld congregation or with St Germain des Prés and its affiliate houses. But the evidence from St Albans and Canterbury in the 1530s would suggest that it had to some extent revived their interest in self-promotion, and reminded them of the need to present themselves and their work to a wider public. Had the Dissolution come a decade later, the debates that surrounded it may have been a good deal less one-sided, even if the outcome had not been different.

PART II

Script, print and textual tradition

5

Law and text: legal authority and judicial accessibility in the late Middle Ages

Anthony Musson

In the future may they have laws that are straightforward as well as brief, and easily available to all and also such that it is easy to possess the books containing them, so that men may not need to obtain with a great expenditure of wealth volumes containing a large quantity of redundant laws, but the means of procuring them for a trifling sum may be given to both rich and poor and great learning be available at a very small cost. (Justinian, C. Tanta, 13).

This paper explores how the embodiment of law in written text affected the authority of the law and knowledge of its precepts both within the legal profession and among the general populace at large. The late Middle Ages marks the transition from a predominantly oral tradition in both substantive and procedural law to a textual tradition where forms of action, their interpretation and elucidation, are invariably given written expression, whether in statutes, treatises or law reports.[1] This paper will range from the thirteenth century, when textual versions of laws and legal procedures started to be produced (in the form of statutes and legal treatises), to the seventeenth, in order to take stock of the initiatives in printed texts. The main questions to be addressed are whether the written text enhanced the law's authority – jurisdictional, jurisprudential, educational and popular – and whether it increased its accessibility, both in terms of the law's wider dissemination and general intelligibility, and with regard to the encouragement this gave to would-be litigants. The prevalence of the spoken word in court and a reliance on oral traditions in many areas of the legal process (especially in relation to evidence and the work of juries) necessitates some consideration of the overlap between oral and textual traditions and the extent to which there were tensions between the two. The advent of printing towards the end of the Middle Ages offered future

---

[1] The foundations of this important move are charted in M. T. Clanchy, *From Memory to Written Record: England 1066–1307*, 2nd edn (Oxford, 1993).

generations new opportunities for dissemination of the written word and a new dimension in which to perceive it.

Let us look now at the various dimensions of legal authority: the jurisdictional, jurisprudential, educational and the popular. For the benefit of non-specialists it is important to make clear at the outset the differences of authority inherent in legal texts, a distinction between the formal sources of law (the respective texts and embodiments of law) and informal ones (examples of legal thought, practice and procedure). The former comprises statutes and case law, but also original writs.[2] Writs have a dual nature: in one sense they were procedural instruments, but they also embodied the substantive law since they were issued from chancery on the basis of decided cases and statutory enactments.[3] The informal legal sources include court records, petitions and legislative memoranda, examples of legal practice such as wills, deeds of settlement or conveyance, and treatises on legal and administrative procedure. First, we need to consider the jurisdictional aspect. In the Middle Ages law represented the exercise of jurisdiction. In addition to areas of local jurisdiction, such as urban centres, manors or other franchise regions, where customary practices formed the basis of law, the two main bodies of law in England were those pertaining to the Church and the crown. To a considerable extent the ecclesiastical jurisdiction was already a textually bound one, relying heavily on the codes and texts forming the governing rules of the Church, the canon law, and aspects of Roman civil law,[4] and it will not concern us further. We will concentrate on royal jurisdictional authority through law.

The law pertaining to the realm of England is generally known as 'the common law', although contemporaries never referred to it as such.[5] The name is derived from the standardised general principles that were applied across the entire kingdom and in territories where the king's writ ran. The common law may be regarded as unwritten law in the sense that it represents the prevailing custom and practice of the realm: unlike Roman civil law or canon law it was not set down as a comprehensive almost unchanging code, but evolved largely on the basis of decided cases and in this period on the basis of the writ actions which they initiated. Its 'unwritten' status does not mean that nothing was ever written down (as various Anglo-Saxon and

---

[2] J. H. Baker, *An Introduction to English Legal History*, 4th edn (2002); J.-Ph. Genet, 'Droit et histoire en Angleterre: la préhistoire de la "Revolution Historique"', *Annales de Bretagne et des Pays de l'Ouest*, 87 (1980), 321–32.

[3] E. de Haas and G. D. G. Hall (eds.), *Early Registers of Writs*, Selden Society 87 (1970).

[4] The key texts were Gratian's *Decretum* and Justinian's *Institutes*.

[5] It should be distinguished from the law of the Western Church that was known as *ius commune*.

Anglo-Norman collections of laws survive),[6] but rather that the law was not set in stone. These early collections can be said to represent 'an index of governing mentalities' rather than the strictures of written law codes.[7]

Royal commands (whether instructions or rules of behaviour) were usually effected by means of oral proclamation. Up until the late thirteenth century it was rare for the crown to commit its legislation to writing. Much of Henry III's legislation, for instance, is lost because the emphasis was on oral proclamation rather than the generation of written text. Our knowledge of many of the early statutes, ordinances and assizes comes in fact from other textual traditions (inclusion in chronicles) or as a result of developing written practices (the letters close containing the instructions for the proclamation of statutes).[8] From Edward I's reign statutes were increasingly committed to writing, providing an almost unbroken stream of legislation preserved for posterity. The promulgation of statutes (described in the thirteenth and early fourteenth centuries as 'new law' or 'special law') provided an additional tier of law to be enforced along with the common law. This supplementary body of law was treated as national legislation and was binding from the moment of its decree. Significantly when interpreting cases in the courts, fourteenth-century judges gave statutes precedence over the common law, referring to the former as the 'law now in force'. This points towards the growing power of textual law and the early recognition of statutes as *primary* law.[9]

The association of sessions of parliament with the issuing of statutes in the early fourteenth century and the emergence of parliament as a body considering and making legislation leant a new weight to the authority of statutes.[10] In the thirteenth and early fourteenth centuries when statute law did not arise directly or solely from parliamentary deliberation judges were quite prepared to override or redefine provisions that were unsatisfactory. Consequently, there was an almost proprietorial air among leading judges. The famous retort to counsel by Ralph Hengham (chief justice of the court of king's bench 1274–89 and of the common bench 1301–9), 'Do not gloss

---

[6] See P. Wormald, *The Making of English Law* (Oxford, 1999); L. J. Downer (ed. and trans.), *Leges Henrici Primi* (Oxford, 1972); and B. O'Brien, *God's Peace and King's Peace: The Laws of Edward the Confessor* (Philadelphia, 1999).

[7] Wormald, *Making of English Law*, pp. 477–83, quotation at p. 481.

[8] Clanchy, *Memory to Written Record*, pp. 168–71, 263–4.

[9] A. Musson, 'Second "English Justinian" or Pragmatic Opportunist? A Re-examination of the Legal Legislation of Edward III's Reign', in J. Bothwell (ed.), *The Age of Edward III* (Woodbridge, 2001), pp. 74–7.

[10] For the growth of a self-conscious attitude towards the deliberations in parliament as legal record see W. M. Ormrod, 'Usage and Abusage: The Parliament Rolls of the Mid-Fourteenth Century', unpubl. paper given at the International Medieval Congress, Kalamazoo, 2002.

the statute; we understand it better than you do, for we made it', is indicative of this organic relationship to legislation.[11]

It is important, however, to draw a distinction between the 'bare' text of a law as found in a statute and its actual judicial interpretation in the courts. Statutory language had to be placed within a framework of rules governing its interpretation, and this did not provide a uniformity of interpretation.[12] As statutes became embedded in the routine work of the courts, so rules of statutory interpretation developed, in many ways paralleling the Church's interpretation of the Scriptures.[13] Fortescue, writing in the mid-fifteenth century, regarded 'human laws' as 'holy' (*sanctum*) and equated the role of judges and lawyers as priests (*sacerdotes*) of the law.[14] Like holy Scripture, statutes could be 'dark and intricate' (as Serjeant Robert Callis, a Reader at Gray's Inn made clear). Indeed, by the sixteenth century the close proximity between judges and legislation had faded and a reverence for the legal text had developed. As Sir Francis Bacon explained in *Chudleigh's Case* (1594): 'for as you my lords judges better know, so with modesty I may put you in remembrance, that your authority over the statutes of this realm is not such as the papists affirm the Church to have over the scriptures, to make them as a shipman's hose or a nose of wax; but such as *we* say the Church has over them, *scil.* To expound them faithfully and apply them properly . . .'[15]

Knowledge and understanding of the common law was largely restricted to the legal profession and those who had experience of the royal courts. To what extent, though, was statutory legislation disseminated within the legal profession and the wider population? Judges and serjeants would have been aware of statutory provisions initially from being present in parliament when they were promulgated. Many statutes would have been drafted by or at least reviewed by royal lawyers. Some legal officials may

---

[11] A. J. Horwood (ed.), *Year Books of the Reign of Edward I: Years 33 and 35*, Rolls Series 31 (1979), p. 82.

[12] C. Holmes, 'Statutory Interpretation in the Early Seventeenth Century: the Court, the Council and the Commissioners of Sewers', in J. A. Guy and H. G. Beale (eds.), *Law and Social Change in British History* (1984), pp. 107–9.

[13] Despite a hostility to legal documents challenges to orthodox notions of textual authority were made by Lollard preachers and polemicists through their borrowing of real and fictitious legal documents (such as Christ's charter and records of heresy trials) see E. Steiner, 'Inventing Legality: Documentary Culture and Lollard Preaching', in E. Steiner and C. Barrington (eds.), *The Letter of the Law* (Ithaca, NY, 2002), pp. 185–201. For an examination of links between the law and the Church (and in particular the dissemination of the printed word) at the time of the Reformation see R. J. Ross, 'The Commoning of the Common Law: the Renaissance Debate over Printing English Law, 1520–1640', *University of Pennsylvania Law Review*, 146 (1998), 329, 338–55.

[14] Sir John Fortescue, *On the Laws and Governance of England*, ed. S. Lockwood (Cambridge, 1997), pp. 6–7.

[15] J. Spedding (ed.), *The Works of Francis Bacon* (Boston, MA, 1861), pp. 15, 168 cited in Holmes, 'Statutory Interpretation', pp. 108–9.

even have retained legislative memoranda for future reference. Parliament aside, the texts of statutes were made available to those who wished to purchase them through teams of manuscript copiers producing first rolls of statutes and later the same in book form. These private collections usually began with Magna Carta, perceptually accorded pride of place as the 'first statute',[16] and then proceeded in chronological order with certain enactments of Henry III, Edward I and Edward II. The earliest collections contained only these *statuta vetera* or *antiqua* (the old statutes), while later ones concentrated on the *nova statuta*, enactments from the beginning of Edward III's reign in 1327 up to the early sixteenth century.[17] The books were produced to order in a handy pocket size for practitioners to refer to readily. The language of the texts (with perhaps the exception of Magna Carta) was Anglo-Norman French rather than Latin. By the mid-fourteenth century French had achieved respectability as a language of government, a status not accorded to English until the fifteenth century.[18]

It was not just the legal profession who purchased or benefited from statute books. Individuals from a variety of backgrounds (landowners, churchmen and merchants) had *statuta Angliae* compiled for them or possessed a copy, including Anthony Bek, bishop of Durham, Isabella de Fortibus (dowager countess of Aumale and countess of Devon) and Sir William Breton, a minor Lincolnshire landowner. Ecclesiastical landowners especially ensured they had access to these texts: in 1421 a copy was among the library books available to Durham Priory, while the chapter library at Lincoln around 1500 possessed a statute book containing the laws of the preceding two centuries.[19] Written texts of certain pieces of legislation were as a matter of course sent to (or obtained by) monastic foundations (copies of Magna Carta, for instance, were sent out in 1215 and still survive in several Cathedral libraries),[20] while the ordinary person would sometimes find laws posted on church doors. In a specific effort to afford accessibility to legislation, in 1279 Archbishop Pecham ordered that copies of Magna Carta were to be publicised in a prominent place in every cathedral church with a fresh copy substituted annually.[21]

[16] J. C. Holt, *Magna Carta and Medieval Government* (1985), pp. 18–19.

[17] D. C. Skemer, 'From Archives to the Book Trade: Private Statute Rolls in England, 1285–1307', *Journal of the Society of Archivists*, 16 (1995), 201, n. 16.

[18] For an examination of the language of legal records, see Clanchy, *Memory to Written Record*, pp. 207–9, 220–3.

[19] A. Bennett, 'Anthony Bek's Copy of Statuta Angliae', in W. M. Ormrod (ed.), *England in the Fourteenth Century*, Proceedings of 1985 Harlaxton Symposium (Woodbridge, 1986), pp. 1–21; Skemer, 'Book Trade', 194–5, 200, n. 7.

[20] R. L. Poole, 'The Publication of Great Charters by the English kings', *EHR*, 28 (1913), 448–53.

[21] Clanchy, *Memory to Written Record*, p. 265.

Significantly, the royal government's practice of drawing up written texts of statutes was followed in manorial and urban jurisdictions from the early fourteenth century. Village by-laws were brought together to form distinct codes which can be found in the manorial court rolls.[22] Similarly, the customs of the city of Norwich (*Leges et Consuetudines antiquitus in civitate Norwicensi usitate*) were drawn together sometime before 1340.[23] In Bristol, too, in the mid-fourteenth century there was a concern to reduce to writing the prevailing mercantile practices in what is known as the *Little Red Book of Bristol*.[24] York's municipal regulations were drawn together in the 1370s in the *York Memorandum Book* and in the city of London in the early fifteenth century a comprehensive code of regulations, customs and practices was drawn up by the common clerk (John Carpenter) and the mayor (Richard Whittington) to form the *Liber Albus*.[25] It is not known how accessible these collections of local 'statutes' were, whether they were available for consultation by people outside the local governing hierarchy or compiled purely for the benefit of civic officials. Manorial and urban jurisdictions may not have regarded codification of prevailing practices as an end in itself, but as Green has argued, their actions may have represented a desperate attempt to save the customary law from what they perceived as the encroaching literate technology.[26]

In spite of the new emphasis on reducing customs and practices to written codes, the spoken word continued to play an important part in the promulgation and dissemination of law. The texts of statutes were made available to the general population through the medium of proclamation. Even in the fourteenth and fifteenth centuries oral proclamation remained the most effective method of communication and the most immediate way of publicising royal intentions and policy. By Edward III's reign all statutes were proclaimed as a matter of course, though special directions were given for their dissemination including an indication of specific places where this should be carried out. Generally statutes were read out at the

---

[22] W. A. Ault, 'Some Early Village Bye-laws', *EHR*, 45 (1930), 209, 211–12.
[23] W. Hudson (ed.), *Leet Jurisdiction in the City of Norwich during the Thirteenth and Fourteenth Centuries*, Selden Society 5 (1892), p. lxxxiv.
[24] F. B. Bickley (ed.), *The Little Red Book of Bristol* (Bristol, 1930); G. Martin, 'English Town Records, 1200–1350', in R. H. Britnell (ed.), *Pragmatic Literacy, East and West, 1200–1330* (Woodbridge, 1997), pp. 126, 129.
[25] M. Sellers (ed.), *York Memorandum Book, Part 1 (1376–1419)*, Surtees Society 120 (1912); S. Rees Jones, 'York's Civic Administration, 1354–1464,' in S. Rees Jones (ed.), *The Government of Medieval York: Essays in Commemoration of the 1396 Royal Charter*, Borthwick Studies in History 3 (York, 1997), pp. 111–12, 115; H. T. Riley (ed.), *Liber Albus: the White Book of the City of London* (1861).
[26] R. F. Green, *A Crisis of Truth: Law and Literature in Ricardian England* (Philadelphia, PA, 1999), p. 126.

monthly county court meetings, and in designated public places (such as town crosses and churchyards) and at fairs and markets. Writs to sheriffs also reveal that threats were sometimes issued by the king to ensure that they (or their deputies) complied with the instructions and duly communicated the relevant parts of the legislation. The crown even checked up on where and on what dates the proclamations had been made. There was, therefore, scope for the public to be aware of major pieces of legislation and of how their provisions affected them.[27] The two most important pieces of legislation, Magna Carta and the Statute of Winchester (the statute detailing arrangements for local policing) were required to be formally recited four times a year. Moreover, the text of royal commissions, which were read out in advance of judicial sessions, also provided details of the particular statutes being enforced. Although the actual written texts of both statutes and judicial commissions were usually in Latin, their substance was capable of reaching a wide audience as they were proclaimed impromptu in the vernaculars (French and English).[28]

The law's jurisdictional authority, then, was potentially enhanced by the developments of written texts because the texts of statutes were regularly disseminated (or distributed) to lawyers and the wider population in both written and oral forms. Neither the written word nor language presented particular barriers to comprehension (even though some of the terminology might have been) since publication occurred (at least) in French and (most likely) in English through impromptu translations by officials. This picture requires qualification in some respects. Oral proclamation remained a key feature of medieval government: there would have been considerable reliance on the ability of the translators, and unless notes were taken, the listener would probably only retain the gist of a piece of legislation rather than the finer points. An exception to this might be those statutes that received regular reinforcement at quarterly intervals, but even these were liable to misinterpretation.[29] Secondly, the accessibility of statutes in a real sense should be questioned. Even though a lay person might know the form of words, they still required judicial interpretation and he or she probably required the services of a lawyer to make legal sense of it. It was only 'bare' statute law that could impinge on the mind since the finer points of case

[27] J. A. Doig, 'Political Propaganda and Royal Proclamations in Late Medieval England', *Historical Research*, 71 (1998), 258–64.

[28] Clanchy, *Memory to Written Record*, pp. 264–5.

[29] See , e.g., the misreading of Magna Carta in M. T. Clanchy, 'Magna Carta and Common Pleas', in H. Mayr-Harting and R. I. Moore (eds.), *Studies in Medieval History Presented to R. H. C. Davies* (1985), pp. 226–7.

law, the judicial interpretation of common law or statute, were neither publicly available, nor probably of interest outside the legal profession. The real authority of the law remained guarded by its priests and in private copies of texts of the law reports.

In many ways the authority of the law stems from more than the mere written text. The key to the wider authority of the law in jurisdictional terms is enforcement. The ability to enforce the law transforms its textual nature and gives it practical existence. Passing statutes as a means of ordering behaviour without considering their workability or attempting to replace long-standing laws without thought to their entrenchment reduces or seriously erodes their power. For example, attempts by Edward I to rescind or abrogate the native laws of Wales and Scotland (following conquest or jurisdictional subjugation) and replace them with English legislation may have been desirable in theory (the laws of Scotland, for instance, were felt to be 'clearly displeasing to God and to reason'), but their negation was virtually impossible to achieve in substantive terms and impractical to enforce in areas where the crown had little direct control territorially.[30] Similarly, over the course of Edward III's reign an increasing amount of legislation was promulgated for substantive areas of social and economic legislation over which the royal government had considerable enforcement problems, particularly with regard to the various sumptuary statutes and the labour legislation. The government had the requisite intention to extend its authority by creating law and telling its subjects about it, but with limited resources the crown was not always able to enforce its laws and writs successfully or at all.[31] Symbolic and literal negation of royal law was given expression during Edward I's reign when a writ which interfered with the liberty of Leominster in Herefordshire was seized and 'trampled in the mud so that it could not be found and the king's command therein could not be executed'.[32] If the legal provision was impractical or unworkable in reality then the ideals were unattainable and it was literally a dead letter.[33] This weakness then in fact served to undermine royal authority.

In terms of our second category, jurisprudential authority, submission of law to written text was beneficial primarily to the legal profession as it

---

[30] C. Neville, *Violence, Custom and the Law: The Anglo-Scottish Border Lands in the Later Middle Ages* (Edinburgh, 1998), pp. 15–17; L. B. Smith, 'Statute of Wales, 1284', *Welsh History Review*, 10 (1980), 151–2.

[31] This discrepancy may of course simply reveal a difference between medieval and modern notions of legislation and what is intended by it.

[32] *Calendar of Patent Rolls: Edward I, AD 1292–1301* (1895), p. 113; M. C. Prestwich, *Edward I* (1988), p. 414.

[33] This is paralleled by servants or messengers being forced to eat the writs they carried; see below.

enabled the development of an intellectual domain based on legal texts.[34] A significant new resource was offered from the mid-thirteenth century through the birth of law reporting (that is the recording by lawyers or 'apprentices' of whole cases, important decisions, or interesting points of law) and the compilation of the Year Books (cases deriving from the law terms in the court of common pleas or occasionally the general eyre). Although not formalised as textual law until 'The Reports' of Sir Edward Coke in the early seventeenth century, the provision of essential details of previous cases facilitated both reference to and an understanding of what had occurred in the legal past and the development of the concept of precedent as a means towards achieving uniformity and consistency in pleading and in judicial decision-making. This in turn had jurisdictional implications. As William Bereford, later chief justice of common pleas, once argued when still only a serjeant-at-law, 'I have seen it adjudged before you yourself: and there ought to be one law for all people in this kingdom'.[35] It also reflected the importance of continuity in decision-making. As a judge in the court of common pleas asked as early 1287: 'On what basis should we give judgment: under the ancient laws customary in the time of those who preceded us, or under the laws alleged by you and others?'.[36] Although the statements in the law reports/Year Books were not binding, nevertheless by the end of the fifteenth century it is clear the profession relied upon them. The continuity previously sustained by reference to memory, continued to be so, but was increasingly supplemented by reference to written documentation.[37] In an action in Henry VII's reign, for example, the serjeant Thomas Kebell 'prayed that the judges would be advised, and he would produce books where this plea was accepted as sound'.[38]

Plea rolls, which were an account of business in the courts as recorded by the clerks, were written repositories of the common law in that they contained the details and outcomes of cases. It should be stressed, however, they did not contain a verbatim account of the trial and tend to provide a rather truncated, business-like view of proceedings. Although they did not always highlight legal principles in the same way that early law reports did, they were nevertheless a source of reference for particular facts and

---

[34] Arguably this was enhanced with the advent of printed texts, which served to promote the intellectual dominance of publisher and author as well as the authority and correctness of texts (Ross, 'Printing English Law', 437–43).

[35] P. Brand (ed.), *The Earliest English Law Reports*, Selden Society 111 and 112 (1996), vol. II, p. 293.

[36] *Ibid.*, vol. II, p. 349.   [37] See Clanchy, *Memory to Written Record.*

[38] E. W. Ives, 'The Origins of the Later Year Books', in D. Jenkins (ed.), *Legal History Studies 1972* (Cardiff, 1975), pp. 136–9.

judicial decisions. They were not generally available for public scrutiny and since the rolls were either deposited in chancery or the exchequer or remained in the possession of particular judges, were primarily utilised by judges and lawyers.[39] An example of the accumulation of such material comes from 1361 when William Shareshull retired from his post as chief justice of king's bench and handed over to his successor, Henry Green, 'rolls, records, processes and indictments and all other memoranda touching the king's bench' stretching back to 1339. There were also 75 bags and 189 boxes full of indictments and items that had been sent into or related to the court.[40]

The general public did, however, have some opportunity for access to judicial decisions. The practice of obtaining 'exemplification', a sealed copy of a judicial decision, which was increasingly employed during the fourteenth century (particularly among peasant communities seeking to show their manor had ancient demesne status), not only enabled ordinary people access to the particular judicial record they required, but engendered some appreciation of the jurisprudential qualities of a legal text or at least the feeling of security that a document sealed with the royal impression could afford.[41] Moreover, by the early thirteenth century the county court rolls, as Professor Palmer notes, 'had already attained the status of a public resource'. Care was taken in their keeping (although in fact few survive today) and it is likely the judges of the court refreshed their memories of the relevant rolls before a session as well as litigants who wanted to avoid procedural slips. Defendants sometimes wanted to prove their defence on the basis of the record of the rolls.[42] Manorial courts too began compiling records of court proceedings from the mid-thirteenth century and there was frequent use of the court rolls by both jurors and litigants to substantiate decisions of claims.[43] The accessibility of the law in the form of the text of previous cases was clearly not an issue. The Peasants' Revolt revealed that people knew where records of both local and central government were kept and

[39] The dramatic events during the Peasants' Revolt reveal that many ordinary people knew where judicial and administrative records were stored: W. M. Ormrod, 'The Peasants' Revolt and the Government of England', *JBS*, 29 (1990), 5–9.

[40] G. O. Sayles (ed.), *Select Cases in the Court of King's Bench*, Selden Society 55, 57, 58, 74, 76, 82, 88 (1936–71), vol. VI, pp. 128–9.

[41] R. Faith, 'The "Great Rumour" of 1377 and Peasant Ideology', in R. H. Hilton and T. H. Aston (eds.), *The English Rising of 1381* (Cambridge, 1981), pp. 47–8.

[42] R. C. Palmer, *The County Courts of Medieval England, 1150–1350* (Princeton, NJ, 1982), pp. 39–40, quotation at p. 39.

[43] L. R. Poos and L. Bonfield (ed.), *Select Cases in Manorial Courts*, Selden Society 114 (1998), pp. lxviii–lxix.

they were familiar enough with them to be able to identify specific things they wished to excise or make their own copies of.[44]

The admissibility and therefore the value of such records in jurispruden-tial terms depended to a large extent on whether the proceedings of the court itself were regarded as being 'of record'. As Chief Justice Bereford retorted to arguments put forward by counsel in 1315 'He proffereth matter of record, while you bring forth naught but your wind'.[45] This was not a question of whether a written record of the sessions was compiled, but whether the status of the proceedings was such that they could be cited in court as authority. So, even though manorial courts kept a record of proceedings only the royal courts were courts of record. This meant the written record (certainly by the fourteenth century) could in certain cir-cumstances preclude the oral evidence of a jury.[46] The significance of this is expounded by William Lambarde in his treatise *Of the Office of the Justice of the Peace* (1581): 'One may affirm a thing, and another may deny it, but if a Record once saye the word, no man shall be received to Averre (or speake) against it . . . And therefore, to avoid all contention that may arise, whilest one saith one thing and one other saith an other thing, the Lawe reposeth it self wholy and solely in the report of the Judge'.[47] Similarly a document that had been drawn up, signed and sealed by a notary public was admissible as legal evidence and deemed to contain 'the historical truth' even if its contents were in fact a fiction.[48] The implication – that the legal record cannot lie (if all the appropriate measures have been taken) – is a significant one as it not only confirms the power that the written word had attained, but also attests to the concentration of that power in the hands of lawyers, royal officials and literate churchmen, who could on occasion manipulate and exploit the apparent sanctity of the written record to their own advantage.[49]

In the fourteenth century the written word was not a replacement for memory, but a supplement. However, it increasingly dominated

[44] Ormrod, 'Peasants' Revolt', 5–16.
[45] W. C. Bolland (ed.), *Year Books of Edward II: 8 Edward II (1314)*, Selden Society 37 (1920), p. 128.
[46] D. W. Sutherland, *The Eyres of Northamptonshire, 1329–30*, Selden Society 97 and 98 (1983), vol. 1, pp. 131–2 (*per* Scrope, CJ).
[47] Lambarde, *Eirenarcha* (1581), p. 71, cited by J. K. Weber in 'The Power of Judicial Records', *Journal of Legal History*, 9 (1988), 180.
[48] Clanchy, *Memory to Written Record*, pp. 304–5.
[49] For lawyers altering plea rolls see P. Brand, *The Origins of the English Legal Profession* (1992), pp. 130, 133; for Richard II's falsification of the parliament roll see J. G. Edwards, 'The Parlia-mentary Committee, 1398', in E. B. Fryde and E. Miller (eds.), *Historical Studies of the English Parliament*, 2 vols. (Cambridge, 1970), vol. 1, pp. 316–28.

proceedings as a way of deciding the correctness of a decision or pointing the way forward. Given the vagaries and fallibility of human memory,[50] there was a definite awareness of the administrative advantages to be gained from possessing the written texts of statutes. Transcripts of Magna Carta were sent to all judges in 1300, while in the 1360s justices of the peace requested copies of recent statutes for their reference.[51] The reduction of law to written text also brought a more critical attitude.[52] The eye and brain were allowed to linger on the written words and this fuelled concern for accurate and authentic statements of the law. In sessions of the court of common pleas, for instance, where statute was cited by counsel, the justices did not rely on memory, but insisted on a copy of the relevant statute being produced in court for careful scrutiny. The relative interest or disinterest of the scribes and the copying of texts from exemplars brought the possibility of differences in word order and spelling as well as corruption to or abridgement of private texts. The compilation of the Great Roll of the Statutes at the Tower of London in 1299 was an attempt to establish an 'official' version, though, as Richardson and Sayles have demonstrated, it depended on many (sometimes garbled) accumulated texts.[53]

The importance of a correct and reliable text from which further textual analysis could then proceed was not restricted to the central courts, but recognised by men such as Andrew Horn, chamberlain of the city of London in the early fourteenth century, who carried out research on the Guildhall's collection of records in order to correct existing copies of legal records and obtain reliable statements of the law.[54] It was not without sincerity, therefore, that Chaucer talked of the Man of Law's professional world as his 'science'.[55] In academic terms at least, then, the authority of the law was venerated and upheld. Yet, it was not just an academic concern

---

[50] For examples of lawyers misquoting statutes see T. F. T. Plucknett, *Statutes and their Interpretation in the First Half of the Fourteenth Century* (Cambridge, 1922), pp. 37, 103–6. Note also in Chaucer's *Canterbury Tales* the Man of Law's distortion of misinterpretation of sources (S. H. Rigby, *Chaucer in Context* (Manchester, 1996), p. 90).

[51] Clanchy, *Memory to Written Record*, p. 265; A. J. Verduyn, 'The Attitude of the Parliamentary Commons to Law and Order under Edward III', D.Phil. thesis, University of Oxford (1991), p. 145.

[52] In his late twelfth century *Dialogue of the Exchequer*, FitzNeal is concerned about the accuracy of texts (Clanchy, *Memory to Written Record*, pp. 130–1). The concern was also a product of their use as archival resources, see for example royal justice Roger Seaton's disparaging remarks about the carelessness of clerks: Sayles (ed.), *Select Cases*, vol. 1, p. clxviii.

[53] G. Sayles, 'The Early Statutes', *Law Quarterly Review*, 50 (1934), 201–23, 540–71.

[54] J. Catto, 'Andrew Horn: Law and History in Fourteenth Century England', in R. H. C. Davis and J. M. Wallace-Hadrill (eds.), *The Writing of History in the Middle Ages* (Oxford, 1981), pp. 367–91.

[55] L. D. Benson (ed.), *The Riverside Chaucer*, new edn (Oxford, 1987), p. 28, line 316.

since the availability of statute books or the familiarity with certain aspects of law through frequent proclamation clearly stimulated the thoughts of ordinary people (though perhaps those with access to legal practitioners) who as litigants and petitioners were able to cite statutes back at the crown.[56]

In jurisprudential terms writs as summonses to court were by the fourteenth century probably no longer carried out orally by summoners, but had become instructions embedded in writing. In the twelfth century the parties to an action were summoned orally and publicly and up to Edward I's reign this was duplicated and supplemented by written authority. The authority of writs lay in the embodiment in writing of the legal command and up until they became stylised and drawn up from a register of writs, they embodied the action itself. The spectacular growth in the number of writs available corresponded with an increase in use of the legal system and its authority to remedy in the royal courts a growing number of wrongs and situations that had not previously been covered by the common law.[57] Some idea of the accessibility of obtaining law in this way can be gained from the methods of obtaining a writ. This could be done through an attorney, or by approaching the clerks themselves and explaining the situation or, alternatively, through a courier. In order to have the opportunity for success in court, it was important to get the correct writ, in other words, the one most suitable for one's situation.[58] The practice of making available copies of the chancery register of writs enabled individuals or corporations who possessed one to locate the most suitable remedy themselves. Indeed, some registers included 'finding aids': little pictures symbolising the rights that were in need of protection.[59]

An alternative form of initiating suits in the royal courts was begun in the mid-thirteenth century when the omnicompetent itinerant court, the general eyre, accepted oral complaints for various petty wrongs previously remediable only in the local courts. Over the course of the fourteenth century the oral complaint, while not dying out completely, was superseded

---

[56] Clanchy, 'Magna Carta and Common Pleas', pp. 226–7; J. R. Maddicott, 'The County Community and the Making of Public Opinion in Fourteenth Century England', *TRHS*, 5th ser. 28 (1978), 36–7; see also extensive references in A. Musson and W. M. Ormrod, *The Evolution of English Justice: Law, Politics and Society in the Fourteenth Century* (Basingstoke, 1998), pp. 234–5, nn. 12–15.

[57] See A. Musson, *Medieval Law in Context: The Growth of Legal Consciousness from Magna Carta to the Peasants' Revolt* (Manchester, 2001), pp. 156–9.

[58] *Early Registers of Writs*, pp. xviii–xix, cxxvii–cxxviii; Sayles (ed.), *Select Cases*, vol. I, pp. 173–4, 175–6.

[59] M. Camille, 'At the Edge of the Law: An Illustrated Register of Writs in the Pierpoint Morgan Library', in N. Rogers (ed.), *England in the Fourteenth Century*, Proceedings of the 1991 Harlaxton Symposium (Stamford, 1993), pp. 7–8.

by bill procedure (the writing down of complaints in the form of a request or petition). In terms of accessibility, the advantage here lay in the lack of formality required and the possibility of remedying a whole range of wrongs. Where in the case of writs, copying mistakes of name or place were not tolerated in court and where the Latin also had to be grammatically correct for legal validity, bills by contrast were in French, rambling phrases were permissible and significantly (unlike writs) could not be held defective for errors in spelling or grammar. Bills were allowed to stand as almost oral transcriptions of complaints. They may have been compiled in a particular way, emphasising certain elements and containing certain formulaic phrases, but they were not imbued with the same degree of formalism as a writ. Bills were already a familiar method of prosecution in the urban and manorial courts, but their adoption by the royal courts enabled the crown significantly to extend its jurisdiction and widen access to justice, while at the same time providing litigants with the benefits of potentially higher awards in damages and of having their suit heard in a court of record.[60]

Changes in jurisprudential practices also had an effect on other informal forms of law which were embodied in writing. By the mid-fourteenth century criminal indictments had to be watertight (containing all the necessary legal details) or they would dismissed by the gaol delivery justices. This was in part associated with the development of the legal profession and the demarcation of this particular role to central court justices, but it was also a recognition that in order to be truly authoritative a legal document needed to be precise in terms of its form. Precision in the wording of indictments was therefore necessary both as requirement of natural justice (a defendant should not be bound and charged if the details are not correct) and as a reflection of new attitudes towards legal text.[61] The later fourteenth century witnessed an expansion in the use of legally binding practices, such as entering into sealed bonds (recognisances), the practice of tenure by lease, wills, enfeoffment to uses and bills for equitable consideration in chancery. Significantly, this new trend was reflected in an increase in the number of writers of legal documents (scriveners and notaries) to cope with the demand.[62]

---

[60] A. H. Hershey, 'Justice and Bureaucracy: the English Royal Writ', *EHR*, 113 (1998), 829–51; A. Harding, 'Plaints and Bills in the History of English law', in Jenkins (ed.), *Legal History Studies*, pp. 74–6.

[61] A. Musson, *Public Order and Law Enforcement: The Local Administration of Criminal Justice, 1294–1350* (Woodbridge, 1996), pp. 176–7.

[62] N. Ramsey, 'Scriveners and Notaries as Legal Intermediaries in Later Medieval England', in J. Kermode (ed.), *Enterprise and Individuals in Fifteenth Century England* (Stroud, 1991), pp. 118–19, 123, 127.

Committing the law to text for the purposes of education, the third aspect to be explored in this study, was a significant feature of the period. By the late fourteenth century it could be said that the legal profession was a book-learned profession at all levels. Legal education, like all teaching, may have been conducted orally and indeed, much legal training was carried out (as it is now) through lectures, disputations and forms of 'roleplay'.[63] Students also learned by listening to and observing what went on in court and by undertaking tasks themselves. The production of manuscript (and later, of course, printed) texts was also part of the educational process.[64] Texts embodying the law as it stood were produced in the late twelfth and early thirteenth century in the works attributed to and known as *Glanvill* and *Bracton*. Revisions of the latter appeared in the late thirteenth and early fourteenth centuries as the treatises *Fleta* and *Britton*. While not explicitly didactic, they comprised compendia of the law as it was thought ought to be practised. 'Course texts' on legal subjects were tailored to the different needs and requirements of the would-be reader. Advanced literature on pleading and forms of action were available in manuscript at the upper end of the market, for the serjeants-at-law and 'apprentices', while at the lower end, texts on conveyancing and court procedure and works on management and accounting were aimed at local legal professionals, royal officials and estate administrators. The law reports were also available as learning tools and indeed, some of them have come down to us in 'lecture' format. The Inns of Court, which by the mid-fourteenth century were beginning to play an educational (rather than purely accommodational) role also contributed by putting on cycles of 'readings' on particular statutes. These formed the basis of the men of court's instruction, with mooting on legal points raised by the 'reading' usually occurring afterwards.

As for the language barrier, *Glanvill* and *Bracton* were written in Latin, but most other educational treatises were in French, which it was assumed that the manorial reeve could understand in 1300.[65] The dissemination of such material is hinted at in the popularity of statute books, which usually included some of the basic treatises. On the basis of surviving books or references to owners, at least 249 owned law books in the late

---

[63] The following paragraph draws on the work of Dr P. Brand and Professor J. H. Baker. See P. A. Brand, *The Making of the Common Law* (1982); J. H. Baker, *The Legal Profession and the Common Law* (1986) and his *The Common Law Tradition* (2000); and essays in J. A. Bush and A. Wijffels (eds.), *Learning the Law: The Teaching and Transmission of English Law, 1150–1900* (1999).

[64] E. W. Ives, 'A Lawyer's Library in 1500', *Law Quarterly Review*, 85 (1969), 104–16. Ives makes the point that demand for the first printed texts of the Year Books was not for ancient tomes of the law, but recent cases.

[65] Clanchy, *Memory to Written Record*, p. 236.

thirteenth and fourteenth centuries.[66] Such treatises were not restricted to male ownership or readership since several works were written specifically for women who had the task of administering estates in the absence, either temporary (through war service) or permanent (through death) of their husbands.[67] Surviving manuals include one by Bishop Robert Grosseteste for the countess of Lincoln and one for Lady Denise Montchensy by Sir Walter Bibbesworth.[68]

In the fifteenth and sixteenth centuries the numbers of people possessing legal literature increased as texts were brought out especially for justices of the peace and other local officials. The earliest surviving such manual compiled in Worcestershire in c.1422 is not a comprehensive account of the duties and jurisdiction of the office, but (in the words of Bertha Putnam) 'does contain almost everything that justices of the quorum and the clerk of the peace ought to know. Moreover, the exclusion from the compilation of extraneous matter means that the documents form an exceedingly useful precedent or formula book easily handled, and therefore accessible for practical purposes.'[69] In about 1460 for example, the corporation of Rochester employed John Ryponden of the Guildhall in London 'to make us a boke of French into Latin and out of Latin in English for the enquiry of all manner of things that belong to the justice of the peace'.[70] In addition to Lambard's manual, mentioned above, the most useful treatise for the early modern justice of the peace was a synthesis of law, tradition and practice by Michael Dalton with the title *The Country Justice, Containing the Practice of the Justices of the Peace out of their Sessions, Gathered, for the Better Helpe of such Justices of the Peace as have not been much Conversant with the Studie of the Lawes of this Realm*. It proved a valuable tool for the next 128 years and went into a second edition a year after its first publication in 1618.[71]

---

[66] I am grateful to Dr J. Arkenberg for allowing me access to his list of book owners.

[67] For example: R. E. Archer, '"How ladies . . . who live on their manors ought to manage their households and estates": Women as Landholders and Administrators in the Later Middle Ages', in P. J. P. Goldberg (ed.), *Women in Medieval English Society*, rev edn (Stroud, 1997), pp. 149–81.

[68] Clanchy, *Memory to Written Record*, pp. 95, 197–9, 276.

[69] B. H. Putnam, *Early Treatises on the Practice of the Justices of the Peace in the Fifteenth and Sixteenth Centuries*, Oxford Studies in Social and Legal History 7 (Oxford, 1924), pp. 60–93. The compiler of the manual was probably John Weston, who was one of the 'working' justices of the peace in Worcestershire and Warwickshire and a justice of gaol delivery for Worcester, Warwick and Coventry gaols in the early fifteenth century. He was a common pleader of London (1402–c.1415), recorder of Coventry (1417–c.1434) and in 1425 became a serjeant-at-law.

[70] Ramsey, 'Scriveners and notaries', p. 122.

[71] L. R. McInnis, 'Michael Dalton: the Training of the Early Modern Justice of the Peace and the Cromwellian Reforms', in Bush and Wijffels (eds.), *Learning the Law*, pp. 255–72.

There is some evidence that the advent of printing had an enormous impact in educational terms in the late fifteenth and early sixteenth centuries. One of the earliest books printed in London and the earliest English legal treatise produced this way, Sir Thomas Littleton's *Tenures* (published in 1481 or 1482), went through over seventy editions before the production of Sir Edward Coke's *First Institutes of the Laws of England* (a commentary on Littleton's *Tenures*) in 1628. Printed abridgements of the Year Books by Statham in the fifteenth century and in the sixteenth by Callow, Fitzherbert and Brooke, although in Law French, clarified points of law for many practitioners and provided a useful resource for the citation of legal authorities. The first law dictionary was compiled and printed by John Rastell in 1527 and the first printed editions of registers of original and judicial writs and of statutes (the latter being *A collection of statutes from the beginning of Magna Carta unto the year of our Lord, 1557*) were produced by Rastell's son, William, in 1531 and 1557 respectively.[72]

The written word not only influenced legal education in terms of the availability of legal texts, but also in terms of its conveyance and function. Encapsulation in print rather than personal recollection precipitated, as Ross has argued, a 'decline of memory and oral tradition as carriers of legal knowledge'.[73] At the same time the growing ascendancy of the printed word altered attitudes towards the law itself, crystallising legal opinions and focusing attention more retrospectively, engendering a 'memorial culture'.[74] As Ives notes, 'When [during the sixteenth and early seventeenth centuries] instruction by book began to impede instruction by ear, the law became a good deal more firmly riveted to its past'.[75]

The explosion of activity during the first part of the sixteenth century and the continued popularity of treatises such as Littleton's, tends to mask the fact that by the 1590s, to quote David Ibbetson, 'legal literature was undoubtedly in something of a crisis'. No new treatises had been written and the Year Books ended their reign in the 1540s with reports from 1535. Some privately made law reports and reports prepared by students were circulated in manuscript among the profession, but until the printing and public dissemination of Coke's *Reports* there was little of educative value.[76] Moreover, it is not to be assumed that the increased potential availability of

---

[72] H. A. Hollond, 'English Legal Authors before 1700', *Cambridge Law Journal*, 9 (1945), 299–307.
[73] R. J. Ross, 'The Memorial Culture of Early Modern English Lawyers: Memory as Keyword, Shelter, and Identity, 1560–1640', *Yale Journal of Law and the Humanities*, 10 (1998), 229–326, quotation at 233.
[74] *Ibid.*, 319–20.   [75] Ives, 'Lawyer's library', 108–9.
[76] D. Ibbetson, 'Law Reporting in the 1590s', in C. Stebbings (ed.), *Law Reporting in Britain* (1995), pp. 73–88 (quotation at p. 73).

legal literature afforded by printing meant that many more people actually benefited from the enterprise (in terms of the availability of texts) since it was presumably largely a speculative enterprise. It therefore differed in commercial terms from the bespoke trade of manuscript book production where each copy had a designated home. On the other hand, it is important to bear in mind that the recorded ownership of legal books represents only the tip of the iceberg so to speak of accessibility, since books could be borrowed for private reading or their contents read aloud to others. Occasionally legal books were stolen from their owners.[77] It was also common for them to be left to others or monastic libraries in wills.[78]

Let us turn to the final area under consideration, the popular authority of the law. Whilst for practitioners the legal text was pre-eminent, for the general populace what the law said was of secondary importance to what it symbolised. The actual detailed provisions of certain statutes or texts of quasi-law (notably Magna Carta and Domesday Book) could be transcended by the symbolic nature accorded them. These sources were regarded by contemporaries (both literate and non-literate) albeit in different contexts as having special authority as containing fundamental rights that made them synonymous with accountability, justice and even freedom.[79] A key example of this phenomenon is the enigmatic 'law of Winchester' claimed as fundamental law by Wat Tyler during the Peasants' Revolt in 1381. I have written elsewhere about the resonances evoked by this particular icon, but even if its symbolism is contentious and difficult to fathom for us today, its authority was nevertheless apparent to the rebels in the late fourteenth century.[80] We can also see how the use of roll format for private copies of statutes associated them with royal records and, as one commentator puts it, 'could have imbued private statute rolls with an aura of quasi-public authority, especially if they were designed to function like those kept by the king's clerks'.[81]

An understanding of the symbolic power of the law was embedded in political and literary culture as evinced by the behaviour of rebellious

---

[77] E.g., J. P. Collas and T. F. T. Plucknett (eds.), *Year Books of Edward II: 12 Edward II (1319)*, Selden Society 70 (1953), p. 122. The case concerns the lack of payment for a Code, a Digest and other books worth £10.

[78] C. T. Allmand, 'Civil Lawyers', in C. T. Clough (ed.), *Profession, Vocation and Culture in Later Medieval England* (Liverpool, 1982), p. 171.

[79] Musson, *Medieval Law*, pp. 251–4.

[80] A. Musson, 'Appealing to the Past: Perceptions of Law in Late-Medieval England', in A. Musson (ed.), *Expectations of the Law in the Middle Ages* (Woodbridge, 2001), pp. 165–79.

[81] Skemer, 'Book Trade', 198.

subjects and its appearance in works of literature. In *Piers Plowman*, for example, Langland cites 'Folville's Laws' as if they genuinely existed and imbues them with the authority of royal law. In fact the citation acquires resonance from the criminal exploits of a band of brothers of the same name who were outlaws operating in the Midlands in the 1320s and early 1330s. 'Folville's Laws' gained symbolic currency in the minds of readers/listeners because in reality they represented the antithesis of (or an alternative to) royal law.[82] In Chaucer's 'Wife of Bath's Tale' written statute yields to the alternative imagined jurisdiction offered by 'the queen herself sitting as a justice' in 'courts of love'.[83] The adoption of royal style for the issuing of proclamations (as was the case in both large and smaller scale uprisings in the fourteenth century) and for mock indictments and libels should not simply be regarded as parodies of legal forms. The prime examples of these, the letter purporting to be from 'Lionel, king of the rout of raveners' sent to Master Richard Snowshill in 1336,[84] and the libel (an ecclesiastical form of bill) defaming John of Gaunt that was posted in various places in the city of London in 1377,[85] demonstrate not only an understanding of the mechanisms of the law and the power of its forms, but also a desire to participate in the political processes and debates.

The symbolic destruction of legal documents also attests their inherent authority. The burning of legal records during the Peasants' Revolt, for instance, should be viewed as a statement of appreciation of the significance of written documents, rather than (more simplistically) as an unthinking demonstration against literacy. Similarly, the public burning of Richard II's 'blank charters' on the end of a pitchfork signified an end to the arbitrary power the king had exercised over the lands of certain individuals. A further example of this appreciation can be found in 1290 when an attempt was made to serve a writ on Bogo de Clare within the precincts of the palace of Westminster (a privilege reserved to the steward and marshal of the king's household) during a session of parliament when he was under the special protection of the king. As a result, one of Bogo's servants forced the

[82] E. L. G. Stones, 'The Folvilles of Ashby-Folville, Leicestershire, and their Associates in Crime, 1326–1347', *TRHS*, 5th ser., 7 (1957), 117–36.
[83] Benson (ed.), *Riverside Chaucer*, p. 119, ll. 1028 and 1048–9; B. Holsinger, 'Vernacular Legality: The English Jurisdictions of *The Owl and the Nightingale*', in Steiner and Barrington (eds.), *Letter of the Law*, pp. 158–9.
[84] This letter was copied into the king's bench plea rolls: King's Bench 27/306 *Rex* m27. For further analysis, see A. Musson, 'Attitudes to Justice in Fourteenth-Century Yorkshire', *Northern History*, 39 (2002), 183–4.
[85] S. Justice, *Writing and Rebellion: England in 1381* (Berkeley and Los Angeles, 1994), p. 29.

messenger to eat the writ seal and all.[86] Ironically the very incomprehensi-
bility of legal jargon and sometimes the proceedings themselves probably
for many ordinary people imbued the law (as it did Scripture) with an air
of mystery that in turn lent it gravitas and authority.[87]

In conclusion: the administration of justice during the later Middle
Ages was underpinned by a growing concern with written text. Not only
did this in many ways enhance the authority of the law, but it was of
importance in jurisprudential and educational terms. Although written
text came to be an accepted part of the operation of the law and indeed
provided a focus for the growing corpus of statutory enactments, the spoken
word remained important, not only in court (where oral pleadings and the
personal evidence of witnesses and jurors were paramount), but also in the
conveyance of royal will through proclamations. In either case language was
not necessarily a barrier to understanding, although the continued use of
Law French as the language of legal literature, even in the fifteenth century
(by which time English had become a language of government), seems to
indicate a desire on the part of the legal profession to restrict accessibility
to law and promote exclusivity.[88] Reducing the essentially 'unwritten' law
to text engendered a more critical attitude and focused attention on the
increasingly important written word and its interpretation. In time printing
added to the significance of the written word by bringing uniformity in the
presentation of text, though it also provided more scope for the perpetuation
of error, and by shifting the culture from a readiness to accept the gist of a
passage to focus on the import of the exact words.[89]

Finally, while the oral tradition and memory retained some vitality even
in the early modern period in the communication of customary practices,[90]
the importance of the period covered by this paper lies in the fact that it
is the precursor of that stage in the development of English legal theory
when the relationship between textual form and the law is fundamentally

---

[86] *Rotuli Parliamentorum*, 6 vols. (1783), vol. I, pp. 24–5; Prestwich, *Edward I*, p. 462. This trope
appears in other contexts such as a private litigant forced to eat his charters (Sayles (ed.), *Select Cases*,
vol. VI, pp. 118–19) and an emissary of the Archbishop of Canterbury was forced to eat his mandate
(A. Gransden, *Historical Writing in England c.1307 to the Early Sixteenth Century* (1982), p. 165).

[87] For argument raised in the seventeenth century that the air of mystery was designed to cultivate a
professional monopoly see Ross, 'Printing English Law', 361–3.

[88] For a fresh perspective of the use of English as a language of law and government see W. M.
Ormrod, 'The Use of English: Language, Law and Political Culture in Fourteenth-Century England'
(forthcoming). I am grateful to Professor Ormrod for allowing me a copy of his as yet unpublished
paper, some parts of which were aired in a paper given at the International Medieval Congress, Leeds,
2002.

[89] Clanchy, *Memory to Written Record*, pp. 265–6, 278–9.

[90] A. Wood, 'Custom and the Social Organisation of Writing in Early Modern England', *TRHS*, 6th
ser. (1999), 257–69.

altered with recognition of the doctrine of judicial precedent. Although it was not until the nineteenth century that the doctrine reached its zenith,[91] it was recognised under this doctrine that the text itself becomes authoritative law and therefore provides the ultimate of textuality and authority.

[91] *London Street Tramways Co.* v. *LCC* [1898] AC 375: In this case it was held that a decision of the House of Lords on a question of law bound the House in subsequent cases.

6

The art of the unprinted: transcription and English antiquity in the age of print[1]

Julia Crick

> Cotton's writing for manuscript circulation was a natural extension of his activities as a librarian, collector of manuscripts, and transcriber, and as such an exceptionally pure example of the continuity of an intellectual culture grounded in the handwritten word.[2]

Robert Cotton, politician, collector, antiquary, died in 1631 having witnessed the confounding of the intellectual culture which had sustained his historical and political endeavours. As a very young man he had co-founded the Society of Antiquaries, an initiative which later shrivelled under royal disapproval.[3] At the end of his life he saw the invasion of his property, the sequestration of his library, his books searched, his possessions catalogued, access barred except under escort.[4] Such violence bespeaks the power of the unprinted in Stuart England. Cotton used print and owned it, of course, and his printed books no doubt included rareties not readily available in England,[5] but what attracted researchers to his library before 1629, when it was shut down, were documents more likely to have been hand-written, unique materials, transcripts of records housed elsewhere, medieval manuscripts. It was manuscript which eluded the regular scrutiny of the state. Indeed, it requires a considerable effort of imagination to envisage the kind of state apparatus necessary to police the proliferation of

---

[1] I have profited from the comments of Professors David Dumville and Simon Keynes who were kind enough to read this article in draft and save me from a number of errors.
[2] H. Love, 'Scribal Publication in Seventeenth-Century England', *Transactions of the Cambridge Bibliographical Society*, 9 (1986–90), 133.
[3] K. Sharpe, *Sir Robert Cotton 1586–1631: History and Politics in Early Modern England* (Oxford, 1979), p. 73.
[4] Sharpe, *Robert Cotton*, pp. 80–1.
[5] He received gifts from foreign scholars and had agents collecting abroad on his behalf: Sharpe, *Robert Cotton*, p. 59. See further Colin G. C. Tite, 'A Catalogue of Sir Robert Cotton's Printed Books', in C. J. Wright (ed.), *Sir Robert Cotton as Collector: Essays on an Early Stuart Courtier and his Legacy* (1997), pp. 183–93.

information in manuscript form.[6] The authorities could limit access to certain kinds of information. Sensitive parts of the public records, the *arcana imperii*, remained closed to public gaze,[7] but short of sporadic acts of intervention, sometimes brutal – silencing individuals by incarcerating them or seizing their books and papers[8] – officers of the Crown had at their disposal few means of control of knowledge. New works were not registered or licensed in the way printed matter was controlled by organised monopoly.[9] Old works, or extracts from them, circulated privately, hand to hand if required. In a world in which political argument was conducted by protagonists armed principally with ancient precedent, where parliamentary select committees were specifically charged with the task of locating new sources,[10] historical knowledge carried a premium.[11] Men with the run of the archives, with detailed knowledge of the public and state records, with access to medieval sources, engaged in potentially political activity.[12] The penalty for the destruction of a record was death.[13] The act of transcription, the means of transfer of information from point of discovery to point of dissemination, may therefore be supposed to have carried a political charge. In such a climate antiquarian transcription deserves consideration as a significant aspect of scribal culture.

In this essay I shall attempt to elevate antiquarian transcription from its usual place in the academic order as a scholarly tool to an object of study in its own right. I do so for the purposes of experiment, not to effect a permanent manoeuvre, and for three reasons. The first is the degree of political

---

[6] Compare the remarks of A. F. Marotti, *Manuscript, Print and the English Renaissance Lyric* (Ithaca and London, 1995), pp. 75–6; H. R. Woudhuysen, *Sir Philip Sidney and the Circulation of Manuscripts 1558–1640* (Oxford, 1996), pp. 12, 15.

[7] R. B. Wernham, 'The Public Records in the Sixteenth and Seventeenth Centuries', in L. Fox (ed.), *English Historical Scholarship in the Sixteenth and Seventeenth Centuries* (Oxford, 1956), p. 30.

[8] The fate of Sir Edward Coke mirrors that of Cotton. 'Papers and manuscripts' were seized from his 'house or place of abode' immediately before his death in 1634: J. H. Baker, 'Coke's Note-books and the Sources of his Reports', *Cambridge Law Journal*, 30 (1972), 78. See also C. Hill, 'Sir Edward Coke – Myth-Maker', in his *Intellectual Origins of the English Revolution* (Oxford, 1965), pp. 244–5.

[9] A. Johns, *The Nature of the Book: Print and Knowledge in the Making* (Chicago and London, 1998), pp. 213–30.

[10] P. Christianson, *Discourse on History, Law, and Governance in the Public Career of John Selden, 1610–1635* (Toronto, 1996), pp. 93, 107.

[11] See, e.g., W. Klein, 'The Ancient Constitution Revisited', in N. Phillipson and Q. Skinner (eds.), *Political Discourse in Early Modern Britain* (Cambridge, 1993), pp. 23–44.

[12] C. E. Wright, 'Sir Edward Dering: A Seventeenth-Century Antiquary and his "Saxon" Charters', in C. Fox and B. Dickins (eds.), *The Early Culture of North-West Europe (H. M. Chadwick Memorial Studies)* (Cambridge, 1950), p. 374. See W. H. Sherman on John Dee, 'But like most antiquarian matters, the deeds were a potent force in the political and legal spheres': *John Dee: The Politics of Reading and Writing in the English Renaissance* (Amherst, 1995), p. 34. I am grateful to my colleague, Tim Rees, for discussion of the operation of communist archives.

[13] Christianson, *Discourse*, p. 140.

passion unleashed by the researches of antiquaries in Tudor and Stuart England.[14] Studies are made of the careers, the writings, and the libraries of antiquaries,[15] but early modern historians have not always pursued with equal vigour the question of the antiquaries' relationship to their sources, particularly medieval ones,[16] even though what these men were reading, what they knew and how, has a bearing on the rest of their endeavour. The raw materials for such a study are readily available. Over the last century, the antiquarian scholarship of the sixteenth and seventeenth centuries has had lavished on it the attention of numerous historians, medievalists as well as early modernists. Medievalists in particular have looked at the patterns of dispersal of medieval materials, pursued texts, considered their use, primarily by church antiquaries, and they and early modernists have studied the intellectual habits of individuals.[17] Throughout attention has tended to be focused at the level of individuals and specific texts, or on the long-term effects of their efforts for the future of the discipline which they founded.[18] Patterns of transcription more generally have attracted relatively little comment.

A second reason for considering transcription as a scribal activity in its own right is its potential place in arguments about script, print, and what Sherman dubbed the script-print interface.[19] Transcription, which I define for the purposes of this essay as the copying of a medieval or classical text by a sixteenth- or seventeenth-century hand, can be understood as a mode of

---

[14] J. G. A. Pocock, *The Ancient Constitution and the Feudal Law: A Study of English Historical Thought in the Seventeenth Century* (Cambridge, 1957); D. R. Woolf, *The Idea of History in Early Stuart England: Erudition, Ideology and the Light of Truth from the Accession of James I to the Civil War* (Toronto, 1990); Sherman, *John Dee.*

[15] See, e.g., Sharpe, *Robert Cotton*, Sherman, *John Dee*, A. G. Watson, *The Library of Sir Simonds D'Ewes* (1966), D. C. Douglas, *English Scholars 1660–1730* (1939; rev. edn, 1951), G. Parry, *The Trophies of Time: English Antiquaries of the Seventeenth Century* (Oxford, 1995). See now K. Thomas, 'The Life of Learning', *Proceedings of the British Academy*, 117 (2002), 201–35, and N. Barker, 'Editing the Past: Classical and Historical Scholarship', in *CHBB 4*, pp. 206–27.

[16] 'Since reading all of the published sources and treatises cited in the margins of Selden's books would take an incredible number of additional years, I have relied on recent secondary works to fill in much of that context': Christianson, *Discourse*, p. 5. For countervailing examples see, e.g., A. Ford, 'James Ussher and the Creation of an Irish Protestant Identity', in B. Bradshaw and P. Roberts (eds.), *British Consciousness and Identity: The Making of Britain, 1533–1707* (Cambridge, 1998), pp. 188–96.

[17] See, e.g., F. Wormald and C. E. Wright (eds.), *The English Library before 1700* (1958); C. T. Berkhout and M. McC. Gatch (eds.), *Anglo-Saxon Scholarship: The First Three Centuries* (Boston, MA, 1982); Sharpe, *Robert Cotton*; R. Sharpe, *Medieval Irish Saints' Lives: An Introduction to Vitae Sanctorum Hiberniae* (Oxford, 1991), pp. 61–8 (on Ussher); E. M. C. Van Houts, 'Camden, Cotton and the Chronicles of the Norman Conquest of England', in Wright (ed.), *Sir Robert Cotton*, pp. 238–52.

[18] E.g., T. Graham (ed.), *The Recovery of Old English: Anglo-Saxon Studies in the Sixteenth and Seventeenth Centuries* (Kalamazoo, MI, 2000). For an important exception see S. Keynes, 'The Cult of King Alfred the Great', *Anglo-Saxon England* 28 (1999), 225–356.

[19] Sherman, *John Dee*, p. 117.

transfer of information, part of a chain linking the post-medieval present to the medieval or even classical past. Various kinds of chain can be envisaged. Script can be the source of the information so conveyed, print the ultimate destination, thus obeying the flow of information which Eisenstein called the shift from script to print.[20] However, the technologies can operate in reverse, with print the source and script the outcome, a situation observed so commonly with antiquarian transcripts of the Latin classics that some scholars have come to expect a printed text to be the exemplar of manuscript-copies made in the age of print.[21] Thus transcription illustrates the permeability of the script-print border which others have observed.[22] A secretary transcribing in the age of print is carrying out essentially the same process as a scribe copying in an earlier period: creating a text for his own use, or that of others, from an existing exemplar, possibly of some antiquity. Transcription is therefore a term of some imprecision. It embraces transcription from print, self-evidently a relatively new phenomenon, and copying from manuscript, a process indistinguishable in terms of intention from the production of manuscripts in an earlier age.

A final justification for making antiquarian transcription an object of study in its own right is its relative neglect in recent investigations of scribal culture in the age of printing.[23] Leading students of the new script culture have primarily focused on a range of texts which, while diverse in content, share certain characteristics. The texts selected evince an authorial presence. Far from the routine or mundane bureaucratic texts which McKenzie has argued made up the bulk of early modern written material,[24] those scribally transmitted texts to which most detailed study has been devoted are finely wrought works of political polemic, creative invention, artistic display, calculated to convince, cajole, or entertain, rather than to inform or instruct.[25] Secondly, the works selected for study circulated in the lifetime of their authors or only shortly after their death, thus obeying rules and responding to trends distinctively different from those associated with manuscript circulation of medieval texts both before and after the

[20] Discussed above, Introduction.
[21] M. D. Reeve, 'Manuscripts Copied from Printed Books', in J. B. Trapp (ed.), *Manuscripts in the Fifty Years after the Invention of Printing: Some Papers Read at a Colloquium at the Warburg Institute on 12–13 March 1982* (1983), pp. 12–20, esp. 12–15. Compare P. O. Kristeller, 'In Search of Renaissance Manuscripts', *The Library*, 6th ser., 10 (1988), 292.
[22] See, e.g., Sherman, above, n. 19; Marotti, *Manuscript*, p. 2.
[23] There is an important exception: Woudhuysen, *Circulation of Manuscripts*, ch. 4. On the anthologising of older texts, see Marotti, *Manuscript*, pp. 30–41.
[24] D. F. McKenzie, 'Speech-Manuscript-Print', *The Library Chronicle of the University of Texas at Austin* 20 (1990), 87–109. See also Woudhuysen, *Circulation of Manuscripts*, pp. 67–81.
[25] Marotti, *Manuscript*, pp. 75–6.

Reformation, when many of the works copied had been written centuries earlier.[26] Antiquarian transcription belongs to neither category. It represents a different facet of the elite milieu of manuscript production, embodying the highest forms of literacy, script and Latinity, potential political sensitivity, but also a certain distance from the text, the creative element being confined to the act of researching and selecting the data to be reproduced.

The next problem is method. How can one interrogate a dull bulk of data, a whole class of material retrospectively defined, as we have seen, and of miscellaneous character and sometimes untraceable origin? The problems are compounded by those of reconstructing the circumstances in which the transcript was made: authorial intention is elusive enough, scribal intention irrecoverable, patterns of readership controversial. In this present experiment evidence of antiquarian interest – copying – will be combined with evidence of reception – reading and ownership – to investigate one class of document which seems particularly to have caught the eye of antiquarian transcribers: the Latin charters of pre-Conquest England. The Latin charters, what Maitland called the landbooks, were not collected in printed form until the three volumes of Dugdale and Dodsworth's *Monasticon* appeared between 1655 and 1673, although individual charters, or extracts from them, found their way into print by other means.[27] But in the long century between the plundering and wasting of monastic records after Dissolution and the publication of selected remnants in the *Monasticon*, the copying of pre-Conquest charters and diplomas continued, indeed it quickened. Of the surviving corpus of texts of pre-Conquest charters, more than a quarter was transcribed in the sixteenth and seventeenth centuries.[28] This proliferation of copies guarantees the importance of such late evidence to medievalists – many texts would be unknown but for the existence of sixteenth- and seventeenth-century copies.[29]

What stimulated this copying remains a question of some significance. The intensity of activity in the century and a half after the dissolution of the monasteries suggests more than a disinterested effort to preserve the

---

[26] The studies by Love, Marotti and Woudhuysen signal in their titles their main focus of interest, Renaissance writers.

[27] See Douglas, *English Scholars*, ch. 2.

[28] See P. H. Sawyer (ed.), *Anglo-Saxon Charters: an Annotated List and Bibliography* (1968). At a conservative estimate, more than 350 of the 1550-odd texts listed survive in antiquarian copies. About 300, dating from the late seventh century onwards, survive as contemporary single sheets: S. Kelly, 'Anglo-Saxon Lay Society and the Written Word', in R. McKitterick (ed.), *The Uses of Literacy in Early Medieval Europe* (Cambridge, 1990), p. 39.

[29] See, e.g., S. Keynes, 'The Lost Cartulary of Abbotsbury', *Anglo-Saxon England*, 18 (1989), 207–43, and his 'A Charter of King Edward the Elder for Islington', *Historical Research*, 66 (1993), 306–7 and n. 62.

remnants of the monastic past: copies of pre-Conquest charters made in this period exceed in quantity those of any equivalent stretch of time up to and after the Norman Conquest, a pattern of survival explained only in part by the scale of archival losses incurred before and after the monasteries were dissolved. One might account for the proliferation of post-Dissolution copies by appealing to print. Pre-Conquest charters were of course transcribed in anticipation of the production of printed texts. They appear in more than twenty of the surviving volumes of transcripts collected by Dugdale and Dodsworth;[30] Madox's volumes of transcripts for his proposed 'Feudal history and Custumier of England' included a number containing pre-Conquest charters.[31] Other transcripts were occasioned by print more directly. It is a commonplace, admittedly a barbed one, that printing allowed the mass circulation of medieval texts, that 'the sixteenth and seventeenth centuries saw more of the Middle Ages than had ever been available to anybody in the Middle Ages'.[32] Copyists of Anglo-Saxon charters sometimes worked from print even before the publication of the great scholarly collections of the mid-seventeenth century. Sir Henry Spelman, who died in 1641 before the publication of the *Monasticon*, noted as one source of charter-texts the 'many extant in printed Authors, as *Ingulf* the *Saxon*, *Malmesbury*'.[33] Weever's *Ancient Funerall Monuments* proves the source of a number of charters transcribed in the papers of Dodsworth himself.[34] But it is a separate question whether the proliferation of copies is explained by printing. Ingulf's *Chronicle*, which Spelman cited as a source, served as a vehicle for the early circulation of numerous pre-Conquest charters forged on behalf of the abbey of Crowland. It was printed by Henry Savile in 1596 but Savile's text appears not to have spawned manuscript copies of the charters – the Crowland charters were relatively little copied in the

---

[30] Bodl. Lib., MSS Dodsworth 9, 10, 24, 25, 38, 39, 55, 65, 68, 78, 85, 97, 105, 110, 120, 160; Dugdale 4, 11, 12, 13, 17, 21.

[31] On Madox's transcripts see S. Keynes, 'The "Dunstan B" Charters', *Anglo-Saxon England* 23 (1994), 170–2.

[32] Michael Clanchy paraphrasing Marshall McLuhan: M. T. Clanchy, 'Looking Back from the Invention of Printing', in D. P. Resnick (ed.), *Literacy in Historical Perspective* (Washington, 1983), p. 8. See also A. Hudson, '"No Newe Thyng": The Printing of Medieval Texts in the Early Reformation Period', in her *Lollards and their Books* (1985), pp. 227–48; E. P. Goldschmidt, *Medieval Texts and their First Appearance in Print* (1943), p. 23.

[33] Quoted by H. A. Cronne, 'The Study and Use of Charters by English Scholars in the Seventeenth Century: Sir Henry Spelman and Sir William Dugdale', in Fox (ed.), *English Scholarship*, p. 80. His source was not *Reliquiæ Spelmanniæ*, as he stated, but the later *The English Works of Sir Henry Spelman, Kt, Published in his Lifetime; together with his Posthumous works, Relating to the Laws and Antiquities of England* (1723). On the tract in question, see Keynes, 'Lost Cartulary', p. 224.

[34] Bodl. Lib., MS Dodsworth 10, S 138 (J. Crick (ed.), *Charters of St Albans*, Anglo-Saxon Charters 10 [Oxford, forthcoming], no. 3), S 1246.

sixteenth and seventeenth centuries.[35] Gervase Holles of Grimsby, colonel in the service of Charles I, had the Crowland charters transcribed for his collection of Lincolnshire documents made in 1638–9, reportedly from manuscript.[36] Copyists in the period after Dissolution did fasten on particular texts. Certain charters were copied with unprecedented frequency, antiquarian copies constituting 50–90% of all extant copies of certain documents.[37] But choice of text was not determined primarily by ease of access through print – much-copied documents circulated before the text was available in print[38] – and thus attention must turn to what they contained and how they were used. It is a striking to observe, for example, how many of the texts which attracted particular interest were medieval forgeries.[39] We need to move away from patterns of copying to patterns of use.

Pre-Conquest charters are a class of document which acquired over time a symbolic and ideological importance out of all proportion to the terms of the original grant. Such documents describe the conveyance of rights to land or other privileges usually made by a king to a religious house or private individual and witnessed by his entourage, clerical and lay. Charters always added up to more than the sum of their parts. Highly solemn statements, written in the language of the Bible and, in the century after their introduction into England frequently in the same script, bearing the sign of the cross, they formed a central part of a ritual of transfer which signified more than the simple handing over of land.[40] But like fine wine, their particular characteristics matured, developed and even changed over time and their value increased with age. They continued to be copied, long after the death of the original grantor, as proof of title of monastic estates, as guarantee of special privilege, as a demonstration of antiquity. This retrospective importance can be seen most clearly in the case of forgeries, where the original transaction is effaced altogether (or at least placed beyond the reach of the historian) and the document served as a vehicle for the claims of a religious house. Such forgeries were made as early as the ninth century, but examples

---

[35] Henry Savile, *Rerum Anglicarum scriptores* (1596), pp. 484–520. On the early modern popularity of Ingulf's *Chronicle* see Keynes, 'Cult of Alfred', p. 242.

[36] BL, MS Lansdowne 207c. The catalogue states that the charters were copied from originals: *A Catalogue of the Lansdowne Manuscripts in the British Museum (Parts I–II)* (1819), p. 74.

[37] Sawyer, *Anglo-Saxon Charters*, nos. [hereafter S] 2 (9 of 18 copies), 731 (17 of 33 copies), 792 (11 of 22), 880 (9 of 19), 906 (5 of 9), 911 (10 of 11), 1000 (9 of 14), 1033 (4 of 7), 1036 (3 of 6), 1220 (8 of 12), 1246 (4 of 4), 1250 (6 of 6). See below, pp. 124–5.

[38] Only four of the texts listed above, n. 37, were printed before the *Monasticon* (S 2, 731, 1250 by Spelman, S 1246 by Weever) but all survive in sixteenth-century copies. See also discussion of S 731, below.

[39] Of the twelve listed in n. 37, all except S 906 and 911.

[40] Kelly, 'Anglo-Saxon Lay Society', pp. 39–47.

can be found from every century up to the time of Dissolution.[41] In the later Middle Ages when abbots and their communities selected their most valuable documents for royal confirmation, they favoured those which expressed most effectively the needs and aspirations of a religious house, ancient documents, frequently forged or interpolated.[42] Even when pre-Conquest documents should have been dead letter, after the appropriation of the monastic estates to which they gave title, their value endured. Sir Henry Spelman reported a positive scarcity: "'They are", he says, "at this Day so rare, as though I have seen diverse, yet could I never obtain one originall'"[43] but this scarcity was born of popularity rather than desuetude. Copying continued, although forging apparently ceased.

The nature of antiquarian interest in Anglo-Saxon charters remains something of an unknown quantity still awaiting comprehensive study.[44] These and similar documents could certainly inflame passions – landowners launched a suit against the *Monasticon*, concerned that its publication undermined title to their own estates[45] – and there is every indication that charters satisfied more than a general curiosity. Sir Edward Dering (1596–1644), MP for Hythe, had Anglo-Saxon charters copied for the library of his mansion at Surrenden, Kent; those which survive suggest a particular interest in Kent and hence local topography.[46] Sir Henry Spelman (c.1564–1641) used charters to illustrate arguments about feudalism and the nature of tenure before the Conquest.[47] In the 1660s Sir John Strangways submitted a portfolio of charters, including 'Saxon deeds', some in translation, in support of his claim to rights formerly enjoyed by the pre-Conquest abbots of Abbotsbury.[48] Here we return to our earlier observation that many of the charters most transcribed in the age of print were forgeries. Contemporaries might regret the perpetuation of erroneous texts – Twysden berated Dugdale for his failure to weed out *spuria* from the documents which he

---

[41] For a fifteenth-century example, see D. Williams, 'The Crowland Chronicle, 616–1500', in D. Williams (ed.), *England in the Fifteenth Century: Proceedings of the 1986 Harlaxton Symposium* (Woodbridge, 1987), pp. 371–90.

[42] Described by M. T. Clanchy, *From Memory to Written Record: England 1066–1307*, 2nd edn (Oxford, 1993), pp. 169–71.

[43] Cronne, 'Study and Use of Charters', p. 80, also quoted by Keynes, 'Lost Cartulary', p. 224.

[44] Professor Simon Keynes of Trinity College Cambridge is preparing a comprehensive survey: *Anglo-Saxon Charters: Archives and Single Sheets*, Anglo-Saxon Charters, Supplementary Ser. 2 (forthcoming). Meanwhile, see Cronne, 'Study and Use of Charters' and H. A. Cronne, 'Charter Scholarship in England', *University of Birmingham Historical Journal*, 8 (1961), 26–61, at 41–52, Keynes (as n. 29), and Keynes, 'Cult of Alfred'.

[45] Douglas, *English Scholars*, p. 35.

[46] Wright, 'Edward Dering', pp. 377–8, 382–6.

[47] Cronne, 'Study and Use of Charters', pp. 81–2, 85. Keynes, 'Lost Cartulary', p. 224.

[48] Keynes, 'Lost Cartulary', pp. 217–19.

printed[49] – but the copying of undetected forgeries suggests more than a lapse in scholarly vigilance. Forgeries offered more to the user than the genuine article: at the time of their creation they aimed to satisfy contemporary aspiration, to stake claims in the past using inflated language or exaggerated descriptions of title. Transcribers, perhaps unconsciously, gravitated towards documents which met particular needs.

Two notorious documents subsequently identified in whole or in part as the work of twelfth-century forgers particularly attracted attention. Early modern transcripts account for nine of fourteen surviving copies of what purports to be a grant which King Edgar made to St Mary's Abbey, Worcester, in 964, and seventeen of thirty-three copies of an alleged charter of Edward the Confessor to Coventry Abbey of 1043. What drew copyists to the Coventry grant remains to be seen but we have ready-supplied a context for the copying of the first, the Worcester document, known from its opening word as the *Altitonantis* charter. As Simon Keynes has shown, *Altitonantis* was known to Aubrey and Pepys and was used to defend English sovereignty of the seas in the seventeenth century.[50] As early as 1577 the same charter was made to serve the same cause at the hands of John Dee, who cited it twice in his *General and Rare Memorials pertayning to the Perfect arte of Navigation*, noting that King Edgar 'Could not chose (I say) But by such Full and Peaceable Possession finde himself, (according to right, and his harts desire) the True and Souerayn Monarch, of all this Brytish Ocean, environing in any way, his Impire of Albion, and Ireland, with the lesser Ilands, next adiacent.'[51] Dee had found in a twelfth-century reworking of a tenth-century royal charter a perfect precedent for the imperial claims of his own monarch,[52] one so good that it was repeated by others, notably Samuel Purchas and John Selden.[53] The number of surviving antiquarian copies reinforces the impression that early modern readers found particular resonances in this forged pre-Conquest document. Besides what it signalled to early modern readers and users, the history of *Altitonantis* in the age of print shows something about script, print and access to ancient documents.

---

[49] Douglas, *English Scholars*, p. 36. On use of forgeries, see Cronne, 'Charter Scholarship', p. 40.

[50] S. Keynes (ed.), *Facsimiles of Anglo-Saxon Charters*, Anglo-Saxon Charters, Supplementary vol. 1 (Oxford, 1992), p. 11. The authenticity of *Altitonantis* has been discussed by E. John, *Land Tenure in Early England: A Discussion of Some Problems* (Leicester, 1960), pp. 106-8.

[51] [John Dee], *General and Rare Memorials pertayning to the Perfect Arte of Navigation* ([1577]), p. 60, see also pp. 58–60.

[52] On Dee and Edgar, see Sherman, *John Dee*, p. 143. Sherman does not discuss Dee's indebtedness to pre-Conquest charters.

[53] Samuel Purchas, *Hakluytus Posthumus or Purchas His Pilgrimes Contayning a History of the World, in Sea Voyages and Lande Travells, by Englishmen and Others* (1625), repr. in 20 vols. (Glasgow 1905–7), vol. XIII, pp. 438–9. On Selden, below, pp. 130–1.

Selden found his text through print – he cited Purchas and Dee – but Dee, writing sixty years before Spelman published a text in his *Concilia*, must have used a manuscript source.[54] The only clue to its nature is provided by his marginal note ('Ex chartæ Fundationis Ecclesiæ cathedralis Wigorniæ') which, together with a similar note for another purported tenth-century charter, this time from Ely, cited on the next page ('FVNDATIO Ecclesiæ cathedralis Eliensis') suggest that Dee used a collection of transcribed foundation charters.[55] Both *Altitonantis*, and the Ely charter cited by Dee in the same section of his *General and Rare Memorials*, are known to have circulated in manuscript form within a collection of monastic foundation charters made by Sir John Prise in the 1530s and copied by his secretary, William Say,[56] but both circulated apparently independently as well.[57] Dee himself kept a collection of charters housed in a case, but we cannot judge their antiquity and nature.[58]

The reception of the *Altitonantis* charter in the age of print suggests something of how a much-transcribed text was used, why it was popular, how it enjoyed currency in both script and print. But until the writings of sixteenth- and seventeenth-century authors are read systematically with an eye to identifying their medieval sources, in this instance their use of pre-Conquest charters, we can only imagine what stimulated interest in other much copied works. With this aim in view the remainder of this paper represents an initial foray, neither comprehensive nor exhaustive, into the writings of contemporaries who set much store by the pre-Conquest past: Edward Coke and John Selden. Coke is an undeniably problematic figure and his writings and thought have stirred up more controversy than it is possible to summarise here.[59] Selden, his younger contemporary, is admired for his scholarly methods and subtlety of mind, although it has to be said that viewed at the level of his interaction with a single class of documents his habits of citation bear more than a passing resemblance to those of Coke.

Called to the bar in 1578, Coke became solicitor general in 1592, attorney general two years later and, near the height of his political influence he

---

[54] Henry Spelman, *Concilia, Decreta, Leges, Constitutiones in re Ecclesiarum Orbis Britannici*, 2 vols. (1639–64), vol. I, p. 432.

[55] S 779: [Dee], *General and Rare Memorials*, p. 59.

[56] Described by S. E. Kelly (ed.), *Charters of St Augustine's Abbey Canterbury and Minster-in-Thanet*, Anglo-Saxon Charters 4 (Oxford, 1995), pp. lix–lx.

[57] Sawyer, *Anglo-Saxon Charters*, pp. 237, 247–8.   [58] Sherman, *John Dee*, p. 34.

[59] Pocock, *Ancient Constitution*, pp. 56–89, C. Brooks and K. Sharpe, 'History, English Law and the Renaissance', *P&P*, 72 (1976), 133–42, S. D. White, *Sir Edward Coke and the Grievances of the Commonwealth* (Manchester, 1979).

acted as the prosecutor at the trials of Sir Walter Ralegh (1603) and the gunpowder plotters (1605). He fell from favour in 1616 and in 1621–2 he spent some nine months in the Tower accused of treason. By the time of his death in 1634 he had published eleven volumes of case reports, a Book of Entries, the first part of his Institutes, the other three following after his death.[60] Coke's writings established him as a fundamental legal voice – Hill claimed that Coke's authority as an interpreter of law outstripped that of any Protestant theologian in interpreting Scripture[61] – but his credentials as an antiquary have left more than a little to be desired. He gained notoriety for twisting English constitutional history into a continuous thread leading back to the Saxon forest, was once depicted as a historical clodhopper oblivious to the best practices of Continental method, charged with the propagation of myth,[62] 'bogus history',[63] 'juridical nationalism', even 'anti-history',[64] although more recently his reputation, together with that of other common lawyers, has been redeemed a little.[65] Although Coke died twenty-one years before the publication of the first volume of the *Monasticon*, it is little surprise that he knew and used pre-Conquest charters. As we have already seen, his elders, like Dee, cited them in print, his contemporaries, like Cotton, collected originals and transcripts, and charters circulated in transcript form, like the Prise-Say register, making them a known historical resource in elite circles in Stuart England. Moreover, they yielded particularly precious information. A vigorous champion of the Ancient Constitution, Coke brought within his purview all aspects of the working of government in the centuries before Norman encroachment[66] and here charters provided, as they still provide, evidence of cardinal importance: they record royal decisions, royal titles, the names and styles of the king's entourage who witnessed the grants. Through them, as through no other source, seventeenth-century readers might have hoped to view English royal government arrayed in its pristine state.

In the proem to the *Fourth Part of the Institutes of the Laws of England*, published posthumously in 1644, Coke described the effort which the construction of this final part of his great work cost him: 'the searching, finding

---

[60] White, *Edward Coke*, pp. 4–11.   [61] Hill, 'Edward Coke', p. 256.   [62] *Ibid.*

[63] M. I. Finley, 'The Ancestral Constitution', in his *The Use and Abuse of History* (1975), p. 40.

[64] D. R. Kelley, 'History, English Law and the Renaissance', *P&P*, 65 (1974), 25, 33.

[65] Woolf, *Idea of History*, p. 27; H. S. Pawlisch, *Sir John Davies and the Conquest of Ireland: A Study in Legal Imperialism* (Cambridge, 1985), p. 166. See also the approach taken by Johns, *Nature of the Book*, pp. 252–3.

[66] P. Styles, 'Politics and Historical Research in the Early Seventeenth Century', in Fox (ed.), *English Scholarship*, pp. 49–72; Keynes, 'Cult of Alfred', p. 249.

out, perusing, and digesting of authoritie in law, Rols of Parliament, Judi-
ciall Records, Warrants in law, and other invisible works *tam laboris quam
ingenii*. Such claims to antiquarian toil merit investigation.[67] Pre-Conquest
charters were hard to come by in Coke's lifetime and his success in acquiring
them raises questions about his sources. In the *Fourth Part of the Institutes* he
cited charters (forged, without exception) on two occasions. On the first he,
as Dee, used them to support the contention that the kings of England had
anciently enjoyed imperial status, listing the royal styles given in charters
in the names of the Anglo-Saxon monarchs Edgar (959–75), Edward the
Confessor (1042–66), and Edgar's brother and predecessor Eadwig, whom
Coke misnames Edwine (955–59).[68] On the second, Coke bolstered his defence of English lordship of Ireland by printing substantial parts of the same
charter of Edgar, a royal diploma dated 964 which contains the remarkable
claim that an English king (Edgar himself) subdued Norway, all the islands
of Oceanus and most of Ireland, including Dublin.[69] The document in
question, inauthentic in its received form, is of course the *Altitonantis*
charter whose utility to early modern commentators has already been
discussed.

How Coke came to know *Altitonantis* is unknown. As we have seen,
Dee had printed extracts in his own discussion of the imperial history of
the monarchy in 1577 but when Coke first cited *Altitonantis* in 1604 in the
Preface to his Fourth Book of Reports, he quoted parts of the attestations
not printed by Dee.[70] As no full text existed in print at this date, we may
safely conclude that he used a medieval or early modern manuscript copy.
In his later references to the charter, he cited a fifteenth-century enrolment
'Vide Rot. Pat. I E. 4. parte 6. m. 23'. The reference looks plausible – the
margins of his *Institutes* demonstrate that Coke had frequent recourse to
Exchequer records for citation of statutes and other forms of document –
and the reference in question even leads to a pre-Conquest document, but
the wrong one, a vernacular writ of Edward the Confessor.[71] Coke's error
is revealing. The printed text of his *Institutes* lays a trail of misattribution

[67] On his notebooks, which included 'historical notes from ancient records', see Baker, 'Coke's
Note-books', p. 67.
[68] Edward Coke, *The Fourth Part of the Institutes of the Laws of England concerning the Jurisdiction of
Courts* (1644), ch. 74, 'Of Ecclesiastical Courts', pp. 343. S 731, S 1030.
[69] Coke, *Fourth Part of the Institutes*, ch. 76, pp. 359–60. See also Pawlisch, *Sir John Davies*, p. 63.
[70] *Le quart part des reportes del Edward Coke Chivalier, l'attorney general le Roy* (1604). He quotes the
proem, dating clause, and extracts from the attestations. Dee had printed the opening of the charter
and the king's attestation.
[71] S 1157.

characteristic of his mode of operation[72] which suggests as much about his materials as about his own failings: the dispersed nature of his sources, the use of notoriously corrupt Exchequer texts, or errors introduced into texts in the process of transcription. In the case of the miscited Exchequer text of *Altitonantis*, Coke perhaps inherited his error from a printed source. Selden three times made precisely the same mistake in citing the same document, the first time in the first edition of his *Titles of Honor* published in 1614.[73] This suggests some common source for the error, a faulty transcription or, more probably, direct borrowing: Selden made the mistake in print before the publication of Coke's text.[74] The facts of the case may be summarised thus. Selden and Coke appear to have encountered the text of *Altitonantis* independently (presumably in medieval or post-medieval manuscript) and to have claimed authority for their text erroneously in the same manuscript source. In 1631 Selden cited Coke's use of the text (in 1604). Coke later incorporated a faulty reference to an Exchequer enrolment, repeating a mistake first made in print in Selden's 1614 edition of *Titles of Honor*. In this tale of repeated citation, script and print have become inextricably entangled.

But if claims to manuscript sources might not be all that they seem, one cannot see print behind every reference either. Coke's 'Charter of King Edwine to the Abby of Crowland' might be expected to have been copied from print, the Crowland charters being disseminated through the medium of Savile's edition of Ingulf's *Chronicle*. But the document in question has no place in Savile's text and was not printed before the *Monasticon* because it, too, has been misattributed: it concerns estates belonging not to Crowland but to neighbouring Thorney.[75] Coke used a manuscript source which may be traced with some certainty to a collection of transcripts housed in his

---

[72] B. H. Rosenwein, *Negotiating Space: Power, Restraint and Privileges of Immunity in Early Medieval Europe* (Manchester, 1999), p. 208 and n. 103. For a comparable instance of miscitation of a printed medieval authority, see D. R. Woolf, 'Little Crosby and the Horizons of Early Modern Historical Culture', in D. R. Kelley and D. H. Sacks (eds.), *The Historical Imagination in Early Modern Britain: History, Rhetoric, and Fiction, 1500–1800* (Cambridge, 1997), pp. 124–5.

[73] Coke, *Fourth Part of the Institutes*, p. 343. 'Pat. 1. Ed. 4. Part. 6. Memb. 23 Pro Pr & Conuentu Wigorn.': Selden, *Titles of Honor* (1614), p. 35: 2nd edn (1631), [hereafter *Titles of Honor* (1631)], p. 18 (in which he cites Coke). In a marginal note alongside his citation of the same charter 'Inspeximus in Rot. Pat. 1. Ed. 4. Part. 6.': Ioannis Seldeni, *Mare Clausum seu de dominio maris* (1635), book II, ch. xii, p. 177.

[74] If Coke's text had circulated in manuscript prior to its printing the relative chronology cannot be established with any certainty. On private circulation, see Baker, 'Coke's Note-books', p. 71, n. 68.

[75] S 595 (AD 956) concerns a grant by one 'Eadwinus' (Coke's *Edwin[us]*) of land at 'Geakeslea' (Coke's *Jeckelea*).

own library,[76] a volume which included three charters from pre-Conquest Abingdon which he quoted extensively in the Preface to his sixth book of Reports, published in 1607.[77] Likewise in the Institutes he cited a charter of the monastery of Ramsey '(which I have)': he owned a twelfth-century copy of the charter in question, one of four Anglo-Saxon charters in single-sheet copies in his possession.[78] The citation of the three charters in Coke's discussion of the imperial claims of the English monarch is accompanied by a marginal note referring to a document not mentioned there at all,[79] but again, the explanation rests in his own library, which once contained 'A Chartre of Kinge Edgar in the lattine and Saxon tongue anno Domini 966. De Dunningtun./'.[80] Coke's personal manuscript collection evidently fed his writing. His volume of transcripts bears every sign of heavy use: it contains many annotations and cross-references, particular attention being devoted to subjects close to his legal interests, immunities and exemption from royal encroachment.[81] In fact, he might have found the texts of all the charters cited in manuscripts in his own library. His volume of transcripts supplied him with two texts, both taken from the same Abingdon volume in Cotton's collection, which he used in his *Reports* and he cited two of four single-sheets in his *Institutes*. In addition he owned several volumes of transcripts of Exchequer documents and cited others through Agarde[82] and it is at least possible that one of these contained the text of *Altitonantis*.

Selden's use of pre-Conquest charters, like that of Coke and Dee, has attracted little comment in print, no doubt because Selden assembled his immense armoury of sources from many cultures, times and places, and viewed against the diversity and range of his collection, any one class of

---

[76] Holkham Hall, MS 677, in which this charter is reproduced with the same erroneous names for the grantor and estate granted (Edwin, *Jeakeslea*). The charter is otherwise known from only two manuscripts. On Holkham 677, see Crick (ed.), *Charters*, forthcoming, also cited Kelly (ed.), *Charters of Abingdon*, p. lxvii. Listed in Seymour de Ricci (ed.), *A Handlist of Manuscripts in the Library of the Earl of Leicester at Holkham Hall Abstracted from the Catalogues of William Roscoe and Frederic Madden* (Oxford, 1932), p. 57.

[77] S 268, 886, 1201, copied from a volume later in Cotton's possession, BL, MS Cotton Claudius B. vi. A diploma of King Æthelred of 995 and a grant of Æthelswith, queen of Mercia, of 868: S 886, 1201. See *La Size part des Reports Sr. Edw. Coke Chivaler, chiefe Iustice del Commonbanke* (1607), Preface.

[78] Holkham Hall, MS 262: de Ricci (ed.), *Handlist of Manuscripts*, 21. S 746, 558, 287: W. O. Hassall (ed.), *A Catalogue of the Library of Sir Edward Coke* (1950), p. 96.

[79] 'The like Charter to the house at Donnington by King Edgar': identifiable as S 746 of AD 966, which does indeed style Edgar *basileus*. See S. Miller (ed.), *Charters of the New Minster, Winchester*, Anglo-Saxon Charters 9 (Oxford, 2001), no. 24, p. 115.

[80] Item 1201 in the catalogue made before Coke's death in 1634: Hassall, *Catalogue*, p. 96, also pp. x–xii on the catalogue. It contained S 898, 268, 886, 1201.

[81] See Rosenwein, *Negotiating Space*, pp. 207–9, 211.

[82] Hassall (ed.), *Catalogue*, pp. vii, 23 (nos. 301, 306).

document looks insignificant.[83] Paul Christianson, in his recent study of
Selden's career and writings, ruled out detailed investigation of his subject's
sources although he did record charters among them, in particular the
Altitonantis charter which has frequently featured in this discussion.[84] At
the time of his death, Selden's library contained a number of volumes containing charters and a collection of his papers discovered in 1939 included
one late tenth-century original, but when he acquired them remains a matter for speculation.[85]

Selden, like Coke, worked at a time when charters remained a resource
available for the most part in manuscript rather than print; his routes of
access and his use of the material make instructive comparison with Coke's
own. Selden has been much praised for his historical method, free from the
taint of 'exuberant nationalism' and ancient constitutionalism usually associated with Coke's historical researches.[86] His early work, *Titles of Honor*,
which concerned the power and rights of the English nobility before and
after 1066, 'displayed a mastery of the humanist historical method, a mature
grasp of Continental evidence and scholarship'.[87] Here pre-Conquest charters constituted prime evidence. Like Coke and Dee, Selden commented
on imperial styles found in tenth-century royal diplomas, notably those
of Edgar, but he extended his interest to the titles of nobles in kings' en-
tourages, noting the occurrence of men styled count and viscount among
the witnesses. In the first edition, published in 1614, Selden confined himself to a dozen or so charters all but one of which were available in print:
Crowland documents printed in Savile's edition of Ingulph's *Chronicle*,
sometimes cited as Ingulph,[88] an extract from *Altitonantis* printed by Dee,
a Malmesbury charter found in William of Malmesbury's *Gesta Regum
Anglorum*, printed by Savile,[89] and one other, for which a manuscript
source was claimed: 'Chart. Archiepisc. Cant. A. Cbr. DCLXXX'.[90] This
last corresponds with the 'Chartulary of diuers deeds & Evidences

---

[83] Christianson, *Discourse*, ch. 1. See, however, Keynes, 'A Charter', and Keynes, 'Cult of Alfred',
p. 250.

[84] On *Altitonantis*, see *ibid.*, pp. 263–6.

[85] See Keynes, 'Charter of King Edward', pp. 304–5; D. M. Barratt, 'The Library of John Selden and
its Later History', *Bodleian Library Record*, 3 (1950–1), 128–42, 208–13, 256–74.

[86] On Selden's historical standpoint, see R. Tuck, '"The Ancient Law of Freedom": John Selden and
the Civil War', in J. Morrill (ed.), *Reactions to the English Civil War 1642–1649* (1982), pp. 137–61 at
139.

[87] Christianson, *Discourse*, p. 55.

[88] S 213, 82, 1230, 741, 538, 965; Selden, *Titles of Honor*, pp. 223–4, 227, 254, 272.

[89] S 796, Seldon, *Titles of Honor*, p. 35. Selden elsewhere cited William of Malmesbury's *Gesta regum*:
ibid., p. 224.

[90] S 230: Selden, *Titles of Honor*, pp. 35, 301.

concerning the Bishopricke of Cant:' listed among his books at his death.[91] The full extent of his indebtedness to print in his charter citations in the first edition is only revealed in the second edition of 1631 in which he supplied detailed marginal references, including page references to Savile's edition of Ingulph and acknowledgement of Coke and Dee's use of *Altitonantis*.[92] But the second edition shows more. Brimming with marginal references, it suggests that Selden struck a new seam – in it he greatly expanded the number and range of his sources, multiplying several-fold his references to pre-Conquest charters. This allowed him to expand his text, building on additions to his original construct using newly discovered material, much of it in manuscript form and much, apparently, from a single source.

Selden made intense use of charters for the first time in a section on kings' wives, for example, which he constructed from a tissue of quotations from the subscriptions of royal women in pre-Conquest charters, genuine and spurious.[93] He described his sources with such care that in many cases it is possible to identify the precise manuscripts which he used. He cited a subscription of King Edgar's queen Ælfthrith, from a charter 'yet remayning in the inestimable library of that learned and worthy Sir Robert Cotton, and written in letters of gold in a hand of that age', clearly the famous New Minster Foundation charter, surviving as an original of 966.[94] Selden cites many of his charters from what he describes as a Worcester register in the Cotton library ('Regist. Wigor. ms. in Bibl. Cott.'), identifiable as the two eleventh-century cartularies of Worcester still in the Cotton collection, of which Selden appears to have owned a partial transcript.[95] This Selden mined, using it for the texts not only of individual documents from it, but making generalisations about queens' subscriptions in the reigns of various Mercian kings.[96] Cotton's library supplied Selden with texts of most of the pre-Conquest charters cited in this section, but Selden also acknowledged the use of public records, correctly citing a charter of King Cnut to Bury St Edmunds Abbey from an inspeximus of Edward III ('cart. 4. Ed. 3. Num. 58'), and an Ely charter of King Edgar from an ancient charter in the Tower of London ('Cart. Antiq. In Arce Lond, B. num. 11').[97] In this second case, the Tower document cannot be identified but it is worth noting that the probable text in question attracted considerable interest

[91] Barratt independently identified this as Bodl. Lib. MS Tanner 223 which contains the charter in question: 'Library', 260.
[92] Selden, *Titles of Honor* (1631), pp. 18, 606, 770.   [93] *Ibid.*, pp. 117–18.
[94] S 745: BL, MS Cotton Vespasian A. viii; Miller, *Charters of the New Minster*, no. 23.
[95] S 217, 1475. Keynes, 'Charter of King Edward', pp. 304–5, n. 13.
[96] Selden, *Titles of Honor* (1631), p. 118.
[97] S 980, and 779 or 794; Selden, *Titles of Honor* (1631), p. 118.

after the dissolution of the monasteries: it was enrolled under Elizabeth and James and eleven transcriptions survive from the sixteenth, seventeenth and eighteenth centuries.[98]

Selden's disquisition on Anglo-Saxon queenship or, more precisely, patterns of attestation of Anglo-Saxon queens in royal charters, thus draws on new texts acquired by two main routes: Cotton's library (originals and medieval copies) and public records (whether through direct access or by means of transcriptions). These patterns of acquisition may be observed throughout the revised *Titles of Honor*. He drew on other originals from Cotton's library – transcribing the entire text of one Worcester charter of AD 736, which he deemed 'as ancient as any original that I haue seen perfit, and is not unworthy to be wholly inserted here'.[99] He made frequent use of the Worcester cartularies, and used documents in royal records, including a vernacular writ of Edward the Confessor which he cited from the patent rolls.[100] In short, by 1631 his text of seventeen years earlier had undergone a transformation, buttressed by ancient precedents of the highest quality. He cited printed texts and discussion but what he stressed and what, we must imagine, lent his revised work authority was the weight of antiquity: the ancient charters lengthily described, the register of the church of Worcester whose venerability and manuscript status he took care to record ('Regis. **ms. & uetustiss.** Eccles. Wigorn.').[101] And this new evidence added significantly to his case.

In many respects Coke and Selden behaved with remarkable similarity in their use of pre-Conquest charters. They cited them for comparable purposes, in discussions of the imperial past of the monarchy; they located texts in comparable circumstances. When Coke sat to down to write the Fourth Book of his Institutes we may imagine him working from materials in his own library: Savile, single-sheet charters, transcripts taken from Cotton's charters and public records. When Selden revised *Title of Honor* he used much the same: print (Savile), manuscript (originals and medieval copies) and transcripts (public records, perhaps other charters). Selden perhaps stood in a less proprietorial relationship to his sources – he acknowledged use of Cotton's originals and medieval copies – but, like Coke, he owned his

---

[98] PRO, Confirmation Rolls 14–18 Eliz., no. 6; PRO Confirmation Rolls, 4 Jac. I, no. 13: all manuscripts listed by Sawyer, *Anglo-Saxon Charters*, pp. 247–8.

[99] Readily identifiable as King Æthelbald of Mercia's grant of Ismere of AD 736: BL, MS Cotton Augustus ii.3. Selden, *Titles of Honor* (1631), pp. 606–7.

[100] 'Pat. 18 H. 6 Part. 2. Memb. 9 n. 12 vide item cart. 4 Ed. 3 membr. 13 &c': Selden, *Titles of Honor*, p. 612. The text corresponds with S 1104, although reference to the Patent Rolls appears to be erroneous.

[101] My emphasis: Selden, *Titles of Honor* (1631), p. 117.

own texts in transcript and original. The similarities should occasion little surprise. As Spelman noted, Anglo-Saxon charters were a scarce resource in the early seventeenth century: private collectors struggled to recover some of what had been lost in the plundering of monastic archives three generations earlier. But Coke and Selden both illustrate the options open to individuals who sought to acquire not so much the physical object – the medieval artefact – although that was highly prized, but the text contained therein. One important route lay in private collections. Coke owned transcriptions of a volume later in Cotton's hands. Selden's debt was the greater as he expressed in his *Historie of Tithes* which he dedicated to Robert Cotton in 1618: 'So great a part of it, was lent me by your most readie Courtesie and able Direction, that I restore it rather than giue it you'.[102] Cotton's status as a purveyor of medieval texts was indeed unrivalled; his collection supplied charters to more than one generation of researchers.[103] His Abingdon cartulary, for example, the source of four texts transcribed for Coke, spawned six surviving seventeenth-century transcripts.[104] But Coke and Selden had recourse to pre-Conquest charters by a second route, of no less importance: public records. Those who pursued pre-Conquest charters found their quarry not just in the physical remnants of the monastic past but in government repositories undisturbed by the ravages of ecclesiastical politics. The archives housed at Westminster and in the Tower included texts of entire pre-Conquest charters enrolled among the records of late medieval government.[105] Access was restricted, recovery of texts, one suspects, unsystematic or even serendipitous, but scholars transcribed whole volumes of pre-Conquest charters from this source.[106] In this instance the release of this material was determined by political, not by technological change, not so much the destruction of one set of medieval archives – the monastic – as the partial opening to scholars of another – state papers.[107]

What part does early modern transcription occupy in the history of scribal culture? In this discussion of the transmission of charters between the break up of monastic archives and their partial reconstitution in print

---

[102] John Selden, *The Historie of Tithes* (1618), p. a.

[103] For charters transcribed from his volumes see BL, MSS Lansdowne 966, Stowe 932, 1085; Bodl. Lib. MSS Dodsworth 78, James 10, 24, 25. See also above, n. 77.

[104] Now BL, MS Cotton Claudius B.vi (S 268, 886, 1201): Kelly (ed.), *Charters of Abingdon*, pp. lxvi–lxvii.

[105] Discussed, e.g., by Wernham, 'Public Records'; John Butt, 'The Facilities for Antiquarian Study in the Seventeenth Century', *Essays and Studies*, 24 (1938 [1939]), 64–79.

[106] Transcriptions of enrolled charters constitute some or all of Bodl. Lib., MSS Dugdale 4, Dodsworth 24, 25, 68, 97, James 23.

[107] The recovery of texts from enrolments perhaps accounts in some part for the significant number of forgeries among the charters surviving in early modern transcription.

in the hands of Dodsworth and Dugdale, print has recurred as the destination, source, and contaminant of scribally transmitted texts. Charters were copied in anticipation of the production of a printed text, copied from print, elements taken from print and combined with manuscript. The printed version featured as a kind of manuscript recension much like a contemporary transcript, providing a text, feeding into the process of textual comparison, providing a point of reference as the miscitation duplicated by Selden and Coke demonstrates. But medieval manuscript appears to have been vested with greater authority and value. Coke supplemented printed texts with documents which he had collected himself; Selden relied on print until manuscript became available as the second edition of *Titles of Honor* demonstrates. He and Coke signalled their use of the genuine artefact, whether medieval copies or originals.

The last word belongs to Selden. In the introduction to *Historie of Tithes* he elaborated the nature of his debt to Cotton: 'For to haue borowd your help, or usd that your inestimable Library (which liues in you) assures a curious Diligence in search after the inmost, least known and most usefull parts of Historicall Truth both of Past and Present Ages'. His words with peculiar accuracy illuminate the behaviour of the antiquary: the 'curious diligence' in the pursuit of 'the inmost, least known and most usefull parts of Historicall Truth both of Past and Present Ages'. To know the present, such men had to own the past; to own the past they had to acquire knowledge of *arcana*, secrets hidden in ancient records, unlocked by diligent research. To a great extent this activity was conducted in and through manuscript: originals in the hands of owners like Cotton and Coke, governmental records in the Tower and in Westminster, transcripts made from both for the convenience of scholars and perhaps their own notes. Particular authority attached to the singular, the hand-written word. Without engaging with manuscript sources how else could men escape from what Selden called a 'kind of Ignorant Infancie', 'the Neglect or only vulgar regard of the fruitful and precious part of it [Antiquitie], which giues necessarie light to the Present in matter of State, Law, Historie, and the understanding of good Autors'?[108]

---

[108] Selden, *Historie of Tithes*, Preface.

7

The authority of the Word: manuscript, print and the text of the Bible in seventeenth-century England

Scott Mandelbrote

"It is true, we have not the Αυτόγραφα [original writings] of *Moses* and the Prophets, of the *Apostles* and Evangelists: but the ἀπόγραφα [copies] which we have . . . containe every *iota* that was in them."[1]

The words of John Owen (1616–83), Cromwell's chaplain and one of the leaders of the Independents, who in 1651 became Dean of Christ Church, Oxford, and was one of the leading advocates of the Republican regime in the university, summed up a position that was widely held among early modern English readers of the Bible.[2] This work had come down to contemporary Protestants from the hands of the inspired prophets and apostles, 'the sacred pen-men of scripture'. It was an entire and complete representation of divine purposes for humanity that comprehended past, present and future. It contained the history of creation, the rules of contemporary duty and living, as well as the promises of rewards and threats of punishments that still awaited people. Yet its teachings were threatened by the perversity of the Catholic Church and of modern heretics, such as the Socinians, who denied its authority.[3]

The Bible's authority as a text that might shape the lives and faiths of men and women was created by its own miraculous past. This bore witness to the divine providence that had generated a means of preserving the continuity of revelation by the rude hands of shepherds or tax-gatherers. It also drew attention to the special care by which the text had then been

---

[1] John Owen, *Of the Divine Originall, Authority, Self-evidencing Light, and Power of the Scriptures* (Oxford, 1659), p. 13.
[2] On Owen's theology and his attitude to the Bible, see P. Toon, *God's Statesman: The Life and Work of John Owen* (Exeter, 1971), especially p. 59; D. K. McKim, 'John Owen's Doctrine of Scripture in Historical Perspective', *Evangelical Quarterly*, 45 (1973), 195–207; C. R. Trueman, 'Faith Seeking Understanding: Some Neglected Aspects of John Owen's Understanding of Scriptural Interpretation', in A. N. S. Lane (ed.), *Interpreting the Bible: Historical and Theological Studies in Honour of David F. Wright* (Leicester, 1997), pp. 147–62; C. R. Trueman, *The Claims of Truth: John Owen's Trinitarian Theology* (Carlisle, 1998).
[3] For a general discussion of these issues, see R. A. Muller, *Post-Reformation Reformed Dogmatics* (Grand Rapids, MI, 1993), vol. II.

maintained entire for future ages. Moreover, the continuing fulfilment of prophecy demonstrated the true authorship and authority of the Bible. Owen's contemporary opponent in public debate over the status of the received text of Scripture, Brian Walton, at the time a delinquent priest, summarised attitudes to the past of the Bible and its place in the history of the Christian Church in the following manner: 'that the speciall providence of God hath watched over these books, to preserve them pure and uncorrupt against all attempts of Sectaries, Hereticks and others'.[4] This special providence, which presided over the manuscript tradition of the Bible, also watched over the transformation of the book into print. Print was itself a providential medium, because it seemed to guarantee the unity of the text in copy after copy. Compared with the precariousness of manuscript, print offered the prospect of the widespread dissemination of a standard text and thus the exposure of errors of faith and religious practice. It promised to maintain the integrity of doctrine that was based on Scripture.[5] The example of John Bagford (1650–1716), a London shoemaker who was intimate with the contemporary book trade, can be used to embody the early modern distinction between the instability of manuscript and the power of print to maintain and distribute God's Word. Whereas Bagford's own deeply idiosyncratic orthography and syntax served to underline the perils that might await texts at the hands of their transcribers, his careful preservation of printed rarities and ephemera testified to the power of the book to objectify the Word: 'it is Gods own book and Copy w[hi]ch he hath equally bequeathed to all men as the foundation and rule of their faith & lives.'[6]

This essay will consider some of the practical and intellectual problems created by the editing of Scripture and the translation and publication of the Bible in English, especially during the seventeenth century. Differences in the status and readership of individual versions of the Bible, in particular between the Authorised Version and the Geneva Bible, were noted by contemporaries and have been studied extensively by historians.[7] They are

---

[4] Brian Walton, *The Considerator Considered* (1659), p. 14.

[5] See, e.g., Thomas James, *A Treatise of the Corruption of Scripture, Councels and Fathers by the Prelats, Pastors, and Pillars of the Church of Rome, for Maintenance of Popery and Irreligion* (1611).

[6] BL, MS Harley 5909, fo. 41r. This manuscript consists of notes on the history of the Bible, compiled by Humfrey Wanley (1672–1726), which draw extensively on Bagford's work. See also MS Sloane 1378, fos. 150–4; M. McC. Gatch, 'John Bagford, Bookseller and Antiquary', *The British Library Journal*, 12 (1986), 150–71.

[7] Above all, C. Hill, *The English Bible and the Seventeenth-Century Revolution* (1993). See also J. D. Alexander, 'The Genevan Version of the Bible: Its Origin, Translation, and Influence', D.Phil. thesis, University of Oxford (1957); M. S. Betteridge, 'The Bitter Notes: The Geneva Bible and its Annotations', *Sixteenth Century Journal*, 14 (1983), 41–62; D. G. Danner, 'The Contribution of the Geneva

not the primary concern here. Instead, this essay focuses on the relationship between the compromises made by printers and scholars in transmitting the text of Scripture and changes in attitudes to the authority of the Bible.

The special status of the Bible determined its unusual relationship with the world of the early modern printing shop. Booksellers attempted to assert ownership and the right to reproduce particular versions of the Bible, as they did with other texts. During the seventeenth century, copyright in English editions of the Bible was vested in the King's Printer, who had held a patent granting the exclusive right to print the Bible and the Book of Common Prayer since 1577 and who shared this privilege, for larger formats such as folios and quartos, with the Universities of Cambridge (from 1629) and Oxford (from 1636).[8] The perceived need to avoid introducing any changes or errors into the text justified the monopoly of one or two individuals or partnerships over its production, despite complaints that this placed an unreasonable restriction on disseminating, and taking profit from, the Word. Time and again, the King's Printers asserted that monopoly practices were demanded by the costs of maintaining the small company of proof readers required to keep the text of the Bible in order. They argued that any reduction in their privileges would lead to the multiplication of dangerous errors.[9] In spite of the counter example provided by errors in their own productions, including the notorious 'Wicked Bible' (1631) in which the seventh commandment appeared as 'Thou shalt commit adultery', the arguments of the King's Printers were probably right.[10] When opportunities for others to publish Bibles arose with the weakening of monopolies during the 1640s, the resulting volumes to some extent bore out their concerns.[11] Even English Catholic writers, the traditions of whose Church were held by Protestants to have been shattered by the power of the vernacular Bible, seemed to find the lure of a providential reading of the provision of Scripture irresistible. According to the mid-seventeenth-century poet Patrick Cary,

Bible of 1560 to the English Protestant Tradition', *Sixteenth Century Journal*, 12 (1981), 5–18; B. Hall, 'The Genevan Version of the English Bible: Its Aims and Achievements', in W. P. Stephens (ed.), *The Bible, the Reformation and the Church* (Sheffield, 1995), pp. 124–49.

8 See B. J. McMullin, 'The Bible Trade', in *CHBB 4*, pp. 455–73.

9 D. McKitterick, *A History of Cambridge University Press*, vol. 1, *Printing and the Book Trade in Cambridge, 1534–1698* (Cambridge, 1992), pp. 322–3; P. Simpson, *Proof-reading in the Sixteenth, Seventeenth and Eighteenth Centuries* (Oxford, 1970), pp. 178–9.

10 On the 'Wicked Bible', see T. H. Darlow and H. F. Moule, *Historical Catalogue of Printed Editions of the English Bible 1525–1961*, rev. A. S. Herbert (1968), pp. 162–3; for later criticism of the work of the Parliamentary printer, John Field, see W. Kilburne, *Dangerous Errors in Several Late Printed Bibles* (Finsbury, 1659).

11 See BL, MSS Sloane 885, fos. 87r–96v; Sloane 1435, fos. 35–6; Archive of the Stationers' Company, London, Court Book D, fos. 1, 10, 15; Cambridge University Archives, C.U.R. 33.2 (109–110); C.U.R. 33.6 (23–7).

who had been brought up in France and Italy, 'Our *Church* still flourishing w'had seene/ If th' *holy-Writt* had ever beene/ Kept out of *Laymens* reach; But when *'twas English'd*, men halfe-witted,/ Nay, *Woemen* too, would bee permitted/ T'expound all *Texts* and preach . . .'[12]

The ideal that a properly supervised printed text would surpass any rival was embodied in the 1638 Cambridge folio Bible, printed for the University by Thomas Buck (d. 1670) and Roger Daniel. This was considered by many to be the best edition of the English Bible ever produced, improving even on the folio that Buck had published at Cambridge in 1629.[13] For John Worthington (1618–71), who became Master of Jesus College, Cambridge, in 1650, it was 'most exactly and correctly performed'.[14] In general, the products of the Cambridge Press largely escaped the criticisms levelled at other early Stuart Bibles during the 1640s and 1650s. This may in part have been because the principal target for critics remained the monopoly that was held by the King's Printer on the production of cheaper Bibles and Testaments in the smaller formats of octavo or duodecimo.[15] Nevertheless, there are certain features even of the Cambridge folio of 1638 that should give us pause in thinking about the transition of the Bible from script to print in the early modern period.

For the 1638 Cambridge folio, the English translation of the Bible had supposedly been corrected by a group of Cambridge divines, who had also had oversight of the presentation of the text. Yet it was an earlier, printed Bible rather than the manuscripts of the translators that served as a copy text for the future. The manuscript of the Authorised Version remained the property of the King's Printer. It could be sold but it was never shared with others who were entitled to print the Bible and, in any case, it seems to have disappeared before the end of the seventeenth century.[16] When working at their corrections, the editors of the Cambridge folio Bible therefore built on conjectures that they formed from other printed copies of the Authorised Version. Some of the improvements of the Cambridge Bible drew attention not only to the care of the translators in producing a literal version but also to the instability of print and the impossibility of a direct rendering from one language to another. For example, the Cambridge editors were careful to revise the use of italics to indicate words that were not present in the

---

[12] V. Delany (ed.), *The Poems of Patrick Carey* (Oxford, 1978), p. 17.
[13] Darlow and Moule, *Historical Catalogue*, pp. 158, 176; B. J. McMullin, 'The 1629 Cambridge Bible', *Transactions of the Cambridge Bibliographical Society*, 8 (1981–4), 381–97; D. McKitterick, 'Customer, Reader and Book-binder: Buying a Bible in 1630', *The Book Collector*, 40 (1991), 382–406; Kilburne, *Dangerous Errors*, p. 6.
[14] Sheffield University Library, Hartlib Papers, 28/2/77A.   [15] See nn. 11 and 13 above.
[16] McKitterick, *History of Cambridge University Press*, vol. I, pp. 195–9, 214–15, 317.

original Hebrew or Greek, thereby reinforcing a typographical convention deployed to an innovatory extent by the Authorised Version from its first edition in 1611.[17] By the late eighteenth century, tens of thousands of 'errors' in the printed text of the Bible could be traced to those italics alone. Print was in fact a much less certain medium than early modern Protestant commentators would have liked it to be. When the first outbreak of the mania for collecting the earliest products of the printing press was at its height at the end of the seventeenth century, connoisseurs admitted: 'We are much at a loss for [th]e true knowledge of [th]e first impressions of both Testaments and Bibles'.[18]

From the turn of the eighteenth century, William Tyndale's New Testament (1526), through which the process of the Bible's migration from script to print in English had properly begun, and of which 3,000 copies had allegedly been printed, was known in a single copy that lacked its title page.[19] Print, like manuscript, preserved only by multiplication. Its products were vulnerable and the process of multiplication was liable to be fraught with error. This was especially true given the habits of the early modern printing shop. The forms that contained the metal type for the text of the Bible were kept standing continuously to cope with the frequency of reprinting so popular a work.[20] They might be stretched, when an edition in a larger format was needed, and their letters bludgeoned into fresh places by the hammer of the compositor. Moreover, printed books, like manuscripts, might be reticent about their origins or about the authority that underwrote their texts. In 1678, when William Nicolson (1655–1727) visited Amsterdam, which was a major source of cheap, printed English Bibles in the seventeenth century, the scene that he witnessed did not necessarily inspire confidence in the accuracy of products of the press. Calling on the workshop of Widow

---

[17] Earlier English Bibles had also deployed this convention, but the Authorised Version introduced a new regularity in its use: see F. H. A. Scrivener, *The Authorised Edition of the English Bible (1611), its Subsequent Reprints and Modern Representatives* (Cambridge, 1884), pp. 20–2; D. Norton, *A History of the Bible as Literature*, 2 vols. (Cambridge, 1992–3), vol. 1, pp. 162–76 and accompanying plates.

[18] BL, MS Harley 5908, fo. 5v.

[19] *A Catalogue of the Genuine and Entire Collection of Scarce Printed Books, and Curious Manuscripts, of Mr. Joseph Ames, F. R. S.* ([London], 1760), p. 89; Darlow and Moule, *Historical Catalogue*, pp. 1–2, also notes the existence of a second, highly incomplete copy; this must now be corrected by D. Daniell, *Let There be Light. William Tyndale and the Making of the English Bible* (1994), recording the acquisition of the more complete known copy by the BL, and by accounts of the discovery in 1995 of a truly complete and previously unknown copy at the Württembergische Landesbibliothek, Stuttgart. See M. Jannetta, 'Good News from Stuttgart: A Previously Unrecorded Copy of William Tyndale's New Testament Translation', *Reformation*, 2 (1997), 1–5; E. Zwink, 'The Stuttgart copy of the 1526 New Testament in English', *Reformation*, 3 (1998), 29–48; P. Arblaster, G. Juhász, and G. Latré (eds.), *Tyndale's Testament* (Turnhout, 2002), pp. 148–9.

[20] BL, MS Harley 5909, fo. 3r; B. J. McMullin, 'The Bible and Continuous Reprinting in the Early Seventeenth Century', *The Library*, 6th ser., 5 (1983), 256–63.

Schippers (1623/4–99), a Roman Catholic whose presses were overseen by the Jewish printer Joseph Athias (1634/5–1700), Nicolson saw '18 hard at work printing, and 6 or 7 setting letters. They print here many English Bibles of all sizes; upon the title-pages of which they sett – *London printed by R. Barker and the Assigns of John Bill* &c. And they were (whilst I lookt on) printing a small English Bible in Octavo, which they sett, printed by the aforesaid A.D. 1669'.[21] Athias was in fact a highly capable printer and he is thought to have pioneered a form of stereotyping, at first sight ideal for the production of multiple editions of an unchanging text. Nevertheless, he seems mainly to have used movable type for most of the English Bibles that he printed. The false imprints that he employed were a necessary disguise for books that were intended to undercut those printed by the King's Printer in London and to sneak onto the English market despite the legal monopoly on the publication of Bibles in smaller formats.[22] Any significant use of stereotyping, which William Ged (1690–1749) had discovered independently in the 1730s, was strenuously resisted by those who held shares in the English Bible patent into the nineteenth century.[23]

The textual guarantees of a printed copy of the English Bible were thus far from ideal. As Richard Baxter (1615–91) remarked, 'God hath not engaged himself to direct every Printer to the worlds end to do his work without any error'.[24] The claims of copies of the Authorised Version were not perhaps as flimsy as those of some of the biblical texts that circulated at both the top and the bottom ends of the market. For example, a little *History of Genesis* which went through numerous cheap editions in the late seventeenth century and early eighteenth century and which was illustrated with several tired woodcuts, was, although it nowhere advertised the fact, no more than a partial translation from the *Histoire du Vieux et du Nouveau Testament* of Nicolas Fontaine, Sieur du Royaumont (1625–1709).[25] Fontaine's work was extremely popular in late seventeenth-century and early eighteenth-century England and several editions with fine, fresh engravings were also

[21] Queen's College, Oxford, MS 68, entry for 7 August 1678; on this manuscript, see P. G. Hoftijzer, 'A Study Tour into the Low Countries and the German States: William Nicolson's *Iter Hollandicum* and *Iter Germanicum* 1678–9', *Lias*, 15 (1988), 73–128.

[22] I. H. van Eeghen, *De Amsterdamse boekhandel 1680–1725*, 5 vols. (Amsterdam, 1960–78), vol. IV, p. 96–106; Harry Carter and George Buday, 'Stereotyping by Joseph Athias: The Evidence of Nicholas Kis', *Quaerendo*, 5 (1975), 312–20; B. J. McMullin, 'Joseph Athias and the Early History of Stereotyping', *Quaerendo*, 23 (1993), 184–207; Gemeentearchief, Amsterdam, MSS 5075/2229.512; 5075/3205.11.

[23] *Biographical Memoirs of William Ged* (1781); *Report from Select Committee on King's Printers' Patents* (1832), pp. 43, 47, 63–4.

[24] Richard Baxter, *The Saints Everlasting Rest*, 6th edn (1656), p. 211.

[25] [R.H.], *The History of Genesis* (1690); R. B. Bottigheimer, *The Bible for Children from the Age of Gutenberg to the Present* (New Haven, 1996), pp. 43–5.

prepared to accompany English versions of his paraphrases of the text of the Bible. Despite claiming to be prepared by 'Orthodox Divines', most of these did little to distance themselves from those parts of Fontaine's work that most obviously betrayed its origin in Jansenist and Counter-Reformation piety. All of them, for example, endorsed the value of the Church Fathers as interpreters of Scripture.[26] The *History of Genesis*, which was explicitly intended for children to read, also repeated Fontaine's message that knowledge of biblical history was necessary because the Fathers had said it was, not because the Bible should be regarded as the foundation for the teaching of the Church. The dynamics of publishing were therefore by no means always in line with the demands of doctrine.

In the case of the English Bible itself, the relationship between text and translation also remained unsure. The past of the English Bible mattered not only out of antiquarian sympathy. For this was the history of the present Bible itself. With touching reverence for the αὐτόγραφα of early Protestants, the words of William Tyndale (d. 1536) survived in the Authorised Version, which drew heavily on his translation of the New Testament and of the historical books of the Old Testament. The phrases of another sixteenth-century editor, Miles Coverdale (1487/8–1569), whose translations had not been based on a reading of Hebrew or Greek but had drawn instead on early sixteenth-century versions in Latin and especially in German, continued to be found in the metrical Psalms of Thomas Sternhold (d. 1549) and John Hopkins (d. 1570). The tunes of Sternhold, Hopkins, and their imitators in the English exile community at Geneva in the 1550s, also betrayed the influence of Coverdale's own efforts to set the Psalms. Despite widespread criticism, they helped to keep that part of the text of Coverdale's Bible in currency well into the eighteenth century.[27] The success and survival of this version of the metrical Psalms derived to some extent from a monopoly, vested in the Stationers' Company, and parallel to that which the King's Printer held over the Authorised Version. It was also a product of the tendency to bind copies of Sternhold and Hopkins with copies of the Bible, especially those in the quarto or octavo formats

---

[26] Various editions of Fontaine's work were published in English translation from 1688: see S. Tyacke, *London Map-sellers 1660–1720* (Tring, 1978), pp. 54, 84–6, 88, 110–11; S. L. C. Clapp, 'The Subscription Enterprises of John Ogilby and Richard Blome', *Modern Philology*, 30 (1932–3), 365–79. On Fontaine's ideas, see J. Mesnard, 'Le Maistre de Sacy et son secrétaire Fontaine', *Chroniques de Port-Royal*, 33 (1984), 5–18; D. E. Singleton, 'A Study of the Port-Royal *Mémoires*, 1640–1760', D.Phil. thesis, University of Oxford (1990), pp. 237–317.

[27] J. F. Mozley, *Coverdale and his Bibles* (1953), pp. 65–109; R. A. Leaver, *'Goostly Psalmes and Spirituall Songes'. English and Dutch Metrical Psalms from Coverdale to Utenhove 1535–1566* (Oxford, 1991); I. Green, *Print and Protestantism in Early Modern England* (Oxford, 2000), pp. 503–52.

that were often marketed as being suitable for family worship. Putting aside the demands of Protestant convictions about the importance of translation from the original languages, the marketing of such confusing and divergent texts could be justified by the assertion that they preserved the 'last dying Breath' of Protestant martyrs 'with which we shall not part for the sake of a *Hebrew* criticism'.[28]

The Authorised Version and the texts associated with it rested in part on the work of Tyndale and Coverdale, and on editions of the English Bible that had been pasted together from their translations during the late 1530s. Those texts had been subjected to multiple, but usually conservative, revisions which were embodied in further translations published during the sixteenth century – the Great Bible (1539), the Geneva Bible (1560), and the Bishops' Bible (1568).[29] Beloved as it was by the most literal of readers of scripture, the Geneva Bible contained much commentary and additional matter that was not in the autograph of the sacred penmen of Scripture.[30] The Authorised Version, which can perhaps claim to be the most successful book written by committee, was also a compilation, created by groups sitting at Westminster, Oxford, and Cambridge.[31] Its translators paid practically no attention to manuscript evidence for the text of the Bible, which was understandable enough given the resources that were available to them, even in the new library that Thomas Bodley (1545–1613) had founded in 1602. Bodley was reluctant to release his librarian, Thomas James (c.1573–1629), in order to assist the translators and was initially opposed to allowing them to borrow any of his books. Moreover, although he was an able Hebraist and eager to make arrangements to supply his library with works of oriental learning, Bodley's initial gifts revealed greater interest in the circulation and paraphrasing of the Latin Bible in the early English Church than in the provision of Hebrew or Greek sources for a modern translation of Scripture into English.[32] In this respect, the concerns of Bodley and James were similar to those that had animated the manuscript collecting

[28] [John Johnson], *Holy David and his Old English Translators Clear'd* (1706), sig. A4r.
[29] C. C. Butterworth, *The Literary Lineage of the King James Bible* (Philadelphia, 1941).
[30] M. Jensen, '"Simply" Reading the Geneva Bible: The Geneva Bible and its Readers', *Literature and Theology*, 9 (1995), 30–45.
[31] On the composition of the Authorised Version, see W. Allen (ed.), *Translating for King James* (Nashville, 1969); W. Allen (ed), *Translating the New Testament Epistles 1604–1611* (Ann Arbor, 1977); W. S. Allen and E. C. Jacobs, *The Coming of the King James Gospels* (Fayetteville, 1995); E. C. Jacobs, 'Two Stages of Old Testament Translation for the King James Bible', *The Library*, 6th ser., 11 (1980), 16–39; E. C. Jacobs, 'King James's Translators: The Bishops' Bible New Testament Revised', *The Library*, 6th ser., 14 (1992), 100–26; D. Norton, 'John Bois's Notes on the Revision of the King James Bible New Testament: A New Manuscript', *The Library*, 6th ser., 18 (1996), 328–46.
[32] G. W. Wheeler (ed.), *Letters of Sir Thomas Bodley to Thomas James* (Oxford, 1926), pp. 105–16, 147–8, 190–1; D. Rogers, *The Bodleian Library and its Treasures 1320–1700* (Henley-on-Thames, 1991), pp. 30–3, 38–9.

of Archbishop Parker (1504–75). They reflected contemporary judgements of the value to anti-Catholic polemic of establishing the antiquity of a vernacular English Bible and Church, rather than the scholarly criteria of the humanist study of the sources for the text of Scripture.[33]

Rather than seeking out ancient manuscripts, the compilers of the Authorised Version relied on earlier English translations, notably Tyndale and the Bishop's Bible, and the fruits of Continental textual scholarship. Their attitude to the authority of printed texts can be seen in their approach to the learning of the leading Genevan theologian, Theodore Beza (1519–1605). The Authorised Version was even more reliant on Beza's work than the revised version of the English Geneva Bible (1576) had been. Perhaps that should be unsurprising since the compilers of the Authorised Version gained from access to the later editions of Beza's Greek New Testament (1582, and more particularly 1589 and 1598). Only in these later editions did the Genevan scholar make any use of the manuscript sources that were available to him, in particular two Greek and Latin codices of the New Testament, Codex Claromontanus and Codex Bezae. In December 1581, Beza donated the latter to the University of Cambridge.[34] In what seems a touching demonstration of faith in the readings of a favoured editor, rather than a reflection of the ease of communication in the early seventeenth century, the Oxford translators were charged with the preparation of the text of the Gospels for the Authorised Version and those working at Westminster oversaw the text of the Epistles.

Although the antiquity of Codex Bezae and other manuscripts was widely attested (and often exaggerated), they were not felt to be suitable starting points for a translation. This was an understandable position, given the difficulties involved in mediating between the differing readings of particular manuscripts, and in the light of the pioneering work that had already been done to establish the text of the New Testament, in particular, by Erasmus and Robert Estienne. In their efforts to interpret the received text of the

---

[33] J. Strype, *The Life and Acts of Matthew Parker* (1711), pp. 38–9, 399–403; M. McKisack, *Medieval History in the Tudor Age* (Oxford, 1971), pp. 26–49; C. de Hamel, *The Parker Library* (Cambridge, 2000), pp. 8–35, 48.

[34] For the use of early Christian manuscript evidence in establishing the text of the New Testament in the sixteenth century, see in general B. Hall, 'Biblical Scholarship: Editions and Commentaries', in S. L. Greenslade (ed.), *The Cambridge History of the Bible*, vol. III, *The West from the Reformation to the Present Day* (Cambridge, 1963), pp. 38–93, and B. M. Metzger, *The Text of the New Testament* (Oxford, 1964), pp. 95–106. The relationship between Beza's work and the Authorised Version is best described by I. D. Backus, 'Influence of Theodore Beza on the English New Testament', D.Phil. thesis, University of Oxford (1975). On Codex Bezae itself, see F. H. Scrivener (ed.), *Bezae codex Cantabrigiensis* (Cambridge, 1864); D. C. Parker, *Codex Bezae: An early Christian Manuscript and its Text* (Cambridge, 1992), esp. pp. 281–4; D. C. Parker and C.-B. Amphoux (eds.), *Codex Bezae* (Leiden, 1996).

Bible, seventeenth-century English translators therefore relied on earlier translations, notably the Vulgate and the Septuagint, which were held to be particularly valuable since they had themselves been made from the original languages.[35] They deployed the fruits of their own patristic scholarship and of the collaborative study of surviving manuscripts that it entailed, making frequent reference, for example, to the biblical quotations in the works of St John Chrysostom.[36] They also depended heavily on contemporary translations and editions, including existing English translations, above all the Bishops' Bible. Their reach in this sphere embraced the work of the exiled Catholic translator of the Rheims version of the Vulgate New Testament. Through the achievements of the editors of the great European polyglot Bibles, published at the instigation of Cardinal Ximenes (1436–1517) at Alcala and by Christopher Plantin (c.1520–89) at Antwerp, and the efforts of early sixteenth-century Hebraists like Sebastian Münster (1488–1552) or Santi Pagnini (1470–1536), there was a broad sense of contentment that printed Latin versions of the texts of the Old Testament also sufficed in general for accurate translation. This position was maintained despite the extent of Greek and Hebrew learning among the revisers of the Authorised Version. Their respect for the work of earlier translators into English reflected their satisfaction with the fruits of Continental humanist scholarship, as well as their endorsement of Tyndale's conviction that 'the greke tonge agreeth moare with the english then with the latyne. And the propirties of the hebrue tonge agreth a thousande tymes moare with the english then with the latyne.'[37] Yet, as others recognised, 'translations of scripture as such cannot in exactnesse of speech be called [th]e word of God'.[38]

---

[35] See n. 31 above. Respect for earlier translations is expressed in the translators' preface to the Authorised Version (1611). For further discussion, see M. Kitagaki, *Principles and Problems of Translation in Seventeenth-Century England* (Kyoto, 1981), pp. 45–102.

[36] Between 1610 and 1613, Sir Henry Savile (1549–1622), who assisted in the editing of the Authorised Version, published a folio edition in eight volumes of the works of Chrysostom, printed at the press that he had established at Eton College. For the extent of contemporary patristic learning, see M. Vessey, 'English Translations of the Latin Fathers, 1517–1611', and J.-L. Quantin, 'The Fathers in Seventeenth Century Anglican Theology', both in I. Backus (ed.), *The Reception of the Church Fathers in the West*, 2 vols. (Leiden, 1997), vol. II, pp. 775–835, 987–1008; N. R. Ker, 'Thomas James' Collation of Gregory, Cyprian, and Ambrose', *Bodleian Library Record*, 4 (1952–3), 16–30; S. van der Woude, 'Sir Henry Savile's Chrysostomus Edition in the Netherlands', in S. van der Woude (ed.), *Studia bibliographica in honorem Herman de la Fontaine Verwey* (Amsterdam, 1966), pp. 437–47; Thomas James, *Concordantiae sanctorum patrum hoc est vera et pia libri canticorum per patres universos tam Graecos quam Latinos expositis* (Oxford, 1607).

[37] William Tyndale, *The Obedie[n]ce of a Christen Man and how Christe[n] Rulers Ought to Governe* ([Antwerp], 1528), fo. 15v.

[38] Harris Manchester College, Oxford, MS Miscellaneous Notebook 11 (Robert Brown's 'Scripture Treasurie', 1664), p. 270.

The most significant cause of criticism of the Authorised Version in the seventeenth century, especially during the 1640s and 1650s, was this failure to return '*ad fontes*'. This had been the original, piqued observation of the Cambridge scholar and Hebraist, Hugh Broughton (1549–1612), who had not been included among the members of the committees to revise the translation.[39] It provided an argument, in the eyes of some of the godly, for preferring the Geneva Bible, even though that translation in reality was no closer in its relationship to the original sources. Dissatisfaction with the Authorised Version led parliament to appoint a committee to revise the English Bible. The political and religious uncertainties of the mid-1650s, however, quickly brought an end to its activities.[40] Similar concerns nevertheless allowed critics like John Owen to assert the continuing primacy of the Hebrew Bible and Greek New Testament for the purposes of private study and devotion, and thus to suggest that there might be a hierarchy among believers, determined by linguistic aptitude.[41] In the case of the New Testament, faith in the authority of the printed Greek text was at least supported by a genuine confidence in the work of its humanist editors. Despite the doubts that were expressed about particular verses, notably the reading of 1 John 5:7 that appeared to give scriptural support to the doctrine of the Trinity, there could be certainty that Erasmus and other editors had devoted themselves to the search for the original and true text of the New Testament.[42] Seventeenth-century scholars, above all John Mill (1645–1707), took up the quest for variant manuscript readings that had been begun by sixteenth-century editors. Although some critics tried to use their findings to undermine the received text, for most readers the comparatively small number of significant variants identified by Mill and others represented further proof of its reliability.[43]

In spite of the achievements of sixteenth-century scholarship, there was, however, far less consensus in the seventeenth century about the text of the Old Testament. The Hebrew Bibles published by Daniel Bomberg

---

[39] Norton, *History of the Bible*, vol. 1, pp. 139–44, 159–61; Hugh Broughton, *An Epistle to the Learned Nobilitie of England* (Middelburg, 1597); Hugh Broughton, *A Censure of the Late Translation for our Churches* ([Middelburg, 1611]).

[40] *CSP Dom. 1652–3*, pp. 73–4; cf. Robert Gell, *An Essay toward the Amendment of the Last English Translation of the Bible* (1659).

[41] E.g, John Goodwin, *The Divine Authority of the Scriptures Asserted* (1648), pp. 5–7.

[42] See Hall, 'Biblical Scholarship'; J. H. Bentley, *Humanists and Holy Writ: New Testament Scholarship in the Renaissance* (Princeton, 1983), pp. 112–219; J. M. Levine, *The Autonomy of History* (Chicago, 1999), pp. 25–51; A. Clarke, *Observations on the Text of the Three Divine Witnesses* (Manchester, 1805).

[43] J. Mill (ed.), *Novum Testamentum cum lectionibus variantibus* (Oxford, 1707); A. Fox, *John Mill and Richard Bentley* (Oxford, 1954); G. D. Kilpatrick, 'Codex Bezae and Mill', *Journal of Theological Studies*, NS, 6 (1955), 235–8.

in 1517 and 1524–5 formed the basis for the study of the Old Testament in the light of rabbinic commentary. They presented the clearest versions of the text, with vowel points and with the full repertory of distinctions that the Masoretes had made between the spelling and the pronunciation of particular words.[44] Yet the contemporary work of Elias Levita (c.1468–1549) had already sown doubts about the antiquity of the Hebrew vowel points and hence of the Masoretic text itself. This was, however, the text that was most often used by those Christians who had learned Hebrew, even when they denounced rabbinical teaching and scholarship.[45] The greatest early seventeenth-century Protestant Hebraist, Johannes Buxtorf (1564–1629), defended it, as did his son, also Johannes (1599–1664), and those, including John Owen, whom the Buxtorfs influenced. Although few scholars argued that the vowel points had a divine original, many agreed with Buxtorf in dating them back to 'the Great Synagogue', over which the scribe Ezra had presided. This meeting had supposedly reformed Hebrew script, giving it its modern character. Most Christian Hebraists recognised that, without the use of vowel points, the difficulties posed by variant readings in different copies of the same text increased.[46] Nevertheless, this was a dangerous position to reach, especially given the strength of Protestant polemic in favour of a return to the original text of the Bible.

John Owen taxed Brian Walton and the other contributors to the mid-seventeenth-century London Polyglot because, like the Catholic Church, they had 'taken from [the Bible's] fulnesse and perfection, its sufficiency and excellency, by their Massora their, *orall law* or *verbum* ἄγραφον [unwritten Word], their unknowne, endlesse, bottomlesse, boundlesse treasure of traditions'. Owen rejected the application of rabbinic and other post-Christian Jewish commentary to Scripture, but defended the integrity of the Hebrew text of the Bible with vowel points. His principal concern was that the

---

[44] T. H. Darlow and H. F. Moule, *Historical Catalogue of the Printed Editions of Holy Scripture in the Library of the British and Foreign Bible Society*, 2 vols. in 4 (1903–11), vol. II, p. 704; I. N. Rashkow, 'Hebrew Bible Translation and the Fear of Judaisation', *Sixteenth Century Journal*, 21 (1990), 217–33.

[45] G. E. Weil, *Élie Lévita. Humaniste et Massorete (1469–1549)* (Leiden, 1963); J. Friedman, *The Most Ancient Testimony: Sixteenth-century Christian-Hebraica in the Age of Renaissance Nostalgia* (Athens, Ohio, 1983); R. A. Muller, 'The Debate over the Vowel Points and the Crisis in Orthodox Hermeneutics', *Journal of Medieval and Renaissance Studies*, 10 (1980), 53–72; M. Goshen-Gottstein, 'Foundations of Biblical Philology in the Seventeenth Century. Christian and Jewish Dimensions', in I. Twersky and B. Septimus (eds.), *Jewish Thought in the Seventeenth Century* (Cambridge, MA, 1987), pp. 77–94.

[46] Johannes Buxtorf, *Tiberias sive commentarius Masorethicus* (Basel, 1620); S. G. Burnett, *From Christian Hebraism to Jewish Studies: Johannes Buxtorf (1564–1629) and Hebrew Learning in the Seventeenth Century* (Leiden, 1996); F. E. Manuel, *The Broken Staff: Judaism through Christian Eyes* (Cambridge, MA, 1992), pp. 82–92; G. Schnedermann, *Die Controverse des Ludovicus Capellus mit den Buxtorfen über das Alter der Hebräischen Punctation* (Leipzig, 1879); A. Grafton, *Joseph Scaliger: A Study in the History of Classical Scholarship*, 2 vols. (Oxford, 1983–93), vol. II, pp. 732–7.

evidence of translations and paraphrases might displace that of a text that he supposed to be original. He recognised this as a danger inherent to all polyglot editions of Scripture, and to translations based on them or on the unreliable testimony of individual manuscripts, such as Codex Bezae.[47] The difficulty that Owen faced, however, was that the tradition of the preservation of the originals of Scripture, to which he subscribed, could be undermined by doubts about the reliability of the Jews as guardians of the text of the Bible, with which he was also in sympathy. For many commentators, the supposed instability of the transmission of the Hebrew text among the Jews weakened its authority compared with that of the earliest translations of the Old Testament: 'and 'tis thought that the *Hebrew*, tho' not so often transcrib'd as the *Septuag[int]* hath suffer'd by the perfidiousness of the Jews'.[48] Regardless of theological persuasion, many English churchmen thus chose to look elsewhere for evidence that would help to establish the authentic text of the Old Testament.

In the debates that had taken place since the time of the Reformation, Catholic critics had often argued that the instability of the manuscript tradition of the Bible indicated that doctrinal certainty could only be derived from ecclesiastical continuity. The scholarship of the Continental polyglot Bibles, in particular the Paris Polyglot (1629–45), seemed to cast doubt on the authority and authenticity of Scripture by drawing attention to the multiplicity of variant readings and the diversity of meaning to be found in ancient translations. These facts could be used to support the decision of the Council of Trent to recognise the Vulgate as the sole, authoritative text of Scripture.[49] The seventeenth-century English churchmen who aspired to emulate Continental scholarship naturally did not share such conclusions. Instead, they developed the view that a polyglot Bible might support the authority of Scripture by demonstrating the relative similarity of the various surviving texts and that it might provide certain ground from which to revise the English translation of the Bible. As early as 1607, William Eyre had called for a multi-lingual study of Scripture, to be accompanied by prolegomena that would set out the nature of the differences between variant

---

47 Owen, *Of the Divine . . . Light, and Power of the Scriptures*, sig. *3r (for quotation), also see esp. sigs. A1–8v, pp. 177–201.
48 CUL, MS Add. 7113, n. 20 (John Jackson to Samuel Clarke, 31 December 1715).
49 F. J. Crehan, SJ, 'The Bible in the Roman Catholic Church from Trent to the Present day', in Greenslade (ed.), *Cambridge History of the Bible*, vol. III, pp. 199–237, esp. pp. 199–222; P. N. Miller, 'Les origines de la Bible polyglotte de Paris: *Philologia sacra*, Contre-Réforme, et raison d'état', *XVIIe siècle*, 49 (1997), 57–66; G. Tavard, *La tradition au XVIIe siècle en France et en Angleterre* (Paris, 1969); G. Fragnito, *La Bibbia al rogo. La censura ecclesiastica e i volgarizzamenti della Scrittura (1471–1605)* (Bologna, 1997).

texts and readings. Eyre was a Fellow of Emmanuel College, Cambridge, and a correspondent of James Ussher (1581–1656), with whom he shared drafts of the Cambridge sections of the translations for the Authorised Version. Ussher was one of the few early seventeenth-century scholars to take seriously the possibility of making an extensive collation of manuscript variants of the Bible.[50] Fifty years later, with the extensive support of Ussher and the protection of the Hebraist and MP, John Selden (1584–1654), Brian Walton brought Eyre's project into being with the publication of the prolegomena that completed the London Polyglot, the work that aroused the ire of John Owen.[51] Walton attacked those who believed that variant readings threatened the purity or authority of Scripture. He argued that 'the *Original Texts* are not corrupted either by *Jews, Christians* or others' because 'the reading of the Text was never arbitrary' and errors or disagreements were 'casuall mistakes of transcribers, yet in matters of no moment'.[52] The existence of variant readings and of differences in the ancient translations of the Bible was no more significant than similar blemishes in the transmission of texts of classical history or literature. It was to be expected, given the age of the texts and the complexity of their compilation.[53] Variants indeed proved that God's providence had been active in preserving the essential truths of Scripture. Similarly, the pit-falls that they presented to the unlearned demonstrated the necessity of a clerical training as the underpinning for acts of interpretation. Walton conceded, however, that the existence of variants between versions of Scripture did not necessarily justify the conjectural reconstruction of the text of the Bible that some had advocated and that might be carried out in editions of the works of classical authors.[54]

Walton was no stranger to the debate over clerical authority in seventeenth-century England. His views on clerical conformity, the

[50] Richard Parr (ed.), *The Life of the most Reverend Father in God, James Usher, late Lord Arch-Bishop of Armagh, Primate and Metropolitan of all Ireland. With a Collection of Three Hundred Letters* (1686), pp. 2–11 (*Letters*); James Ussher and William Eyre, *De textus Hebraici Veteris Testamenti variantibus lectionibus ad Ludovicum Cappelum epistola* (1652); E. Boran, 'An Early Friendship Network of James Ussher, Archbishop of Armagh, 1626–1656', in H. Robinson-Hammerstein (ed.), *European Universities in the Age of Reformation and Counter Reformation* (Dublin, 1998), pp. 116–34; Bodl. Lib., MS Rawlinson C 849, fos. 262–3 (Eyre to Ussher, Dec. 1608).

[51] The clearest narratives of the preparation and publication of the London Polyglot remain A. Clarke, *A Succinct Account of Polyglot Bibles* (Liverpool, 1802); H. J. Todd, *Memoirs of the Life and Writings of the Right Rev. Brian Walton, DD*, 2 vols. (1821), I, G. J. Toomer, *Eastern Wisedome and Learning: The Study of Arabic in Seventeenth-Century England* (Oxford, 1996), pp. 202–10, provides a succinct version of the story, as does N. Barker, 'The Polyglot Bible', in *CHBB 4*, pp. 648–51.

[52] Walton, *Considerator Considered*, pp. 14, 11.

[53] See P. N. Miller, 'The "Antiquarianization" of Biblical Scholarship and the London Polyglot Bible (1653–57)', *Journal of the History of Ideas*, 62 (2001), 463–82.

[54] Walton, *Considerator Considered*, pp. 95–7. Although Owen's criticisms might suggest the opposite, Walton in fact remained sympathetic to most of the conclusions of the younger Buxtorf, see Öffentliche Bibliothek der Universität Basel, MS G I 62, fos. 4–10.

collection of tithe, and the promotion of the beauty of holiness had led to attacks in both London and Colchester during 1641, and he was later deprived of his livings at St Martin Orgar and at Sandon, Essex.[55] At the end of the 1650s, he remembered the foolishness of 'some *Citizens*, yea women in *London*, who having learned to read *Hebrew*, were so conceited of themselves, that they have despised the ablest *Divines* about the *City*, and have almost doubted of the salvation of all persons that could not read *Hebrew*'.[56] For Walton, the Hebrew text of the Old Testament was not the sole embodiment of the authority of Scripture. This rested instead in the combined testimony of all the versions of the Bible that had survived since antiquity. Taken together, these allowed the learned commentator to consider the true meaning of the text and to prepare suitable interpretations and translations for the people. One effect of Walton's position was to bolster the status of the clergy as interpreters of Scripture. Later commentators advanced clerical claims even further and in surprising ways. Thus, Jeremy Collier (1650–1726) was able to praise the fifteenth-century archbishop of Canterbury, Thomas Arundel, for prohibiting private translations of the Bible and to attack the abortive attempt made to improve and revise the Authorised Version in 1653.[57]

If the London Polyglot in the end boosted the status of the Authorised Version, it did so despite casting some doubt on the authority of the received texts of Scripture. The work itself acquired an extraordinary reputation among English scholars. That reputation rested in part on its achievements as a monument of printed learning and culture. Yet it also depended on the success with which the Polyglot established the credentials of a particular manuscript. In compiling the London Polyglot, Walton had sought aid from across Europe to add further manuscripts to the few whose readings, like those of Codex Bezae or Codex Claromontanus, were already well known. He also had access to numerous eastern manuscripts, collected by Archbishop Laud and his agents, notably John Greaves (1602–52), in the 1630s.[58] Walton's work continued a process of European collaboration that had earlier sent the Cottonian Genesis, which Ussher considered the most ancient manuscript in the world, on a journey from London to Paris

---

[55] Todd, *Memoirs*, vol. 1, pp. 7–26; see also K. Lindley, *Popular Politics and Religion in Civil War London* (Aldershot, 1997), p. 53; J. Walter, *Understanding Popular Violence in the English Revolution: The Colchester Plunderers*. (Cambridge, 1999), p. 186; D. Como and P. Lake, 'Puritans, Antinomians and Laudians in Caroline London: The Strange Case of Peter Shaw and its Contexts', *JEH*, 50 (1999), 684–715.

[56] Walton, *Considerator Considered*, pp. 30–1.

[57] J. Collier, *An Ecclesiastical History of Great Britain*, 2 vols. (1708–14), vol. 1, p. 635; vol. 11, p. 869.

[58] For the activities of Greaves and other collectors in the Middle East, see Toomer, *Eastern Wisedome and Learning*, pp. 108–11, 127–46.

where it remained for five years for collation and study by the Jesuit scholar, Fronto du Duc.[59] Walton was also perpetuating the idea, enunciated by the translators of the Authorised Version, that ancient vernacular traditions of Scripture might embody truths that had otherwise been lost. This was a view that gained strength in opposition to post-Tridentine Catholic defences of the Vulgate. The early eighteenth-century author of 'An essay upon the English translation of the Bible', for example, praised the Anglo-Saxon Gospels in part because they were 'done from the ancient Vulgar before it was revised by St Jerome'.[60]

The text that most obviously testified to an alternative biblical tradition, independent of the dubious attentions of Jews and Catholics, was the Septuagint or Greek Old Testament. This survived in a number of manuscripts that were known to Walton and his contemporaries, including Codex Vaticanus, a version of which was published in England by the Socinian John Biddle (1615–62) in 1653.[61] Distaste for the association thus created between anti-Trinitarianism and the Septuagint explained some of the hostile reception that later greeted Walton's work. The London Polyglot, however, revised the text that Catholics and heretics had presented and attempted to correct the readings of Codex Vaticanus against those of another manuscript, Codex Alexandrinus. Tradition ascribed this manuscript to the hand of the martyred Thecla and dated it to shortly after the great orthodox Council of Nice (325), which had established the doctrine of the Trinity.[62] Codex Alexandrinus had been given to James I by Cyril Lucaris (1572–1638), Patriarch of Constantinople. The eventual arrival of the manuscript in England in 1628 sparked a flurry of interest in the possibility of locating similar texts on Mount Athos, where Lucaris was supposed by some to have found Codex Alexandrinus.[63] It also generated

---

[59] See K. Sharpe, *Sir Robert Cotton 1586–1631: History and Politics in Early Modern England* (Oxford, 1979), pp. 96–7; Ussher's estimation of the manuscript is reported by Walton, *Considerator Considered*, p. 141; see also Bodl. Lib., MS Rawlinson D 1290, fo. 98r. After 1629, the Cottonian Genesis was lent to Thomas Howard, Earl of Arundel, from whose widow it was later recovered: see Colin Tite, '"Lost or Stolen or Strayed": A Survey of Manuscripts Formerly in the Cotton Library', in C. J. Wright (ed.), *Sir Robert Cotton as Collector* (1997), pp. 262–306, esp. p. 271.

[60] 'An Essay upon the English Translation of the Bible', *Bibliotheca literaria*, 4 (1723), 1–23.

[61] [John Biddle (ed.)], *Vetus Testamentum Graecum ex versione Septuaginta interpretum, juxta exemplar Vaticanum Romae editum* (1653).

[62] On Codex Alexandrinus (now BL, MSS Royal I D.v–viii), see E. Maunde Thompson (ed.), *Facsimile of the Codex Alexandrinus*, 4 vols. (1879–83); T. S. Pattie, 'The Creation of the Great Codices', in J. L. Sharpe III and K. van Kampen (eds.), *The Bible as Book: The Manuscript Tradition* (1998), pp. 61–72; T. C. Skeat, 'The Provenance of the Codex Alexandrinus', *Journal of Theological Studies*, NS, 6 (1955), 233–5.

[63] Others assumed that Lucaris had brought Codex Alexandrinus with him from Alexandria, where he had been Bishop until 1621. See Thomas Smith, *Collectanea de Cyrillo Lucario, Patriarcha*

the belief that this was 'the true Septuagint, or at least nearest to the true Septuagint of any now extant'.[64] The work of Patrick Young (1584–1652), the Royal Librarian, encouraged the Westminster Assembly to consider an edition of the Septuagint based on Codex Alexandrinus. It introduced the possibility of recovering for the canon of the New Testament the Clementine Epistles, whose text formed part of the manuscript.[65] Nothing came of these schemes, however, and there were scholars, including Ussher, who recognised that neither Codex Alexandrinus nor Codex Vaticanus represented a pure copy of a Greek translation of the pre-Masoretic Hebrew text.[66] Nevertheless Codex Alexandrinus provided a powerful tool with which to assert the antiquity of the tradition of vernacular translation of Scripture and a means to circumvent doubts about the transmission of the Old Testament. Its authority was confirmed by Walton's comments about its antiquity and reliability in the prolegomena to the London Polyglot.[67]

In 1731, flames consumed Ashburnham House and with it much of the Cottonian Library, including the manuscript of Genesis that Ussher had so admired. The royal librarian, Richard Bentley (1662–1742), strode down the burning staircase in his nightclothes clutching Codex Alexandrinus to his breast.[68] The readings provided by Codex Alexandrinus, which Bentley was collating, offered the possibility of reaching beyond the received text of the Bible and fulfilling the Protestant dream of direct access to the inspired word of God. The status of this manuscript thus went some way towards bridging the gap between the attitudes of those like Owen, who defended the received text of the Bible, and those like Walton, who had argued for the revision of Scripture based on a study of surviving versions and manuscripts. Moreover, in the hands of Bentley or of Johann Ernst Grabe

Constantinopolitano (1707); G. A. Hadjiantoniou, *Protestant Patriarch: The Life of Cyril Lucaris (1572–1638), Patriarch of Constantinople* (Richmond, VA, 1961); M. Strachan, *Sir Thomas Roe 1581–1644: A Life* (Salisbury, 1989), pp. 172, 175; S. Runciman, *The Great Church in Captivity* (Cambridge, 1968), pp. 259–88; and esp. H. Trevor-Roper, *From Counter-Reformation to Glorious Revolution* (1992), pp. 83–111, which corrects many of the errors to be found in earlier accounts.

[64] J. Kemke (ed.), *Patricius Junius (Patrick Young) Bibliothekar der Könige Jacob 1. und Carl 1. von England* (Leipzig, 1898), pp. 79–80 (Mr Glen to Young, 23 May 1636); for the identity of Glen, see N. Malcolm (ed.), *The Correspondence of Thomas Hobbes*, 2 vols. (Oxford, 1994), vol. II, p. 837.

[65] Kemke (ed.), *Patricius Junius*, pp. xxiii–iv; cf. *CSP Dom. 1651–2*, pp. 421–2.

[66] Ussher and Eyre, *De textus Hebraici Veteris Testamenti*; James Ussher, *Historia dogmatica controversiae inter orthodoxos & pontificios de scripturis et sacris vernaculis*, ed. Henry Wharton (1690), pp. 316–18.

[67] Brian Walton (ed.), *Biblia sacra polyglotta*, 6 vols. (1653–7), vol. I, fo. 65v.

[68] A. Prescott, '"Their Miserable State of Cremation": The Restoration of the Cotton Library', in Wright (ed.), *Sir Robert Cotton as Collector*, pp. 391–454; Bentley's collations from the Cottonian Genesis survive, see Trinity College, Cambridge, MS B.17.20, fos. 89–92.

(1666–1711), it helped to generate a new burst of textual scholarship that promised to replace the work of sixteenth-century editors.[69]

For scholars, the London Polyglot helped to demonstrate the shortcomings of editions and translations of Scripture. For ordinary churchmen, however, it provided fresh justification for the provision of the Bible in the vernacular and for the authority of the Authorised Version. In this curious way, the enthronement of manuscript traditions could contribute to the vitality of a particular version of the printed Bible. Antiquity endorsed the decisions that had been made by the translators of the Authorised Version, both to present Scripture in the vernacular and to follow the testimony of ancient translations of the Bible. The doctrinal foundations of English Protestantism came to rest more and more openly on tradition partly because of the construction of intellectual lineages such as this. Even moderate Presbyterians, like Baxter, accepted that 'the most Learned Criticks know the true signification of any one word of the Hebrew or Greek (in Scripture or any other book) yea Latine or English, or any language, but only by Tradition and Humane Faith'.[70] The longevity of the Authorised Version can be explained in part by the commercial interests of its printers, but it was also the product of changing attitudes to the sources of Scripture. Scholarly discoveries multiplied the difficulty of establishing a definitive text, but at the same time they gave support to the principle of vernacular translations underpinned by the authority of national Churches. The idea of revising the English Bible did not go away during the eighteenth century, but it seemed a less pressing concern for many orthodox commentators than it had during the middle years of the seventeenth century. Bemused visitors to England commented on this change: 'they all agree that their Bible is full of hard terms which have passed out of use; however in this country which is full of capable critics, and where there is so great a liberty of writing, there can yet be found no-one since the reformation who might produce a new version of the Bible or the New Testament'.[71] English authors, by contrast, endorsed the view that 'the *English Translation* of the Bible is the best Translation in the world'.[72]

[69] Christ Church, Oxford, MS Wake Letters 20, fos. 76r–7v (Bentley to William Wake, 15 April 1716); Trinity College, Cambridge, MS B.17.20., fos. 148–9; Johann Ernst Grabe *et al.* (eds.), *Septuaginta interpretum*, 4 vols. (Oxford, 1707–20); see also the praise for Codex Alexandrinus of the great librarian, Humfrey Wanley, CUL, MS Mm. 50, fos. 293–7 (Wanley to John Covel, 24 January 1716).
[70] Baxter, *The Saints Everlasting Rest*, sig. R2r–v.
[71] Georges Louis Le Sage, *Remarques sur l'Angleterre faites par un voyageur, dans les années 1710 & 1711* (Amsterdam, 1715), p. 172, my translation.
[72] John Lewis, *A Complete History of the Several Translations of the Holy Bible, and New Testament, into English*, 2nd edn (1739), pp. 353–4. Lewis was quoting John Selden, *Table-talk*, ed. Edward Arber (1869 [1st edn, 1689]), p. 20.

The actions and decisions of seventeenth-century scholars and printers helped to generate and perpetuate a conservative attitude to the revision of the English Bible. Reverence for traditions embodied in print to a large extent displaced whatever public concern there might have been for the ideal of a return to the original sources, although particular manuscripts might be invoked to demonstrate the intellectual or doctrinal validity of maintaining the status quo. Nevertheless there was a painful awareness among scholars and critics of the danger of creating and perpetuating errors through various kinds of carelessness that might be associated with the processes of print. Thus, printed books seemed to suffer from many of the failings of manuscripts and, almost paradoxically, manuscripts and their histories retained an ability to challenge and undermine, as well as to uphold, traditions that were supported by print.[73] The experience of seventeenth-century English editors and translators suggested that providence might have a use for institutions and traditions, as well as for particular forms of the written word.

---

[73] Many critics of orthodox religion, including Thomas Hobbes, Isaac Newton, and John Toland, were well aware of this. See, for example, N. Malcolm, *Aspects of Hobbes* (Oxford, 2002), pp. 383–431; J. A. I. Champion, '"Acceptable to Inquisitive Men": Some Simonian Contexts for Newton's Biblical Criticism, 1680–1692', in J. E. Force and R. H. Popkin (eds.), *Newton and Religion* (Dordrecht, 1999), pp. 77–96; John Toland, *Nazarenus*, ed. Justin Champion (Oxford, 1999).

PART III

Script, print and speech

8

The functions of script in the speech community of a late medieval town,

c.1300–1550

Andrew Butcher

I

The cultural achievement of medieval clerks, writing what are now called urban records, has been widely unappreciated. A positivistic scrutiny of their writings for particular recorded evidences has been undertaken at the expense of a consideration of their significance as cultural artefacts and of their producers as cultural mediators and creators. As a result, a retrospectively determined perception of origin, function, and dynamics has tended to limit the historical understanding of medieval and post-medieval urban society. These writings, however, deserve closer imaginative consideration, an investigation of contemporary individual and collective practice which explores the roles and functions of writings within whatever constitutes the urban community. Such an investigation might give full value to social particularity and identity and to the contribution of the writings to the community's processes of self-replication and transformation.

The kinds of these writings considered here are not personal. They are intended rather to express the community to and for itself, but they do incorporate personal utterances and are frequently derived from them, being constituted often of a selected and edited collection of personal statements. Such texts acknowledge, moreover, the social force of these statements, privileging their testimony, accommodating them linguistically, recording their content for future consultation, recognising their political and moral significance. Self-consciously intertextual, they refer to other personal statements and other records of such statements, the 'narrationes' of court depositions, the accumulated memoranda of personal and collective legal and administrative submissions. Far from being expressive only of a single domain of urban government, a narrowly defined genre of legal, administrative, or financial writing, they are the skilled product of writers who recognise the importance of the personal and the oral in their compositions, and who are intent on the commemorative description of significant action taken at all levels of political, legal, and administrative production.

Reading the writings of the medieval town clerks in a modern archive office, it is easy to imagine them at work as I work, directly generating the script on the page. The text I am reading, however, is at least as far removed from its many processes of production as is this text from the notes I have taken, involving at least as many literate and oral stages in its production as this text. It is easy to fall foul of a kind of reductive fallacy in relation to the scribes' work, and to forget the complexity of the productive process and the socially embedded nature of their textual production. It is easy also to ignore the textually enmeshed character of the writings, the abundant internal reference to direct and indirect evidence of texts and utterances which no longer survive, destroyed perhaps in the accidental processes of time or in the necessary processes of transformation and final construction.

To insist on the local and particular nature of these writings is not to suggest that we neglect to try to understand the more general forces at work in the generation of script and record. It must, of course, be acknowledged that within late medieval English urban society, for example, and within late medieval European society generally, there are similarities of practice which make it possible to talk of a culture of textual production. A town such as Hythe, which is the subject of this study, is part of a federation of towns, the Cinque Ports, which all have similar practices, and is intimately connected with local, regional, and national networks of communities, all of which recognise the nature of its production and share many of its practices, methods, and understandings.[1] To insist on the local and particular, rather, is to insist that despite a shared, general cultural experience, which makes possible, for example, the movement of clerks between communities, readily able to adapt their methods of record production to new circumstances, there is a significantly particular character which is vitally part of the structure of record, memory, and tradition, within each urban community. Whatever the similarities, therefore, between Hythe and Sandwich, New Romney, Folkestone, Dover, Rye, Hastings, Winchelsea, and Faversham,[2] there are also strong differences; and though Hythe might

---

[1] This essay sets out the conceptual framework for arguments to be explored more fully in my forthcoming book *Writing Urban Culture*. That volume is based on a fully documented study of the surviving manuscripts in the archive of Hythe and includes detailed consideration of the work of the town's scribes.

[2] See K. M. E. Murray, *The Constitutional History of the Cinque Ports* (Manchester, 1935).

be in regular communication with Canterbury, only fifteen miles away, its practices are even more distinctive from those of the cathedral city and are functionally suited to express such cultural distinctions.

II

Under the influence of Clanchy's magisterial *From Memory to Written Record* these writings of urban clerks have come to be understood as part of the development of 'practical literacy', and of the general development of literacy in England and Europe up until the twentieth century.[3] Laymen, Clanchy argued, became more literate to meet the demands of a growing volume of written business. Along with an increasing volume of documents came the development of bureaucracies, writing skills, and archive techniques. Older systems of writing and recording were adapted to utilitarian demands. In place of a reliance on oral testimony developed the habit of referring to accumulated information in book and archive. The emergence of a 'literate mentality' was a gradual process. Traditional, non-literate ways did not suddenly and inevitably disappear and the symbolic and ritualistic and the spoken word continued to be retained.

The term 'pragmatic literacy' has been coined to describe this literacy as it developed from the twelfth century onwards. Writing of 'Pragmatic Literacy in Latin Christendom', Britnell makes a distinction between what he describes as 'two different modes of written text': 'One is the literary manuscript – the work of philosophy, theology, history, law, poetry or romance – which had the capacity to instruct, edify or entertain an indefinite number of readers. Such works were . . . usually marketable, and many passed from hand to hand by gift and exchange.' A pragmatic text, on the other hand, contributed to some legal or administrative operation and was produced for the use of a particular administrator or property-owner; records of this kind 'had no marketable value, and if they were copied, it was for administrative convenience, not to satisfy a wider range of readers', and 'rarely passed from hand to hand independently of the land or office to which they were related'.[4] There is about the term almost something of an apology – 'pragmatic' is of the everyday, the mundane, the stuff of the implementation of social and political control, of economic and legal and administrative function – it is not the stuff of the imagination.

---

[3] M. T. Clanchy, *From Memory to Written Record: England 1066–1307*, 2nd edn (Oxford, 1993).
[4] R. Britnell (ed.), *Pragmatic Literacy, East and West 1200–1330* (Woodbridge, 1997), p. 3.

The historical role of pragmatic literacy as described and distinguished by Clanchy and Britnell, however, fails to engage fully with its social and cultural significance. An approach to language and literacy from modern anthropology, however, might be usefully incorporated.[5] As Besnier has insisted: 'one must first recognize that literacy, rather than transcending the social and cultural, is embroiled in social and cultural processes . . . In the realm of culture, literacy is semiotically connected to many of the categories that social actors invoke to make sense of the world around them (e.g., personhood, emotionality, religious symbolism). No account of literacy, or for that matter of any other aspect of human nature, can ignore either social or cultural aspects of the phenomenon.' What is required is an approach which emphasises the nature of literacy as social practice.[6] In this instance, such an approach demands the deconstruction of the ideas of 'practical' and 'pragmatic' and a wider recognition of the expressive capacity of these writings that survive to articulate person and community in English society from the thirteenth century onwards.

The historically and culturally specific nature of the functions of these writings embodies connections between oral, ritual and ceremonial, and manuscript culture; and asserts the differences of a phase of literate development markedly distinct from those of modern society – even though to understand such differences may be to understand better our own literacy. To engage with this culture, however, is to need to reconsider the nature of legal, financial, and administrative practice, and the perception of 'audience', and 'authorial intention'. I want to suggest that the nature of administrative, financial or legal use is intimately connected with ideas of community and individual, of tradition, history, and memory, and of the political implications of these concepts. The nature of the audience for such materials is linked to this more complex notion of use. Their audience is not of the same order as that of a written text produced for present-day consumption. Defined in this way, its audiences are very small, perhaps even essentially scribal or clerkly, perhaps a small group of specialists concerned with the immediate matters of legal or administrative business, but their audience, redefined as suggested, is an audience which is locatable in a past and present continuum of custom and tradition and communal memory. This is not to say that such texts lack individuality of production, a production of the moment, the individual context, for clerks seek to impose

---

[5] See, e.g., M. Z. Rosaldo, *Knowledge and Passion: Ilongot Notions of Self and Social Life* (Cambridge, 1980) and N. Besnier, *Literacy, Emotion, and Authority: Reading and Writing on a Polynesian Atoll* (Cambridge, 1995).

[6] Besnier, *Literacy,* p. 169.

their own individual skill and understanding upon these texts even as they construct them according to generic forms. But this is, primarily and self-consciously, a social and communal literature. It is also a literature which systematically incorporates its individual contributors as social beings defined in terms of their essential contributions to the community, individuals as single persons and as members of households.

Redefined in this way, what has been called 'pragmatic' may be understood to have wider significance than its original description suggests, and it may also be seen to have greater continuities with 'non-pragmatic' literatures than might at first be imagined. The distinction, for example, between some administrative literature and chronicles may often be only slight, a matter of descriptive mode rather than kind. Similarly, the political content of administrative texts may be clear and self-conscious. Equally, the moral and political content of such urban texts is often a vital guide to contemporary perceptions of community, and custumals, for example, occupy a special role in the self-consciousness and self-determination of community. Implicit in this reconsideration is a challenge to the idea of the text that Britnell proposes as essentially retrospective and anachronistic, a suggestion which has similar implications for 'non-pragmatic' literatures. Britnell's textual categorisations, indeed, may not be very helpful when it comes to understanding the functions of text and, indeed, script in medieval culture.

At the same time, it may prove valuable to identify more closely the units of linguistic and textual analysis within which our understanding of speech and literacy is to be constructed. Here the work of linguistic anthropologists may prove valuable and particularly their development of the concept of the 'speech community', a fundamental analytical tool in the study of language and text in culture and society.[7] Concerned with the spoken word, the idea of speech community gives identity to the practices of fellow speakers engaged discursively and interactively with one another as they use their language system, behaving 'as though they operate within a shared set of norms, local knowledge, beliefs, and values'.[8] Essential to this speech community is an awareness of linguistic diversity and its social correlatives and the idea of interaction as a social process. Though, for those

---

[7] See A. Duranti, *Linguistic Anthropology* (Cambridge, 1997), esp. pp. 72–83; A. Duranti (ed.), *Key Terms in Language and Culture* (Oxford, 2001), esp. M. M. Morgan, 'Community', pp. 31–3; A. Duranti (ed.), *Linguistic Anthropology: A Reader* (Oxford, 2001), esp. A. Duranti, 'Linguistic Anthropology: History, Ideas, and Issues', pp. 1–38, J. J. Gumperz, 'The Speech Community', pp. 43–52, and D. Hymes, 'On Communicative Competence', pp. 53–73.

[8] Morgan, 'Community', p. 31.

concerned with historical communites, speech is not available and even evidence of speech is rare, there can be little doubt that the implications of its analysis have wide application. It would seem useful, indeed, to draw metaphorically upon the linguistic structures and processes of speech relations in terms of a 'text community', an interactive system of texts and text users, and maybe even to think of that significant hybrid, the 'speech/text community', representing the discursive interaction of speech and text within a single cultural entity.

The undoubted complexity of the 'speech/text community' is manifested in the writings of which it is constituted. To comprehend the working of its discursive interaction requires an awareness of the general role of text within it and of the particular roles, for example, of Latin, French, and English social/communal texts. In such a complex community, each act of text-making, and each linguistic choice, and each discourse is political. Each textual act is an expression of authority and power, an expression which is deeply embedded historically. The written record, as such social/communal texts may be called, needs to be deconstructed in order to comprehend its social function. 'Record' implies a text used for the useful collection of materials which may subsequently be consulted, but to record is to choose ways of recording, it is not a neutral collection but a socially and individually selective one. In the process of selection the record reveals itself to be part of a system of collective memory and political distinction.

The detail of the written record and its accumulation are highly significant, and deserve closer consideration than they have hitherto been given. We need to ask why the records contain so much apparently 'superfluous' detail and why communities go to such lengths to preserve and store such records. The answer to these questions may well suggest that their 'purpose' goes far beyond simply recording details of immediate or short-term administrative use, providing a record of relationships and persons and families, and moral and political justifications, but also recording detail which expresses the nature of the community in perpetuity, and the ways in which that community changes in relation to its customs and traditions, and, in turn, in relation to the perception of those customs and traditions by the outside world, a world of other authorities and powers. We need, also, to think in detail about the organisational structure and formulae employed with the written records of the 'speech/text community', and the ways in which these change over time. And, not least, the disposition of the text upon on the page, the quality and kind of the script used, the degree and character of decoration, all need to be recognised as having social and cultural significance.

III

At the centre of the particular 'speech/text community', the town and port of Hythe possessed a population probably not much larger than 1500 persons at any time during the period 1300–1550. As a port, however, it had an extensive hinterland and trading region. Its overseas connections linked it with France and the Low Countries and also with the North Sea basin and especially the east coast of England from as far north as Newcastle. Along the south coast its coastal trading linked it with the West Country and Ireland. It drew immigrants from northern Europe as well as much of England: from northern France, the Rhinelands, and the Low Countries, in particular. Like New Romney,[9] its local hinterland probably extended some twenty to thirty miles into Kent and Sussex, but it had regular legal, administrative, and political connections further afield, in part as a member of the Cinque Ports (including connections with Yarmouth and Scarborough as well as with the Cinque Ports of Kent and Sussex), in part with the household of the Archbishop of Canterbury, its overlord, and in part with London, with royal government and parliament. Its citizens might also come from Scotland, Ireland, Wales, and from a wide range of English counties.

It drew the majority of its citizens, however, from within the more immediate local hinterland, and the families of that hinterland enjoyed close economic and kin relations with the people of Hythe, using the town and port as a centre for many of their economic, social, political, and religious activities – its courts recording the relations of a population far in excess of its residents. The activities of many members of aristocratic households, administrative and legal officials of the crown and other authorities, as well as merchants and players, were focused here. It was intimately connected with its immediate hinterland (in the Romney Marshes, for example) by the landed and livestock possessions of the butcher-graziers who formed leading members of its governing councils, and by the fishermen and boat-owning cattle sellers.

The consequence of the interconnections indicated here was a 'speech/text community' of some size and complexity. Linguistically it possessed considerable diversity and, in the broadest sense, a multiple ethnicity, consisting not only of representatives of various national identities but of significant groupings based in local economic and cultural interests and kin alliances. It possessed the potential for literate connections and textual influences from metropolitan and mercantile connections as well as those

---

[9] A. F. Butcher, 'The Origins of Romney Freemen', *Economic History Review*, 2nd ser., 27 (1974), 16–27.

of aristocratic and noble households, and its probable links with vernacular texts may have brought it into contact with heterodox groups (including Lollards) in its locality, as well as those associated with new groups among the orthodox pious and those connected with its significant ecclesiastical centre in the fraternities and cults of its own substantial parish church of St Leonards.[10]

IV

The surviving archive for Hythe owes its existence, almost entirely, to the textual fulfilment of the necessities of custom.[11] In this case, custom may be understood as the product of the interaction between local practice, the constitutional structure of the urban community derived from the devolution of royal and archiepiscopal power, and the autonomy of the Cinque Port federation. The nature of this written archive embodies structurally this interrelationship and derives from it a significant potential for change, a change expressed in both content and form. In Hythe, for example, content and form change markedly between the late fourteenth and the fifteenth centuries, probably in response to a combination of circumstances and especially devastating French and Castillian coastal raiding, alterations in the location of the town's harbour, and profound demographic change in town, locality and region, all of which resulted in economic contraction and restructuring. The surviving fragmentary accounts for the late fourteenth century seem to indicate an economic community notably larger than that recorded later but also more distinctly differentiated and organised occupationally, perhaps more highly specialised.[12] At the same time the written record represents these economic characteristics in appropriate administrative and accounting forms, notably different from those of the later years of relative decline, and expressive of different administrative structures of implementation.[13] No doubt in other ways too, form and content have a reciprocal relationship with cultural change. Such mutual adaptation, in which changes in the nature of the community are translated into changes

[10] A. Hudson, *The Premature Reformation: Wycliffite Texts and Lollard History* (Oxford, 1988), p. 121; R. G. A. Lutton, 'Heterodox and Orthodox Piety in Tenterden, c.1420–1540', Ph.D. thesis, University of Kent at Canterbury (1997); and for the church of St Leonard see, e.g., Hythe Borough Archives 1346.

[11] For discussion of the custumals of the Cinque Ports, and especially those of Sandwich and Faversham, see J. P. Croft, 'The Custumals of the Cinque Ports c.1290–1500. Studies in the Cultural Production of the Urban Record', Ph.D. thesis, University of Kent at Canterbury (1997). Also M. Bateson (ed.), *Borough Customs*, 2 vols., Selden Society 18, 21 (1904, 1906).

[12] Hythe Borough Archives 1056–60.   [13] Hythe Borough Archives 1061.

in the written record, encourages a perception of script and record as, in an important sense, symbolic or metaphorical.

As well as the structural embodiment of custom and adaptability of these writings, it is of their nature to incorporate other discourses, or to provide a discourse within which those others might survive, albeit in fragmentary form. The household taxation accounts ('maletotes'), for example, the court books, or the cartulary of urban properties, bring together evidences themselves derived from other oral and written testimonies, whether they are concerned with details of production or commercial transactions, the evaluations of distrained goods, or the boundaries of tenements.[14] It is possible to read accounts of personal, household, and community activities, reconstructed by the clerks, often obviously translating from those other testimonies into the expected, conventional Latin syntax and vocabulary of the record, at other times retaining the original English or even French forms, expressive of local registers and parlances to produce a kind of macaronic. Within the moral and poltical economy of the community these composite intertextual writings perform a special cultural function.

The precise form of the writings, moreover, involves the use and development of abbreviated Latin, technical vocabulary and conventional phraseology appropriate to each specific kind of record which, though broadly similar to that used in other like communities, is often specifically local in its formulations, though capable of change. And if such writings are essentially intertextual they are also infratextual, making cross-reference within themselves as well as beyond, to the texts and performances of persons, groups and institutions, events and social developments, making sense of the interrelationships in terms of their formal structures. To write (and to read) the 'maletotes', for example, is to enter into administrative structures of ward and household and to make links and comparisons between all the active persons and households within the community, expressed in terms of individual or collective economic, administrative or political action. In their construction and performance these writings, arguably, have a crucial role to play in the negotiation of cultural change.

The complex process of the textual construction of civic memory and identity, the defence and expression of power and authority, and the recording of adaptation and change, provides vital reasons for why towns might take such care to produce and to keep such records. They provided a site for these processes at the point at which the local intersects with the other influential authorities and negotiates the changing balances of power of

---

[14] See, e.g., Hythe Borough Archives 1058, 1020, 1026.

vital interest to the community. On an annual, or even more frequent basis, for example, the 'maletote' accounts or the case records of the court books, permit a complex reconsideration of the perceived state of the community, previously observed in performance in the presence of the clerks and the principal officers of the town (the mayors and jurats).

The making of these writings was, of course, in the hands of the clerks but though the imperative for their making was communal custom, the implications of that imperative were to affect the behaviour of every townsperson and involve the citizens in processes which patterned their lives and necessitated their conformity to the regular demands of civic authority. The burden of local taxation, for example, had consequences for production and prosperity, but the anticipation of an annual public accounting and declaration of household economic activity under oath must have required acts of individual and household memory or record, acts themselves conditioned by the expected form of the presentation, as written in the civic record. No independent individual or household record survives for the citizens of Hythe but their existence seems probable, and at times the form of the clerks' record perhaps intimates the pre-existence of rough household accounts, which make an incoherent list of quantities, sums, and persons, where the clerk has not converted his information into the usual form. The civic record then may be seen to embody the self-conscious acts of memory, oral, literate, and numerate, of the citizens and their households. More than this, however, the occasions of accounting (in the case of the 'maletotes'), as oral transmissions delivered publicly, in person, have the character of ritual or ceremonial performance, and perhaps also act as episodes of moral mutuality when the citizens recognise their collective obligations to community and when the community acknowledges its obligation to them; and a time also for informal gathering, for discussion of personal, commercial, and civic affairs. For the clerks, the jurats, citizens and non-citizens, the written record kept in the Common Hall was the record of these occasions as well as of the activities of the past year, with all their significance for the maintenance of social order and identity.

If we must imagine what precedes the surviving records, we may more readily determine from the surviving fair copy manuscripts the work of the clerks themselves. The existence of the fair copy predicates the written or oral transmission of household accounts but also the clerks' drafts and the copying, editing, clarification and conversion (not least perhaps from some forms of English into Latin), a process requiring careful checking and verification, the making of corrections and additions, before the final making of the fair copy, often in a book specially devoted to the permanent record. The fair copies were made in parchment or paper (paper exclusively after the early fifteenth century) in gatherings which would later be sewn separately and gathered together in books with either parchment wrappers or covered boards. These books were then kept by the clerks and frequently given letter symbols to distinguish them in what seems to be some kind of shelving system. Whether any system of keeping evidences and drafts existed (as it did for the courts) is not revealed by surviving materials, though there are frequent references to books of various sizes no longer present in the borough archives. Indeed, what soon becomes clear, working on the extensive archive surviving for Hythe is how much has disappeared: the drafts and pre-existing memoranda, the bills, the 'narrationes' and 'fabulae' of the missing court files, all are gone. What survives must be seen not just as accident but as a matter of archival choice.

For the clerks to compile these fair copies required considerable knowledge and skill. The necessary techniques of recording and the legal and administrative procedures would have to be learnt by any incoming clerk, and there was a steady, occasionally rapid, turnover of clerks. Some of the legal and administrative knowledge might have been known by long-serving jurats and other town officers, many of whom were men of considerable commercial, governmental, and political experience in their own rights, but to master the whole meant a specialist training. The surviving records suggest that some clerks were undoubtedly better than others – in the way they organised material, the detail which they incorporated, the skill with which they presented, and not least in the production of a record which satisfied the visual and ritualistic demands of the community. Among those clerks whose careers were of some duration and whose achievements must have been well regarded, there was a demonstration not only of their ability to translate present circumstance for posterity in terms of civic jurisdiction and control but to do so with an appropriate command of calligraphic skill, a skill which permitted an individual virtuosity which lent authority to memory and achievement. Furthermore, this scribal practice implicated the considerable extent of the knowledge which the clerks possessed of the community and which they used in the production of the record. The clerks were a crucial repository of collective knowledge or memory and their writings were an embodiment of that particular and general knowledge within the community.

Though the work of the scribes as a whole indicates a multi-layered representative complexity, the 'maletote' accounts provide the most detailed and the richest examples of the functions of script within the community of Hythe. Court proceedings, charters, letters and other accounts, as they now survive, are often more remote from the intimacies of their own production. Even so, the characteristics of the whole discourse of the 'maletotes' are never contained within the activities of a single household, they are essentially of the whole community. Some entries, for example, might contain detailed references to the activities of the fishing industry, a fundamental economic activity for the majority of the citizens, providing, sometimes in Latin, sometimes in English, description of the fishing seasons and their saints' days, the names of fishing ports around the North Sea, the names of fish and the sizes of catches, the names of fellow fishermen and customers, and the names of boats, and nets, and hooks. Similar details might be recorded by those citizens whose principal livelihood was made in pastoral farming in the urban hinterland: the seasons of buying and selling and killing and the names of suppliers and customers, the details of horses, cattle, and sheep, and the kinds and quantities of skins and fleeces. For those who served as officers of the town, the record of their business on the town's behalf in London and parliament, in the Cinque Ports at the Dover sessions and the administrative assemblies of the 'Brodhull', in meetings with lawyers and townsmen and gentry and members of the households of the aristocracy, in legal, administrative, and political affairs. And even for a household of lesser significance, the detail is indicative. John Cheseman, junior, of Middleward, submitted his accounts under oath on 20 January 1413.[15] He paid 2s 2d for the customary payment for his right to practise as a tailor ('de malitota art' sue sissor hoc anno'); 12d for selling woollen cloth to the value of £6 ('de malit' panni lanii vend hoc ao ad val' £6'); 1d for one cow sold that year; and he also accounted for 9d and three farthings on behalf of Margery, formerly his father's wife, by way of payment of the customary fine for his father's occupation as a watercarrier for three quarters of the year ('nuper ux' Joh' patris sui de 9d ob q malitota art' sue Watyrledaryscraft p iij qrt anni'). The total of his debt to the community on this account was 4s and three farthings. Against this sum Cheseman claimed and was allowed 3s 5d for hire of his horse by the town's representatives to various places during the year as had been recorded on a certain paper ('ut pate' in papiro'). He paid 8d to settle his account, leaving the community owing him one farthing ('Et communitas ei debet q'). He also successfully claimed back 4d for a day's work for which he had not been paid, digging in the construction of the new harbour ('p def' j diei in lez Delvez'), and as a result the community owed him 3d three farthings at the end of his account for that year.

[15] Hythe Borough Archives MS 1052, fo. 4v.

As Cheseman's account suggests, the 'maletote' accounts in the fifteenth century often employ a kind of macaronic. In this case, the use of a text which employs within a dominantly Latin form English words and phrases as well as French constructions. This linguistic plurality reflects different voices and authorities, the traditional voice of the official record, borrowed from royal and ecclesiastical legal and administrative precedent, and the voice of popular authority and clerical education. Early in the sixteenth century, some forms of these writings experience a language shift, into English, a shift significantly political, variously marked elsewhere in the region, as in Canterbury. English has its own social, moral, and political identity, and indeed is not singular but multiple in itself, a matter of choosing between Englishes. Throughout the period it is used textually to convey the content of oral transmission within Hythe's Common House; and similarly to record the proceedings of the Brodhull at New Romney, at the meetings of the Cinque Port representatives, to discuss and formulate common policy. By the 1540s it seems to have effected a substantial usurpation of Latin in the town accounts, apparently asserting a new, popular civic voice, the shift manifesting the resolution of a linguistic tension long present in the community and the record.

v

The social and cultural significance of the writings of civic clerks needs to be understood within the locally determined field of text and speech which constitutes the community. The 'speech/text' community of the town is a multi-ethnic complex involving a network of discursive interrelationships of personal, collective, and institutional kinds, and the writings themselves are to be regarded as performative of economic, social, religious, moral, and civic practices and processes, and not merely representative of a narrowly defined 'pragmatic' literacy. The linguistic nature of these texts is to be seen as an essential part of these processes and practices, with different languages and parlances derived from national, regional, and local groupings and tensions, manifesting themselves at times in macaronic texts, and showing in the early sixteenth century language shift towards English a moment of significant political resolution.

Playing a vital role in the perception of the community in the making of its customs, traditions, and history, its identity and authority, these texts are to be recognised as capable of incorporating subtle change and adaptation. The individual contribution of the clerk(s) in the processes of interpretation, in editorial practice, and in the development of distinctive characteristics of textual form, and of script, plays a crucial part in the construction of collective consciousness.

The relationship between the clerk/text and the persons for whom and of whom these texts are produced is, in significant part, a relationship of social control in the performance of their construction, a relationship which embodies obligation and reciprocity. This control is also constitutive of the perception of the person and of the civic or communal. The role of the making, preserving, and using of these texts is a moral and political one, intimately concerned with the nature of personal conduct within and on behalf of the community. To be involved in a manuscript culture is to be part of a written system of moral representation in which the material culture of script and text is an intimate, expressive, responsive, and formative part of the political discourse at every level, and in which the boundaries between literatures are frequently functionally imprecise.

9

The sound of print in early modern England: the broadside ballad as song

Christopher Marsh

In a volume devoted to script and print, it may seem somewhat perverse to include a chapter investigating early modern ballad tunes, the one key component of the broadside that was very rarely published. It will be argued here, however, that the study of melodies and their associations ought to be integral to the interpretation of ballads, single-sheet publications that were by all accounts an important category within early modern cheap literature. Printed ballads fulfilled a number of functions in the period, and at the more basic end of the spectrum were used variously as material for lining tins, fuel for the fire, and toilet paper. More significantly, they were songs designed for performance, and they thus serve to remind us that seventeenth-century literature was aural and oral to a degree that is difficult to imagine today. Unless this is appreciated and investigated, scholars may find themselves frequently missing the point of the ballads into which they regularly dip for illustrative evidence. Melody made meaning.

The vast majority of ballads were printed as verbal texts only, with the tunes identified by name but not by musical notation. In 1676, Thomas Mace said that there were many such tunes, 'very *Excellent*, and *well contriv'd Pieces*, *Neat*, and *Spruce*', adding that they were 'Commonly known by the *Boys*, and *Common People, Singing them in the Streets*'. Indeed, most of these melodies were sufficiently well known that a mere title could be expected to activate the musical instincts of the potential consumer. Samuel Pepys even had a blackbird who could whistle the opening phrases of many tunes, 'but there leaves them and goes no further'.[1] A human customer would, ideally, remember the entire tune from its previous incarnations, and be able, perhaps with the help of friends, to fit the printed words to the recalled melody.

---

[1] Thomas Mace, *Musick's Monument* (1676), p. 129; R. Latham and W. Matthews (eds.), *The Diary of Samuel Pepys*, 11 vols. (1995), vol. IV, p. 152.

It was not only the common people who knew the tunes, however, and we can be thankful that many melodies *were* written down by publishers such as John Playford, or by composers from Byrd to Purcell. Of course, it is not always easy to identify the bare tunes within the elaborate treatments which they received from musically sophisticated professionals, and it is clear that individual tunes could sound in a great variety of guises depending on the purpose of a performance and the social level on which it occurred. Nevertheless, it is possible in many cases to recover plausible core versions of the tunes, and to re-unite them with their ballads.[2]

Towards the end of the seventeenth century some ballad publishers did begin to print musical notation on their broadsides. In a few cases, this notation was legible and suitable, and presents another source for the salvaging of endangered melodies. More often than not, however, the printed music that was introduced onto the ballads was, in Richard Luckett's phrase, 'a mere meaningless jumble, presumably intended to flatter the musically illiterate'. 'The boon companions', for instance, was set to the tune of 'Fond Boy', but the music that was printed on the sheet was a random series of notes, way ahead of its time in 1692.[3] 'Meaningless' may, however, be too dismissive a term. In cases such as this one, the printed music functioned as a visual symbol of melodic sound, expected to interest viewers merely because it represented music to them – it served a purpose equivalent to that fulfilled by the pictorial images of musicians found on many other ballads.

The use of such decorations by printers indicates the selling power of music amongst their target audience. In the 1790s, an anti-republican correspondent noted 'that any thing written in voice & especially to an Old English tune ... made a more fixed Impression on the Minds of the Younger and Lower Class of People, than any written in Prose'. A successful printed ballad, he continued, was likely to be 'Re-echoed by Every Little Boy in the Streets'.[4] Melodies mattered, and the editor of *The Rump*, a famous song collection of 1660, warned his customers, 'If thou *read* these ballads (and not sing them), the poor ballads are undone'. Here, the author pleads with his audience to consume the ballads as music rather than merely as texts. This plea locates him within that grand, never-ending transition from a culture centred on orality and aurality (in which ballads were almost invariably sung and heard) towards one centred more on literacy (in which

---

[2] See C. M. Simpson, *The British Broadside Ballad and its Music* (New Brunswick, 1966).
[3] R. Luckett, 'The Collection: Origins and History', in R. Latham (ed.), *Catalogue of the Pepys Library at Magdalene College, Cambridge*, 7 vols. (Woodbridge, 1978–84), vol. II, Pt. 2, p. xv; W. G. Day (ed.), *The Pepys Ballads*, 5 vols. (Woodbridge, 1987), vol. V, p. 95.
[4] Letter to John Reeves, 4 December 1792, BL, MS Add. 16922, fo. 45, cited in R. Palmer, *The Sound of History: Songs and Social Comment* (Oxford, 1988; Pimlico edn., London, 1996), p. 17.

they might also be read in silent privacy). He asserts the importance of the music in very strong terms: without it, the ballads will be impoverished to the point at which they fail completely to fulfil their purpose. In the first part of the remark, however, he also reveals his awareness that reading ballads without singing them was increasingly an option, and a troubling one.[5]

Despite this anxiety, it remained true throughout the seventeenth century that, for the vast majority of people, ballads were things that flew through the air, vibrating eardrums as they went, rather than so many silent words on paper, designed to be processed within the relative peace and quiet of an individual's head. Many plays of the period present the interaction between people and ballads as fundamentally aural. In *The Winter's Tale*, for example, the ballad-singer Autolycus reports gleefully that he has mesmerised the members of a crowd until 'all their other senses stuck in ears'.[6] It is a little surprising, therefore, that historians of early modern English popular culture and cheap print have paid so little attention to the ballad as song. Natascha Würzbach dismissed the melodies in a single paragraph, on the grounds that they showed 'no definite functional interrelation' with the all-important texts, though she did note their mnemonic function. Bernard Capp and Barry Reay both paused to assert the importance of the tunes, but passed on rather swiftly. For Richard Luckett, a ballad's tune was 'merely a vehicle' for the words.[7] Tessa Watt, Bruce Smith, Roy Palmer, Diane Dugaw, Patrick Collinson and Adam Fox have all been more constructive, but even in their works we do not progress all that far beyond a basic awareness of the musical identity of ballads, and a partially developed sense of the ways in which a song's tune may have contributed to its impact.[8] 'Until a sociological and historical aesthetics of music properly develops,' wrote Michael Pickering and Tony Green in 1987, 'the study of vernacular song as a musico-literary entity will remain biased towards its verbal dimension of signification.' The remark was aimed primarily at sociologists, but early modern scholars might also be encouraged to prick up their ears.[9]

---

[5] *The Rump, or a Collection of Songs and Ballads* (1660), preface 'To the Reader'.

[6] W. Shakespeare, *The Winter's Tale* (1623; Harmondsworth, 1969), Act IV, Scene iv.

[7] N. Würzbach, *The Rise of the English Street Ballad 1550–1650*, trans. G. Walls (Cambridge, 1990), pp. 9, 16; B. Capp, 'Popular Literature', in B. Reay (ed.), *Popular Culture in Seventeenth Century England* (1985), p. 204; B. Reay, *Popular Cultures in England 1550–1750* (London and New York, 1998), pp. 59, 91; R. Luckett, 'Collection', p. xii.

[8] T. Watt, *Cheap Print and Popular Piety 1550–1640* (Cambridge, 1991), pp. 23, 329; B. R. Smith, *The Acoustic World of Early Modern England: Attending to the O-Factor* (Chicago, 1999), pp. 188, 191; Palmer, *Sound of History*; D. Dugaw, *Warrior Women and Popular Balladry 1650–1850* (Chicago, 1989), pp. 48, 56; P. Collinson, *The Birthpangs of Protestant England* (Basingstoke, 1988), pp. 108–11; A. Fox, *Oral and Literate Culture in England 1500–1700* (Oxford, 2000), pp. 318–20.

[9] M. Pickering and T. Green (eds.), *Everyday Culture: Popular Song and the Vernacular Milieu* (Milton Keynes, 1987), pp. 175–8.

This essay is written not only in response to the appeals of seventeenth-century authors, but because the relevant historiography seems to neglect the place that music, in general, occupied in the lives of the early modern majority. Within a culture that was still much more oral and aural than literate, and which knew nothing of electronically recorded sound, we might expect to find ourselves interested by some of the ways in which music and its associations were used. Physicians knew that melody had the power to revive patients and ease melancholy.[10] Other writers sometimes expressed the opinion that those people who understood music were more likely to live orderly and harmonious lives.[11] Explorers were aware of the value of melody in establishing contacts with the natives of distant lands, and in locating lost compatriots.[12] Music also played a variety of roles in the punishment of those who broke laws or otherwise offended their contemporaries.[13] Lastly, everyday speech seems to have been peppered with words and expressions which drew their meaning from music.[14] Some of these examples find echoes in modern culture, while others are more surprising. Either way, social historians have not yet devoted much energy to the investigation of music. It is as if the commonplace music of the early modern age is considered 'incidental'.

It has frequently been noticed that cultures within which the oral and aural predominate tend to make extensive use of repetition, formulae, stock themes and other methods of remembering. Creativity consists more in re-configuring established building blocks in new and interesting ways than in seeking to say something unprecedented. When print intrudes into such an environment, it operates first as a part of that environment, and its contents – to a considerable degree – are framed according to the conventions of that environment.[15] There is, therefore, a case for arguing that almost all print was imagined and interpreted as oral and aural, even if it was read in silence. For George Puttenham, poetry was 'a kind of Musicke', and his guide to the art of writing it abounds with phrases such as 'our rime and

---

[10] R. Brockleby, *Reflections on Ancient and Modern Musick, with the Application to the Cure of Diseases* (1749).

[11] Thomas Elyot, *The Boke Named the Governour* (1531), fo. 24r.

[12] Discussed by the musicologist Ian Woodfield in *English Musicians in the Age of Exploration* (Stuyvesant, NY, 1995). In 1590, a group of men searching for the lost Roanoke colony rowed close to the shore, playing trumpet calls and 'many familiar English tunes of songs' (p. 10).

[13] Consider, e.g., 'rough music', the 'drumming out' of deviant soldiers, and the songs associated with executions.

[14] E.g.: to 'sing the praises' of another; to 'fiddle still on the same string'; to 'run division' with one's tongue; to be 'all out of tune'; to 'bear the burthen'.

[15] W. Ong, *Orality and Literacy* (1982), pp. 18–26. The inter-twining of oral and literate culture is emphasised by R. A. Houston in *Literacy in Early Modern Europe* (1988), pp. 219–29, and by Fox in *Oral and Literate Culture*.

tunable concords or simphomie'. In the *Arte of English Poesie* he apologises to Elizabeth I for having 'presumed to hold your eares so long annoyed with a tedious trifle'.[16] Later scholars have also noted, with Roger Chartier, that 'an oralisation of the text' was implicit in much seventeenth-century literature, and Walter Ong reminds us that sound is 'the natural habitat of language'.[17] Despite such comments, however, historians have not yet paid sufficient attention to the sound of print (how strange the expression *looks*!). The historian who sits silently to read ballads in a library (where they are usually catalogued as literature rather than music) is a world away from the bustle of a seventeenth-century alehouse or marketplace, in which an individual would often have heard the tune first, and the words only if he or she decided to go closer to the performer. The seventeenth-century listener experienced ballads almost inevitably within a social setting; the twenty-first century scholarly reader almost inevitably does not. In early modern England, ballads flew around in crowded space, jostling for the attention of people whose attitudes to any given theme were varied. Ballads, in such a social setting, were designed to incite debate, banter and contest. They were intended to provoke responses, and this is why so many ballads are tussles between man and wife, tailors and maidens, the old and the young, or countrymen and townsmen. We should probably not be 'looking' for the author's one intended meaning (as historians still tend to), but 'listening' for the many possible meanings that might have registered amongst the audience.

Seventeenth-century thought patterns were also richly associational. Recent scholars have emphasised the important role played by 'resemblance' and 'correspondence' in the construction of knowledge during the early modern period. For Foucault, the perception of resemblance operated in such a way that a new cultural representation might 'reanimate a former one, and juxtapose itself to it'. Two different representations might appear even as 'quasi-likenesses', brought together by 'the insistent murmur of resemblance' and 'the perpetual possibility of imaginative recall'.[18] For Sir Thomas Browne, writing in 1642, even the vulgar music of the tavern was touched by divinity and possessed of the power to move souls: 'It is an Hieroglyphicall and shadowed lesson of the whole world'. The soul, he added, 'is harmonicall, and hath its nearest sympathy unto musicke'. The

---

[16] George Puttenham, *The Arte of English Poesie* (1589), ed. G. Doidge Willcock and A. Walker (Cambridge, 1936), pp. 5, 307.
[17] R. Chartier, *The Order of Books*, trans. L. G. Cochrane (Cambridge, 1994), p. 9; Ong, *Orality and Literacy*, p. 8.
[18] M. Foucault, *The Order of Things* (New York, 1970), p. 69.

imaginative world of John Taylor too was made meaningful (and amusing) by such connective thinking.[19]

In all these respects, we can hear links with balladry: in its constant recycling of tunes; in its many verbal and thematic formulae; and in the frequent inter-connecting of different ballads through explicit and implicit references. Surely, it seems inherently unlikely that the tune was 'merely a vehicle' for the words. We should at least consider the possibility that there is, in the popular tunes of the period, a hidden code of meanings and associations with which scholars have so far not occupied themselves. If there was not such a code, then how could a ballad unsung be a ballad 'undone'?

Of course, there are a number of interpretative difficulties. Many tunes have been lost, and it is often difficult to establish the original publication dates of individual ballads. Detailed evidence relating to the actual reception of songs is difficult to find. Furthermore, it apparently does not come naturally to most of us to think carefully about the more complex social and cultural functions of music. This may be partly because we are nowadays conditioned to be so literate, so visually-minded, imprisoned within 'our text-bound minds'.[20] Amongst historians, it may also be that only a minority consider themselves sufficiently musical to tackle the subject.[21] More generally, it may be partly because our engagement with melody has lost something in an age when music plays at the flick of a switch, or in lifts, or as we wait for a phone connection. At times, music still provides us with an escape; but on many occasions, it now seems inescapable. 'Greensleeves', hugely popular for nearly five hundred years, has recently been voted the most annoying telephone hold tune in England. 'Every time it comes on the line, I want to smash the phone with a pick-axe', commented one man (the editor of a website devoted to the management of stress).[22]

Ultimately, however, our reluctance to think carefully about music may have more to do with the ways in which the human brain processes musical sound. Music does not often engage our conscious minds by stimulating us to think articulate thoughts about its role in our lives. Instead, this is a matter only for a small band of scholarly specialists, few of whom

---

[19] Thomas Browne, *Religio Medici* (1643), ed. L.C. Martin (Oxford, 1964), p. 67; see, e.g., *All the Works of John Taylor the Water Poet*, 3 vols. (Manchester, 1869), vol. II, p. 294.

[20] Ong, *Orality and Literacy*, p. 156.

[21] On this point, however, it should be noted that a considerable body of recent research in psychology indicates that most people are far more musically astute than they realise. See, e.g., A. R. Halpern *et al.*, 'Perception of Mode, Rhythm and Contour in Unfamiliar Melodies: Effects of Age and Experience', *Music Perception*, 5 (1998), 335–55.

[22] *The Guardian*, 2 July 2001.

are historians. Music, it seems, influences us and affects us through other pathways in our brains, and we rarely attempt to drag an awareness of its power to the forefront of our minds. According to James Mursell, an educational writer and philosopher, 'music is the most purely and typically emotional of all the arts' and does not convey intellectual meanings.[23] Psychologists tell us that people tend not to think as they listen to music, and that they apply to music personal knowledge that is 'procedural' rather than 'declarative'.[24] One thinks also of recent research concerning the preferences of people shopping for wine in a supermarket. On days when background music with clearly French associations was played, the proportion of French wine that was purchased increased significantly. When German music was played instead, a shift to German wine was measured. When shoppers were asked, post-purchase, whether the music had influenced their choices, the vast majority answered 'no'. Within the brains of these unwitting consumers, 'superordinate knowledge structures' had been automatically activated, directing their behaviour without engaging their conscious minds.[25] Of course, the Elizabethan writer Thomas Wright knew all this well enough when, in 1601, he remarked, 'musicke hath a certain secret passage into mens soules'. A century later, the clergyman Thomas Naish noted the mysterious power of melody to enhance the communication of spiritual truths to listeners: 'By what smooth, and soft, and easie passages doth it convey as it were by stealth, the Treasure of good things to the Mind of Man? Its Force is not easily resisted.'[26] If most people are not aware of the stealthy influence that music has over them, then they are unlikely – with occasional and welcome exceptions – to speak about it in terms sufficiently articulate for any scholar, let alone a poor historian, to examine in depth. The exercise must, therefore, be somewhat conjectural, but it also seems to be worth trying.[27]

---

[23] Quoted in B. Reimer and J. E. Wright (eds.), *On the Nature of Musical Experience* (Colorado, 1992), p. 123.

[24] E. Narmour, 'Music Expectation by Cognitive Rule-Mapping', *Music Perception*, 17 (2000), 330–1; W. J. Dowling, 'Procedural and Declarative Knowledge in Music Cognition and Education', in T. J. Tighe and W. J. Dowling (eds.), *Psychology and Music: The Understanding of Melody and Rhythm* (Hillsdale, NJ, 1993), p. 6. 'Declarative' knowledge is consciously accessible and can be easily discussed; 'procedural' knowledge is more automatic, being consciously accessible only through its results.

[25] A. C. North *et al.*, 'In-store Music Affects Product Choice', *Nature*, 390 (1997), no. 6656, p. 132.

[26] Thomas Wright, *The Passions of the Minde in Generall* (1601; London, 1604), ch. 5, section 2; Thomas Naish, *A Sermon Preach'd at the Cathedral Church of Sarum, November 22 1700. Before a Society of Lovers of Musick* (1701), p. 21.

[27] This discussion is based upon a sample of several hundred of the most popular tunes of the period, compiled by counting the citations in the following ballad collections: A. Clark (ed.), *The Shirburn Ballads 1585–1616* (Oxford, 1907); Day (ed.), *Pepys Ballads*; Roxburghe Ballads, BL, C20 F7–10; *The*

There are a number of ways in which an awareness of melody might alter our understanding of ballads (and perhaps, by distant implication, of print more generally). Most obviously, the mood of a tune conditioned the range of available meanings.[28] A good example of this occurs in a ballad of c.1620, entitled *A merry new catch of all trades*, to be sung 'To the tune of the cleane Contrary way'. It was analysed by Natascha Würzbach, who found in it a somewhat perplexing list of mainly urban occupations, and who suggested that it may have been the sort of song that was designed for children to sing in the nursery. Dr Würzbach did not investigate the music, and, given this fact, her conclusion seemed perfectly reasonable. A typically trite verse runs,

The Taylor sowes, the Smith he blowes,
The Tinker beates his pan:
The Pewterer ranke, cries tinke a tanke tanke,
The Apothecary ranta tan tan. The Apoth. etc.[29]

When the tune is called into play, however, the entire song gradually begins to take on a rather different aspect (Figure 1).[30] In 1994, I presented transcripts of *A merry new catch* and its melody to a group of Queen's University music students, most of whom had backgrounds in Irish traditional music, and asked them to prepare it for a recording. In their hands, lungs and mouths, the song was steadily transformed into a rhythmic, fast,

---

Euing Collection of English Broadside Ballads in the Library of the University of Glasgow (Glasgow, 1971); Bagford Ballads, BL, C40 M9–11.

[28] We should not, of course, assume that our interpretation of melodic mood is a wholly accurate guide to early modern perceptions. Seventeenth-century ballads with gloomy textual themes were sometimes set to tunes which, to our ears, sound incongruously cheerful. It is also true that, in any age, two people can hear the same rendition of the same tune in surprisingly different ways. In early modern England, the subject was complicated by the influence, probably declining, of the medieval modes, and by the fact that individual tunes were sometimes played in both major and minor keys. Having said all this, it does seem that there is a basic affinity between modern and early modern feelings for melodic mood. In most cases, the adjectives applied to specific tunes by contemporaries ('dainty', 'pleasant', 'delightful', 'heavy', 'light') remain adequate as descriptive labels, and the comments recorded on the subject of melody by seventeenth-century musical theorists generally still seem to make sense today. See, e.g., Charles Butler, *The Principles of Musik, in Singing and Setting: with the Two-fold Use therof* (1636), p. 96; William Holder, *A Treatise on the Natural Grounds and Principles of Harmony* (1694), p. 198.

[29] Day (ed.), *Pepys Ballads*, vol. 1, p. 164–5; Würzbach, *Rise of the English Street Ballad*, pp. 207–8.

[30] The tune is discussed in Simpson, *British Broadside Ballad*, pp. 109, 778. Professor Simpson was unconvinced that the tune he transcribed as 'The clean contrary way' actually fitted the ballads calling for this melody. Early modern ballad singers may, however, have been rather more resourceful than he allows in fitting words to tunes. The ballad does indeed make necessary a somewhat awkward repetition of the fourth and eighth lines of the melody (perhaps in the manner of a communal refrain), but singers may simply have dispensed with this device if it proved unsatisfactory. They surely did not share the anachronistic modern view that the text bound them tightly to a single possibility.

Figure 1 'The clean contrary way' (CUL, MS Dd.6.48, fo. 17v; quoted in Simpson, *British Broadside Ballad*, p. 109).

relentless, accelerating and pulsating thing. It is highly charged and infectiously repetitive.[31] An awareness of the tune thus creates for the words a new aura, and it becomes ever more clear that the ballad – like so many others – is a semi-coded assemblage of bawdy innuendo: 'The Tinker beates his pan', 'The Carpenter doth love his rule,/ and the Hatmaker loves his felt', and so on. The tune title also emerges as a signal to us that we are to hear the first line, as it were, backwards, in 'the cleane Contrary way'.[32] 'All things are not alike' because we all have different occupations and tools, and yet – ultimately – the chief occupation of each and every one of us is to seek sexual satisfaction. One tool is much like another. Fornication makes the world go round. Is this really one for the nursery?

Other tunes carried with them powerful associations, and a detailed consideration of these would add immeasurably to our understanding of balladry.[33] Individual melodies frequently retained their popularity for decades, even centuries, and were designated on ballad sheets again and again. Over time, they tended to pick up an association with one or two particular textual themes – there were bawdy tunes, godly tunes, patriotic tunes and festive tunes.[34] A character in Phillip Massinger's *The Bondman* spoke of 'villanous' tunes, indicating at one and the same time his personal distaste and his awareness that certain melodies were associated with the executions of criminals (these were also known as 'hanging tunes').[35] It seems that the

[31] We produced eighty copies of a teaching pack entitled 'Songs of the Seventeenth Century'. There are very few of these left, but I will happily make a recording of 'A merry new catch' for anyone who sends me a blank cassette.

[32] This expression was in common currency during the seventeenth century. See, e.g. *Works of John Taylor Not Included in the Folio Volume*, 5 vols. (Manchester, 1870), vol. 1, fo. A2r, 'Mad fashions'. Here, Taylor's commentary on a topsy-turvy picture runs, 'All things are turn'd the Cleane contrary way'.

[33] The potential significance of melodic associations is touched upon, but not developed, in Watt, *Cheap Print*, p. 329; Smith, *Acoustic World*, p. 188; and Dugaw, *Warrior Women*, pp. 48, 56.

[34] This paper concentrates on such tunes, but it should be noted that by no means all melodies had deep-rooted associations. Many ballads were set to 'new' tunes, and older tunes (like 'Packington's Pound') sometimes avoided becoming connected predominantly with specific textual themes.

[35] P. Edwards and C. Gibson (eds.), *The Plays of Philip Massinger*, 5 vols. (Oxford, 1976), vol. 1, p. 395.

tunes were selected with some degree of care, and it is said that the great
nineteenth-century ballad publisher, James Catnach, employed a fiddler to
experiment with a variety of tunes in order to assess the market potential of
ballads, and presumably to select the melodies that were most likely to be
effective. In 1636, Charles Butler may have been implying a similar degree
of precision when he referred to 'the infinite multitude of Balads (set to
sundry pleasant and delightfull tunes, by cunning and witti Composers)'.[36]

The previous associations of a tune could contribute to a ballad's potential
impact in a variety of ways. Where the text fitted into a clear thematic
category, the most obvious technique available to the writer or publisher
was to name a tune that identified and reinforced that theme. In such
songs, the tune added new momentum and depth to the meanings of the
text and connected it with all the ballads that had previously been sung
to the same melody. The human brain is particularly adept at processing
music that it recognises, and we can assume that – as for the modern
supermarket shoppers – the sound of a familiar ballad tune drifting across an
early modern marketplace would have activated 'superordinate knowledge
structures' amongst those who heard it.[37] Prior associations would have
found their way uninvited into the mind, and the listener's attitude to
the song would have been profoundly influenced by his or her previous
knowledge of the tune. In this way, the tune was also a marketing device,
designed to attract to the ballad singer/seller those potential customers who
had a taste for songs on that particular theme.

Perhaps the best example of this stock technique is provided by the remarkably successful melody, 'Fortune my foe', which, under various names,
remained popular for two hundred years or more.[38] It is not, to most modern ears, a particularly appealing melody, but it was evidently built to last
(Figure 2). Its associations were extremely strong and clear, and there can
have been few people in seventeenth-century England who did not connect
it, whenever they heard it, with disasters, murders and, perhaps above all,
with the 'last speeches' of those condemned to capital punishment. This
was the 'hanging tune' *par excellence*.

In 1616, for example, Anne Wallen was executed for the murder of her
husband, and the balladeers cashed in with a broadside 'lamentation', set
to 'Fortune my foe'. It included the exquisite line, 'Amongst his intrailes I
this Chissell threw', and concluded thus:

[36] Palmer, *Sound of History*, p. 22; Butler, *Principles of Musik*, p. 8.
[37] J. D. Smith *et al.*, 'What Child is this? What Interval was that? Familiar Tunes and Music Perception
    in Novice Listeners', *Cognition*, 52 (1994), 50; see also n. 25.
[38] Simpson, *British Broadside Ballad*, pp. 225–31. The most common alternative name was 'Aim not
    too high'.

Figure 2 'Fortune my foe' (Paris Conservatoire, MS Res. 1186, fo. 24; quoted in Simpson, *British Broadside Ballad*, p. 227).

My judgement then it was pronounced plain,
Because my dearest husband I had slain:
In burning flames of fire I should fry,
Receive my soule sweet Jesus now I die.[39]

When such a ballad was performed to early modern audiences, it was much more than a sensational song to a 'heavy' tune. It was also a link with all those who, in previous decades and centuries, had paid the price for their sins. This gave the 'last confession' ballads a rooted and universal quality that contemporary listeners evidently found difficult to resist. Many other tunes performed a similar reinforcing effect in the printed ballads for which they were selected.[40]

In other cases, the prior associations of a melody were called upon, but were simultaneously re-directed in some way. For example, when 'Fortune my foe' was named as the tune for what Simpson calls 'dull, moralising ballads' – warnings to youth to behave well, and so forth – it carried with it a stern and threatening reminder of what became of the dissolute. Arguably, no words could convey this message as powerfully as this very distinctive melody. One text set to this tune, *The Virgins ABC*, is transformed by it from a piece of clumsy patriarchal moralising into something with dark and threatening undertones. It opens,

All youthfull Virgins,
to this song give ear,
And learn these lessons,
which are taught you here:
An Alphabet of Vertues,
here are set,
And being learn'd
will make a Maid compleat.

---

[39] Day (ed.), *Pepys Ballads*, vol. 1, p. 125.
[40] E.g., martial ballads called for melodies such as 'Let the Soldiers Rejoice', while a good choice for romantic ballads was 'The Spinning Wheel'.

There follows a weighty, uncompromising statement of the standards by which young women are expected to lead their lives. The tone is overwhelmingly negative, and the words 'not', 'never' 'no' and 'nor' are heard twenty-two times.[41]

When a tune's associations were strong and deep, a point could be made without the articulate deployment of words. In such cases, the sound of a melody alone was sufficient to call to mind a wealth of older expressions and sensations. Naturally, it was rare for examples of this practice to be recorded verbally for posterity, but there is evidence sufficient to imply that the tactic was a common one. In the 1660s, Martin Parker's celebrated tune, 'When the king enjoys his own again', was frequently played in order to express patriotism and loyalty. After General Monck arrived in London in 1660, his musicians reportedly 'play'd that Tune every Morning . . . , till the King came himself, and then, you know, there was no more Occasion for it.' During celebrations at Bruton (Somerset) on 29 May 1660, this great melody sounded all day long. Around the same time, English ships sometimes greeted one another with trumpet renditions of the tune.[42] Moreover, the associations of the best known melodies were known even beyond England's shores. Pepys was understandably upset when the Dutch fleet sailed up the Medway to Chatham in June 1667, capturing a famous and symbolic ship, the 'Royal Charles'. He well understood the non-verbal language that was used by the raiders: 'and presently a man went up and struck her flag and Jacke, and a trumpeter sounded upon her "Joan's placket is torn"'. This brilliant piece of melodic mockery can only be fully understood when the tune's associations with romantic conquest and, by implication, sexual penetration are called to mind.[43]

The associations of a melody could also offer listeners a clue regarding a broadside ballad's hidden layers of meaning. These possibilities were not necessarily made explicit in the text of a song, especially when they were in some way indecent or improper, but they were clearly registered in the melody. A ballad of c.1675 has at its head an assurance that it contains no mention of warfare, courtship, monsters, wonders and death, 'Nor any

---

[41] Roxburghe Ballads, vol. 1, pp. 430–1. Here, the tune title is given as 'The Young Mans ABC', yet another alternative name. For another example of a ballad in which the tune's associations were re-directed, try *Couragious Betty of Chick-Lane*, sung to the tune 'Lillyburlero'. *Ibid.*, vol. IV, p. 294.

[42] Defoe, 'Ballad-maker's Plea', cited by Würzbach, *Rise of the English Street Ballad*, pp. 283–4; W. L. Sachse (ed.), *The Diurnal of Thomas Rugg 1659–1661*, Camden 3rd ser. 91 (1961), p. 179; *A Narrative or Journal of the Proceedings of their Excellencies, the Right Honourable the Lord Holles, and the Lord Coventry* (1667), p. 5, cited by Woodfield, *English Musicians*, p. 60, n. 29.

[43] Latham and Matthews (eds.), *Diary of Samuel Pepys*, vol. VIII, p. 283; Simpson, *British Broadside Ballad*, pp. 388–90.

Figure 3 'Bobbing Joan' (John Playford, *The English Dancing Master* (1651); quoted in Jeremy Barlow (ed.), *The Complete Country Dance Tunes from Playford's Dancing Master* (1985), p. 18). I have modified the melody very slightly in order to demonstrate how it might be accommodated to the words of 'My dog and I'.

thing under the Sky, But onely of my Dog and I' (these last four words provide the ballad's title and refrain). The text opens with a man singing fondly and, for all a modern reader knows, innocently of his beloved pet:

I of no doged (*sic*) nature am,
But loving, gentle, kind and tame,
And have no bigger Family,
But only two, my Dog and I,
My Dog and I, my Dog and I,
But only two, my Dog and I.[44]

The tune, however, tells us immediately that this is a thoroughly bawdy ballad in which dog = penis. 'Bobbing Joan', a simple and beautiful melody that was used both for songs and dances, was associated first and foremost with sex (Figure 3).[45] It seems possible that the ballad-writer, in this and comparable cases, aimed to deceive the official licenser by deliberately excluding the obvious smut from the title and initial verses, burying it instead in the melody and the body of the text, where it could later be rediscovered by well-informed listeners.[46] The role of such tunes may help to explain why early modern ballads, which sometimes look rather bland to modern eyes, were regularly categorised *en masse* by contemporary moralists as dangerously licentious. Thomas Brice, for example, spoke of the 'wanton sound, and filthie sense' of ballads, and to Henry Chettle the maddening sheets were 'full of ribaudrie and all scurrilous vanity'.[47]

A tune could also be applied to themes that were more decisively beyond its main sphere of influence. In some instances, this technique was

---

[44] Day (ed.), *Pepys Ballads*, vol. IV, p. 229.   [45] Simpson, *British Broadside Ballad*, pp. 46–7.

[46] On 22 September 1585, Christopher Hoddeson sent Francis Walsingham a suspicious ballad, noting that 'Allthoughe therbe in the beginning Fayre gloss yet if hit please your honour to Read hit to the eand I hope you will conceive I doo butt my deutye to send hit to be concidred off' (PRO, SP 12/182/25). Unfortunately, the text itself has not survived and the tune cannot therefore be identified.

[47] Thomas Brice, *Against Filthy Writing, and such like Delighting* (1561); Henry Chettle, *Kind-Hart's Dreame* (1592), sig. C1 r.

consciously conceived as an attempt to kidnap popular melodies by over-whelming their existing associations with newer, supposedly better ones. Most famously, Elizabethan puritans sought to popularise Protestantism by attaching much-loved ballad tunes to godly texts. The effort does not appear to have been very successful, and was abandoned around 1580. Godly strategists, in attempting to drown out the established connotations of tunes such as 'Row well ye mariners', were evidently labouring against a powerful tide.[48] A century later, James II's publicists made an attempt to steal 'Lilliburlero' by setting new words to the top Protestant tune of the moment, but, again, the results were disappointing.[49] It seems that English people of the period had clear ideas about proper and improper uses of melodies, and the borderline between the two could be a sensitive area. Those who sang 'psalms to hornpipes' or 'Trenchmore to the tune of Laugh and lye downe' were misguided in some way. In 1597, a vicar from Kent was troubled by the allegation that he had led a rendition of the 25th psalm to the tune of 'Greensleeves', and sued his congregation for slander.[50]

Despite such sensitivities, ballad writers periodically set their songs to tunes with seemingly inappropriate associations. In most cases, the inten-tion was probably not to obliterate those associations, but, more modestly, to harness them to a new theme in the hope of commercial success. Some of the most interesting examples are those in which a well-established tune suddenly crossed a thematic borderline, taking on a new role in another area. In such cases, the tune adds to the text meanings that do not exist in the text itself, and unsettles more obvious meanings. In our Jacobean marketplace, the listener, attracted to the ballad-singer by the tune, must have been surprised when his or her expectations were challenged rather than reinforced. Frequently, one suspects, the early modern listener would have found humour in the twinning of a familiar tune with an unfamiliar or unexpected theme.

For example, the tune 'Fortune my foe' (Figure 2) seems to have been wittily realigned by the talented ballad-writer, Martin Parker, in c.1630.[51]

---

[48] Collinson, *Birthpangs*, pp. 108–11; Watt, *Cheap Print*, pp. 40, 47, 69, 72–3.

[49] *Poems on Affairs of State. Augustan Satirical Verse 1660–1714*, 7 vols. (New Haven, 1963–75), vol. IV (ed. G. M. Crump), pp. 314–15.

[50] Shakespeare, *Winter's Tale*, Act IV, Scene iii; *Works of John Taylor Not Included in the Folio Volume*, vol. II, p. 17, 'Ale Ale-vated into the Ale-titude'; Cathedral Archives and Library, Canterbury, MS. X.4.1 (i), fo. 51, cited by P. Collinson, *From Iconoclasm to Iconophobia: the Cultural Impact of the Second English Reformation* (Reading, 1986), p. 18.

[51] Unfortunately, we cannot be absolutely certain about the identification of the tune in this case. Parker called for 'The Maids ABC', and no separate melody bearing this title has been found. However, 'Fortune my Foe' was sometimes known as 'The Virgins ABC', and it seems probable that this was the intended tune. See Simpson, *British Broadside Ballad*, p. 230.

He apparently applied it to a ballad, *The honest plain dealing porter*, in which a man, once rich but now poor, explains that he is profoundly happy to have lost all his possessions and to have taken humble, back-breaking employment instead. Without the tune, and in the library, we would 'read' this ballad as a thoroughly conventional reiteration of the values ideally associated with the 'great chain of being'; but with the tune, and in the alehouse (Parker's domain), it was more probably heard as a spoof upon such reiterations. The associations of the tune were so gloomy that it becomes impossible to listen to this ballad without a satiric smile:

Such pleasure in my worke I find,
that I live more content in mind,
To earne my living with my hands,
then [than] when I lived upon my Lands.
For many cares are incident
to wealthy men when sweet content
Doth fall unto the meane mans lot,
though need doth make the old wife trot.[52]

Other examples include a ballad in which a man declares his undying love for a woman to the notes of 'Russel's farewell', the most popular 'hanging tune' of the late seventeenth century. Surely, we are to understand that this poor lovesick man is doomed, even if the words do not quite tell us so (he remains hopeful).[53] And why is it that a vehemently anti-Catholic ballad of the mid-1620s, during which time Charles Stuart was busy courting foreign Catholic princesses (and domestic controversy), was set to 'Thomas you cannot', a tune associated with male sexual failure?[54] Is it possible that the tune was being deployed in order to make the kind of political and personal criticism that humble ballad-mongers could not afford to articulate verbally?[55] In the words of one medieval troubadour, 'Of things I would rather keep in silence I must sing'.[56]

A final example will place us on somewhat firmer ground. In the late 1680s and early 1690s, the supporters of William III faced the unenviable task of convincing the English that an apparently cold and suspicious Dutchman who, according to Gilbert Burnet, 'hears things with a dry silence', was

---

[52] Day (ed.), *Pepys Ballads*, vol. 1, pp. 194–5.   [53] *Ibid.*, vol. v, p. 203.

[54] *A New-Yeeres-Gift for the Pope. Ibid.*, vol. 1, p. 62. For the original song, see/hear F. J. Furnivall (ed.), *Bishop Percy's Folio Manuscript: Loose and Humourous Songs* (1868), pp. 116–18. The tune can be found in Simpson, *British Broadside Ballad*, p. 704.

[55] On the control of ballad content in the early modern period, see Watt, *Cheap Print*, pp. 43–4.

[56] Countess of Dis (born c.1140), quoted in D. Watson (ed.), *Chambers Music Quotations* (Edinburgh, 1991), p. 296.

Figure 4 'With a fading' or 'An orange' (*Wit and Mirth. An Antidote against Melancholy* (1682), p. 18; quoted in Simpson, *British Broadside Ballad*, p. 793. Again, I have made minor alterations to the tune).

in reality the bold, brave, glittering, lovable answer to all their prayers.[57] William's balladeering friends were determined that their hero should not go 'unsung'. They selected an old tune, previously known as 'With a fading' or 'The pudding', and applied it to a series of intensely royalist ballad texts. It is a catchy tune, and it worked – for the old tune titles were rapidly displaced in favour of a new one, 'The Orange' (Figure 4). In 1689, one typical ballad, *The Famous Orange: Or, An Excellent Antidote against Romish Poison*, opened with the lines:

There's none can express,
Your great Happiness,
The like was ne're seen since the Days of Queen Bess,
A Nation enslav'd,
And Justice outbrav'd,
To be thus redeemed, and gallantly sav'd, By an Orange.[58]

The tune's apparent success as a propaganda tool must have had something to do with its distinctive and infectious lilt, but there was rather more to the melody than this. Its previous associations, established over a century, were with kissing, courtship, drink, dance and innuendo. One ballad, issued in the earlier part of the seventeenth century, asserted the universal importance to all humans of the kiss:

The aged man of three score yeeres,
oft takes to wife a girle of twenty,
The cause whereof you may suppose,
which make him take this girle so dainty,
is kissing.[59]

---

[57] BL, MS Add. 63057B, fo. 103, cited by C. Rose, *England in the 1690s: Revolution, Religion and War* (Oxford, 1999), p. 38.
[58] Day (ed.), *Pepys Ballads*, vol. II, p. 260.
[59] *The Merry Forrester*, in Day (ed.), *Pepys Ballads*, vol. I, pp. 224–5.

Sexual associations were still attached to the melody during the 1680s, when another ballad, *The passionate damsel*, began with the verse:

I am a young maid of Beauty bright,
That have a desire indeed to be Wed,
That I might take part of such pleasant delight
That e'ry young woman enjoys in the Bed
With a Husband.[60]

It seems possible, therefore, that the ballad-writers who attempted to popularise William following the events of 1688 were using a well-known melody in order to manipulate his image in such a way that accusations concerning his defects (frostiness and sexual inadequacy) were repudiated by musical association. In defiance of the Jacobite slur that William 'is not qualified for his wife', the balladeers were presenting the Dutchman as hot and sexy. In response to the rumour that William had been castrated at birth by a midwife, his supporters sang loudly of his balls.[61] The fact that they did so by musical implication made it possible to bypass the conventions which prevented them from proclaiming the king's sexual prowess in clear and verbal terms. These were clearly new songs, and the rhyme scheme was changed in an act of appropriation, but the tune's associations were very well established.

Furthermore, the associations of this melody ran deeper still. The first musical phrase of 'An Orange' is virtually identical to that of another melody, 'Jog on', and this equally popular tune was itself strongly associated with songs celebrating the defeat of the Spanish Armada exactly 100 years earlier (Figure 5). This tune was also known as '88', and retained its marketability right through into the eighteenth century.[62] It spoke of English nationhood, Protestantism and a monarch of truly famous memory. It seems difficult to believe that the precise affinity between the unusual opening bars of the two tunes was a mere coincidence, particularly if we note the passing verbal references to Elizabeth I (in another of the 'Orange' ballads, the Spanish Armada was also mentioned explicitly).[63] Instead, it is at least worth arguing that one of the reasons for the selection of the 'Orange' tune was that it included this musical reference to the Armada, thus allying 1688 with 1588, and William III by association with a great,

---

[60] Bodl. Lib., Douce Ballads, 2 (176a).
[61] 'Coronation Ballad', quoted by P. Kléber Monod, *Jacobitism and the English People 1688–1788* (Cambridge, 1989), p. 55.
[62] 'Jog on' is discussed in Simpson, *British Broadside Ballads*, p. 392, though the author makes no connection with 'An Orange'.
[63] Day (ed.), *Pepys Ballads*, vol. v, p. 132.

Figure 5 'Jog on' (Playford, *English Dancing Master*, quoted in Barlow (ed.), *Complete Country Dance Tunes*, p. 26. I have transposed the tune down a fifth in order to facilitate comparison with figure 4).

home-grown, Protestant heroine. Having made William sexy, the balladeers were also making him English.

We should not assume, however, that this positive interpretation was the only one that contemporaries could have placed upon these ballads. The light and arguably flippant nature of the songs almost invited listeners to attend to other, more satirical, possibilities. The receivers of ballads were just as important as the composers when it came to constructing meaning. In the minds of many English people, William was not, after all, a new Eliza. Those listeners who rejected the parallel might have concentrated instead on the comparison drawn in the ballads between the dull, dry new king and an exotic, juicy fruit. Like all such fruit, the 'Orange' had the potential to turn rotten, and at least one ballad-writer was aware of the danger.[64] Sadly, we can take this matter no further, for it is not possible to say with any certainty whether this derisory alternative interpretation was popular, nor whether it contributed to the commercial success of the ballads. What proportion of the population welcomed William with a smirk?

There is, therefore, plentiful and suggestive evidence of a hitherto un-investigated system of associations by which melody added significantly to the meaning of printed ballads in early modern England. The web of ballad tunes involved a complex vocabulary that contemporaries did not need to explain to one another because, in all likelihood, they learnt it gradually and automatically over the course of their lives. Modern scholars, in contrast, must piece it all together with deliberate thought, and they face certain handicaps in attempting so to do. Academics are, by definition, an extraordinarily literate group with profoundly literate ways of thinking. Paradoxically, this may leave them poorly qualified to understand early modern society through its cheaper forms of print. Ballads and chapbooks were shot through, both in presentation and reception, with features more

---

[64] *Ibid.*, vol. v, p. 109. One verse runs, 'Perhaps you may think to *Peters* they Stink, Because from our Neighbours they'r brought over Sea, Yet sure, 'tis presum'd, They may be perfum'd, By'th scent of good *cloves*, for they may be stuck in an *Orange*.'

characteristic of predominantly oral and aural cultures. Our advanced literacy stands as a barrier between us and the original 'audience' members. Our 'view' of early modern culture is inevitably influenced by our position close to one end of the transition from orality towards literacy. Of course, this is a very elusive subject, and is all too easily over-simplified. Modern 'literate' culture is full of non-chirographic symbols, speech and other aural signals, just as early modern 'oral' culture was full of written words.[65] Furthermore, it would be mistaken to suppose that musical association and melodic cross-referencing have no part to play in modern life. Certainly, commercial pop music no longer makes frequent and systematic use of the technique, and the artist who records a song that 'sounds just like' something else risks falling foul of the intellectual property laws (the 'cover version' is a different phenomenon because the words and the melody both remain the same). In music, associational habits of mind seem to have receded somewhat, but they are far from dead. Football crowds and political demonstrators, in particular, regularly set new words to existing tunes. Advanced literacy has not, therefore, eclipsed older creative thought-patterns. The transition from orality towards literacy involved a very gradual shift in the cultural centre of gravity, rather than the replacement of one way of knowing and representing by another. Nevertheless, profound and meaningful changes did occur, and, in common parlance, the 'eye-witness' drove the 'ear-witness' into the shadows.[66]

Students of balladry have shown a marked tendency to ignore the un-printed messages that can be partially reconstructed only by close attention to melody. An awareness of the tunes breathes new life into the medium, opening up a world of controversial allusions, contrary possibilities and deeply satirical humour. A well-aimed tune could reinforce or undermine textual messages and, by alluding to additional interpretative possibilities, it could encourage or allow listeners to think the unprintable. The meanings of songs constructed and attended to in this way must often have been highly unstable, because each listener presumably had different levels of relevant knowledge, different prior associations, and consequently a different 'take' on the many shifting alliances of text and tune that were presented by the balladeers. In these songs, moral and political messages were not only presented, but manipulated, teased and even undermined. Sometimes, this may have been a tactic deliberately adopted in order to

---

[65] On the latter point, see Fox, *Oral and Literate Culture*, pp. 406–12.

[66] Who today would express himself thus: 'his mother in law was *eye and ear witnes* of his fathers abuse by this blessed child'? See *Kemps Nine Daies Wonder: Performed in a Daunce from London to Norwich* (1840; first publ. 1600), p. 22.

evade controls, whether official or unofficial. More often, one suspects, the
method was utterly instinctive and came naturally to people who had been
raised within a riddling, rhyming, resonating culture that was only partially
literate.

For those living inside this culture, printed materials of all sorts may
have been imagined as louder, more 'situational' and 'agonistic' than we can
readily understand.[67] It seems probable that early modern readers perceived
written words as if spoken aloud, and inevitably connected them with face-
to-face, mouth-to-ear interaction of some sort. When Thomas Mace argued
in print that the English needed to improve the quality of their church
music, he imagined the irresistible persuasiveness of his case amongst his
readers in the following terms: 'And now againe methinks I see some of
you *tossing* up your *Caps*, and crying aloud, We will have an *Organ*, and
an *Organist* too'.[68] A typical text was rhetorical, and was probably not
clearly imagined as a permanent creation, a finished article or the final
word on a subject. The diarist Thomas Rugge referred regularly to 'Jeering
books' and 'jeering printed sheets', expressions which indicate nicely the
noisiness of Restoration literature.[69] Where ballads are concerned, it seems
that an awareness of sound can have a transformative effect upon the range
of potential messages, and can advance our understanding of the ways in
which literature was used. For other kinds of print, the implications are
more difficult to establish. If we could read as our forbears read, is it possible
that the significance of much early modern literature would shift, before
our very ears?

[67] These terms are used by Ong, *Orality and Literacy*, ch. 3.
[68] Mace, *Musick's Monument*, p. 12.   [69] Sachse (ed.), *Diurnal of Thomas Rugg*, p. 23.

10

Communicating with authority: the uses of script, print and speech in Bristol 1640–1714

Jonathan Barry

This essay seeks to forward the themes of this collection in a number of ways. It challenges the assumption that specific forms of the media (script, print, speech) determine processes of communication, preferring a model in which types of media are seen as both contingent and contested and in which the more important questions relate to the 'authority' which a particular communication could command, a matter in which media form was significant but not determinant, and in which the local context of social and political relationships between the parties to the communication was the principal factor. In that context, it emphasises the complex interplay between different forms of communication in a local setting, and the dangers of isolating a particular mode of communication, both for understanding what that specific message might mean and for our overall picture of the nature of communication in that period and place. This, in turn suggests caution about the influential paradigm which sees a 'public sphere' of print emerging (at some point between the Civil War and the early eighteenth century) that was qualitatively distinct from earlier practices of communication and supported a different form of political culture. Whilst not denying that significant changes were occurring, the essay argues for considerable continuity in forms of authority in communication, but that these took on new meanings due to the intensification of a contested civic culture of communication, subject to the pressures of more intense and more overt ideological division.

In arguing this case, I am reinforcing many recent studies which have emphasised the dangers of polarised cultural models and the complex interplay between different forms of communication. Most of these accounts, however, have either been national surveys or have focused on the very particular case of London (especially studies of news and political debate). The interplay between oral and literate culture has largely been examined as it affected 'popular' culture, through the study of traditions, ballads, rumours and the like, while the relationship between manuscript and print has been of interest to historians of 'elite' culture, but mostly in a literary or ideological context.[1]

This essay seeks to complement that excellent work by looking more broadly at the full range of communications in the context of a specific provincial town, Bristol, during the period most commonly identified with the emergence of this new public sphere, namely 1640–1714.[2] I will try to sketch a picture of the different types of communication available to Bristolians, both in their dealings with the wider world and within the city. However, I will focus on the disputes caused by political and religious divisions and their interplay with the spread and manipulation of 'news'. This is the best documented aspect of the subject and also the one which bears most immediately on the notion of a public sphere. I will also argue that it was these ideological disputes, and the way they were mediated by institutions such as the Bristol corporation and the churches, both established and dissenting, which tended to shape the use of new forms of communication, as well as determining the authority of old ones, rather than the utilitarian demands of trade and industry, which were still well served by traditional

---

[1] H. Love, *Scribal Publication in Seventeenth-Century England* (Oxford, 1993); S. Pincus, '"Coffee Politicians does Create": Coffeehouses and Restoration Political Culture', *Journal of Modern History*, 67 (1995) 807–34; C. J. Sommerville, *The News Revolution in England* (Oxford, 1996); J. Raymond, *The Invention of the Newspaper* (Oxford, 1996); H. M. Weber, *Paper Bullets* (Lexington, Kentucky, 1996); D. Freist, *Governed by Opinion: Politics, Religion and the Dynamics of Communication in Stuart London 1637–45* (London and New York, 1997); A. Johns, *The Nature of the Book: Printing and Knowledge in the Making* (Chicago and London, 1998); J. Raymond (ed.), *News, Newspapers and Society in Early Modern Britain*, special issue of *Prose Studies* 21 no. 2 (1998); B. R. Smith, *The Acoustic World of Early Modern England: Attending to the O-Factor* (Chicago and London, 1999); M. J. M. Ezell, *Social Authorship and the Advent of Print* (Baltimore and London, 1999); D. Zaret, *Origins of Democratic Culture: Printing, Petitions and the Public Sphere in Early Modern England* (Princeton, 2000); A. Fox, *Oral and Literate Culture in England 1500–1700* (Oxford, 2000); B. Dooley and S. Baron (eds.), *The Politics of Information in Early Modern Europe* (2001); T. Harris, 'Understanding Popular Politics in Restoration Britain', in A. Houston and S. Pincus (eds.), *A Nation Transformed: England after the Restoration* (Cambridge, 2001) pp. 125–53; A. Fox and D. Woolf (eds.), *The Spoken Word: Oral Culture in Britain 1500–1850* (Manchester, 2002).

[2] This study builds on my earlier work and fuller accounts and references can be found in: 'Popular Culture in Seventeenth-Century Bristol', in B. Reay (ed.), *Popular Culture in Seventeenth-Century England* (1985), pp. 59–90; 'The Parish in Civic Life', in S. Wright (ed.), *Parish, Church and People* (1988), pp. 152–70; 'The Politics of Religion in Restoration Bristol', in T. Harris *et al.* (eds.), *The Politics of Religion in Restoration England* (Oxford, 1990), pp. 163–90; 'The Press and the Politics of Culture in Bristol, 1660–1775', in J. Black and J. Gregory (eds.), *Culture, Politics and Society in Britain 1660–1800* (Manchester, 1991), pp. 49–81; 'Cultural Patronage and the Anglican Crisis: Bristol c.1689–1775', in J. D. Walsh *et al.* (eds.), *The Church of England c.1689–c.1833* (Cambridge, 1993), pp. 191–208; 'Bristol Pride', in M. Dresser and P. Ollerenshaw (eds.), *The Making of Modern Bristol* (Tiverton, 1996), pp. 25–47 and a forthcoming essay, 'Begging, Swearing and Cursing: the Politics of Religion in Bristol 1689–1715' in J. Barry, *Religion in Bristol c.1640–1775*. The other major studies of this period are D. H. Sacks, *The Widening Gate: Bristol and the Atlantic Economy* (Berkeley, 1991) and his 'Bristol's "Wars of Religion"', in R. C. Richardson (ed.), *Town and Countryside in the English Revolution* (Manchester, 1992), pp. 100–29.

methods. That said, there is an urgent need to ground our sense of communication firmly in the forms of daily life and also in relation to the economic and social pressures faced by those involved, especially those whose trade was the communication or mediation of knowledge. As we shall see, it is impossible to separate the ideological authority of communications from the social authority of those engaged in communication, but in turn, their authority depended in part on the authority that forms of communication could command. Thus clergymen and booksellers, as well as churches and forms of media, were in a state of mutual interdependence and potential competition. For the clergy, in particular, whose own authority depended heavily on their superior investment in the interpretation and ownership of printed material, the use of print by others, to challenge the message they could offer from the pulpit, was a complex challenge to which to respond.

In a brief essay it is only possible to sketch an account of communication over more than seventy turbulent years in a city whose population probably rose from some 12–15,000 in 1640 to about 25,000 in 1714. At one level, almost all the surviving records could be pertinent to this topic. On the other hand, there are major limitations on our understanding posed by the nature of that evidence. In 1683 a Bristol informer urged that his letter not be shown to any Bristolians 'for they tell every man his friend, so that in a day it will be public',[3] but we have very few personal papers of Bristolians and no records such as diaries that might allow us to recreate flows of communication on a daily basis. Some letters of merchants, gentry and other leading figures survive, but even these are limited in scale and duration. Bristol is also poorly supplied with depositions from court records which might offer some systematic coverage of social interchange. There are many more records which allow us to monitor the flow of people or goods – through migration, marriage, trade or financial connections – and enough historical work has been done on these to enable one to conjecture on their implications for communication. But most of the extant evidence that bears directly on communication as an issue is produced by institutions such as the corporation or the churches, or survives in the form of the products of those media that have proved durable, notably printed material collected into libraries and now easily accessible to all scholars through online facsimiles. Given the themes of this essay, there is clearly a danger that the nature of such evidence will predetermine the outcome. One of my arguments will be that historians have been unduly

---

[3] *CSP Dom. 1683–4*, p. 97.

influenced by the historical visibility of print culture and its growing accessibility, but paradoxically much of my argument will depend on using those very sources to show how they, themselves, reveal the secondary importance of print within civic culture. However, my own argument for the centrality of a civic culture and of political and religious aspects of communication is vulnerable to similar criticism that I have allowed the records of bodies central to such a civic culture to shape my view of the whole topic.

The main institutional records are those of the city corporation, which had the legal status of a chartered incorporation wielding, among other things, the legal powers of a county, as Bristol had been since 1373 a county of itself outside the jurisdiction of Somerset and Gloucestershire, on whose borders it sat. The corporation had a mayor and aldermen who acted as the city's JPs and a wider common council of forty-three members from whom they were chosen. The city was also divided into twelve wards, each the special responsibility of one alderman. The city also had seventeen parishes and an extra-parochial area, the Castle, which was developed for building after the Castle was demolished in the 1650s. Some of the parishes stretched outside the city boundaries. The parishes were subject to the deanery of Bristol, one of two deaneries of the diocese of Bristol (the other, oddly, being Dorset), whose seat was the cathedral on College Green, although the bishops and diocesan government divided their time between the two parts of the diocese. Many of the city parishes were in the gift of the city corporation, although some belonged to private patrons, the crown or the church. As JPs the city magistrates held considerable power over the parishes, and from 1696 the parishes also lost one of their major powers, that of relief of the poor, to a statutory Corporation of the Poor, which emerged as a body partly responsible to both corporation and parishes and partly an independent body elected by local ratepayers. All of these bodies have left extensive records except for aspects of diocesan government lost in fires in 1731 and 1831 and the Corporation of the Poor, destroyed by bombing in the Second World War. At the national level the correspondence between the central government, notably the secretaries of state, and various groups in the city (see below) as deposited in the State Papers Domestic, form the major evidence, not just for the interchange of information between Bristol and the state but also for the concerns of all parties about the nature and impact of that communication, and much of what follows will draw on that evidence. It is worth noting that the higher standard of calendaring and indexing of these papers before 1700 than afterwards has undoubtedly reinforced historians' tendency to see these records as central for that period but not later, when printed evidence is used more often to establish the nature of local/central interaction.

In 1640 Bristol already had a well-established book trade, which led to a steady stream of sermons and the occasional pamphlet being published in London, while Bristol stories and ballads with a Bristol seafaring theme quite often featured in ballads and chapbooks.[4] The Civil War saw the start of Bristol printing, as the king's printers had a press in the city during the royalist occupation from 1643 to 1645, while news of Bristol's military and political actions were of sufficient national importance to both sides that there were numerous printings of petitions, official notices and rival news items and justificatory statements about events in Bristol during the civil war period. By the 1650s this was replaced by London publication of a series of interlocking controversies between rival religious groups, with disputes between Presbyterians and independents/Baptists then overlaid by disputes between Quakers and all the other groups, often involving clergy and others from neighbouring counties and from London, and with close connections to the evolving politics of the corporation, various parliamentary committees in the region and military garrisons. This set the pattern for the post-Restoration decades when the same topics dominated publications about and from Bristol, which had to be of sufficient wider interest to be published in London or Oxford, even if sponsored and sold locally by booksellers or local interest groups. The main subjects are political and religious, with elections, the persecution of dissenters and Bristol input into the Popish Plot and subsequent crises until 1689 as the most frequent topics. Most other items, such as almanacs, reports of prodigies or literary publications, turn out on closer inspection to have more or less overt ideological overtones, often being prompted by public events such as elections, anniversaries or public occasions.

It was not until 1695 that Bristol regained its own printing press, after fifty years, when the lapsing of the Licensing Act led the blind William Bonny to leave London to set up the first provincial press of the new era. Sometime between 1700 and 1702 he then established one of the first provincial newspapers, the *Bristol Postboy*. By 1714 he had for some years been facing a rival paper, the first of many run by members of the Farley family, a West Country dynasty whose papers were generally opposed to the Whig regimes of the next half-century. For some decades after 1695 Bristol authors and material remained as likely to be published nationally

---

[4] E. R. N. Mathews, *Bristol Bibliography* (Bristol, 1916) remains the starting point, but I have compiled a much fuller bibliography based on the short-title catalogues, on which the analyses here are based.

as locally, but gradually a local market grew, just as the newspapers began to develop a larger local content. But even in 1714 it remains the case that the products of the press in and about Bristol must be understood largely as a record of aspects of Bristol life that interested a wider audience or informed Bristolians about external events (as the early newspapers largely did), not as a sample of the communications of Bristolians between themselves or about their own affairs.

If we examine, for example, all the extant issues of the *Bristol Postboy* and *Sam Farley's Bristol Postman* until 1715 (a few stray issues until 1713 and some reasonable runs for 1714–15),[5] the only Bristol items, apart from advertisements, are a small number of letters with news from ships, one letter from Paris to a Bristol merchant reporting the arrival of a prominent Jacobite (the Duke of Ormonde), a report of the outcomes of the assize trial of those charged with murder following the coronation day riots in Bristol, lists of the Lenten preachers, a prayer to be read in all churches during the Jacobite rebellion, copies of various addresses to the King by the Loyal Society, the corporation and the sheriffs and Grand Jury, and copies of Grand Jury presentments.[6] There is also a corporation notice regarding a £20 reward for information leading to conviction of the author, writer or publisher of 'several malicious scandalous, false and traitorous libels published and dispersed in Bristol and several written copies thereof put clandestinely at night in and under doors of several houses in city'.[7] Instead, both papers offered an account of 'the most material news both foreign and domestick',[8] laid out in a style borrowed largely from manuscript newsletters. *Sam Farley's Bristol Postman* follows the layout of a letter, starting 'Sir', and abstracting the 'following advices' or 'intelligences' from the post, in which it is not clear which items are from printed sources and which from manuscript newsletters or ordinary letters. The issue for 24 December 1715 typically declares 'since our last we have received the following advices . . . by this day's post we have received two mails from Holland with the following advices'. It is clear that contemporaries did not draw any fixed line between news conveyed in private letters, manuscript newsletters or what we call newspapers. Instead, they viewed them all as products of 'the post', hence

---

[5] C. E. Clark, *The Public Prints* (New York and Oxford, 1994), pp. 62–6 discusses the contents of the early Bristol papers, but is unaware of the copies in the Codrington Library, All Souls, Oxford, and so makes several errors: see my 'Press and Politics of Culture'. My account builds on D. F. Gallop, 'Chapters in the History of the Provincial Newspaper Press: 1700–1855', MA thesis, University of Bristol (1954).

[6] *Bristol Postboy*, nos. 808, 791, 706, 668, 718, 802, 705, 794, 798 and 795 and *Sam Farley's Bristol Postman*, nos. 6 and 27.

[7] *Bristol Postboy*, no. 808 (10 December 1715).   [8] *Ibid.*, nos. 91, 619.

the titles of the early newspapers. In 1683 it was noted that 'almost every private and public letter related a design on the king's life'.[9] In 1702 the mayor was asked to compare the handwriting on the superscription of a Jacobite libel with 'the hand of the public newspapers that are writ to your town'.[10]

Both printers also advertised their own services. Bonny undertakes 'to print any thing in Hebrew, Greek, Latin or English, in Divinity, Physick or Law or any Science or Art, as well and as cheap as in London or any other place. Justices-Warrants and summons and all other usual blanks, Also Polices, Bills of Lading etc and all sorts of advertisements will be printed' while Sam Farley claims 'I shall always have by me ready printed' a whole range of legal and administrative warrants (including for the poor law and for informers against profane swearers), tax forms, blank appearances for attorneys, and druggists' labels.[11] From this it is clear that the chief customers of the printers were expected to be mercantile or professional and that the local material conveyed was overwhelmingly generated by the public bodies of the town, with the papers reproducing authoritative texts generated elsewhere: precisely the same kinds of documents constitute most of the surviving ephemeral printing of this period (indeed one suspects that the same printer set up the text for a public notice and then transferred it into his newspaper).

We can also approach the nature of communications more structurally (and so hypothetically) by considering the forms of communication, both in and out of Bristol and within the city, that must have flowed from the nature of Bristol's economy, society and governmental position. Rather than operating independently, the media may be seen as operating in the context of the movement of people and goods, and hence of information, through Bristol. News was spread by people in their travels and by the networks and meetings of people involved in the exchange of goods. Bristol's status as the entrepot of the west was made most visible in its two annual fairs, in January (St Paul's) and July (St James) when traders from all over the West Country came as buyers and many Londoners came to sell, including London booksellers such as Benjamin Harris and John Dunton. The authorities knew these events to be crucial to the city's economy (indeed relied on the revenue that their stalls generated) yet also feared the effects of mass migration into the city. Groups such as the Quakers used the fairs as a time to hold their regional meetings and circulated their literature within

---

[9] *CSP Dom. 1683 (1)*, p. 341.　　[10] *CSP Dom. 1700–2*, p. 490.
[11] *Bristol Postboy*, no. 619; *Sam Farley's Bristol Postman*, nos. 6, 25.

the crowded city, leading a clerical opponent to liken one such publication to a monster exhibited at the fair. But the fairs were merely the most intense expression of the continuous flow of people and goods generated by trade. It has been shown that the patterns of migration into and out of the city mirrored Bristol's chief trading routes, with flows from the immediate hinterlands of South Gloucestershire, west Wiltshire and north Somerset, plus the two coasts of the Bristol channel and the counties bordering the Severn, all of which looked to Bristol both for coastal trade and as their main link into wider trading patterns. Of these, Bristol's most important connections were with London, with Ireland, with southern Europe and, of ever-growing importance over the period, with the Caribbean and American colonies.[12]

Much of the news collected in Bristol of greatest interest both to Bristolians and others was of events in these places, with economic issues not easily distinguishable from military and political news, since trade was not only affected by these other matters but also provided the carriers by which such news travelled. Much of the unpublished state correspondence reflects the passing-on of such news to London (with customs officials as key correspondents), and so does a steady stream of printed news items reproducing letters received in Bristol from merchants or others. In 1689, for example, a London publication reproduced news of the deposed King James's landing in Ireland from a Bristol merchant's eyewitness letter.[13] However, until the 1690s there is little direct reflection of mercantile activity in Bristolians' printed output: a few navigational works, a gauging handbook, and a letter regarding the East India Company, though after 1695 there is some growth of trade literature, largely from the pen of John Cary.[14]

In assessing the importance of such communications, we must realise that the economy both of the port and of the traders, especially the merchants, was largely determined by the accuracy of their information, or, in contemporary parlance, by the 'credit' of their networks.[15] In the absence of impersonal financial systems, and with their profits depending largely on judging relative price movements in unstable trading highly dependent

---

[12] See Sacks, *Widening Gate*; K. O. Morgan, *Bristol and the Atlantic Trade in the Eighteenth Century* (Cambridge, 1993); D. Hussey, *Coastal and River Trade in Pre-Industrial England* (Exeter, 2000).

[13] *A Full and True Account of the Landing and Reception of the Late King James at Kinsale* (1689), Wing F2306.

[14] S. Sturmy, *The Mariner's Magazine* (1669 and later editions), Wing S9096–8; H. Turford, *The Merchant's Aid or a Help to the Unskilful Accomptant* (1674), Wing 3261A; R. Collins, *The Countrey Gaugers Vade Mecum* (1677), Wing C5383; *An Answer to Two Letters concerning the East-India Company* (1676), Wing A3457; Cary's works are discussed below.

[15] See J. Barry, 'Bourgeois Collectivism', in J. Barry and C. Brooks (eds.), *The Middling Sort of People* (Basingstoke, 1994), pp. 84–112; C. Muldrew, *The Economy of Obligation* (Basingstoke, 1998).

on external factors, many of them political but others natural, merchants rose or fell (and many failed, itself a key piece of news) on the strength of their knowledge of multiple markets and on the basis of other people's estimation of the credit of their knowledge. Hence the authority invested in their letters in the eyes of the wider world, but also, paradoxically, the value to them of keeping such knowledge to themselves. Thus the exchange of Bristol, as in London and elsewhere, was simultaneously the key locus of communication, where one went to hear the news and read letters from elsewhere, but also a place where communication had its most obvious price, excluding many. During the eighteenth century, the growth in printed information about all aspects of trade as well as the rise in banking and other means of assuring credit, served to lessen this impact, while making the trading community the obvious target audience for newspaper editors or coffeehouse proprietors eager to trade on the news they could offer. But in 1714 these media were still more dependent on the traders for news than the traders were on them. As a consequence, within Bristol it was through family, social circles, associations and churches that traders simultaneously acquired information of credit, since it came from trusted sources and also established their own credit economically and socially. On a smaller scale, the same story might be told of craftsmen and small retailers, and of their search for both credit and knowledge through guilds, societies and often through neighbourhood. Equally, although advertisements began to appear in the papers, and printers presumably produced ephemeral items to serve business, this seems to have been very small-scale until the 1730s, at least, and to have related to housing, luxury and service retailing, rather than commercial or industrial activity.[16]

The other main structural determinant of the flow of information was the governmental structure outlined above, which was in part a hierarchy intended to ensure the flow of information up and down the network. Among the early examples of the uses of print were a range of materials generated by such processes, including visitation articles designed to elicit both written responses from parish officers and clergy and to structure discussions at visits, and petitions sent from Bristol to parliament or the crown presenting information and requesting action.[17] The 'presentment', in which an authorised body provided information to another and sought

---

[16] Some examples of early Bristol printed ephemera are found in BL, 816 m.16 and Bristol Archives Office [hereafter BAO], 04217.

[17] Printed articles survive for 1640 (*STC* 10145.3), 1662 (Wing C4018), 1673 (see n. 19), 1678 (Wing C4019A), 1682 (Wing C4020), 1686 (Wing C4020A). The parish presentments to the church courts are in BAO, EP/V/3.

action in return, might indeed be regarded as the paradigmatic form of communication in early modern government, underlying all kinds of courts and administrative processes. The most authoritative form within city government was the Grand Jury presentment to quarter sessions or assizes, and interestingly a whole series of these were published in the 1670s and 1680s as rival party groups sought to represent the city interest. In such cases it is clear that the Jury was itself carefully chosen by the sheriffs to ensure that its members would communicate certain facts and draw certain conclusions. These presentments may be preserved in written and sometimes printed form, but of course their primary expression was in speech, and speech given to a specific audience on a specific occasion, from which its authority was drawn.[18] The 1673 visitation articles make this interpenetration of the media very clear: the clergyman is instructed to read the articles of enquiry 'distinctly' to the churchwardens, suggesting some might be illiterate (very few churchwardens still were in Bristol), but the relevant articles were also printed within the text in black letter, the form of print used for proclamations and other notices, perhaps for their air of authority, or perhaps because the less educated found this lettering easier to read than the italic form. Emphasis is laid on the sacred duty of the laypeople to present their answers fully and truthfully, with the warning that failure to do so would subject their parish to God's judgement.[19]

The same point might be made about most of the other governmental forms of communication. The city corporation used a wide range of written methods to communicate both within the city and elsewhere, especially to London, and the town clerk with his written archives had been a key figure since the fifteenth century at least. But the corporation invested heavily in a range of modes of communication, while spending only modestly on script and very little on print, even after Bonny's arrival, except in political emergencies when multiple copying of an exact message could be seen as valuable. At first sight the figure of £27 spent by one side on printing in the Bristol election of 1713 sounds impressive, but it seems modest in a total expenditure of £2257, or even compared to the £78 18s spent on 'knots' or party favours.[20] Normally communication still centred on proclamations (given both orally by the bellman and in writing posted up at certain set

---

[18] BAO, 04451–2(1) contain the jury presentments for the period to 1700 (1641–56, 1661, 1663 and 1667–75 presentments are missing). There are printed presentments or addresses for 1675 (Wing G1501), April and October 1681 (Wing G1500/A, T3529), April 1682 (Wing P3286A, S3879), March 1683 (Wing P3285/6), Midsummer 1696 (Wing H3591A). See also *CSP Dom. 1679–80*, pp. 440–1, 488, 619–20; *CSP Dom. 1680–1*, pp. 250, 277, 681; *CSP Dom. 1683(1)*, p. 95.

[19] *Articles of Enquiry [of Guy Carleton]* (1673), Wing C4019, 'Direction to the Clergy' and p. 5.

[20] W. Barrett, *The History and Antiquities of the City of Bristol* (Bristol, 1789), p. 148.

locations around the town) and on the use of rituals and symbols, such as bellringing, public celebrations and regular processions and rounds of meetings to recognise key events and anniversaries. In the 1680 election, supporters of the exclusionist candidate, Robert Henley, complained that the morning before the election the Corporation 'did cause papers to be posted up at several parts of the town purporting, That none but a freeman could be elected, and at the bottom of those papers was written, No Henly; No Henly; and when some of the electors pulled down those papers, they were, for so doing, bound over to the sessions'.[21] In 1667 the customs collector Fitzherbert, who was the central government's chief conduit for news from Bristol (and in return received the official papers), noted that until the proclamation of peace, nobody had really trusted the news and traders had not dared sail, but 'many formerly diffident may now believe'.[22] During the Popish Plot another ultra-royalist informer, Richard Ellsworth, complained bitterly that the Assizes speech of the Whig city recorder, Sir Robert Atkins, in 1679 had 'begotten in all those that heard the same and all others from the report such a real belief in its verity, as well as its notoriously intended villainy, that 'tis a crime . . . to gainsay or question its credit . . . so that . . . they are now thereby strangely confirmed in their beliefs of that which they had before taken up only at trust from printed papers and bare reports and at a great distance too'.[23]

We know very little about what was said on such occasions and how far the visual and aural messages were made explicit in speeches: but such events obviously mattered, as there was often conflict over who did what, where and when. Perhaps the most extraordinary event of this entire period was the charge delivered by Judge Jeffreys at the Bristol assize on 21 September 1685, following Monmouth's rebellion, as reported in a pamphlet. Jeffreys began: 'Gentlemen, I find here a great many auditors, who are very intent, as if they expected some formal or declared speech, but assure yourselves, we come not to make neither set speeches nor formal declarations, nor to follow a couple of puffing trumpeters; for, Lord, we have seen those things twenty times before: No, we come to do the King's business'. He proceeded to lambast the city and its authorities for their inclination to rebellion, especially attacking the 'trimmers' among the elite. He then demanded that each constable be reminded of his duty to bring in his presentment 'or that you present him' before, in an astonishing piece of theatre, himself

---

[21] *The Case of the Election for the City of Bristol* (1680), Wing C1067A.
[22] *CSP Dom. 1667*, pp. 427, 448.
[23] HMC, *Report on the MSS of Allan George Finch, of Burley-on-the-Hill, Rutland*, 4 vols. (1913–65), vol. II, p. 57.

turning to the bench of city magistrates to arrest the mayor and aldermen for kidnapping, 'their Bills [of indictment] being privately preferred to the Grand Jury by John Rumsey [the town clerk] and being found [i.e. found a true bill]'.[24] It is hard to imagine a more effective overturning of civil cultural expectations, nor to be surprised that the next civic speech committed to print from Bristol is that in 1689, when civic dignitaries were dispatched to London with an address of thanks to the Prince of Orange![25]

At the same time, the civic authorities both worked with, and were jealous of, the other official channel of communication, namely the Church. Church processions, attendance and sermons were a crucial part of civic propaganda, but the churches could also send out their own messages. The ringing of bells, for example, was highly contentious: in February 1660 one alderman was reproved by the mayor for having his parish bells rung for the readmission of the secluded members,[26] while in 1683 the vestry of St Philip and Jacob forbad any ringing for public events without their express permission, except on 5 November and 29 May (Restoration Day).[27] Relations between city and cathedral were particularly fraught, but parish pulpits were also fought over. After all, the authoritative commentators on the significance of news and events were the clergy, particularly through their sermons, and such sermons formed the largest single type of printed material, though only a tiny fraction of sermons got into print.[28] Some that did so were printed because of the controversy which their oral presentation had created. A tremendous furore surrounded the claim that Bristol Dean Richard Thompson had preached in the Cathedral, on 30 January 1679, that there was no Popish Plot but rather a Presbyterian one, along with (if his opponents be believed) disparaging remarks on Henry and Elizabeth as despoilers of the church.[29] When a Whig parish clergyman, John Chetwynd, tried to preach his sermon in the Cathedral on 5 November 1681, calling for Protestant unity against popery, he was unable to deliver

---

[24] *The Charge Given by the Lord Chief Justice Jefferies* (1685), Wing J527, pp. 1, 4. Bristol Central Library, Bristol Collection 4502 gives an annalist's hostile response to Jeffreys.

[25] *The Speech of the Recorder of Bristol to his Highness the Prince of Orange* (1689), Wing P3115A.

[26] HMC, *Report on the Manuscripts of F. W. Leyborne-Popham, Esq., of Littlecote, Co. Wilts* (1899), p. 160.

[27] BAO, P/St P and J/V1, 1683.

[28] On this see T. Claydon, 'The Sermon, the "Public Sphere" and the Political Culture of Late Seventeenth-Century England', in L. A. Ferrell and P. McCullough (eds.), *The English Sermon Revised* (Manchester, 2000), pp. 208–34.

[29] *The Report from the Committee of the Commons to Consider the Petition of Richard Thompson* (1680) (not in Wing, but three copies in Bristol Central Library); *The Visor Pluck't off from Richard Thompson of Bristol Clerk* (1680) (Wing V661).

the sermon and had to finish it the next day in his own parish of Temple; he then had it printed in London for sale by Thomas Wall, the Whig Bristol bookseller.[30]

It is very hard to tell how far the normal sermon had the heavy political and immediate relevance one finds in many printed sermons, since it may have been their exceptional ideological content and topicality which led to their publication. We do not have any collection of unpublished sermons to compare them with until the very end of the period when some of the sermon notes of an independent minister (Andrew Gifford) have survived: these are relatively politically charged, but dissenting clergy may have been more explicit about this than the parochial clergy.[31] From the 1640s the latter faced a growing range of rival communicators in the shape both of alternative ministers and groups of laity who decided to do without a professional communicator, such as the Quakers. Much of the debate about the media was fostered by the clerical reaction to this competition, and although it might take the form of a critique of the press as a seditious force undermining the clergy, this challenge was seen as a minor part of the larger problem of meetings of people outside clerical control ('hearers' as contemporary sources significantly called them) and their manipulation by preachers.

Many examples of complaints about both the news and the press in the period revolve around the fear and accusation that religious organisations of one kind or another were in fact controlling the flow of information, often through connections to London and other external bodies. In these controversies anxiety about the challenge to established authority posed by people with access to alternative means of communication was the key theme, from which complaints about specific media methods and content took on their force. For example, there are a series of 'Tory' grand jury presentments between 1675 and 1685 (themselves often printed, paradoxically but significantly) which attacked the influence of news spread by seditious groups,[32] including the role played by coffeehouses in providing news, which it was suggested was seducing the ordinary people from their business into 'debating state matters and hearing news which often proves false and yet is glibly swallowed by the credulous' to the detriment of both trade and peace within the city.[33] It is easy to take these attacks as signs of a powerful new influence at work, and the authorities certainly took

---

[30] J. Chetwynd, *Eben-ezer* (1682), Wing C3796.
[31] Regent's Park College, Oxford, Angus Library, FPC D.21.
[32] See above n. 18, especially *CSP Dom. 1679–80*, pp. 440–1, and presentment of April 1682.
[33] *CSP Dom. 1680–1*, p. 250.

the threats seriously, for example raiding one coffeehouse and sending a newsletter found there up to London.[34] Efforts were made to catch the publishers of 'libels' against the Bristol authorities and correct false claims: in July 1682 they complained of a 'pamphlet printed and set forth' denying a Bristol Quaker had recanted and taken the oaths: he was to take them again 'to give publick satisfaction' and this should be 'made public in the [London] Gazette or otherwise' and one libel was publicly burned at the High Cross.[35]

But it is crucial to note that these occasional attacks, verbal and actual, on dissenting print culture were a minor skirmish in an ongoing battle against dissenting churches and related clubs, which faced the brunt of prosecution. The 1681 presentment of John Kimber's coffeehouse identified its clients as 'many schismatical, seditious and disloyal persons': Kimber's widow was a Baptist.[36] In 1683 a leading persecutor claimed all the disorders and 'seditious contrivances' 'were hatched at that meeting-house' [the Castle Green independent church] and moved from thence into 'coffeehouses and clubs'.[37] The 1675 presentment defined the danger as from 'schismatical, seditious and disloyal seducers and sectaries, who are the very pests and firebrands of our cities and the principal (if not only) disturbers and breakers of the peace therein', their 'heads' being 'diverse strangers' 'pretending themselves to be ministers of Jesus Christ . . . lately come to settle in this city'.[38]

As I have described elsewhere, the heart of this struggle was over the effort of their opponents to identify the dissenters and their allies as out-siders, subverting the civic community, and of the other side to portray themselves as core members of the civic community.[39] In this struggle, the dissemination of news and print was simultaneously a metaphor for the wider problem and a means of carrying on the contest. Hence the Presbyterians were frequently identified, for example by the nearby Beaufort family, as using their London ties to spread news against the crown and its supporters.[40] Tory satirists also tried repeatedly to undermine the

---

[34] *CSP Dom. 1682*, pp. 321, 327.   [35] BAO, 04452 (1), July 1682.

[36] *CSP Dom. 1680–1*, p. 250; BAO, 04434(1), recognizance 13 February 1676 and indictment of Kimber May 1682; Quarter-Sessions Minute Book 1672–81, letter of 2 July 1679 at end, and Minute Book 1681–1705, July 1682 and March 1684; E.P./V/3 St Ewen's, 1680–1 and All Saints, 1684; E.P./J/4 inventories of J. Kimber (1681) and A. Payne (1687). R. Hayden (ed.), *The Records of a Church of Christ in Bristol 1640–87*, Bristol Record Society 27 (1974), pp. 204, 252, 297.

[37] *CSP Dom. 1683(2)*, pp. 265–6.

[38] *The Grand Jurors of the City of Bristoll, their Address* (1675), Wing G1501, p. 2.

[39] Barry, 'Politics of Religion'.

[40] HMC, *Twelfth Report, Appendix, Part IX, The MSS of the Duke of Beaufort, K.G., the Earl of Donough-more and others* (1891), pp. 77–81, 93; *CSP Dom. 1666–7*, p. 273; *CSP Dom. 1667*, p. 389.

respectability of the leading city bookseller, Thomas Wall, by accusing him of drunkenness and adultery, as well as Presbyterian intrigue, as if to undermine his moral claims to trade and publish legitimately within the civic community.[41] The moral attack was the more powerful because 'sobriety' and moral reformation were the watchwords of dissenters and their allies in justifying their own conduct and attacking their persecutors: for example, their printed response to the 1675 presentment is called *A Sober Answer to an Address of the Grand Jurors*.[42] When the Quaker merchant Thomas Speed published his *Reason against Rage* in 1691, responding to a 'late scurrilous libel' prefixed to a reprint of a republican sermon he had given in 1651, intended to smear Quakers and other Whigs with fanaticism during the 1690 election campaign, he defended his appearance 'to the World in print' as purely defensive, faced with a 'libel whose contents are fitter to be turned into a song, to be sung by a crew of drunkards at an ale-bench, than to be exposed to the view and perusal of any judicious and serious readers'.[43]

At the same time, there was a lot of competition and tension between the established authorities about their respective authority and the nature of the messages they had to offer – such divisions were arguably the chief reason why effective control over communication was never established. Neither the lay nor the clerical establishment ever presented a unified message to the people of Bristol at any time after 1640, despite their continued commitment to the claim that such a message should exist, if only the proper authority was respected. This problem equally affected the flow of news out of Bristol to government. Successive regimes found it very hard to know whose information to trust; by 1681 Secretary Jenkins told the Mayor that, while he had to write to all those who complained, it was not 'incumbent to give credit till all are heard'.[44] When Jeffreys left the dramatic scene described earlier, he immediately wrote to the royal court urging that the king not be 'surprised' into pardoning those arrested before he had come in person to tell the full story, but in fact the arrested mayor

---

[41] *Advice to a Painter in a Poem to a Friend* (1681), Wing A639, p. 15; E. Phileroy, *A Satyrical Vision* (1684), Wing P1985, pp. 10–11; J. Dunton, *Life and Errors* (1705), p. 316.

[42] *A Sober Answer* (1675), Wing S4407.

[43] T. Speed, *Reason against Rage* (1691), Wing S4906, 'To the honest-hearted impartial Reader', pp. 1–2, 10, 16, 18. The original sermon printed in 1651 is Wing S4907; the reprint is in Bristol Central Library, Bristol collection 9706. For the 1650s controversy between Speed and the clergy see: T. Speed, *Christ's Innocency Pleaded* (1655), Wing S4904/A; C. Fowler and S. Ford, *A Sober Answer* (1656), Wing F1694; W. Thomas, *Rayling Rebuked* (1656), Wing T989; T. Speed, *The Guilt-Covered Clergyman Unveiled* (1657), Wing S4905; W. Thomas, *A Vindication of Scripture and Ministry* (1657), Wing T991.

[44] *CSP Dom. 1680–1*, pp. 628–9.

petitioned successfully, using his connections as a father-in-law of one of the North family.[45] The Duchess of Beaufort urged her husband to stop his servants writing news to those in the country, as things reported from Badminton were given 'authority' by the place. Rumours of a French invasion in December 1678 were, according to her, spread by the machinations of nonconformists and Whigs such as Atkins, but also by the influence of the mayor who, though not ill-intentioned, had given official credence to the report by acting on it.[46] Rival forms of authority could nearly always be deployed to communicate different messages, whether it was different Anglican clergy preaching different political messages, or grand juries in successive quarter sessions offering contradictory views or the inherent ambiguities in the public celebration of events such as 5 November.

It is in this context, I would argue, that we should consider the usefulness, and limitations, of the notion of a 'public sphere'. There is no doubt that concepts of public authority and communication were central to the arguments just noted. The ideal was the virtuous and godly public magistrate, such as alderman Joseph Jackson, as described in his funeral sermon of 1661, who 'knew well the state of this city's affairs and aimed at the publique weal thereof, without self-seeking. He was a man of a very publique spirit, desiring the publique good; and what evil he was not able publiquely to redress, he was wont privately to lament.'[47] The critique of those people, places and times that were used to communicate outside the control of the establishment was that they lacked public authority and so represented the work of factions or parties. These were private and self-interested groups whose claim to represent or communicate within the public sphere of civic culture was illegitimate in motive, form and consequence. Yet in an increasingly pluralist city it was hard to find a stable core of agreed public authority against which to make these accusations of faction last for any length of time or with any lasting effect. And those in opposition to a particular establishment could equally appeal to their 'public spirit' as the motivation for their actions, including their decision to publish their opinions for the information of Bristolians and others. James Holloway, a Bristol merchant executed as a Rye House plotter, presented himself in his printed confession as an ordinary Bristolian who had unluckily 'concerned myself in things

---

[45] *CSP Dom. 1685*, nos. 1663, 1767, 1843; R. North, *The Lives of the Norths*, ed. A. Jessopp, 3 vols. (1890), vol. 1, p. 284; J. Latimer, *Annals of Bristol in the Seventeenth Century* (1900), pp. 433–4.

[46] HMC, *Twelfth Report, Appendix, Part VIII, MSS of the Duke of Athole, K. T., and the Earl of Home* (1891), pp. 76–81.

[47] F. Roberts, *The Christian's Advantage* (1662), Wing R1582, p. 29. See G. Baldwin, 'The "Public" as a Rhetorical Community in Early Modern England', in A. Shepard and P. Withington (eds.), *Communities in Early Modern England* (Manchester, 2000), pp. 199–215.

much above me', but there was a definite double edge to his statement that 'it has been my bad fortune to hear too much of public affairs and to have too much a public spirit for one of my capacity', and in more defiant mood Holloway sent the King a long account of the state of public opinion about the plot and the monarchy, clearly believing Charles needed to take account of the public view.[48]

In strict Habermasian terms, Bristol in this period certainly did not see a public sphere of private people coming together in free association by rules of rational debate and information exchange to establish a public sphere separate from the traditional authority structures of society, state and Church. One may question whether sociologically such a sphere is plausible anywhere, but it was not even a conceivable project within Bristol in this period.[49] Instead the ideal was of a civic culture where the public sphere is rooted in the established forms of social and political authority and operates through all sorts of inherited symbolic forms, based on the traditions of civic life, which are the reverse of Habermas' model. However, that does not mean that this civic culture was monolithic and consensual. It never was, and it became less so as pluralistic forces in Bristol grew stronger. That did not, I argue, remove the ideal or many of the practices of a civic culture, but it did make the nature of communication within the city ever more complex and contested.

One final example may illustrate this point. In all the printed material produced in Bristol, one set of publications stand out in character, and might easily serve as an example of the rise of a public sphere dependent on print. These are the writings of John Cary, Bristol merchant and pioneer writer on economics, whose publications on trade and poverty, and proposals to establish a Bristol workhouse, are self-conscious appeals to a universal public based on rational arguments. The fact that Cary had urged his correspondent Locke and others to oppose the renewal of the licensing act, so allowing Bonny to establish a press in Bristol, and that Cary's writings were among Bonny's first commissions, makes the case even more perfect. Yet a closer look reveals that Cary's use of print was only one aspect of a much more complex strategy, in which personal contacts (both in London, where he was a lobbyist for various Bristol interests, and in Bristol, where he had many influential friends among the radical circles of the elite) and use of other media played an equal part: indeed, it could be argued that the

---

[48] J. Holloway, *A Free and Voluntary Confession* (1684), Wing H2509; *CSP Dom. 1683–4*, pp. 238–41, 366–70, 380.
[49] See J. Barry, 'A Historical Postscript', in D. Castiglione and L. Sharpe (eds.), *Shifting the Boundaries* (Exeter, 1995), pp. 220–34.

turn to print was a strategy of last resort rather than a principled choice. Furthermore, both his trade arguments and his proposals on poverty were clearly understood at the time as reflecting very specific interests, both economic and ideological. In particular, the Corporation of the Poor was designed to remove power from the Anglican parishes and diminish the influence of the city corporation, or at least its Tory members, and to empower dissenting and mercantile groups. In practice, its establishment and subsequent developments owed more to electoral and corporate politics (including an ill fated attempt by Cary to stand as MP in 1698) than to his publications. All of this is not to downplay the importance of ideas in the political process, but to note that the printed word is a very partial guide to the nature and complexity of those ideas and how they were both generated and received.[50]

I have argued that it is more useful to interpret all the various types of communication found in Bristol over this period as contingent responses to the complex culture of local society. Uses of the media were debated because of the people, places and times with which they were associated, although those debates certainly addressed the form as well as the content of each communication. It is unhelpful to single out a particular form of the media and see its growth or decline as the main trend, offering both the object and means of explanation of change. So, rather than see the rise of print or the decline of the scribal or oral as the main theme, requiring explanation and suggesting what form such an explanation should take, we should look instead at the wider debates within which the uses of print were situated in actual cases. At the same time we need to be alive to the practical and ideological considerations, for and against, that lay behind the decision to use print or script in some forms of communication and not in others.

---

[50] See Barry, 'Parish in Civic Life', pp. 168–9 and 'Begging, Swearing and Cursing' for fuller accounts of Cary and the Corporation of the Poor. Some of his papers are in BL, Add. MSS 5540. His writings include: *An Essay on the State of England in Relation to its Trade, its Poor and its Taxes* (Bristol, 1695), Wing C730; *An Essay on the Coin and Credit of England* (Bristol, 1696), Wing C729; *To the Freeholders and Burgesses of the City of Bristol* ([Bristol?], 1698), Wing C733A; *A Vindication of the Parliament of England* (1698), Wing C734–5; *A Proposal offered to the Committee of the House of Commons* (1699/1700?), Wing C732; *An Account of the Proceedings of the Corporation of the Poor* (1700), Wing C724A. See also *Proposals for the Better Maintaining and Employing the Poor in Bristol* (Bristol, 1696), Wing P3747 and other notices in BAO, 04217; *Some Considerations Offer'd to the Citizens of Bristol* ([Bristol?], 1711), *ESTC*, t127579; *The Case of the Poor within the City of Bristol* (1714), *ESTC*, t188810; *The Case of the Workhouse and Hospital of the City of Bristol* ([1718?]), *ESTC*, t063579.

PART IV

Script, print and persecution

11

Preaching without speaking: script, print and religious dissent

Alexandra Walsham

The idea of an apostolate of writing has its roots in early Christian history. Cassiodorus gave classic expression to this conceit in the advice he issued to the religious community he founded in Calabria in the mid-sixth century. He directed his monks 'to preach unto men by means of the hand, to untie the tongue by . . . the fingers . . . to fight the Devil with pen and ink'. 'Every word of the Lord written by the scribe', he said, 'is a wound inflicted on Satan'. In succeeding centuries, this ancient topos was frequently reiterated by the members of cloistered orders whose vows bound them to shun pulpit oratory. 'Without breaking silence', wrote Peter the Venerable, the solitary ascetic could thereby 'make the Lord's teaching resound in the ears of the nations'. 'Since we cannot preach God's word by mouth', declared a Carthusian prior around 1112, 'let us preach it with our hands. Every time we write a book, we make ourselves heralds of the Truth.' In the fifteenth century, echoes of the same commonplace emerged in the circles of the *devotio moderna*: a tract printed in 1476 referred to the Rostock Brethren of the Common Life as *fratres non verbo sed scripto predicantes* ('brothers who preach, not by speaking but by writing').[1]

In these cases silence and exile was chosen and self-imposed: medieval monks voluntarily surrendered the power of speech. In the first half of this essay, however, I want to extend the theme of a ministry of books to individuals and groups whose retreat and marginalisation from the world was not of their own making. I shall use it to illuminate the role which script and print played in the dissemination of religious dissent in pre- and post-Reformation England. In a context of persecution, where the ordained clergy were molested, muzzled, imprisoned, deported, and even put to death, written and printed texts could likewise operate as a proxy

---

[1] Quoted in E. L. Eisenstein, *The Printing Press as an Agent of Change: Communications and Cultural Transformations in Early Modern Europe*, 2 vols. in 1 (Cambridge, 1980 edn), pp. 316–17, 373–4; M. A. Rouse and R. H. Rouse, *Authentic Witnesses: Approaches to Medieval Texts and Manuscripts* (Notre Dame, 1991), pp. 458–9.

and prosthesis for the living voice. They provided minorities whom the
authorities were intent upon rendering mute with a powerful device for
communicating with both their co-religionists and the wider world. They
also helped to forge ties of association which counteracted the dissevering
effects of repressive legislation. The condition of proscription stimulated
creative and imaginative use of the pen and the press in a culture in which
communication was still predominantly oral and in which modes of scribal
publication continued to thrive alongside the technology of typographical
reproduction. In part two, I shall suggest that these insights may necessitate
a partial reassessment of some ingrained assumptions about the intrinsic
links between Protestantism and printing and between the Reformation
and the book.

The ensuing discussion emphasises the overlapping features of
manuscript and print, both being media in which the eye displaced the
ear as the organ of cognitive reception. But it also recognises their distinctive characteristics and functions. Script had the advantage of being more
immediate and intimate and offering authors greater scope for selecting and
controlling their audience. It was also a much safer vehicle for heterodox
material: it could more readily evade the net of government censors and in
an emergency it was much easier to hide a pen than a heavy and cumber-
some press. Print, though, clearly had superior qualities as a mass medium:
it was able to carry multiple copies of texts to readers more quickly and
cheaply than even the most briskly efficient commercial scriptorium. At
the same time it must be stressed that neither printing nor writing worked
in isolation from the spoken word. Rather they operated in conjunction
with it. What Brian Stock has observed of heretical 'textual communities'
in the eleventh and twelfth centuries still applies to clusters and congregations of dissenters in the fifteenth, sixteenth, and seventeenth: speech
frequently remained essential in authenticating and mediating texts to a
body of auditors. Reading could be a catalyst of communal sociability no
less than a stimulus to private introspection. Nor was literacy necessarily a
prerequisite for enrolment in these fellowships.[2]

I

We may begin in the period before the advent of printing. In late medieval
England, Lollardy and literacy were inextricably intertwined in the eyes

---

[2] B. Stock, *The Implications of Literacy: Written Language and Models of Interpretation in the Eleventh
and Twelfth Centuries* (Princeton, 1983), esp. ch. 2.

of the authorities. The act *De heretico comburendo* of 1401 identified the production of texts as a hallmark of heresy.[3] Mere possession of vernacular tracts was enough to incriminate one, as indicated by John Phip's well known quip upon his abjuration in 1521 that 'he had rather burn his books than that his books should burn him'.[4] Some scholars have doubted the existence of anything like a 'tractarian factory' and downplayed the idea of Lollardy as 'the earliest mail order book club',[5] but there is much to suggest that an organised system of scribal copying was fundamental in spreading the sect. As Anne Hudson has shown, manuscript translations of the Scriptures, sermon cycles, instructional manuals, and flysheets all played a crucial part in welding together Wyclif's disciples. Bills listing the Twelve Conclusions of the Lollards were nailed to the doors of Westminster Hall and St Paul's Cathedral during the session of Parliament in the early months of 1395. 'Letters of Satan' in which the devil heaped praise on the established Church circulated widely, together with martyrological narratives of the tribulations of William Thorpe and Sir John Oldcastle and consolatory epistles in the mode of Christ's apostles.[6] Peripatetic teachers left books behind them as they scurried around the countryside, to compensate for their premature departure. As one remarked: 'Now siris the dai is al ydo and I mai tarie you no lenger, and I have no tyme to make now a recapitulacioun of my sermon. Netheles I purpose to leve it writun among you'.[7] It was in this sense that Joan Baker of London declared defiantly to her episcopal inquisitors in 1511 that 'she cold here a better sermond in hur howse than any doctor or prist colde make at Poulis crosse or any other place'. She echoed the sentiments of Richard Gilmyn of Coventry who, in 1486, insisted *nullus presbiter melius loquitur in pulpito quam ille liber loquitur* (no minister speaks better in the pulpit than does the book).[8]

Even in the later stages of Lollardy, books remained supremely important as conduits of this illicit faith. Those who attended 'scoles of heresy' in 'privy chambers and places' were shown manuscript tracts and exhorted to 'copy the same'.[9] Individual heretics commissioned and purchased transcriptions of key texts like *The Lantern of Light* and *Wycliffes Wicket* for their personal use. The fact that some of those who owned such books were unable

[3] 2 Hen. IV c. 15.   [4] John Foxe, *Actes and Monuments*, 2 vols. (1583), vol. 1, p. 833.
[5] R. N. Swanson, *Church and Society in Late Medieval England*, paperback edn. (Oxford, 1993), p. 332; R. G. Davies, 'Lollardy and Locality', *TRHS*, 6th ser., 1 (1991), 202.
[6] A. Hudson, *The Premature Reformation: Wycliffite Texts and Lollard History* (Oxford, 1988), at pp. 200, 220–4. See also her *Lollards and their Books* (London and Ronceverte, 1985).
[7] Quoted in J. Catto, 'Dissidents in an Age of Faith? Wyclif and the Lollards', *History Today*, 37/11 (1987), 50.
[8] Hudson, *Premature Reformation*, pp. 199–200, 187 respectively.   [9] *Ibid.* pp. 470–1.

to read reminds us of the crucial role played by vicarious literacy and memorisation.[10] A number of female Lollards in East Anglia and the West Midlands became renowned for having committed the Scriptures to heart, at least partly as a precaution against persecution.[11] By this means, in the words of the extra prologue to the Wycliffite Bible, 'though wickid men hadden brent alle oure bookis, God hath writen his lawe in cristen mennis soulis and consciencis'.[12] On the eve of the Reformation, Robert Swanson has conjectured, Lollardy may have been more dependent on the 'incarnate textuality' of such laypeople than on the evangelical initiatives of designated teachers.[13]

The importance of written and printed texts to England's first Protestants is also eloquently attested by their enemies. In the early Henrician period, heretics were envisaged as 'particoler persons who carried in there bosomes certan bokes'.[14] Some went to extraordinary lengths to deceive snooping officials: Humphrey Monmouth, patron of Tyndale, even had items in his library bound with false titles 'to blynde and abuse' inquisitive visitors.[15] Proclamations listed the 'blasphemous and pestiferous books' which the king regarded as his responsibility as a Christian prince to eradicate from his realm and Luther's 'poisonous' tracts were ceremoniously incinerated in London in 1521.[16] In 1530 four men who had illicitly distributed Tyndale's *New Testament* in the capital were forced to ride facing backwards from the Tower to Cheapside, their coats 'pinned thick' with this and other 'infected' works, and there to toss them symbolically into the flames.[17] Imported from abroad and printed secretly in England, such tracts frequently carried spurious imprints designed to mislead: in 1553–4, for instance, John Day issued fifteen texts under the pseudonyms of 'Nicholas Dorcaster' and 'Michael Wood, Rouen'.[18] Published in small octavo formats (for ease of

---

[10] See A. Hudson, 'Lollard Book Production', in J. Griffiths and D. Pearsall (eds.), *Book Production and Publishing in Britain 1375–1475* (Cambridge, 1989), esp. pp. 125–6.

[11] C. Cross, '"Great Reasoners in Scripture": The Activities of Women Lollards 1380–1530', in D. Baker (ed.), *Medieval Women*, SCH Subsidia I (Oxford, 1978), pp. 363, 366–7 and *passim*.

[12] Hudson, *Premature Reformation*, p. 103.

[13] R. N. Swanson, 'Literacy, Heresy, History and Orthodoxy: Perspectives and Permutations for the Late Middle Ages', in P. Biller and A. Hudson (eds.), *Heresy and Literacy, 1000–1530* (Cambridge, 1994), p. 286.

[14] Quoted in A. G. Dickens, *Lollards and Protestants in the Diocese of York 1509–1558* (Oxford, 1959), p. 29.

[15] John Strype, *Ecclesiastical Memorials*, 3 vols. in 6 (Oxford, 1822), vol. i.i, p. 489.

[16] P. L. Hughes and J. F. Larkin (eds.), *Tudor Royal Proclamations*, 3 vols. (New Haven and London, 1964–9), nos. 122 (1521), 129 (1530), 272 (1546); C. S. Meyer, 'Henry VIII Burns Luther's Books, 12 May 1521', *JEH* 9 (1958), 173–87.

[17] R. Brown *et al.* (eds.), *CSP Venetian*, 9 vols. (1864–98), vol. iii, p. 642.

[18] See *STC*, vol. iii, pp. 52, 55, 187; L. P. Fairfield, 'The Mysterious Press of "Michael Wood" (1553–1554)', *The Library*, 5th ser., 27 (1972), 220–32; J. King, 'John Day: Master Printer of the English

concealment and in the interests of greater portability), Reformation texts could fulfil the function of mobile missionaries. The future Anabaptist Joan Bocher was able to disperse polemical pamphlets against the Real Presence in the royal court by tying them to strings and hiding them under her skirts.[19] In the 1530s, Rose Hickman's mother first came to 'some light of the gospell by meanes of some English books' sent to her from beyond the seas, 'whereuppon' she called her three daughters into her chamber and read these out to them, 'very privately for feare of troble'.[20] Also reminding us that the written word continued to be inscribed within a culture of speech, during the reign of Mary I, both the English Bible and the banned Edwardian Book of Common Prayer became the focus of the communal devotion and solidarity of beleaguered underground congregations. Ralph Allerton and other prisoners in Newgate used the latter daily in defiance of the Catholic liturgy and an Islington man attempted to smuggle in a Coverdale version of the Scriptures to sustain those detained in the same gaol by wrapping it in a handkerchief and informing the warden that it was a piece of powdered beef. Books became badges and icons of the proscribed Protestant faith, precious heirlooms to be preserved at any price: in 1554, Edward Underhill employed a Whitechapel bricklayer to build his into a fireplace in the corner of his bedroom.[21]

Nor should we ignore the role played by script in facilitating resistance, creating chains of communication, and fostering inner fraternalism. Handwritten bills scattered in the streets were intended to stir passions, ignite reaction and provoke debate and in 1532 Thomas Bennett nailed a poster to the door of Exeter Cathedral proclaiming 'The Pope is Antichrist, and we ought to worshippe God onely and no Saintes'.[22] The correspondence of incarcerated preachers like John Philpot comforted and instructed their lay followers, resolving their questions of conscience and stiffening their resistance to the temptation of bowing to Baal and becoming 'mass gospellers'. According to the earl of Derby, John Bradford had 'done more hurt by his letters . . . than ever he did when he was abroad by preaching'. It is not surprising that these were gathered up as relics, carefully edited and published by John Foxe, Miles Coverdale and others as 'monuments' of the martyrs.

Reformation', in P. Marshall and A. Ryrie (eds.), *The Beginnings of English Protestantism* (Cambridge, 2002), pp. 180–208.

[19] Strype, *Ecclesiastical Memorials*, vol. II.i, p. 335.

[20] M. Dowling and J. Shakespeare, 'Religion and Politics in Mid-Tudor England through the Eyes of an English Protestant Woman: The Recollections of Rose Hickman', *Bulletin of the Institute of Historical Research*, 55 (1982), 97.

[21] P. Tudor, 'Protestant Books in London in Mary Tudor's Reign', *The London Journal*, 15 (1990), 20–1.

[22] Foxe, *Actes and Monuments*, vol. II, p. 1037.

Reminiscent of St Paul's epistles to the afflicted early Christians, these intimate missives powerfully reinforced the claim that Protestants were part of a brotherhood of believers stretching back to the primitive Church.[23]

The uses to which early Protestants put the pen and the press find many echoes when we turn to consider Elizabethan and early Stuart puritanism. The first stages of the Vestiarian controversy were fuelled by *A Brief Discourse against the Outward Apparell of the Popish Churche* (1566) and, published in Emden, *Two Short and Comfortable Epistles* in the Pauline mould offered solace and sympathy to the 'persecuted brethren' prosecuted in the wake of Matthew Parker's *Advertisements*. The heroic sufferings of puritan ministers who laboured 'to roote out the weedes of Poperie' were catalogued in *A Parte of a Register* published in Middelburg in 1593; a second instalment remained in manuscript until the early part of the twentieth century.[24] Print enabled John Field and Thomas Wilcox to speak to the political nation in their provocative *Admonition to Parliament* (1572) and to criticise England's partial and incomplete Reformation with less fear of immediate reprisal. In the late 1580s, with Robert Waldegrave acting as midwife, it also transformed the viciously satirical Marprelate Tracts from scribal libels into a national scandal. The government sought to extinguish the subversive effects of these texts by making them the victims of rites of destruction by fire.[25]

After the collapse of the Presbyterian movement the following decade the godly clergy partly redirected their energies into the production of practical divinity: in the absence of a true system of ecclesiastical discipline some 'painefull' preachers turned to the written word to assist them in their mission of spiritually awakening the English populace. Edward Dering and others compiled collections of prayers for use in private households, churches in miniature which lacked an ordained ministry.[26] Those ejected

---

[23] See Thomas Freeman's essay, below; also S. Wabuda, 'Henry Bull, Miles Coverdale and the Making of Foxe's *Book of Martyrs*', in D. Wood (ed.), *Martyrs and Martyrologies*, SCH 30 (Oxford, 1993), pp. 245–58. The remark about Bradford can be found in A. Townsend (ed.), *Writings of John Bradford*, Parker Society, 2 vols. (Cambridge, 1848–53), vol. I, p. 469.

[24] [Anthony Gilby and James Pilkington], *To my Lovynge Brethren that is Troublyed about the Popishe Aparell, Two Short Epistels* (Emden, 1566). *A Parte of a Register* ([Middelburg, 1593?]); A. Peel (ed.), *The Seconde Parte of a Register being a Calendar of Manuscripts under that Title Intended for Publication by the Puritans about 1593*, 2 vols. (Cambridge, 1915).

[25] See P. Milward, *Religious Controversies of the Elizabethan Age: A Survey of Printed Sources* (1978), pp. 25–33, 86–93; L. Rostenberg, *The Minority Press and the English Crown 1558–1625: A Study in Repression* (Nieuwkoop, 1971), chs. 13, 14. P. Collinson, 'Ecclesiastical Vitriol: Religious Satire in the 1590s and the Invention of Puritanism', in J. Guy (ed.), *The Reign of Elizabeth I: Court and Culture in the Last Decade* (Cambridge, 1995), pp. 150–70.

[26] Edward Dering, *Godlye Private Praiers for Housholders* (1574). P. Collinson, *The Elizabethan Puritan Movement* (1967), p. 360.

from their benefices in the purges conducted by Whitgift and Bancroft quickly cast aside any inhibitions they had hitherto had about printing. 'We are now willing to make some worke for the Presse because we have no imployment in the pulpit', declared John Dod and Robert Cleaver in the preface to a biblical commentary published in 1606 after both had been deprived of their Oxfordshire livings.[27]

Radical Protestants exploited the press with even more alacrity. Books were the lifeblood of the hated nicodemite sect of the Family of Love. The tiny evangelical tracts by H. N. which Christopher Vittels imported from Cologne rolled up inside Flemish carpets played a vital part in proselytising. The crown drew no distinction between their producers and distributors, branding both 'fathers of damnable lies'.[28] Dispersing heterodox tracts was tantamount to the crime of illicit evangelising: the Brownists John Copping and Elias Thacker were executed for disseminating seditious writings by their leader in 1593.[29] Separatists exiled in the Netherlands were quick to take advantage of the sophisticated Low Countries printing industry, issuing dozens of works denouncing the Church of England as a limb of Antichrist and defending their flight into schism. Nor did they disdain to use print as a vehicle for pursuing their vicious internal quarrels, a strategy which, unsurprisingly, proved somewhat counterproductive.[30] Men like Francis Johnson and John Smyth who had seceded from the state Church and formed discrete congregations in Amsterdam compared the printed book with a trumpet and described it as 'a publique writing, proclaymed as it were uppon the house top'. Their works succoured and cemented scattered bands of separatists who had not yet made their exodus out of England.[31] Similarly, in the late 1580s Henry Barrow had written pastoral letters from prison, admonishing his followers to remember the warning the Lord had given to the lukewarm church of Laodicea and closing with the words from 1 John 5: 'Beloved, kepe your sellves from idolls. Amen'.[32]

---

[27] John Dod and Robert Cleaver, *A Plaine and Familiar Exposition of the Ninth and Tenth Chapters of the Proverbs of Salomon* (1606), sig. A3r.

[28] Hughes and Larkin (eds.), *Tudor Royal Proclamations*, no. 652 (1580). On familist printing, T. W. Hayes, 'The Peaceful Apocalypse: Familism and Literacy in Sixteenth-Century England', *Sixteenth Century Journal*, 17 (1986), 131–43; C. W. Marsh, *The Family of Love in English Society, 1550–1630* (Cambridge, 1994), pp. 79–85.

[29] John Stow, *The Annales of England* (1605), p. 1174.

[30] See Milward, *Religious Controversies of the Elizabethan Age*, pp. 35–8, 96–9, 172–4, and his *Religious Controversies of the Jacobean Age* (1978), ch. 2.

[31] John Smyth, *Paralleles* (Middelburg, 1609), sig. A2r. See K. L. Sprunger, *Trumpets from the Tower: English Puritan Printing in the Netherlands 1600–1640* (Leiden, 1994).

[32] L. H. Carlson (ed.), *The Writings of Henry Barrow 1587–1590*, Elizabethan Nonconformist Texts 3 (1962), pp. 108–17.

Dutch printers also did much to assist the literary campaign to discredit Laudian policies in the 1630s, along with the London stationer Michael Sparke, who circulated the fugitive works of Prynne, Bastwick and Burton.[33] However, many Caroline puritans preferred to disseminate their attacks on crypto-popish innovations scribally rather than risk their rejection by episcopal licensers, as the sheer volume of pamphlets which exploded from the presses after 1641 reveals. Whether silenced by the Star Chamber or High Commission or by some form of self-denying ordinance, they harnessed the medium of script as a substitute for speaking. As John Vicars remarked, 'MS[S] are nowe the best help Gods people have to vindicate the Truth, printing being now a dayes prohibited to them'.[34] At a lower level, handwritten lampoons were a powerful vehicle for attacking the latest incarnation of Satan: during the Personal Rule a notice was fixed to Cheapside Cross declaring that 'the Arch-Wolf of Cant[erbury] had his hand in persecuting the saints and shedding the blood of martyrs'.[35]

Texts were pivotal in the voluntary religion of Protestants who felt obliged to remain loosely within the embrace of the halfly-reformed Church of England. Gatherings of the godly in private houses like those held in Harpsden, Oxfordshire, in the reign of Charles I, where parishioners read Scripture, repeated sermons from shorthand notes, and listened to the edifying works of puritan preachers like John Preston and Richard Sibbes, were always in danger of being denounced as seditious conventicles.[36] Iconic centrepieces of household devotion, books were also vital in the emotional lives of individuals who imagined themselves as members of a small remnant of the elect surrounded by a sea of hostile reprobates. The siege mentality which characterised the puritan psyche gave rise to prodigious feats of memory: Mrs Mary Gunter learnt 'many select chapters, and specially *Psalmes*' by heart because 'shee knew not what daies of triall or persecution might come, wherein shee might be deprived of her Bible, and other good books and helpes'.[37] Imprinted in their hearts, texts could provide a haven from the tribulations suffered by the faithful. When these fears became more

---

[33] See Sprunger, *Trumpets*; Rostenberg, *Minority Press*, ch. 15; S. Foster, *Notes from the Caroline Underground: Alexander Leighton, the Puritan Triumvirate, and the Laudian Reaction to Nonconformity* (Hamden, CT, 1978), esp. ch. 6.

[34] F. S. Boas (ed.), *The Diary of Thomas Crosfield M.A., B.D. Fellow of Queen's College, Oxford* (1935), p. 89. See A. Milton, 'Licensing, Censorship and Religious Orthodoxy in Early Stuart England', *Historical Journal*, 41 (1998), 640 and 625–51 *passim*.

[35] William Laud, *Works*, ed. W. Scott and J. Bliss, 7 vols. in 9, Library of Anglo-Catholic Theology (Oxford, 1847–60), vol. III, p. 228.

[36] E. R. Brinkworth, 'The Study and Use of Archdeacons' Court Records', *TRHS*, 4th ser., 25 (1943), 114.

[37] Thomas Taylor, *Three Treatises* (1633), p. 173.

real in the decade preceding the outbreak of the Civil War, classic works
like Foxe's *Actes and Monuments* acquired fresh significance as inducements
to steadfastness and fortitude.[38] Studied silently, the book could provide
a 'refuge beyond the reach of visible institutional disciplinary procedures',
to quote Roger Chartier.[39] If persecution (imagined or real) encouraged
reading it also stimulated writing. This too could be a means of retreating into the safety of solitude. In his voluminous notebooks, the London
turner Nehemiah Wallington preserved long accounts of the ordeals of
Prynne, Bastwick and Burton at the hands of the prelates and during the
metaphorical trial of a lingering illness Lady Brilliana Harley translated
John Calvin's *Life of Luther*.[40] Copying could thus become a poignant act
of piety comparable to that of the medieval monk who employed his pen
as an instrument of prayer.

After the tables were turned in 1642, it was Anglicans who were imbued
with a fresh awareness of the merits of script and print. Books once more
had to deputise for the sermons of the 'scandalous and ignorant' ministers
evicted from their livings by Parliament, to take the place of vocal discourse.
As the Royalist clergymen Daniel Featley commented in a tract published
in 1645: 'And preach the Gospel I can no otherwise, for both my pulpits are
taken from me. Now therefore since I cannot *lingua*, I must be content as
I am able to *evangelizare calumo*, to preach with my pen.'[41] Used illicitly to
facilitate corporate worship and administer baptism, marriage and burial,
the Book of Common Prayer once again became a touchstone for dissent,
the mascot of a Church under the cross.[42] It is a testament to its perceived
centrality that Roundhead soldiers in Colchester made this text the target
of their sacrilegious violence in 1642: 'some of the leaves they tread under
feet, some they cast into the kennel, some they pissed upon, and some they
fixed on the end of their Clubs and Cudgels'.[43]

---

[38] D. Nussbaum, 'Appropriating Martyrdom: Fears of Renewed Persecution and the 1632 edition of *Acts and Monuments*', in D. Loades (ed.), *John Foxe and the English Reformation* (Aldershot, 1997), pp. 178–209.

[39] R. Chartier (ed.), *The Culture of Print: Power and the Uses of Print in Early Modern Europe* (Oxford, 1991), p. 139.

[40] P. Seaver, *Wallington's World: A Puritan Artisan in Seventeenth-Century London* (1985), p. 200; J. Eales, *Puritans and Roundheads: The Harleys of Brampton Bryan and the Outbreak of the English Civil War* (Cambridge, 1990), p. 52.

[41] Daniel Featley, *The Dippers Dipt* (1645), sig. C1r.

[42] See J. Morrill, 'The Church of England, 1642–9', in J. Morrill (ed.), *Reactions to the English Civil War 1642–1649* (Basingstoke, 1982), pp. 104–5; J. Spurr, *The Restoration Church of England, 1646–1689* (New Haven and London, 1991), pp. 14–17. Forthcoming work by Judith Maltby will illuminate this further.

[43] *Mercurius Rusticus* (3 June 1643), p. 20 and (20 February 1643), p. 156.

The same argument may be extended to the sects of the Civil War and Interregnum, especially the Quakers, who produced some 300 tracts in the first four years of the movement, between 1652 and 1656, as an arm of their mission to 'publish the truth'. These pamphlets were expected to function not only in conjunction with acoustic preaching but also in lieu of it, to operate not merely as amplifiers of the spoken word but as alternatives to it. Deemed to carry the authority of the inward spirit within them, they were envisaged as potent instruments of 'convincement'.[44] By this means, suggests Adrian Davies, Quakers were able simultaneously to evangelise unbelievers and to escape the contagion which might follow from contact with profane worldlings.[45] Mainstream Protestant divines accused them of exalting their own writings above Scripture itself: adapting an image originally used to denigrate Catholicism's reverence for 'unwritten traditions', one Baptist propagandist portrayed dozens of flimsy Quaker tracts being outweighed by a single copy of the Holy Bible (Illustration 5).[46] According to the Somerset rector William Thomas, the 'corrupt' and 'flying Books' issued by the Society of Friends were nothing less than 'Satan's Library', 'purposely made little, that they may be made nimble, and pass with more speed, and at an easy rate to infect the Nation'.[47]

As well as 'poisoning' the souls of simple parishioners, Quaker pamphlets did much to create a coherent identity for the sect. They embodied a bold contribution to the public debate about the nature of the post-regicide religious settlement and a provocative attempt to mobilise the populace to participate in the final establishment of Christ's kingdom on earth. Sensitive to the fact that the weapon of print could easily backfire, from the outset George Fox actively vetted and censored them prior to consigning them to the press, 'to see that young Friends' books . . . might be stood by'.[48] Later Thomas Ellwood judiciously edited Fox's more enthusiastic reminiscences from the first edition of the journal in 1694 in case they blighted the reputation of a movement anxious to efface the memory of its embarrassing earlier antics.[49]

For Quakers who spent long periods in custody, books were an important replacement for communal interaction. When the young Thomas Story was

---

[44] See M. K. Peters, 'Quaker Pamphleteering and the Development of the Quaker Movement, 1652–1656', Ph.D. thesis, University of Cambridge (1996), esp. pp. 41–3.

[45] A. Davies, *The Quakers in English Society 1655–1725* (Oxford, 2000), pp. 109, 122.

[46] Benjamin Keach, *The Grand Imposter Discovered* (1675), facing p. 193.

[47] William Thomas, *Rayling Rebuked* (1656), epistle, quoted in Davies, *Quakers*, p. 110.

[48] Quoted in N. Keeble, *The Literary Culture of Nonconformity in Later Seventeenth-Century England* (Leicester, 1987), p. 111.

[49] B. Reay, *The Quakers and the English Revolution* (1985), p. 112.

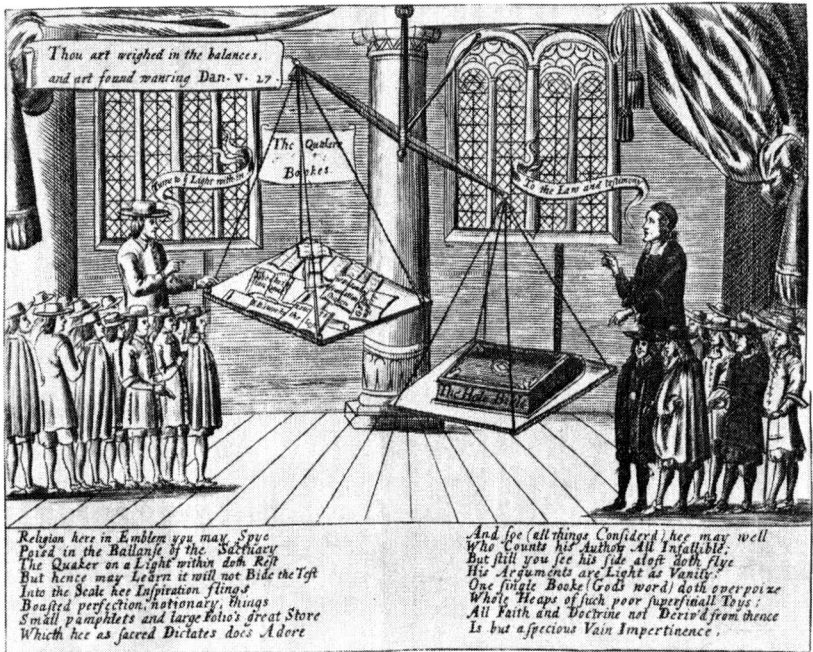

Illustration 5   Quaker books outweighed by the Bible: Benjamin Keach, *The Grand Impostor Discover'd* (1675), facing p. 193.

prohibited by his father from keeping company with members of the sect, he was sent a small parcel of books to sustain him in isolation.[50] Such experiences must have functioned as a stimulus to literacy, though the oral performance of texts ensured that an inability to read was no bar to involvement. Letters were also significant in fusing its followers: William Robinson, who emigrated to New England and was executed at Boston in 1659, 'left many Worthy Testimonyes of his love and faithfullness to the Truth, and severall Consolatory Epistles, behind him writing, wch were afterwards printed and dispersed amongst the Churches of Christ'.[51] Many manuscript registers of the stoical 'sufferings' of early Quakers lovingly compiled by local meetings subsequently found their way into the public domain by means of mechanical reproduction.

Like the Baptists, the Quakers were quick to harness the media of script and print as instruments of intra- and inter-sectarian dispute, as

[50] Davies, *Quakers*, p. 110.
[51] N. Penney (ed.), *'The First Publishers of Truth': Being Early Records (Now First Printed) of the Introduction of Quakerism into the Counties of England and Wales* (1907), pp. 159–60.

mechanisms for dissociating themselves from the dangerous enthusiasm of groups like the Ranters and tarring their competitors with the brush of lurid fanaticism. By publishing vitriolic tracts and scribally disseminating 'thundering letters', Friends like William Penn prosecuted private vendettas against their archrivals.[52] In turn, such sects proved equally adept at exploiting the powers of the pen and press. Thus a letter of damnation written by Ludowick Muggleton to the Lord Mayor of London and copied for the recorder and several other officers of the Court of Aldermen was printed at the charge of a friend in 1653.[53] Muggleton's autobiographical *Acts of the Witnesses* was an elaborate exercise in self-promotion: through it he sought to erase the impression that John Reeve had been the first to receive his divine commission and to inflate his own intellectual stature.[54] Through their correspondence both prophets corrected sinners, comforted the dying, and reassured the melancholic. Writing was indispensable to the leaders of a movement who rarely engaged in proactive proselytising, but rather waited for potential followers to contact them via a chandler's shop in Great Trinity Lane. Even so, in a letter communicating his visions to Mrs Alice Webb, Muggleton confessed that script was secondary to speech: 'Much more might I write, but speaking Face to Face, if it may be, is farre more profitable'.[55]

After the Restoration, writing and printing became essential to those forced out of the re-established Church of England because of their refusal to comply with the Act of Uniformity. Neil Keeble has argued that the preservation of nonconformity was due, above all else, to the written word. 'It was upon publication that its ultimate survival depended.' The vitality and creativity of its literary culture, of which John Bunyan's *Pilgrim's Progress* is an emblem, owes much to its experience of victimisation after 1662. Despite renewed censorship and the continuing practice of lighting 'bibliographical bonfires', printed books did much to feed and nurture Dissent.[56] By the late seventeenth century, surreptitious publishing was too deeply entrenched to be uprooted and eradicated: printers taunted the

---

[52] See J. F. McGregor, 'The Baptists: Fount of All Heresy', in J. F. McGregor and B. Reay (eds.), *Radical Religion in the English Revolution* (Oxford, 1984), p. 60; J. C. Davis, *Fear, Myth and History: The Ranters and the Historians* (Cambridge, 1986), pp. 88–92, 110–11. For Penn, see T. L. Underwood (ed.), *The Acts of the Witnesses: The Autobiography of Lodowick Muggleton and Other Early Muggletonian Writings* (New York, 1999), pp. 105–6.

[53] Underwood (ed.), *Acts of the Witnesses*, p. 74. See also pp. 78, 79, 93.

[54] C. Hill, 'Debate: The Muggletonians', *P&P*, 104 (1984), 153–8; Underwood (ed.), *Acts of the Witnesses*, pp. 7–9.

[55] Underwood (ed.), *Acts of the Witnesses*, pp. 193–214, 10, 196 respectively. See also W. Lamont, 'The Muggletonians 1652–1979: A "Vertical Approach"', *P&P*, 99 (1983), 35–8.

[56] Keeble, *Literary Culture*, at pp. 78, 82, 101.

authorities with witty imprints like that which adorned Andrew Marvell's *Rehearsal Transpos'd* (1672) which was allegedly printed 'for the Assigns of John Calvin and Theodore Beza'. This savage piece of satire depicted the Anglican bishop Samuel Parker lamenting that though 'There have been wayes found out to banish Ministers . . . no Art yet could prevent these seditious meetings of Letters. Two or three brawny Fellows in a Corner, with meer Ink and Elbow-grease do more harm than an hundred Systematicall Divines with their Sweaty Preaching.'[57]

Manuscript too remained imperative as an agent of clandestine communication. By means of 'tender and affectionate letters', well-wishers were able to make 'Epistolary Visits' to imprisoned ministers and to maintain a sense of community which the Clarendon Code had been devised to defuse.[58] In the case of Obadiah Grew, the written word enabled him to carry out his ministry without exposing his flock to the danger of prosecution under the Conventicle Act: after he lost his eyesight he dictated his sermons to an amanuensis and sent them to be read 'to four or more writers in short-hand', who in turn transcribed and passed them on, so that they were 'afterwards read at twenty several meetings'.[59] Like the ejected Presbyterian Roger Morrice, some diarists and correspondents thought it wise to write in 'character' or 'cypher'.[60] Allegory, allusion and other tactics of circumvention allowed many texts to pass the hands of the censors and enter into the realm of mainstream discourse like a Trojan Horse. The fact that catechetical and devotional literature was low on the list of the priorities of the licensers accounts for the continuing ability of deprived ministers to secure authorisation for their works after 1662. As Eamon Duffy has remarked, for many nonconformist clergy publishing became a replacement for the preaching vocation they were now forbidden to exercise.[61] Although an awareness by dissenting ministers of the benefits of 'wholsome and excellent Books' predated their mass expulsion,[62] persecution greatly intensified it. It encouraged them to prepare posthumous editions of the sermons and letters of fervent preachers and pastors like Thomas Wadsworth and Abraham Cheare for the edification of the laity

---

[57] Andrew Marvell, *The Rehearsall Transpos'd and The Rehearsall Transpos'd The Second Part*, ed. D. I. B. Smith (Oxford, 1971), pp. 4–5.

[58] Cited by Keeble, *Literary Culture*, p. 79.

[59] M. Watts, *The Dissenters from the Reformation to the French Revolution* (Oxford, 1978), pp. 229–30.

[60] Keeble, *Literary Culture*, p. 110.

[61] E. Duffy, 'The Godly and the Multitude in Stuart England', *The Seventeenth Century*, 1 (1986), 48.

[62] See, e.g., the remarks by Richard Baxter in a commendatory letter appended to Richard Younge, *A Christian Library . . . of Practical Divinity, in Ten Treatises* (1655), calendared in N. H. Keeble and G. F. Nuttall, *Calendar of the Correspondence of Richard Baxter*, vol. 1: *1638–1660* (Oxford, 1991), p. 160.

and to anticipate the methods of the SPCK, disseminating Bibles, catechisms, and edifying tracts like Joseph Alleine's *Alarm to the Unconverted*
(1672), to rouse the heathens who lurked in the bowels of England out of
their spiritual stupor. Joshua Richardson, who had lost his cure in Myddle
two years after Charles II's accession, bequeathed a similar work by Richard
Baxter to the poor people of his former parish; Thomas Gouge, former incumbent of St Sepulchre's in London, founded a trust to print the Bible
in Welsh and distribute catechisms and puritan classics like Bishop Bayly's
Practice of Piety.[63] Persecution also facilitated an unlikely liaison between
nonconformist ministers and profit-seeking publishers who hijacked and
marketed their works in the format of godly chapbooks. The role of businessmen in disseminating such texts to satisfy public demand illuminates
Ian Green's observation that the press was 'increasingly used to disseminate
forms of Protestantism of which the clergy did not fully approve'.[64]

So far this discussion has focused upon Protestant dissenters and those
whom they retrospectively embraced as their courageous precursors. But if
we cross over to the other side of the confessional divide, we find that
English Catholicism also made a virtue out of the necessity of its de-
pendence on the pen and the press.[65] In the context of its repression by
successive Tudor and Stuart governments, it too became a religion of the
printed and manuscript book. Texts played a vital part not only in keeping traditional religion alive but also in disseminating Tridentine ideals.
Published abroad or illegally at home, smuggled across the Channel and
dispersed to outlying areas by an intrepid band of carriers, a whole range of
polemical and devotional works helped to stiffen the resolve of the recusant
laity and to create a conscious sense of a community united in adversity –
from weighty volumes of theological controversy and provocative political treatises like *Leicester's Commonwealth*, to primers, manuals on mental
prayer, penance, reception of the sacraments, and guides to the Christian
life. Scribal copies of accounts of the courageous deaths of the martyrs
circulated around the Catholic underground, along with rousing ballads,
stories of miracles worked on behalf of the Church of Rome, and circular
letters from the clergy urging constancy and condemning the heinous sin

---

[63] See E. Duffy, 'The Long Reformation', in N. Tyacke (ed.), *England's Long Reformation 1500–1800*
(1998), pp. 53 (Wadsworth), 55 (Gouge); B. R. White, *The English Baptists of the Seventeenth Century*
(1983), pp. 113–14 (Cheare); Richard Gough, *The History of Myddle*, ed. D. Hey (Harmondsworth,
1981 edn), p. 43 (Richardson).
[64] Duffy, 'Godly and the Multitude', pp. 47–9. Ian Green, *Print and Protestantism in Early Modern
England* (Oxford, 2000), p. 444 and *passim*.
[65] See my '"Domme Preachers"? Post-Reformation English Catholicism and the Culture of Print',
P&P, 168 (2000), 72–123.

of schism.[66] Discussion of contentious issues like equivocation and occasional conformity was also confined to the more confidential medium of manuscript, for fear of exposing Catholicism to ridicule as a deceitful and lying religion.[67] The Counter Reformation leaders regarded the written word as an essential weapon in their struggle to reclaim England to the Roman fold. With the Spaniard Luis de Granada, they envisaged books operating in the guise of 'domme preachers'.[68] In his *Apologie* for the English seminaries published in 1581, William Allen celebrated the success of his colleagues' 'combat in writing bookes' and the same year Edmund Campion hoped that 'books written with ink' would soon succeed those which were 'daily being published, written in blood' by priests on the gallows.[69] As John Wilson, director of the St Omer press reported in 1616, texts 'penetrate where priests and religious cannot enter and serve as precursors to undeceive many'.[70] Quoting Psalm 45, Robert Southwell summed up his clerical vocation in a marginal note made while he was a student in Rome: 'My tongue is the pen of a scrivener that writeth swiftly'.[71]

With their secular colleagues, the Jesuits employed sophisticated techniques of mass dissemination and made prudent use of various subterfuges. Catholic propaganda was brought into the capital in parcels of 150 and introduced into the homes, shops and palaces of heretics to deflect attention away from their presence in the houses of recusants.[72] Such works were required to assume an almost sacerdotal role in a country in which priests were in desperately short supply and in constant danger of apprehension

[66] On post-Reformation Catholicism and scribal copying, see N. Pollard Brown, 'Paperchase: The Dissemination of Catholic Texts in Elizabethan England', in P. Beal and J. Griffiths (eds.), *English Manuscript Studies 1100–1700* (Oxford, 1989), vol. I, pp. 120–43; M. Sena, 'William Blundell and the Networks of Catholic Dissent in Post-Reformation England', in A. Shepard and P. Withington (eds.), *Communities in Early Modern England* (Manchester, 2000), pp. 54–75; A. F. Marotti, 'Manuscript Transmission and the Catholic Martyrdom Account in Early Modern England', in A. F. Marotti and M. D. Bristol (eds.), *Print, Manuscript and Performance: The Changing Relations of the Media in Early Modern England* (Columbus, OH, 2000), pp. 172–99; G. Kilroy, 'Paper, Ink and Penne: The Literary Memoria of the Recusant Community', *Downside Review*, 119 (2001), 95–124; M. Greengrass, 'Two Sixteenth-Century Religious Minorities and their Scribal Networks' (forthcoming).
[67] See N. Pollard Brown, 'Robert Southwell: The Mission of the Written Word', in T. M. McCoog (ed.), *The Reckoned Expense: Edmund Campion and the Early English Jesuits* (Woodbridge, 1996), pp. 196–7; P. J. Holmes (ed.), *Elizabethan Casuistry*, Catholic Record Society 67 (1981).
[68] Luis de Granada, *A Memoriall of a Christian Life*, trans. R. Hopkins (Rouen, 1586), p. 12.
[69] William Allen, *An Apologie and True Declaration of the Institution and Endevours of the Two English Colleges* (1581), fo. 58v; Campion, cited in Pollard Brown, 'Robert Southwell', p. 195.
[70] A. B. Hinds (ed.), *CSP Milan 1385–1618* (1912), p. 654.
[71] Quoted in Pollard Brown, 'Robert Southwell', p. 213.
[72] L. Hicks (ed.), *Letters and Memorials of Father Robert Persons, SJ*, vol. I *(to 1585)*, Catholic Record Society 39 (1992), p. 85.

and execution by the authorities. In the hands of the laity, however, they were equally capable of becoming agents of independence from clerical control. Vocalised to a group of assembled listeners, texts might become a partial substitute for liturgy and rite. In this 'catacomb culture', the singing of motets and remembered portions of the mass were acts of communal affirmation.[73] Deprived of public worship, laypeople pored over primers, Tridentine devotional guides and spiritual classics like Thomas a Kempis' *Imitation of Christ* in the privacy of their chambers and closets. Imprisonment could provide an unexpected opportunity and impetus to become literate: it was during her captivity in York, for instance, that the future martyr Margaret Clitherow first learnt to read and write.[74]

Like other dissenting groups, then, English Catholics forged an intimate alliance with the media of writing and printing at least in part because they were obliged to do so in order to survive. Persecution catalysed enthusiasm for the press as a valuable missionary tool and stimulated renewed appreciation of the advantages of scribal publication in a climate of censorship. It created communities whose identity centred on a shared experience of the texts thus engendered, as well as provided individuals with a powerful incentive to acquire skills which would enable them to escape into a temporary inner sanctuary of peace and tranquillity. The bias of dissenting groups towards script and print both predated the Reformation and transcended the confessional barriers erected by it.

II

These observations arguably unsettle some tenacious and closely inter-related historiographical commonplaces. They qualify the still lingering conviction that post-Reformation Catholicism nurtured an innate hostility towards the new technology of mechanical reproduction, indicating that Tridentine attitudes towards the medium of printing by movable type were far more complex and contingent than is often implied. They also perhaps inject an additional strand of analysis into our understanding of the relationship between Protestantism and the written and printed book, at least in the context of England, further refining the powerful paradigm which instinctively links the success of the Reformation with the press and

---

[73] I am grateful to Alison Shell for sharing with me a chapter on this theme from her forthcoming book.

[74] John Mush, 'A True Report of the Life and Martyrdom of Mrs Margaret Clitherow', in J. Morris (ed.), *The Troubles of our Catholic Forefathers*, 3 vols. (1872–7), vol. III, p. 375.

sees it as a critical factor in the expansion of literacy.[75] These notions, of course, are in part legacies of a process of Protestant myth-making. In his *Table Talk*, Martin Luther declared that it was through 'the writing-pen' that God had preserved His truth upon the earth and heralded printing as the Lord's 'ultimate and greatest gift', 'the last flicker of the flame which glows before the end of this world'.[76] John Foxe similarly heralded printing as a 'divine and miraculous invention' in a famous passage in his *Actes and Monuments*, seeing it as a science bestowed by God's 'marvellous providence' for the advancement of glory, the subversion of Antichrist, and the abolishing of ignorance and idolatry.[77] But the evidence assembled above suggests that the claim that reformed religious culture possessed a natural predisposition towards reading and writing may need to be balanced by the observation that an orientation towards these media was frequently a side-effect of the constraining circumstances in which churches and sects found themselves, a point which must now be explored in more detail.

It would be foolish to deny that there was a strong incentive towards literacy inherent within the Protestant religion. The Reformation made direct, personal access to the text of Scripture a central tenet of its original manifesto. The effect of the doctrine of 'sola scriptura' was to promote reverence for the written Word and to elevate the Bible on a pedestal. Protestant ministers saw literacy as a key to conquering impiety and a remedy for superstition and barbarity. Sometimes they even implied that without it one might be in danger of damnation: 'How many for want of reading have lost their precious souls?' lamented George Swinnock, for instance, in 1663.[78] Nor can we ignore the fact that Protestantism gave rise to a very considerable body of pious and polemical literature in the century and a half following Henry VIII's break with Rome. In its position as the official Church of England, it engendered a vast quantity of practical divinity: literally thousands of catechisms, commentaries, didactic handbooks, devotional tracts, and moralistic pamphlets spilled from the presses, together with hundreds

---

[75] For older reiterations of this theme L. Stone, 'Literacy and Education in England 1640–1900', *P&P*, 142 (1969), 77–8; A. G. Dickens, *The German Nation and Martin Luther* (1974), p. 103; Eisenstein, *Printing Press*, p. 310; S. Ozment, *The Age of Reform 1250–1550* (New Haven, 1980), p. 199. Important revisionist discussions include G. Strauss and R. Gawthrop, 'Protestantism and Literacy in Early Modern Germany', *P&P*, 104 (1984), 31–55; J.-F. Gilmont (ed.), *The Reformation and the Book*, trans. K. Maag (Aldershot, 1998); J.-F. Gilmont, 'Protestant Reformations and Reading', in G. Cavallo and R. Chartier (eds.), *A History of Reading in the West*, trans. L. G. Cochrane (Cambridge, 1999), pp. 213–37.

[76] H. Bell (ed.), *Selections from the Table Talk of Martin Luther* (1892), p. 54; Gilmont (ed.), *Reformation and the Book*, p. 1.

[77] Foxe, *Actes and Monuments*, vol. II, pp. 707–8.

[78] George Swinnock, *The Christian Mans Calling . . . the Second Part* (1663), p. 22.

of volumes of doctrinal controversy.[79] Many Protestant writers acknowledged the unique capacity which print possessed to preserve and disperse
the Word. The Canterbury divine Thomas Jackson admitted that printing
was of 'longer continuance' and 'larger extent' than vocal oratory, while the
Ipswich preacher Samuel Ward compared sermons with 'showers of Rayne
that water for the instant' and books with 'Snow that lyes longer on the
earth'.[80]

However, this evidence must be set against the backdrop of contemporary
anxiety about technological innovation. Reformed clergymen frequently
shared with their peers a deep psychological unease about the new-fangled
medium of print. Poets like Sir Philip Sidney and John Donne often displayed a lofty distaste for this vulgar mode of publishing and refused to
sink to it, determined to avoid the 'stigma' it would bestow upon their
work. They and others exhibited a distinct preference for manuscript.[81]
The prototype of the noble art of the scrivener was the sacred secretarial labour of the Gospel writers, especially St John the Divine, to whom
the angel had dictated Revelation. But writing itself could evoke distrust.
Following St Augustine, it could be seen as a symbol of human sinful-
ness, a token of the Fall of man from Paradise, where perfect oral discourse
had prevailed. For some it was tainted by association with the Scribes and
Pharisees who had perverted the Law in the time of Jesus Christ and with
the scholastic theologians who had used it to imprison Scripture in medieval monasteries.[82] Linked with this was the idea that lack of learning
was a sign of purity: the topoi of the illiterate heretic and the evangelical peasant both had their roots in the tradition of the unlettered early
apostles.[83]

It is also important to recognise that many Protestant ministers continued
to place a premium on what Walter Ong called the verbal 'presence of the

[79] See I. Green, *The Christian's ABC: Catechisms and Catechising in England c.1530–1740* (Oxford, 1996) and *Print and Protestantism.*
[80] Thomas Jackson, *Judah must into Captivitie* (1622), sig. A1r–v; Samuel Ward, *The Happinesse of Practice* (1621), sig. A3r.
[81] See J. W. Saunders, 'The Stigma of Print: A Note on the Social Bases of Tudor Poetry', *Essays in Criticism* 1 (1951), 139–64; D. F. McKenzie, 'Speech-Manuscript-Print', *Library Chronicle of the University of Texas at Austin* 20 (1990), 87–109; H. Love, *Scribal Publication in Seventeenth-Century England* (Oxford, 1993); A. F. Marotti, *Manuscript, Print and the English Renaissance Lyric* (Ithaca and London, 1995); H. R. Woudhuysen, *Sir Philip Sidney and the Circulation of Manuscripts 1558–1640* (Oxford, 1996); P. Beal, *In Praise of Scribes: Manuscripts and their Makers in Seventeenth-Century England* (Oxford, 1998), esp. ch. 1.
[82] Beal, *In Praise of Scribes*, pp. 7–8.
[83] See P. Biller, 'Heresy and Literacy: Earlier History of the Theme', in Biller and Hudson (eds.), *Heresy and Literacy*, esp. pp. 3–5, 9, 11. For the tradition of Karsthans, the godly peasant, see R. W. Scribner, 'Images of the Peasant, 1514–1525', in J. Bak (ed.), *The German Peasant War of 1525* (1976), pp. 29–47.

word'.[84] They continued to regard the pen and press as inferior to the organ of the mouth as mechanisms for conveying divine truth, to privilege sound over sight, the ear over the eye, as a route to spiritual revelation and enlightenment. The enthusiastic sects of the mid-seventeenth century carried these assumptions to their extreme logical conclusions. Rejecting the rigidity of a textual liturgy in favour of extemporaneous utterance, Seekers, Ranters and Muggletonians valued the charismatic witness of the 'indwelling spirit' and 'inner light' far above the mere 'dry husk' of the Bible.[85] But even mainstream Calvinist preachers can be found according the spoken word an almost sacramental quality. Quoting 2 Corinthinians 3:6 ('The letter killeth, but the spirit giveth life') and Romans 10:17 ('Faith cometh by hearing'), they insisted that 'bare reading' of the Word was quite insufficient. It was but a blunt sword in a scabbard unless 'drawne out by application'.[86] Conceiving of themselves as the Lord's ambassadors, with Samuel Hieron they believed that preaching was 'the choice and principal meanes, by which the Lord would bring his people unto the true and savinge knowledge of himselfe'. It contained 'a speciall gift of grace', declared Miles Mosse, which enabled the minister to speak with 'such power to the Conscience, as no pen of man by writing can expresse'. The 'lively voice of the Prophet', said Richard Greenham, 'feedeth most effectually, searching even the secret chambers of the soule, and working greatest impressions in the heart'.[87] Handbooks like those compiled by Richard Bernard and William Perkins stressed that sermons should be delivered from memory rather than from a pre-prepared script[88] and in the prefaces to the published versions of their lectures, the clergy repeatedly expressed their reluctance to exchange the animated instrument of the tongue for the 'dead letter' of the press.[89]

---

[84] W. J. Ong, *The Presence of the Word: Some Prolegomena for Cultural and Religious History* (New Haven, 1967).

[85] See McGregor, 'Baptists', pp. 57–8; N. Smith, *Perfection Proclaimed: Language and Literature in English Radical Religion 1640–1660* (Oxford, 1989), pp. 5–6.

[86] Charles Richardson, *A Workeman that Needeth not to be Ashamed* (1616), p. 69.

[87] Samuel Hieron, *Six Sermons* (1608), sig. B1r; Miles Mosse, *Justifying and Saving Faith Distinguished from the Faith of the Devils* (Cambridge, 1614), sigs. ¶¶1v–¶¶2r; Richard Greenham, *The Works*, (1599), sig. A4r.

[88] Richard Bernard, *The Faithfull Shepheard Amended and Enlarged* (1609 edn), pp. 12, 82–5; William Perkins, *The Arte of Prophecying*, in *The Workes*, 3 vols. (Cambridge, 1608–9 edn), vol. II, p. 758.

[89] See, e.g., John King, *Lectures upon Jonas* (Oxford, 1599), sig. *4r; John Lawrence, *A Golden Trumpet to Rowse up a Drowsie Magistrate* (1624), sig. A4r. These issues are further discussed by D. R. Woolf, 'Speech, Text, and Time: The Sense of Hearing and the Sense of the Past in Renaissance England', *Albion*, 18 (1986), 173–4; A. Hunt, 'The Art of Hearing: Preachers and their Audiences 1590–1640', Ph.D. thesis, University of Cambridge (2000); E. J. Carlson, 'The Boring of the Ear: Shaping the Pastoral Vision of Preaching in England, 1540–1640', in L. Taylor (ed.), *Preachers and People in the Reformation and Early Modern Period* (Leiden, 2001), pp. 278–82. See also N. Smith, 'Nonconformist Voices and Books', in *CHBB 4*, pp. 413–15 and *passim*, which complements the discussion offered in section I, above.

For many, a written or printed text was but a surrogate agent of homiletic instruction, a mere understudy and feeble substitute for pulpit oratory.

We need, then, to pay careful attention to the circumstances in which Protestants embraced the book. On what occasions did they concede that the potential benefits of script and print outweighed their drawbacks and defects? In which situations were they able to overcome their reservations about the weaknesses and limitations of mechanical (and indeed scribal) reproduction? In the light of the preceding discussion, it may be proposed that they sometimes did so as much through force as choice. They turned to script and print when they were ejected from and denied access to their pulpits. Persecution seems to have been one of the experiences which persuaded Protestants to accept writing and printing as a locum for preaching. It helped to convince ministers imbued with the belief that speech had sacred potency that texts could be an adequate substitute for prophesying, catechising, and casuistical guidance. Where ordained clergymen were scarce and subject to constant harassment by the authorities, books and letters could stand in for faithful shepherds and wear the shoes of spiritual directors. Just as Elnathan Parr's treatise *The Grounds of Divinitie* (1614) was 'the fruit of my sicknesse, whereby in the beginning of this winter I was made unserviceable for my publique duety', so too did divines prevented from carrying out their ecclesiastical functions by deprivation, exile or incarceration feel themselves bound to 'redeeme the time' by employing their pens to God's glory and the devil's destruction.[90]

It was in contexts in which Protestantism was a Church under the cross that the written word assumed particular importance as a source of inspiration, advice, solace, and encouragement. Letters and tracts filled a vital gap when laypeople were deprived of personal contact with evangelists and pastors. While texts could foster introspection and privacy, they could also compensate for the loss of corporate worship and facilitate illicit collective celebration of the liturgy. They often remained firmly entrenched within the context of the heard and spoken word, continuing to be thought of as forms of silent speech, as sound reduced to a set of symbols on a page. This is apparent from the prevalence of the vocative sense in many of the remarks quoted above. The heavy 'oral residue' in contemporary prose alerts us to the continuing importance early modern Protestant culture attached to the organs of the voice and the ear.[91]

---

[90] Elnathan Parr, *The Grounds of Divinitie* (1614), sig. A5r.
[91] On this theme, see W. J. Ong, 'Oral Residue in Tudor Prose Style', *PMLA*, 80 (1965), 145–54; Woolf, 'Speech, Text and Time'.

If we look closely at some of the most celebrated sixteenth- and seventeenth-century statements about the virtues of printing, these points become even clearer. Foxe's discussion of the 'divine invention' of the press, for example, comes in the context of his chronicle of the providential interventions by which the Almighty had helped persecuted true believers to conquer the dominant falsehood of Catholicism. It was brought forth at a time 'so daungerous and desperate, where mans power could do no more, there the blessed wisedome & omnipotent power of the Lord began to work for his church; not with sword and tergate to subdue his exalted adversary, but with Printing, writing and reading. So that by this meanes of printing, the secret operation of God hath heaped upon that proud kingdome a double confusion.' Comparing printing with 'the gift of tongues', Foxe boasted that although the vicar of Rome had 'stopped the mouth of John Hus' and Jerome of Prague before him, 'God hath opened the presse to preach, whose voyce the Pope is never able to stop with all the puissance of his triple crown.'[92] In the preface to his edition of the works of 'the Apostle of England', William Tyndale, and his fellow martyrs, John Frith and Robert Barnes, he celebrated the way that it enabled the victims of Romish tyranny to speak, as it were, from the grave, notwithstanding the attempts of the papacy to suppress them.[93]

No less strikingly, the syndicate of preachers who oversaw the belated publication of the London divine Thomas Taylor's collected works in 1653 vindicated their decision to print them by rejoicing in the ability of the press to make this 'Burning and Shining Light' which the 'iniquity of former times' had conspired to eclipse 'once again speak to the good of the Church after so many years silence'. Referring to an old proverb regarding Luther, 'The Goose quill hath strook Antichrist through the fifth rib', they insisted that it was the duty of every Christian to contend not only by the spoken word but also by writing. Paradoxically, persecution assisted in this enterprise: God 'many times suffered the violence of men to silence their tongues, that they might have a greater vacancy for this kinde of instruction'.[94] Ministers needed leave of absence from their pulpits if they were to write books – no less than university lecturers require relief from teaching to finish their monographs.

Read carefully, the most prominent feature of the classic panegyric on print incorporated in Richard Baxter's *Christian Directory* of 1673 is also its

---

[92] Foxe, *Actes and Monuments*, vol. II, pp. 707–8.
[93] John Foxe (ed.), *The Whole Workes of W. Tyndall, John Frith, and Doct. Barnes* (1573), sigs. A2r–3r.
[94] Thomas Taylor, *The Works of that Faithful Servant of Jesus Christ, Dr Thom. Taylor*, ed. Edmund Calamy *et al.* (1653), title-page, sigs. A3r, b1r–v.

emphasis on the press as an artificial voice box: 'The Writings of Divines are nothing less else but a preaching the Gospel to the eye, as the voice preacheth it to the ear. Vocal preaching hath the preheminence in moving the affections . . . But Books have the advantage in many other respects: you may read an able Preacher when you have but a mean one to hear. Every Congregation cannot hear the most judicious or powerful Preachers: but every single person may read the[ir] Books . . . Preachers may be silenced or banished, when Books may be at hand . . .' Once again the background to Baxter's tract is significant: in the preface he stressed that it had been written in 1664–5 for the reason 'That when I could not Preach the Gospel as I would, I might do it as I could'. He went to some lengths to confute proud objectors who cried out against those who hindered them from preaching in the pulpit and yet at the same time reproached their brethren for preaching by the press.[95] It is tempting to conclude that the relationship between Protestantism and print, the reformed faith and writing, was sometimes in practice not so much a consequence of magnetic attraction as of expediency and pragmatism, less a match made in heaven than a marriage of convenience.

III

The argument that persecution induced a distinct proclivity towards the written word has one further intriguing corollary which deserves our attention: when religious communities achieved a position of monopoly and dominance, in relative terms, they had less need for manuscript and printed texts. Where they controlled the pulpits and airwaves, they were less likely to resort to the book as a prosthesis for the voice, as a surrogate for the minister or priest, and as a crutch to hold up a threatened tradition of corporate worship. When they ceased to be a hunted minority, they were also comparatively less reliant upon literacy.

These suggestions should not be taken too far, but they find some reinforcement in the observation that the spoken word lay at the heart of the laity's experience of the post-Reformation Church of England. Oral communication was critical to its mission to the populace: sermons were the linchpin of the service, catechising involved techniques of

---

[95] Richard Baxter, *A Christian Directory: or, a Summe of Practical Theologie* (1673), p. 60 and sig. A3r–v. Baxter curiously echoes Johannes Trithemius' encomium of scribal copying: *In Praise of Scribes: De Laude Scriptorum*, ed. K. Arnold, trans. R. Behrendt (Lawrence, KA, 1974), p. 59. As noted above (n. 62), Baxter's enthusiasm for the press predated his ejection. See also his *True Christianity* (1656), sig. A4r.

memorisation, recitation and dialogue, and the liturgy and Bible were read aloud by vicars and curates to their parishioners.[96] The same reasoning may also help to explain Marian Catholicism's alleged failure to recognise the importance of printing.[97] Having reclaimed the privilege of public speech, the ecclesiastical hierarchy could afford to make writing less of a priority. The books which bishops like Edmund Bonner did produce were designed to aid the clergy in their work of verbal teaching rather than provide laypeople with tools for self-education; hence the concentration upon catechisms, homilies and collections of model sermons which could assist parish priests in mediating the precious pearls of Scripture to their congregations.[98]

Under Elizabeth, Protestantism itself was widely perceived to be lagging behind its popish adversaries in the publication of pastoral divinity. Its own ministers, like Daniel Featley, were obliged to acknowledge that in this sphere of activity the Church of Rome was in fact 'more fruitfull'.[99] Occupied about the business of preaching, catechising, and casuistical instruction, godly ministers had little opportunity and no pressing need to take up their pens – unlike Catholic exiles biding their time on the Continent. In consequence, the Reformed clergy sometimes resorted to appropriating and 'purging' classic works of popery like Robert Persons' famous *First Booke of Christian Exercise*[100] – a technique of sterilisation to which Wycliffite texts had themselves been subjected in the fifteenth century. And just as the circulation of Lollard books had stirred Reginald Pecock and Nicholas Love to prepare vernacular works for laypeople themselves,[101] so too in the post-Reformation period did the initiative of their dissenting enemies provoke orthodox divines to set about preparing edifying tracts to compete with them. It also encouraged them to undertake polemical refutations. Such

---

96 J. N. Wall emphasises the ways in which printing promoted oral, corporate worship in 'The Reformation in England and the Typographical Revolution', in G. P. Tyson and S. S. Wagonheim (eds.), *Print and Culture in the Renaissance: Essays on the Advent of Printing in Europe* (Newark, 1986), pp. 208–21. See also B. R. Smith, *The Acoustic World of Early Modern England: Attending to the O-Factor* (Chicago, 1999), esp. pp. 261–9.

97 J. W. Martin, 'The Marian Regime's Failure to Understand the Importance of Printing', in his *Religious Radicals in Tudor England* (1989), pp. 107–23.

98 J. Loach, 'The Marian Establishment and the Printing Press', *EHR*, 101 (1986), esp. pp. 139–41; E. Duffy, *The Stripping of the Altars: Traditional Religion in England c.1400–c.1580* (New Haven, 1992), pp. 534–43.

99 Daniel Featley, *Ancilla Pietatis* (1626), sig. A6r.

100 Robert Persons, *A Booke of Christian Exercise . . . Perused . . . by Edmund Bunny* (1584). See B. S. Gregory, 'The "True and Zealouse Service of God": Robert Parsons, Edmund Bunny, and the *First Booke of Christian Exercise*', *JEH*, 45 (1994). For a Lollard example, see A. Hudson, 'The Expurgation of a Lollard Sermon-Cycle', in her *Lollards and their Books*, pp. 201–15.

101 See A. Hudson, '"Laicus Litteratus": The Paradox of Lollardy', in Biller and Hudson (eds.), *Heresy and Literacy*, pp. 234–5.

works often took the form of line-by-line dissections of heterodox passages; others printed the 'seditious' and 'superstitious' pamphlets and libels which were the objects of their fury before answering them; some simply repub-lished them, confident that their mere exposure to public scrutiny was 'a sufficient Antidote' to the errors embedded therein.[102] As a consequence, such works became repositories of heresy, sources of the very poisons they were intended to neutralise. In short, they operated as a form of second-hand evangelism.[103] By publishing texts which had hitherto been dispersed solely in manuscript and reproducing scarce items which the government was simultaneously incinerating, these propagandists were ironically assist-ing religious minorities in their ministry of books. They were assisting them in their efforts to preach without speaking.

---

[102] Quotation from Justus Lipsius, *Miracles of the B. Virgin* (Protestant edn 1688), sig. A2r. For other examples, see William Fulke, *A Confutation of a Popishe, and Sclanderous Libelle* (1571); John Rogers, *An Anwere unto a Wicked & Infamous Libel made by Christopher Vitel* (1579); Samuel Hieron, *An Answer to a Popish Rhyme, Lately Scattered abroad in the West Parts* (1604); Thomas Bell, *The Popes Funerall* (1606); Edward Gee (ed.), *The Jesuit's Memorial, for the Intended Reformation of England* (1690), sig. A3v.

[103] See also the comments of Swanson, 'Literacy, Heresy, History and Orthodoxy', p. 281.

12

Publish and perish: the scribal culture of the Marian Martyrs

Thomas S. Freeman

I

For centuries scholars have persistently linked Protestantism with printing, maintaining that the new technology was a necessary precondition for
the Reformation.[1] None have done so more eloquently than John Foxe,
the martyrologist. In passages which have been quoted repeatedly, Foxe
extolled printing as a divinely ordained instrument for propagating the
gospel and subverting the power of the papacy: 'how many printing presses
there bee in the world, so many blockhouses there be against the high castle of S. Angell'.[2] Yet paradoxically, the most celebrated section of Foxe's
martyrology, his account of the persecution of Protestants during the reign
of Mary Tudor, was based almost entirely on oral and manuscript, not
printed, sources. For it is an underappreciated fact that, although English
exiles during Mary's reign printed various works in Protestant centres on
the Continent, the Marian Protestants relied more heavily on the written
than the printed word as a means of communicating with their followers.
Moreover, their success with the older medium was considerable. Through
treatises, sermons and letters, all in manuscript, incarcerated English Protestant leaders were able to wage a propaganda war with the Catholics and
to stiffen the resistance of their co-religionists to the Catholic authorities.
From their cells they were able to maintain intimate pastoral relations with
their lay followers from Sussex to Lancashire. Perhaps more remarkably, the

---

[1] For a classic statement of this position see E. L. Eisenstein, *The Printing Press as an Agent of Change:
Communications and Cultural Transformations in Early Modern Europe*, 2 vols. in 1 (Cambridge, 1980
edn), pp. 303–450. Eisenstein's views on the links between Protestantism and printing have been
modified by an increasing, and increasingly subtle, body of scholarship on the subject; see J.-F.
Gilmont (ed.), *The Reformation and the Book*, trans. K. Maag (Aldershot, 1998).

[2] John Foxe, *The Ecclesiastical History contayning the Actes and Monumentes of these latter and perillous
dayes . . .* (1570), STC 11223, pp. 837–8. Each of the four editions of the *Actes and Monuments* which
were printed in Foxe's lifetime will hereafter be designated by the year of their publication, i.e., *1563,
1570, 1576* or *1583*. All references to this work will be made to the first edition in which the material
being quoted or cited appears.

captive Protestant leaders were, solely by the power of the pen, without any means of physical coercion, or even the technology of the printing press, able to establish their control over myriad local congregations and to crush internal dissent.

Scholars have recently given a great deal of attention to networks of scribal communication, not only emphasising their importance and persistence throughout the seventeenth century, but their efficiency and extent.[3] Yet these networks were legal and were maintained by people at liberty, without fear of official harassment, arrest or even death. Nevertheless from the outset of Mary's reign, the leading English Protestants were in prison or in exile. In prison, even the basic act of putting pen to paper can be difficult, especially when pen, paper and ink are liable to confiscation by the authorities. And if composition under these circumstances is an arduous task, then the copying and dissemination of these works is a Herculean labour. How were the Marian Protestants able to write, copy, and circulate millions of words of polemic and propaganda when they were imprisoned by authorities determined to silence them?

There is another, even more important question. The Marian Protestant achievement, impressive as it was, was rivalled by the networks of scribal communication established by Elizabethan and Jacobean Catholics.[4] Englishmen of both confessions had access to printing presses, if not in England, then in cities on the Continent. Yet often (and as we shall see, this was particularly true of the Marian Protestants) they preferred to leave their writings in manuscript. In this essay, I will suggest that script had important advantages over print for those who were persecuted, and that any comparison of the two media should not overlook the role of manuscript transmission in the religious conflicts of early modern Europe.

II

The security of any prison is never as watertight as the authorities would like and sixteenth-century prisons were positively porous. Along with oral

---

[3] P. Beal, *In Praise of Scribes: Manuscripts and their Makers in Seventeenth-Century England* (Oxford, 1998); M. Hobbs, *Early Seventeenth-Century Verse Miscellany Manuscripts* (Aldershot, 1992); H. Love, *Scribal Publication in Seventeenth-Century England* (Oxford, 1993); A. F. Marotti, *Manuscript, Print and the English Renaissance Lyric* (Ithaca and London, 1995), and H. R. Woudhuysen, *Sir Philip Sidney and the Circulation of Manuscripts 1558–1640* (Oxford, 1996).

[4] See A. F. Marotti, 'Manuscript Transmission and the Catholic Martyrdom Account in Early Modern England', in A. F. Marrotti and M. D. Bristol (eds.), *Print, Manuscript, Performance: The Changing Relations of the Media in Early Modern England* (Columbus, OH, 2000), pp. 172–99 and N. Pollard Brown, 'Paperchase: The Dissemination of Catholic Texts in Elizabethan England', *English Manuscript Studies* 1 (1989), 120–43.

messages and letters, larger works written by the most prominent Protestant captives flowed in and out of various prisons during Mary's reign. John Bradford, imprisoned in London, sent copies of treatises on the Eucharist and on predestination which he had written, his account of his interrogations and a copy of a treatise on free will written by a mutual opponent, to Nicholas Ridley, imprisoned in Oxford.[5] Ridley, in turn, sent treatises he had written in captivity to Thomas Cranmer, also imprisoned in Oxford, and to John Bradford.[6] And John Hooper sent a copy of a treatise he had written from the Fleet Prison, where he was confined, to Bradford, then being held in the King's Bench.[7] In an impressive display of co-ordinated activity a dozen prisoners – including the former bishops John Hooper, Robert Ferrar and Miles Coverdale – held in four separate London prisons, drew up and signed a declaration in May 1554, protesting against a planned disputation between Protestant and Catholic theologians which was to be held in Cambridge.[8]

All of this was typical of Tudor prisons; they were squalid and cruel but conditions were potentially ameliorated by administrative inefficiency, deference to the social hierarchy and sometimes by the biases and abilities of their governors. Most of the Protestant prisoners were held, during at least part of their incarceration, in one of the two royal prisons in Southwark, the King's Bench and the Marshalsea. During Mary's reign, the governors of both prisons had been appointed by Edward VI and were Protestant sympathisers. Sir William Fitzwilliam, the Marshal of the King's Bench, was married to a woman who was a friend and supporter of the Henrician martyr Anne Askew and the Marian martyr Laurence Saunders.[9] If Fitzwilliam was lenient to his charges, Sir Thomas Holcroft, the Marshal of the Marshalsea, went further, scheming and bribing his way to securing the release of one of his most important captives, Edwin Sandys, the future archbishop

---

[5] Henry Bull (ed.), *Certain most godly, fruitful and comfortable letters of such true saintes and holy martyres . . .*, (1564), *STC* 5886, [hereafter *LM*], pp. 60 and 65. See also BL, Add. MS 19400, fo. 42r–v; printed in *LM*, pp. 357–9. Throughout this article, whenever a particular letter was printed by both Bull and Foxe, reference will be made only to the earliest work in which it appeared. If multiple contemporary manuscript copies of a document exist only the holograph will be cited. If no holograph exists, all contemporary copies of the manuscript will be cited. Reference will be made to modern printings of writings of the Marian Protestants only when this document was printed by neither Foxe nor Bull. If such a document has been printed in more than one modern work, reference will be made only to the most generally accessible version.

[6] Emmanuel College Library, Cambridge, [hereafter ECL] MS 260, fo. 117r; printed in H. Christmas (ed.), *The Works of Nicholas Ridley*, Parker Society (Cambridge, 1841), p. 539 and *1570*, pp. 1633–4.

[7] *LM*, p. 146.   [8] *1563*, pp. 1001–3.

[9] Anne Askew, *The lattre examination of Anne Askew*, ed. J. Bale (Wesel, 1547), *STC* 850, fo. 40v and *LM*, pp. 191–3. For further evidence of Sir William's Protestant sympathies see *LM*, pp. 386–8; ECL, MS 260, fos. 148r and 164v; *LM*, p. 226.

of York.[10] Nor was this an isolated incident; ordered to arrest Thomas Mountain, a Protestant minister, Holcroft instead secretly sent Mountain a warning to flee London.[11]

The irony inherent in having prisons administered by those sympathetic to the prisoners reached its mordant height during Mary's reign when two Londoners were sent to Bridewell to be whipped for buying and selling a vernacular New Testament. The governor of Bridewell was none other than Richard Grafton, who had printed the first officially sponsored English language Bible. Aware that Grafton might not regard possession of the Scriptures in English as a transgression which cried to the heavens for vengeance, Edmund Bonner, the bishop of London, sent his own official to preside over the beating.[12]

The inability of the Marian authorities to curtail the laxity of some of the governors of their prisons was not due to ignorance of the problem or incompetence: it was the consequence of a system of penal administration in which it was difficult to discharge officeholders, even penal officeholders. Elizabeth's government experienced similar problems with gaolers who sympathised with their Catholic prisoners.[13] Nevertheless a house of correction divided against itself cannot stand and the fact that the Marian government was forced, in several important cases, to rely on Protestant sympathisers to guard Protestant prisoners guaranteed that those prisoners were able to communicate with their followers and with each other.

Close confinement was at least partially effective but it was difficult to maintain and did not completely prevent the flow of communication in and out of prison.[14] After John Hooper's servant was caught and imprisoned for smuggling letters written by his master out of prison, Hooper was no longer allowed visitors. Yet although only a single keeper ('a symple rude man' in Hooper's words) had access to him, Hooper continued to write letters and even a treatise on the Eucharist, which were all smuggled out of

---

[10] *1583*, p. 2088.

[11] BL, MS Harley 425, fo. 115r–v; printed in J. G. Nichols (ed.), *Narratives of the Days of the Reformation*, Camden Society, 1st ser., 77 (1859), p. 210.

[12] *1563*, p. 1703.

[13] E. D. Pendry, *Elizabethan Prisons and Prison Scenes*, Salzburg Studies in English Literature, 17 (Salzburg, 1974), pp. 129 and 259–60. For an extreme case, see P. Lake and M. Questier, 'Prisons, Priests and People', in Nicholas Tyacke (ed.), *England's Long Reformation 1500–1800* (1988), pp. 203–4.

[14] For example, after John Philpot was transferred into Bishop Bonner's custody he found it much more difficult (although not impossible) to communicate with his co-religionists. A number of letters to and from Philpot were intercepted and confiscated only to be found in the bishop's papers and printed by Foxe (*1563*, pp. 1427–8, 1444–5 and 1459). A letter, written by the martyr Richard Roth while he was confined in Bonner's palace, was similarly intercepted and discovered by Foxe among the bishop's papers (*1563*, p. 1631).

prison.[15] At a time when Ridley claimed that he was so carefully watched that his servants were afraid to carry anything unauthorised to or from him, he still managed to obtain a treatise sent to him from Bradford.[16]

A letter from another martyr, Robert Smith, written during a severe crack-down on all Newgate's Protestant prisoners, casts some light on how this was possible. Smith wrote to his wife:

> I have receaved your letter, and I prayse God, without any daunger. Nevertheless if Gods marvelous goodness had not brought it to Peter the keeper, there might have risen a great trouble upon the same. For well ye know that George is a wicked man, utterly without al feare of God and if he had gotten it, the [Privy] Counsel had surely sene it. But Peter, lyke an honest man, never opened it.

After instructing his wife on how future letters could be sent to him safely Smith added 'I wold ye could make a meanes by your money to send a chese to Peter, for I find much kindnes at his handes'.[17]

In sum, a Marian prison was only as secure as its gaolers. The assistance that sympathetic warders could render to Protestants was illustrated in a complaint sent to royal commissioners in 1556, that Robert Bird, an Ipswich gaoler of Protestant sympathies, 'by evil counesel doth animate the prisoners of his sect'.[18] Some gaolers, such as Bird, were genuinely sympathetic to the religious convictions of their prisoners. Nevertheless, bribery was probably the most important factor in securing compliant gaolers. Apart from intermittent structural maintenance, Tudor prisons were expected to be self-supporting. Gaolers derived their income either largely or entirely from money collected from the prisoners themselves. In return for numerous fees, gaolers would provide better living conditions, greater freedom of movement and access to visitors for those prisoners who could pay for them.[19] It was very difficult to deny these privileges to Protestant prisoners, since the money raised in this way was an established privilege of the gaolers and, more than that, a necessary perquisite of maintaining the prisons. As long as the Protestants had enough money, the vast majority of their prisoners could not be isolated, short of a complete restructuring of the penal system. Bishop Bonner, displaying a keen understanding of the situation, ordered that Protestant prisoners in the Marshalsea should not be allowed to share in the alms which the bishops of London customarily sent to those incarcerated there.[20]

---

[15] *1563*, pp. 1055 and 1063. Hooper's treatise was printed in John Foxe, *Rerum in ecclesia gestarum . . . Commentarii* (Basel, 1559), pp. 309–92.

[16] ECL, MS 260, fo. 272r; printed in *LM*, pp. 69–70.   [17] *1563*, p. 1266.   [18] *1576*, p. 1981.

[19] S. McConville, *A History of English Prison Administration*, vol. 1, *1750–1877* (1981), pp. 8–10 and 15–21.

[20] BL, MS Harley 425, fo. 109r; printed in Nichols (ed.), *Narratives*, p. 185.

But Bonner's efforts hardly deprived the Protestant prisoners of funds. Some of the martyrs were people of substantial means and those who were not were supported by a network of co-religionists, ready to supply more than cheeses to the cause. An underground Protestant congregation headed by Thomas Rose typically raised ten pounds a meeting expressly for the relief of Protestant prisoners.[21] The chief underground congregation in London appointed two deacons to distribute money to Protestant prisoners in London and to act as executors for those who were martyred.[22] Augustine Bernher, one of the leaders of the London congregation, sent a letter to his deacons ordering them to raise money on behalf of their imprisoned co-religionists: 'I requyre you [in] Gods behalfe to consyder the great ned the prisoners of God ar in the prisons att london and meack [make] som gatheringes amongst your neighbors for the relyfe of them'.[23] It would be surprising if large sums were not raised by these deacons: Brett Usher has demonstrated how deeply Protestantism had penetrated London's mercantile elite by the beginning of Mary's reign.[24] And, in fact, powerful, because grudging, testimony to their largesse came from John Careless. In the middle of a fervent exhortation to London Protestants to shun all Catholic services and a scathing denunciation of the 'carnal gospellers' who were unwilling to risk their lives for the cause, Careless fielded a possible objection to his position:

But now mee thinketh, I heare some of you say to me: 'Why syr we do suffer with Christ, as becommeth Christians, in helpyng you to beare the crosse with our liberal relief. If we had loved our goods more than we do Christe, as you seeme to laye to our charge, then woulde we not have bestowed so muche of them uppon you and other, as we have done, yea, and daungered ourselves to bryng it to you', etc. Indeede, dear frendes, in thys poynte, I muste needes confesse that you have done youre dewtye towardes us; the Lorde God graunte you to do the rest belonging to him as well.[25]

Aristocratic sympathisers including the dowager duchess of Suffolk, Lord Russell the son of the earl of Bedford, Lady Fane, Lady Wyatt and Lady

[21] *1576*, p. 1978.   [22] *1563*, p. 1632.
[23] ECL, MS 260, fo. 27r; printed in A. Townsend (ed.), *The Writings of John Bradford*, Parker Society, 2 vols. (Cambridge, 1848–53), vol. II, p. 400. The letter is actually addressed to a 'Master D' and Townsend assumed that this was a person's name, but the letter lacks the personal details (e.g. salutations to mutual friends) common in such letters. It is also unusually impersonal and peremptory in tone, implying that this is a letter from a superior to an inferior. For these reasons, as well as the contents of the letter, I would maintain that 'Master D' means 'Master Deacon' and that this letter was sent to some, if not all, of the deacons in the London congregation. For Bernher's leadership of the London congregation see *1563*, p. 1700.
[24] B. Usher, 'Backing Protestantism: The London Godly, the Exchequer and the Foxe Circle', in D. Loades (ed.), *John Foxe: An Historical Perspective* (Aldershot, 1999), pp. 105–34.
[25] ECL, MS 262, fo. 208v; printed in *LM*, p. 598.

Knevett, all sent money to the imprisoned Protestants as did numerous gentry folk, including the 'honest gentleman' who sent £11.13s.4d to Hugh Latimer's family for his relief and that of Cranmer and Ridley.[26]

III

Poorer Protestant prisoners also earned money by copying the manuscripts of their incarcerated brethren. Robert Smith mentioned in a letter to his wife that that he was copying treatises, written by one of the martyrs, for Lady Fane.[27] The martyr Thomas Whittle, confined in Bonner's London palace, wrote to Careless, imprisoned in the King's Bench, asking Careless to copy Philpot's account of his examinations for a friend of Whittle's; Whittle promised to send payment to Careless.[28] Philpot, also imprisoned in Bonner's palace, sent a work of Calvin's to Careless to be copied out for a friend.[29] So busy was Careless with his copying that he repeatedly apologised to his correspondents for not replying to their letters, blaming his tardiness 'partlye on the inconvencye of the place wherein I nowe am . . . and partlye by the earnest calling on my dear fryndes (which dayly do releve me and my pore breatherne) to coppy owte suche thinges as they do brynge me'.[30]

The Protestant manuscript network was further extended by people outside the prisons who continued the copying process. There are, for example, copies of letters by Bradford and Ridley written in Bernher's hand.[31] On several occasions, the Protestant martyrs inspired such copying by exhorting their followers to disseminate their works. At the close of one of his treatises, Hooper urged his readers to circulate it as widely as possible, while the Lancashire martyr George Marsh asked his followers to show a copy of his account of his examinations to Protestants in the Manchester area before delivering it to its intended recipient.[32]

In fact, one of the chief purposes of this copying activity was to distribute the works of the martyrs to as wide an audience as possible. Transcriptions of Bradford's treatise 'The Hurt of Hearing Mass' circulated in manuscript in London, Kent and Lancashire.[33] In January 1555, Ridley sent Bradford a

---

[26] BL, MS Add. 19400, fo. 80r; see also *LM*, pp. 73, 75 and 280. For the importance of the financial support godly women gave to the martyrs see Thomas S. Freeman, '"The Good Ministrye of Godlye and Vertuouse Women": The Elizabethan Martyrologists and the Female Supporters of the Marian Martyrs', *JBS*, 39 (2000), 10–11.

[27] *1563*, p. 1266.   [28] BL, MS Add. 19400, fo. 58v.   [29] ECL, MS 260, fo. 65v.

[30] BL, MS Add. 19400, fo. 69r. Careless made a similar apology in *LM*, pp. 616–17.

[31] ECL, MS 260, fos. 18r–v and 283r.

[32] Hooper's plea is in ECL, MS 261, fo. 9v; printed in John Hooper, *An apologye made by the reverende father and constante martyr of Christe John Hooper . . .*, ed. H. Bull, (1562), STC 13742, sig. C5v. For Marsh's request see *1570*, p. 1744.

[33] *LM*, p. 355; ECL, MS 260, fos. 40v (printed in *LM*, p. 385), 81v and 171v (printed in *LM*, p. 563).

letter he had written to Hooper, asking that Bradford have it copied and then sent on to Hooper.[34] Copies of letters by William Tyms and John Philpot to individuals (John Careless and an anonymous gentlewoman respectively) made by Careless, with even their signatures transcribed in Careless's hand-writing, demonstrate the copying network in operation.[35] Of particular interest is a copy of a letter from Nicholas Ridley to his 'brethren in Christ', written in a copyist's hand but signed by Ridley.[36] Since Ridley was held in detention in the house of William Irish, the mayor of Oxford, he must have had the original letter smuggled out to be duplicated and had the copies returned to him for his signature.

The martyrs also used amanuenses to help them handle their extensive correspondence and maintain the wide-ranging network of contacts on which the survival of their Church depended. Several of Bradford's letters survive in which most of the text of the letter was written by a copyist, with corrections made and closing lines added by Bradford.[37] These letters were presumably dictated by Bradford to an amanuensis and then edited by Bradford before being disseminated; this is clearly demonstrated in a letter from Bradford, most of which is written in a copyist's hand, but which contains a conclusion with personal messages for that particular correspondent.[38] In a related example, a copy of part of Bradford's account of his examinations is transcribed in Careless's handwriting, continued in Bradford's and finishes with a note by Careless beginning 'Oh my deare father Master L.' After imploring Master L. to 'Remembre mee when you talke with youre good God that he may geve me the strengthe of His Spirit', the note concludes 'Oh that you knewe how good your faythefull servant Austen is to me'.[39] 'Faithfull servant Austen' can only be Augustine Bernher, which means that Master L. was Hugh Latimer. (Bernher had been Latimer's amanuensis). Bradford must have had Careless copy out his account of his examinations for the benefit of Latimer, imprisoned in Oxford. When Careless was unable to finish them, or perhaps finish them quickly enough, Bradford acted as his own copyist, while Careless added his own personal missive to Latimer.

So well organised was the copying network which the Protestant prisoners established that Bradford was able to invite Ridley to send the works he

---

[34] *LM*, p. 63 [*recte* 68].
[35] ECL, MS 260, fos. 27r and 167r. Careless's annotation in the upper left-hand corner of the letter, reading 'A letter of Master Philpot to a gentlewoman' indicates that the copy was being made for someone other than Philpot or the original recipient.
[36] BL, MS Add. 19400, fos. 52r–53r.   [37] E.g., ECL, MS 260, fos. 25r–26v.
[38] ECL, MS 260, fo. 136r–v.   [39] ECL, MS 262, fos. 95v–96v.

wrote while in custody to Bradford and his fellow inmates to be copied. Ridley sent two treatises, a hortatory letter to persecuted Protestants and a rebuttal of Thomas Watson's two sermons defending the doctrine of the Real Presence.[40]

Perhaps the most important achievement of this copying network was to ensure the survival of works which, as long as they remained in the prison cell, were subject to destruction whenever the authorities conducted a search. Once the original manuscripts had been copied and disseminated, their destruction became vastly more difficult. As William Tyms wrote from the King's Bench: 'I desyre some good brother to wryte this new, for I wrote it (as I do many times) with feare. For if the keepers had found me, they would have taken it from me, and my pen and incke also.'[41]

Tyms's fears raise an obvious question: Why didn't the authorities put a stop to this propaganda by simply depriving the prisoners of pen, ink and paper? It was not that they were unconcerned; the earl of Derby complained in Parliament that Bradford 'hath done more hurt by his letters, and exhorting those that came to him in religion, then ever he did when he was abroad, by his preaching'.[42] And, in fact, the letters of the martyrs frequently mention the confiscation of writing materials and refer to cell searches for letters and contraband paper, pen and ink.[43] But once again, the Marian authorities were prisoners of their own prison system. As long as access to the prisoners was maintained, through bribery or other means, writing materials could be smuggled in, as letters and treatises were smuggled out. Bonner's men, for example, found dried ink and a knife (presumably for sharpening quills) concealed in a roasted pig sent in to Philpot.[44] Yet except in unusual cases, prisoners could not be denied access to outsiders, since this was how the prisoners received the money that was as essential to the running of the prisons as petrol to the running of a car.

Even when outside aid failed, it was possible to improvise. Ralph Allerton and Richard Roth, his fellow prisoner, wrote a number of letters, as well as Allerton's account of his interrogations, in their own blood.[45] Strips of lead from the windows were used as substitute pens.[46] The biggest problem,

---

[40] ECL, MS 260, fo. 118r; printed in Christmas (ed.), *Works of Ridley*, pp. 537–8.

[41] *1570*, p. 2082.

[42] *1563*, pp. 1186–7. When he interrogated Bradford on 29 January 1555 Stephen Gardiner made it clear that he was aware of the scope of Bradford's epistolary activities during his imprisonment (*1563*, p. 1190).

[43] E.g., *LM*, pp. 195–6 and *1563*, pp. 1056, 1191 and 1419.   [44] *1563*, pp. 1417, 1418 and 1444.

[45] *1563*, pp. 1621 and 1631. Lest this be dismissed as hyperbole, letters written in the blood of Allerton and Roth were produced at their trials (*1563*, pp. 1627–8).

[46] *LM*, sig. A4r.

however, was a lack of paper; Allerton complained that want of paper alone prevented him from copying a letter of Roth's for the edification of his friends.[47] On one occasion, Ridley answered a letter of Bernher's by writing his reply on the back of it and returning it to him.[48]

IV

A great deal of time, money and ingenuity was spent in composing and disseminating these writings, while considerable hardships were borne and dangers faced in disseminating them. Smuggling documents in and out of prison was a hazardous enterprise. Hooper's servant William Downton was imprisoned for carrying his master's letters out of prison, and Ridley's brother-in-law George Shipside suffered the same fate.[49] Robert Glover, Latimer's kinsman by marriage and a martyr himself, wrote to Bernher urging him to leave Oxford because his services to Latimer were attracting attention: Glover feared that if Bernher was arrested and questioned about his beliefs his trial for heresy would necessarily follow.[50]

What made these letters worth all this hardship, risk and expense? Why were they written at all? These are questions worth considering if for no other reason than that the production, circulation and preservation of prison writings on this scale was without precedent in English history; the Lollards and the Henrician Protestants did not produce such a bountiful harvest of prison literature.[51] But the Marian Protestants, unlike

---

[47] *1563*, p. 1628.

[48] ECL, MS 260, fo. 278r–v. Bernher's letter is on fo. 278r; Ridley's reply begins on fo. 278v and ends on the bottom of 278r.

[49] *1563*, p. 1055 and ECL, MS 260, fo. 115r; printed in *LM*, p. 54. Interestingly, Shipside was only detected when he delivered copies of a large part of Ridley's writings to one of the bishop's former chaplains, who betrayed Shipside to the authorities (*LM*, pp. 56–7).

[50] BL, MS Add. 19400, fo. 80r. Something similar happened to Harry Adlington, who was arrested while visiting Stephen Gratwick, a fellow Protestant. Adlington was interrogated, tried, condemned and finally burned at Stratford-le-Bow on 27 June 1556 (*1563*, pp. 1524–5).

[51] The only two Lollard works which appear to have been written in prison are William Thorpe's account of his examinations and Richard Wyche's account of his examination. The former was well known and has been printed in A. Hudson (ed.), *Two Wycliffite Texts*, EETS, OS 301 (Oxford, 1993), pp. 24–93; also see Hudson's discussion of this text on pp. liii–lix. In contrast, Wyche's account survived in a single copy (Prague University Library, MS III. G. fos. 89v–94v) and was unknown to contemporaries and during the Reformation. For an analysis of Wyche's account, see C. Nolcken, 'Richard Wyche, a Certain Knight, and the Beginning of the End', in M. Aston and C. Richmond (eds.), *Lollardy and the Gentry in the Later Middle Ages* (New York, 1997), pp. 127–54. Some important works were written by people imprisoned for religious reasons during Henry VIII's reign, and disseminated by their co-religionists; Anne Askew's examinations provide a notable example of this. Yet the elaborate communications network between imprisoned martyrs and their colleagues and supporters which existed in Mary's reign was not established in Henry's reign. An interesting, and unique, harbinger of things to come was William Tyndale's correspondence, sent while he was

the Lollards and their Henrician forebears, were members of tightly organised congregations led by professional, university educated, clergy, many
of whom had enjoyed close links to leading Continental Reformers. The
underlying purpose of their prison writings was to enable this clergy, along
with certain lay supporters such as Careless, to guide and direct their flocks.
By means of the manuscripts which they wrote in prison, the imprisoned
members of the Edwardian ecclesiastical hierarchy were able to conduct
an extensive pastoral ministry with their followers, forging enduring and
profound bonds of spiritual intimacy. They were also able to maintain the
organisation and structure of their Church, as well as their control over it.[52]
These tasks were made especially pressing in Mary's reign by a number of
developments.

V

One of these developments was the vehement, and virtually unanimous,
insistence of the leading Marian Protestants that their co-religionists must
refuse to attend Catholic services. Even vespers and matins, to say nothing of the Mass, were to be rigorously shunned as sources of spiritual
pollution.[53] This rigorism, inspired by the strictures of John Calvin and
Heinrich Bullinger against Nicodemism, was unprecedented among English religious dissenters.[54] It would have been unrealistic to expect such
new and radical teachings to have gone unchallenged under the best of
circumstances. But the anti-Nicodemite convictions of the English Protestant leadership imposed unpalatable choices upon their followers: exile,
death or apostasy. For women the dilemma imposed by the insistence on
absolute non-conformity was often even more severe, entailing defiance of

incarcerated in the Low Countries, with John Frith, imprisoned in the Tower of London, encouraging and advising his younger colleague (*1570*, pp. 1231–2). Also virtually unique in this reign, but
very typical of later writings, is Frith's epistle sent from the Tower to his friends and co-religionists
(*1570*, pp. 1177–8).

[52] For Quakers using letters and manuscript tracts for the same purposes a century later, see M. K.
Peters, 'Quaker Pamphleteering and the Development of the Quaker Movement, 1652–1656', Ph.D.
thesis, University of Cambridge (1996), pp. 29–37, 42 and 49–58.

[53] *LM*, pp. 401–3 and 414–18.

[54] The term Nicodemism, coined by Calvin, referred to the Pharisee who visited Jesus by night (see
John 3:1–2) and was used in derision of those Protestants who outwardly conformed to Catholicism
while inwardly harboring Protestant sympathies. See P. Zagorin, *Ways of Lying: Dissimulation, Per-
secution and Conformity in Early Modern Europe* (Cambridge, MA, 1990), especially pp. 63–82 and
B. Gregory, *Salvation at Stake: Christian Martyrdom in Early Modern Europe* (Cambridge, MA, 1999),
esp. pp. 154–62. Also see A. Pettegree, 'Nicodemism and the English Reformation', in *Marian
Protestantism: Six Studies* (Aldershot, 1996), pp. 86–117 and A. Hudson, *The Premature Reformation*
(Oxford, 1988), p. 158.

husbands and fathers as well as magistrates.[55] As a result, the martyrs spent – indeed felt compelled to spend – prodigious amounts of time and energy to ensure that their co-religionists, especially those who were spiritually intimate with them, did not fall into the sin of idolatry. The crusade to prevent their followers from attending Catholic services as well as the need to deal with the problems this created for their followers (loss of honour, status, wealth, children, spouses and even life itself, as well as guilt, doubt and despair from defying those in authority or from committing idolatry) generated a very large portion of the writings of the imprisoned Protestant leaders.[56] The networks for the copying and circulation of the writings of their writings proved invaluable in the struggle against Nicodemism; these networks enabled John Bradford to disseminate copies of his treatise 'The Hurt of Hearing Mass'. From surviving evidence we know that Bradford sent copies to three households and that he offered to send it to a fourth.[57] The actual distribution of Bradford's treatise was probably much wider than this.

If it was necessary to guide, direct and support the faithful in their rejection of idolatry it was also essential, for different reasons, to instruct and encourage those ready to die for the gospel through the course of their martyrdom. The Marian Protestant leaders recognised the enormous propaganda windfall arising from martyrdoms and the powerful role they might play in rallying the faithful, provided that such martyrs displayed the necessary constancy and fortitude.

But more than courage was demanded of the martyrs: they also needed the theological expertise to articulate and defend the beliefs for which they were prepared to die. If, however, those sacrificing their lives appeared ignorant they provided the Catholics with the opportunity to brand them as fools and even lunatics rather than true martyrs.[58] Although usually literate, the Marian martyrs often came from relatively humble backgrounds and they lacked theological training. These martyrs were carefully coached by their more educated brethren in what to do or say during their examinations. Bradford, for example, wrote to one prisoner, carefully detailing how he was to answer questions on the Eucharist, while on another occasion he wrote to a woman instructing her on what to say when she was examined by

---

[55] For the problems anti-Nicodemism created for Marian Protestant women see Freeman, 'Good Ministrye', 13–16.

[56] See Freeman, 'Good Ministrye', pp. 12–13 and 15–17.

[57] ECL, MS 260, fos. 40v (printed in *LM*, p. 335), 81v and 171v (printed in *LM*, p. 363).

[58] See Gregory, *Salvation at Stake*, pp. 134–8 and 315–41 and my 'The Importance of Dying Earnestly: The Metamorphosis of the Account of James Bainham in "Foxe's Book of Martyrs"', in R. N. Swanson (ed.), *The Church Retrospective*, SCH 33, (Woodbridge, 1997), pp. 267–88.

an unnamed 'deabolycall doctor' and royal commissioners on her religious beliefs.[59]

In a letter to Harry Adlington, a sawyer, who was eventually executed for heresy in 1556, Careless wrote that he had read the account which Adlington had sent him of his examinations and he congratulated Adlington for maintaining that there were only two sacraments. He then gave Adlington a definition of a sacrament in case he should be questioned on the subject at his next examination. Careless then wrote a prefabricated oration for Adlington to deliver after he was sentenced to death. It went on for hundreds of words, touching the major theological bases (Adlington was especially to affirm his belief in the Trinity and to announce that he detested all sects of Arians and Anabaptists) before concluding: 'And if for these things you take away my life, and make your selves giltye of my blood . . . bee you sure, your iudgement sleepeth not, but when you crye peace, and all is safe, then shall your plagues beginne lyke the sorrowes of a women travelyng with child, according to Christes infallible promise.' Careless then advised Adlington not be drawn into further discussion with his judges, observing that 'This kind of answer wil cut their combes most and edify the people that by stand by, so that the same be done with sobrietie, mekenes and patience'.[60]

Careless' observation underscores a final area in which the martyrs required guidance. In addition to courage and knowledge of doctrinal issues it was expected that true martyrs would display a stoic patience, a heroic and reasoned indifference to pain and suffering, characteristic of the Aristotelian virtues which infused early Christian martyrologies – notably those of Eusebius and Lactantius, enthusiastically revived during the Reformation.[61] This stoicism entailed moderate behaviour and temperate speech even when a martyr was faced with the prospect of torture and death.

Sharing the same values and expectations, leading Protestants wrote to their colleagues who were about to die, reminding of them of the need for temperance and calm. Careless wrote from the King's Bench to William Tyms in Newgate, congratulating him, and those condemned with him, for their 'hearty boldnes and modest behaviour'.[62] A few months later, Careless wrote to two prisoners, congratulating them, for their conduct during their trials and for having 'well learned the lesson of mekenes and

[59] *LM*, pp. 389–91; ECL MS 260, fo. 136r, Townsend (ed.), *Bradford*, vol. II, p. 101.
[60] *LM*, pp. 613–15.
[61] P. Collinson, '"A Magazine of Religious Patterns": An Erasmian Topic Transposed in English Protestantism' in his *Godly People: Essays on English Protestantism and Puritanism* (1983), pp. 511–13.
[62] ECL, MS 260, fos. 130r–131v; printed in *1563*, pp. 1449–50.

pacience of suche as weare His trewe mynisters appoynted to teach you'. Careless deplored the fact that two prisoners tried with them, had, in contrast, 'rayled verye sore uppon suche as sought theyre cruell condempnacion'. Careless asked them to send him a report of what these intemperate martyrs had said and done, if at all possible.[63] Because of the ability of the Protestant prisoners to communicate with each other through a manuscript network which ran from prison to prison, leading Protestants were able to choreograph the regime's trials and executions, transforming figures who potentially could have been dismissed as ignorant and eccentric cranks into athletes and warriors of Christ.

The Marian Protestant leaders were also faced with a bitter schism in their own ranks over the doctrine of predestination: a zealous minority, commonly referred to as the freewillers or freewill men, challenged the predestinarian theology of the Protestant leadership.[64] The predestinarians eventually triumphed: many freewillers reconverted and freewill opposition had been virtually eradicated by the beginning of Elizabeth's reign.[65] But it was a fierce struggle with leading Protestants, including Ridley, Bradford, Careless and Philpot, waging a propaganda war against articulate and organised fellow Protestants.

From the London prisons the tentacles of the Protestant manuscript network reached out to co-religionists across England. Careless wrote to a friend in the Oxford area, instructing her on how to deal with radical Protestants (characterised by Careless as 'blynde prophets'): namely, to read a confession of faith which Careless had already sent to a fellow Protestant in Witney 'and in all points to be ruled thereby'.[66] A letter dated 26 February 1558 was sent by 'the ministers and senyors [i.e., elders] with the deacons' of the London congregation to certain 'well beloved brethren'. (We do not know where these brethren were, but in a reply one of them stated that they were 'farre from you and unacquaynted in the fleshe'.) The leaders of the London congregation informed their co-religionists that they were sending them a manuscript book 'wherein is contayned not only a treatyse of that blessed martyr of God, Master Bradford, but also other works of godly men agaynst the sayd errors of thos men which impugne Gods electyon and ascrybe freewill unto man'. The letter went on pointedly to ask the

[63] BL, MS Add. 19400, fo. 67r.

[64] See my 'Dissenters from a Dissenting Church: The Challenge of the Freewillers, 1550–1558', in P. Marshall and A. Ryrie (eds.), *The Beginnings of English Protestantism* (Cambridge, 2002), pp. 129–56. For contemporary use of the term 'freewill men', see *1563*, p. 1605.

[65] See Freeman, 'Dissenters,' pp. 145–56.

[66] Nicholas Ridley, *A pituous lamentation of the miserable estate of the Churche . . .*, (1566), STC 21052, sig. F7r–v.

recipients to 'let us know your mynd in the said controversie, not for this cause, as though we do doubt in the matter . . . but rather to the entent that our ioye might be encreased in hearyng that you be sound in the doctryne of Jesus Christ'.[67]

The Protestants imprisoned in England were also able to correspond with their co-religionists on the Continent; networks as elaborate as those which copied the manuscripts of the martyrs and disseminated them in England also transported them out of the country to Protestant centres abroad. In fact, manuscripts written by Protestants could reach the Continent with surprising speed. Andrew Pettegree has pointed out that Nicholas Ridley's *Brief Declaration of the Lord's Supper*, written, according to its preface, 'a little before' his death on 16 October 1555 was published in Emden by the end of the year.[68] In May 1555 Edmund Grindal wrote to Ridley from Frankfurt, discussing, among other things, Ridley's account of his disputation, a copy of which was in Grindal's possession although the disputation had taken place only a month earlier.[69]

Edward VI's reign had seen a Protestant clerical leadership establish a Church which was organised, with a committed core of believers scattered throughout most of England, and a clearly defined orthodoxy. During Mary's reign, committed Protestants continued to turn to the Edwardian religious elite for guidance, although their former leaders were behind bars or beyond the seas. At the same time, the Protestant clerics were compelled to communicate with their followers, not only to provide pastoral guidance, but also to preserve the Church they had built. For these reasons, English Protestants, free and captive, lay and cleric, created, and participated in, at considerable risk, an elaborate well-organised system of manuscript communication.

Yet despite the imperative need for communication, the English Protestant leaders did not communicate with their followers in print. It was not that they lacked the means to do so. In the next reign, both Catholics and radical Protestants would operate clandestine presses with considerable success; there was no reason why this could not have been done in Mary's reign. In fact, no less a figure than William Cecil financed the underground 'Michael Wood' press, operated by John Day, which printed heretical books in Lincolnshire in the early years of Mary's reign.[70] But this enterprise was

---

[67] The letter is Bodl. Lib., MS Bodley 53, fo. 146v; the reply is fos. 147r–48v.

[68] A. Pettegree, 'The English Church at Emden', in *Marian Protestantism*, p. 29.

[69] ECL, MS 260, fos. 114r–15v; printed in *LM*, pp. 49–56.

[70] The location of the 'Michael Wood' press, and the involvement of Cecil and Day in its operation, have been conclusively demonstrated by the brilliant detective work of Elizabeth Evenden. This will be published in a forthcoming edition of the *Sixteenth Century Journal*.

unique and did not involve Protestant clerics, nor did it print any writings by the leading Marian martyrs and confessors.

Since manuscripts by Protestants incarcerated in England flowed to the Continent, it would certainly have been possible for these works to have been printed abroad and smuggled back into England. Yet to a surprisingly large extent this did not happen. Out of well over 150 works published, in English and Latin, by English Protestants during Mary's reign less than ten were works written in prison.[71] Furthermore almost all of these few works were published in Emden, whose English congregation and Protestant printers were more aggressive in printing polemical works than their counterparts in other Protestant centres.[72] Much has been made of the putative failure of the Marian authorities, particularly the Marian religious authorities, to appreciate the importance of printing and to utilise the printing press, but similar charges could be made against the Marian Protestants.[73] The celebrity, or notoriety, of the works of Ponet, Goodman and Knox should not blind us to the fact that the works of Ridley, Bradford, Philpot and Careless which were central to the concerns of Marian Protestants were published slowly, sporadically or not (in this reign) at all.

---

[71] Lists of books printed by English Protestants during Mary's reign, both in England and abroad, are given in E. J. Baskerville, *A Chronological Bibliography of Propaganda and Polemic Published in England between 1553 and 1558* (Philadelphia, 1979), pp. 34–87. See also his 'Some Lost Works of Propaganda and Polemic from the Marian Period', *The Library*, 6th ser., 8 (1996), 47–52 and A. Pettegree, 'Checklist of Latin Polemic Published by the Marian Exiles Abroad, 1553–1559', in *Marian Protestantism*, pp. 183–96. (Both the lists of Pettegree and Baskerville are restricted to religious topics and do not cover the full range of English Protestant publication.) It is difficult to be more precise about the numbers involved, because the criteria remain subjective. For example, should an English translation of a Latin work be counted as a separate work? Or should Jane Grey's letters be considered as prison writings? Furthermore Jean Crespin printed manuscripts of the martyrs in his 1556 martyrology: *Troisième partie du recueil des martyres* (Geneva, 1556), pp. 482–3, 506–14, 540 and 543–59. This work, however, was not directed to an English speaking audience.

[72] Some of the reasons for Emden's prominence as a publishing centre for the Marian exiles are discussed in Pettegree, 'English Church at Emden', pp. 27–8. It might also be observed that the German and Swiss printers were reluctant to print works which dealt with topics, such as the Eucharist, capable of exacerbating the already strained relations between the Lutherans and the Swiss Protestants. Paradoxically the remoteness of Emden may also have contributed to its becoming a centre for Marian exile publication as it was beyond the influence of Bullinger, Peter Martyr and Grindal, who were more cautious about printing the works of the English martyrs.

[73] For claims that the Marian authorities failed to appreciate the propaganda potential of printing see J. W. Martin, 'The Marian Regime's Failure to Understand the Importance of Printing', in his *Religious Radicals in Tudor England* (1989), pp. 107–23; A. G. Dickens, *The English Reformation*, 2nd edn (1989) and D. M. Loades, *The Reign of Mary Tudor* (1979), pp. 162–4 and 338–40. For dissenting views see J. Loach, 'Pamphlets and Politics, 1553–8', *Bulletin of the Institute of Historical Research*, 48 (1975), 31–45 and E. Duffy, *The Stripping of the Altars: Traditional Religion in England 1400–1580* (New Haven, 1992), pp. 525 and 532–43.

VI

There were several reasons why so few of the letters of the martyrs were published during Mary's reign and they illustrate some of the advantages of script as opposed to print. The first consideration that inhibited the printing of Marian Protestant prison writings was the fear that publication would lead to reprisals against their authors – indeed against all incarcerated Protestants. Premature publication might provoke the authorities into measures that would cripple, if not curtail, the composition of such works. As Ridley wrote to Bernher: 'I suppose many harmes mai fal thereupon if anything be [set] forth onder the title and name of any prisoner, not to hymself onely, but also to the rest. As ye knoo, I have alwaies counsayled Master Hooper not to be hasty to set forth any thyng under the title of his own name.'[74] Ridley's protégé Edmund Grindal wrote to his mentor in May 1555, stating that while the English exiles had manuscript copies of many of Ridley's works: 'It hath bene thought best not to printe them till we see what God will do with you, bothe for incensyng of their malicious fury, and also for restraining you and others from writing hereafter, which should be a greater losse to the church of Christe, than forbearing of these for a tyme.'[75] Bullinger also used his very considerable influence to restrain publication of the works of the martyrs; he intervened to prevent the publication of Jane Grey's writings, arguing that publication would be 'injurious to many individuals'.[76] The leading martyrs were hostages who kept their own works from being published, at least until their executions put them beyond reprisal.

Circulating the works of the Protestant prisoners in manuscript was, in contrast, much safer than having them printed. The recipients of manuscripts, at least in the initial stages of transmission, could be carefully selected and manuscript circulation was easier to keep clandestine and harder for the authorities to trace. But while manuscripts could reach a wide audience they could not reach as many people as printed works could. As soon as it was safe to do so, the letters of the martyrs were accordingly published. The Marian authorities could not prevent the production and dissemination of illicit manuscripts, even within their own prisons, but

[74] ECL, MS 260, 271r; printed in Townsend (ed.), *Bradford*, vol. II, p. 172. One letter which Ridley wrote to Hooper urged him not 'to hasten the publishing of your works' for fear that 'your mouth should be stopped hereafter and al things taken away from the rest of the prisoners' (*1563*, p. 1052).

[75] *LM*, p. 51.

[76] H. Robinson (ed.), *Original Letters Relative to the English Reformation*, Parker Society (Cambridge, 1846), p. 306.

their efforts to suppress heretical literature were not completely ineffective. By creating circumstances which inhibited the printing of the martyrs' letters, the authorities restricted the audience for these works even if they were unable to suppress them entirely.

The fear of reprisals against imprisoned authors underscored a major advantage manuscripts had over print: manuscripts circulated in what was, to appropriate Habermas's terminology, a restricted, or semi-public, sphere. As with print, manuscript copying and distribution provided a medium for communicating with large audiences, for putting ideas, arguments and assertions into the public sphere. But unlike print, manuscripts also permitted those disseminating them to select their audiences and place ideas, arguments and assertions into a restricted, or semi-public, sphere. This allowed the Marian Protestants to conduct doctrinal disputes without the outside world, particularly their Catholic adversaries, finding out about them.[77]

Another consideration blocking the printing of the letters was the perceived need to remove errors and potentially embarrassing passages from texts that had been written in haste by authors with, at best, a limited access to books. The fact that some of these works were written as part of controversies (for example, about freewill and predestination) from which the Continental Protestants were anxious to distance themselves only increased the perceived need for censorship.[78]

It is impossible to exercise editorial control on manuscripts once they have begun to circulate. The process of printing, on the other hand, permitted the imposition of editorial control and the rewriting of texts. While Foxe was preparing his 1559 martyrology, the immediate precursor of the *Actes and Monuments*, Grindal wrote to him, expressing disapproval of a recent publication of Philpot's account of his examinations because it did not amend Philpot's statements and correct his errors. Grindal urged Foxe not to repeat this mistake and passed on the opinion of Bullinger and Peter Martyr that Hooper's writings should be similarly edited.[79] In the event

---

[77] Peter Lake and David Como have described a similar manuscript network existing among puritans in early seventeenth-century London in '"Orthodoxy" and its Discontents: Dispute Settlement and the Production of "Consensus" in the London (Puritan) "Underground"', *JBS*, 39 (2000), 34–70, esp. 38–9, 44–5, 47, 64–5 and 68–70.

[78] When a work by John Knox, defending predestination, was printed in Geneva in 1560, the Consistory consented to its publication only upon the conditions that the work be examined by senior ministers of the city and that any passages which these divines felt were 'contre la doctrine cattolique et orthodox' be removed: J.-F. Gilmont, *Bibliographie des éditions de Jean Crespin 1550–1572*, 2 vols. (Verviers, 1981), vol. I, p. 133.

[79] BL, MS Harley 417, fo. 112r; trans. and printed in W. Nicholson (ed.), *The Remains of Edmund Grindal*, Parker Society (Cambridge, 1843), p. 223.

this was well-heeded advice. Foxe and his fellow martyrologist, Henry Bull, exercised an editorial control over the letters of the martyrs so thorough that it stopped just short of being obsessive. Passages, indeed whole paragraphs, were added or deleted from the original texts; references to backsliding, Nicodemism, the freewillers and even the personal lives of the martyrs were ruthlessly expunged as the letters were printed. The very genders of the martyrs' correspondents were occasionally altered in the printed letters, in order to suit the polemical purposes of Foxe and Bull.[80]

A great deal has been said about the opportunities that the printing press presented for the dissemination of new ideas; relatively little has been said about the opportunities printing offered, at least to those who controlled the medium, for the editing and shaping of those ideas. Printing a text standardises it; myriad diverse scribal copies of a text, each containing its individual variations, are replaced by a single uniform text. The importance of this to censorship and the regulation of ideas cannot be overstated. Essentially the printing press is a bottleneck in the transmission of ideas. This was certainly the case with the writings of the Marian martyrs: the diverse manuscripts were gathered by Foxe and Bull, and rewritten, with 'improvements' and with problematic or embarrassing passages all airbrushed away. The new printed texts of Bull and Foxe became authoritative, replacing the original writings of the martyrs with their anodyne versions. It is ironic, but hardly accidental, that Bull and Foxe succeeded in doing what Bishop Bonner could not: they controlled and regulated the writings of the Marian martyrs.

Despite the yoking of Protestantism with printing, the Reformers did not rely exclusively on the new technology, instead they pragmatically used whichever of the competing mediums was best suited to their purposes in particular circumstances. Manuscript communication had real advantages over print; for one thing, it was far easier in the sixteenth century to copy a text by hand than to print it. Despite the work of Harold Love and others, there is still a too-frequent tendency to forget that scribal networks could produce hundreds of copies of a particular work.[81] As we have seen, manuscript communication was more suited to the clandestine

---

[80] S. Wabuda, 'Henry Bull, Miles Coverdale and the Making of Foxe's Book of Martyrs', in D. Wood (ed.), *Martyrs and Martyrologies*, SCH 30 (Oxford 1993), pp. 255–7 and Freeman, 'Good Ministrye', pp. 24–30.

[81] Several hundred manuscript copies survive of one translation of a popular Greek text. This means that many hundreds, possibly thousands, of copies of this work must have been made which have been lost or destroyed. See J. Soudek, 'Leonardo Bruni and his Public: A Statistical and Interpretative Study of his Annotated Latin Version of the (Pseudo-) Aristotelian Economics', *Studies in Medieval and Renaissance History*, 5 (1968), 49–136.

dissemination of ideas than print was; in Elizabeth's reign Catholics would rely on the circulation of manuscripts much as the Protestants had in the preceding reign.[82] The overwhelming advantage of print was its ability to reach large audiences: if it was easier to copy a work than to print it, it was easier to print multiple copies of a work than to copy them out by hand. Once the English Protestants were free from the danger of persecution, and no longer had to communicate covertly, then they turned to the mass medium to spread their message. In doing so, they also reaped the additional benefit of being able to control and shape the texts they were disseminating. Foxe extolled printing as God's instrument for preserving godly writings from oblivion, but he knew better than anyone the ability of the press to alter, amend and even conceal other godly writings.

[82] Brown, 'Paperchase,' 120–43.

13

Print, persecution and polemic: Thomas Edwards' Gangraena (1646) and Civil War sectarianism

Ann Hughes

Shortly after the New Model Army had occupied London in August 1647 to overawe their Presbyterian opponents in Parliament and the city, the radical Independent minister Hugh Peter defended the soldiers' restraint by declaring: 'I doe professe I conceive even *Gangraena* himselfe might have marcht through the Army unmolested'.[1] *Gangraena* himself was the London Presbyterian and lecturer, Thomas Edwards, whom the army regarded as one of their principal defamers. Edwards had denounced the religious heterodoxy of parliament's army at great length in his notorious *Gangraena: or A Catalogue and Discovery of many of the Errours, Heresies, Blasphemies and pernicious Practices of the Sectaries of this time, vented and acted in England in these four last years*, published in three parts in February, May and December 1646 (Illustration 6).[2] *Gangraena* – one of the most important printed works of the 1640s – was central to the conflicts over the future of Church and state that bedevilled the victorious parliamentarians at the end of the first Civil War. It was a vital text for Presbyterians agitating for a compulsory national church and a peace settlement with the king. For its subjects and opponents, *Gangraena* was a call for ruthless persecution of the godly; for its author and his allies it was an urgent defence of truth against heresy and schism. In over 800 pages Edwards listed the outrageous errors spread by contemporary sectaries, described their disorderly and often immoral behaviour, and offered the orthodox a programme to resist an independent and sectarian onslaught.

Gangraena can be presented as a classic exemplar of the power of print in mid-seventeenth-century England. Through print Edwards acquired an

---

[1] Hugh Peter, *A Word for the Army and Two Words to the Kingdome* (1647), pp. 7–8.

[2] For convenience *Gangraena* is quoted from the facsimile reprint of all three parts published by the Rota and the University of Exeter in 1977. For discussion of seventeenth-century editions see the Appendix to my *Gangraena and the Struggle for the English Revolution* (Oxford, forthcoming). I am grateful to the Leverhulme Trust, the British Academy and the former Humanities Research Board for their generous support for my work on *Gangraena*, and to Dr Kate Peters for her most effective research assistance.

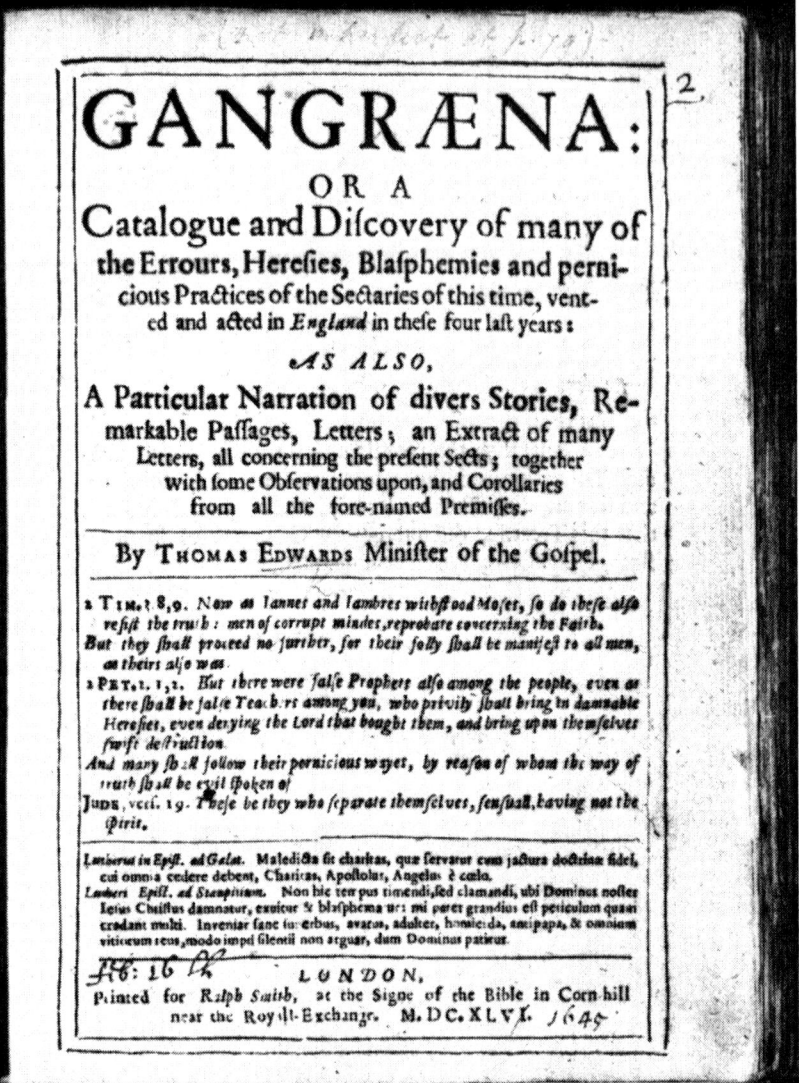

GANGRÆNA:

OR A

Catalogue and Discovery of many of the Errours, Herefies, Blafphemies and pernicious Practices of the Sectaries of this time, vented and acted in *England* in thefe four laft years:

AS ALSO,

A Particular Narration of divers Stories, Remarkable Paffages, Letters; an Extract of many Letters, all concerning the prefent Sects; together with fome Obfervations upon, and Corollaries from all the fore-named Premiffes.

By THOMAS EDWARDS Minifter of the Gofpel.

2 TIM. 3,9. *Now as Iannes and Iambres withftood Mofes, fo do thefe alfo refift the truth: men of corrupt mindes, reprobate concerning the Faith. But they fhall proceed no further, for their folly fhall be manifeft to all men, as theirs alfo was.*
2 PET. 2. 1,2. *But there were falfe Prophets alfo among the people, even as there fhall be falfe Teachers among you, who privily fhall bring in damnable Herefies, even denying the Lord that bought them, and bring upon themfelves fwift deftruction. And many fhall follow their pernicious wayes, by reafon of whom the way of truth fhall be evil fpoken of.*
JUDE, verf. 19. *Thefe be they who feparate themfelves, fenfuall, having not the Spirit.*

Lutherus in Epift. ad Galat. Maledicta fit charitas, quæ fervatur cum jactura doctrinæ fidei, cui omnia cedere debent, Charitas, Apoftolus, Angelus è cælo.
Lutheri Epift. ad Staupitium. Non hic tempus timendi, fed clamandi, ubi Dominus nofter Iefus Chriftus damnatur, exuitur & blafphema ur: mi puret grandius eft periculum quam credant multi. Inveniar fane fuperbus, avarus, adulter, homicida, antipapa, & omnium vitiorum reus, modo impd filentii non arguar, dum Dominus patitur.

Heb: 16 th LONDON,
Printed for *Ralph Smith*, at the Signe of the Bible in Corn-hill near the Royall-Exchange. M.DC.XLVI. *1645*

Illustration 6 Thomas Edwards, *Gangraena: or A Catalogue and Discovery of many of the Errours, Heresies, Blasphemies and pernicious Practices of the Sectaries of this time, vented and acted in England in these four last years* (1646), title-page.

authorial notoriety, identified indelibly with his most famous book – the work is always Edwards' *Gangraena*, while he is usually *Gangraena* Edwards. For Edwards' critics, *Gangraena* vividly demonstrated the power of print – to define, persuade and mobilise. As one of his most eminent targets alleged, it was through print in *Gangraena* that Edwards constructed a misleading identity for the godly men he denounced. Thus John Milton condemned this public defaming:

Men whose life, learning, faith and pure intent
Would have been held in high esteem with Paul
Must now be named and printed heretics
By shallow Edwards and Scotch What-d'ye-call.[3]

For Edwards this was (or would have been) a compliment; he shared with his opponents a belief in the power of print, aiming to expose the dangers of heresy and schism so that those deceived could be disillusioned: 'By my Books, especially *Gangraena*, many Sectaries being so discovered by name and places of abode, laid open in severall of their opinions and wayes, will not be able for the future to do so much hurt and mischiefe among the people; their Sheeps skins are by this pull'd over their Wolves ears, and many will now shun, and be afraid of them, who before knew them not'.[4] Edwards offered many examples of the power of printed books to reclaim people from error. Both 'in Histories and in the experience of our own times . . . many Sectaries have been regained' through books; examples ranged from the anabaptists in the sixteenth century who had been 'reclaimed by learned Musculus' to 'a good Scholar, Fellow of a Colledge', a member of a London Independent congregation, who became 'a profest Presbyterian', after reading 'some Books against Independencie'. Hope Sherrard, the minister of Sandwich, a town that featured several times in *Gangraena*, had been pastor of an Independent congregation when, 'I was in the Iland of Providence alone, and in the dark', but through reading 'books, as Master Rutherford, etc', he had come to see 'the Independent way' as 'a moth-eaten garment' with 'many flawes in it'.[5] Edwards included, of course, examples of the efficacy of his own book, recounting with approval the direct action taken by the minister at Bath who had refused to allow the radical anti-formalist Puritan John Saltmarsh to preach in his

---

[3] Milton's book, *The Doctrine and Discipline of Divorce*, was cited in *Gangraena*, part I, p. 34; for his sonnet, 'On the New Forcers of Conscience under the Long Parliament', which ends, 'New Presbyter is but old Priest writ large', see, e.g., S. Orgel and J. Goldberg (eds.), *John Milton* (Oxford, 1990), pp. 83–4. 'Scotch What-d'ye-call' is probably the Scottish minister Robert Baillie, resident in London in the 1640s and an associate of Edwards.

[4] *Gangraena*, part II, p. 46.   [5] *Gangraena*, part II, p. 204; part III, pp. 108–9.

church. When Saltmarsh remonstrated with him, 'especially seeing he had never seen him before; unto whom the Minister replyed, he had heard of him by M. John Ley, and Master Thomas Edwards, and was fully satisfied concerning him'.[6]

Orthodox Presbyterians had to expose and publicise the errors of the sectaries precisely because those sectaries had made such effective use of print. The spreading of evil doctrines through print often headed Edwards' lists of their baleful influence: 'There have been more Books writ, Sermons preached, words spoken, besides plottings and actings for a Toleration, within these foure last yeers, then for all other things. Every day now brings forth Books for Toleration.' To drive home his point, Edwards repeated in the margin: 'Within the space of five or sixe dayes there came out five Bookes that I saw either wholly or in part pleading for Toleration'.[7] Print represented a shameless courting of publicity, and a ruthless political campaign: heretical doctrines were not simply, 'preached with us in the ear, but on the house-top, we declare our errours, as Sodom, and are not ashamed; yea, abominable errours are Printed, the Books sold up and down in Westminster-Hall, London, and dispersed in all places; yea, given into the hands of Parliament men in Westminster-Hall'.[8] Unlike ephemeral speech, print fixed errors in a public domain and spread them without restraint. The harmful power of print was endorsed by another orthodox cleric, Richard Vines, in the published version of his sermon delivered on the fast day called in March 1647 to combat heresy: the pulpit was powerless, argued Vines, while the 'poison is carried up and downe in books and cryed at men's door every day'.[9] Hence, important sermons needed to extend their impact from the oral event through a more enduring printed version.

Consequently, Edwards' *Gangraena* was directed against 'audacious men and their daring books'.[10] Sectarian publications formed a major source for the errors exposed in *Gangraena*: as Edwards explained in part I, he had drawn both on the writings of the sectaries and the works of 'persons of note and worth for learning and piety, who either after conferences with them, or hearing them preach upon certain knowledge have printed and attested them to the world, diverse of which printed books, especially those made

---

[6] *Gangraena*, part III, p. 114; John Ley published three attacks on Saltmarsh: *The New Quere and Determination upon it* (1645); *Light for Smoke* (1646) and *An After-reckoning with Mr Saltmarsh* (1646).

[7] *Gangraena*, part I, p. 122.   [8] *Gangraena*, part I, p. 149.

[9] Richard Vines, *The Authours, Nature and Danger of Haeresie* (1647), p. 67.

[10] *Gangraena*, part III, p. 217.

by the sectaries, I quote upon the margent by the errours'. 'Quoting Books knowne to hundreds', was, he insisted in part III, a prime guarantee of the validity of his work.[11] Religious debate and competition were transformed by the widespread resort to the press in the 1640s and the *de facto* freedom to express any views in print. In the 1620s and 1630s, radical Puritan ideas rarely found their way into print but spread through preaching, discussion and manuscript circulation. Consequently orthodox Puritan heresy hunters relied on manuscript lists of errors or notes taken from dubious sermons for evidence of error.[12] In the 1640s, as sectarians used the press to spread their views beyond their immediate milieu, so Presbyterians like Edwards scoured printed material for evidence for his case. In compiling *Gangraena*, then, Edwards took advantage of other printed attacks on sectarianism such as Thomas Gataker's *God's Eye on his Israel*, a denunciation of the antino-mians Giles Randall and John Simpson or Prynne's more wide-ranging, *A Fresh Discovery of Some Prodigious New Wandring Blasing-Stars & Fire-brands, Stiling Themselves New-Lights*.[13] He quoted at length also from the works of Independents, Baptists and other separatists and radicals, from at least twelve works by John Lilburne, ten by John Goodwin, six by John Saltmarsh, and three by Jeremiah Burroughs. Edwards' analysis of one tract by one of his prime targets, Hugh Peter, *Master Peters Last Report of the English Wars*, covered twenty pages of repetitive quotation and comment – almost twice the length of the original work.[14]

Printed publication made sectarians doubly notorious. Their fame was spread through their treatment in *Gangraena*, but for Edwards they already had a prior identification as the authors of dangerous books. The titles of these books took pride of place in Edwards' pen portraits, forming a crucial element in the defining or 'naming' of dangerous radicals, as in: 'There is one Lawrence Clarkson, a Seeker, spoken of in my *Gangraena*, pag 104 and 105, who put forth a pamphlet called *The Pilgrimage of Saints*'.[15] Edwards' treatment of three Kent radicals, for example, was based on their 'wicked' books rather than their activities as pastors of separate congrega-tions. John Turner's recently published *Heavenly Conference*, was the source

---

[11] *Gangraena*, part I, p. 6; part III, Preface, sig. *3v. As Anthony Grafton has suggested, 'savage polemics produced the richest growths of source-notes': *The Footnote* (1997), p. 202.

[12] D. Como and P. Lake, '"Orthodoxy" and its Discontents: Dispute Settlement and the Production of "Consensus" in the London (Puritan) "Underground"', *JBS*, 39 (2000), 34–70.

[13] Thomas Gataker, *God's Eye on his Israel* (1645); William Prynne, *A Fresh Discovery of Some Prodigious New Wandring Blasing-stars & Firebrands, Stiling Themselves New-lights* (1645).

[14] *Master Peters Last Report of the English Wars* (1646), took up twelve pages; for the critique, *Gangraena*, part III, pp. 128–46.

[15] *Gangraena*, part II, p. 7.

for error 172 in *Gangraena* part I, and its arguments against the imposition of the Westminster Assembly's Presbyterian 'Directory of Worship' were repeated at least twice more. There was no mention of Turner's leadership of a 'conventicle' meeting near Sutton Valence, a role that had lasted almost twenty years.[16] Two Baptist conventiclers, Francis Cornwall and Christopher Blackwood, also featured as pamphleteers:

> There is one Cornwell in Kent an Anabaptist, who hath put forth divers Pamphlets, one against Baptising of Children, others lately printed, Dedicated to particular members of the House of Commons: The first pamphlet called, *The Vindication of the Royall Commission of King Jesus*, set forth about three years ago, was given to divers Members at the doore of the House of Commons.[17]

Blackwood's attack on infant baptism, *The Storming of Antichrist*, was similarly prominent.[18] Inevitably, and ironically, Edwards' accounts gave further publicity to the doctrines and practices he condemned.

It could therefore be argued that *Gangraena*, and the pamphlet controversies it generated, demonstrate a 'modern' use of print within a generalised, national campaign over abstract principles.[19] Edwards denied any personal animus, or even much personal contact with the sectaries he denounced; he was concerned only with their offences against 'the truth and the glory of God', offences committed in particular through the medium of print.[20] Likewise, those who went into print to denounce *Gangraena* as slander mounted a general campaign against Edwards. John Goodwin, his most prominent target, and most active critic, defended himself and his friends but also wrote in support of men unknown to him before their common featuring in the pages of *Gangraena*.[21] While an Independent-sectarian community of those attacked by Edwards and his supporters was defined in print, an orthodox-Presbyterian alliance was similarly

---

[16] Thomason's copy of Turner's book, E1171 (2), is dated 11 December 1645. It is quoted in *Gangraena*, part I, p. 36; p. 53 (first sequence), and part III, p. 321. For Turner's early career see R. J. Acheson, 'The Development of Religious Separatism in the Diocese of Canterbury 1590–1640', Ph.D. thesis, University of Kent (1983) pp. 62–6, 142–3, 151–6; for his activities in the 1640s see, e.g, J. S. Cockburn (ed.), *Calendar of Assize Records. Kent Indictments Charles I* (1995), pp. 439, 518.

[17] *Gangraena*, part III, p. 98. *The Vindication* was published in 1645; it is not in Thomason. Cockburn (ed.), *Kent Indictments*, pp. 420, 438, 486–7 for Cornwall's activities in the 1640s.

[18] *Gangraena*, part III, p. 98.

[19] This paragraph is based on my chapter 'Approaches to Presbyterian Print Culture: Thomas Edwards' *Gangraena* as Source and Text', in E. Sauer and J. Andersen (eds.), *Books and Readers in Early Modern England* (Philadelphia, 2001), pp. 97–116, esp. pp. 108–10.

[20] *Gangraena*, part I, p. 178.

[21] John Goodwin, *Cretensis or A Briefe Answer to an Ulcerous Treatise . . . intituled Gangaena* (1646) is the crucial example; a similarly broad response is found in [Marchamont Nedham], *Independencie no Schisme, or An Answer to a Scandalous Book* (1646) and John Lanseter, *Lanseter's Lance for Edwardses Gangrene* (1646).

constructed – through affectionate mutual citation by Edwards and allies such as Prynne, Bastwick, John Vicars and Josiah Ricraft.[22] Edwards' enterprise might thus be used as evidence to support Elizabeth Eisenstein's classic formulation of the triumphalist impact of print working to forge impersonal communities linked through ideology rather than personal connections, with authors addressing 'an invisible public from afar'. It might also be linked to David Zaret's recent account of how the printing of opposing petitions encouraged new forms of political mobilisation and judicious participation during the English revolution, as a broad 'public' were presented with conflicting proposals in printed petitions and invited to adhere to one side or the other.[23]

Nonetheless, the account given so far is much too straightforward. For if Edwards' *Gangraena* provides ample evidence for the importance of print in the religious conflicts of the 1640s, it offers little support for arguments that printed communication was in the process of replacing oral or written forms of discussion and debate, or for views that would distinguish print sharply from speech or the written word. Edwards did not take print for granted – *Gangraena*'s many passages of self-conscious prose about the making of books reveal the novelty and provisional nature of the medium. Edwards connected the protracted process of moving from text to print to the difficulties of controlling the never-ending stream of information about sectarian misdeeds: 'There is one Master Feake, an Independent named in page 81 of this Book, of whom because when I writ that sheet I had not my full profe of particulars as I desired, I passed him over lightly till another time, but having since received full and particular information of him, I think it good to pay my debt of promise sooner then I made account of.'[24] In explaining why some passages earlier in part III might be construed as 'speaking evil' of the recently dead Independent Jeremiah Burroughs, Edwards stressed to readers, 'they were both written and printed off long before Master Burroughs sicknesses and death . . . no understanding man will once imagine a Booke of above Forty sheets could be made, written out, and printed in a month'. Indeed, the third part of *Gangraena* had been in the

---

[22] Examples include John Bastwick, *The Utter Routing of the Whole Army of all the Independents and Sectaries* (1646); John Vicars, *The Schismatick Sifted, or the Picture of Independent Freshly and Fairly Washt-over Again* (1646); Josiah Ricraft, *A Nosegay of Rank-smelling Flowers* (1646); and William Prynne, *The Sword of Christian Magistracie Supported* (1647).

[23] E. L. Eisenstein, *The Printing Revolution in Early Modern Europe* (Cambridge, 1983), pp. 95–6; D. Zaret, *The Origins of Democratic Culture: Printing, Petitions and the Public Sphere in Early Modern England* (Princeton, 2000). This is not to accept Zaret's focus on petitioning as the only genre of print that functioned in this fashion, or his sharp distinction between print and manuscript.

[24] *Gangraena*, part III, p. 147.

press for three months as the bookseller and printer could testify.[25] Edwards' reflexiveness, his painful awareness of the complex processes whereby investigation and writing were turned into printed books, has something in common with recent post-modern self-consciousness about texts and readers. Edwards lacked a straightforward modernist confidence in the integrity and impact of printed communication.

Furthermore, *Gangraena* vividly illustrates an environment in which print remained an intimate and personal medium, closely connected to other, more obviously direct forms of communication. Edwards' contacts within the Stationers' Company offered privileged access to partisan book production. Edwards thus saw a pre-publication manuscript of a reply to *Gangraena* by the sectary Thomas Webb: this 'by a providence came to my hand without ever seeking it, or indeed imagining that ever Web (such an Heretick and Blasphemer) durst have appeared in print, or been taken notice of to be in London'. With this manuscript Edwards was able to conduct a detailed analysis of the influence of the radical licensor John Bachelor:

I perused this Answer after it was licensed with Master Bachilers hand, and compared the hand of 'Imprimatur, John Bachiler,' with the hand where other words were put in, and found it the same hand, and writ out with my hand, severall amendments made by John Bachiler, which I have by mee in writing, and then subscribed my hand under them, with the day of the moneth when I extracted them out of the originall Copie; and one being with mee, who was a witnesse of all this, I also intreated his hand to attest it, which hee willingly did; all which I can produce to satisfie any man who desires it.[26]

Edwards' account of his dealings with Webb's manuscript (soon to be a printed book) piles on detail in his drive to make his material credible to readers. His own manuscript record is vouched for by the signature of a first hand witness. The Webb incident is typical of the methods Edwards used in *Gangraena* to explain and validate the sources for his 'catalogue'. Print was by no means Edwards' only source of information; *Gangraena* included an enormous range of oral and manuscript material, as well as extracts from other books, presented characteristically in complex interrelationships. In an elaborate account of his methods at the start of part I, Edwards stressed he had cast his net widely in searching out sectarian enormities. For 'grounds of proof' of the 'opinions and errors' condemned he had sought to present: 'their own words and phrases syllabically . . . as themselves have expressed them in books, manuscripts, Sermons, conferences, which either are extant

[25] *Gangraena*, part III, p. 290.   [26] *Gangraena*, part II, pp. 137–9.

of their own setting forth, or set forth by other learned godly men in print, or as I have received them from credible sufficient witnesses'.[27]

Gangraena is full of talk – descriptions of casual debates in London bookshops and streets, arguments in Westminster Hall or the Guildhall, preaching, disputations, testimony before Justices and Committees. Some material had begun as oral testimony to 'the Parliament, Committees of Parliament, Assembly of Divines, and others in authority', but had then been transmitted in manuscript to Edwards: 'of which errours I have had either perfect copies given me from Ministers both of the Assembly and City, or relations from their mouths who have known particularly the story and truth of them, which copies I keep by me to produce if need be, and out of which amongst many other papers and books, I made up this Catalogue.' Talk generated manuscripts which in turn were given renewed oral confirmation. Other material was based on direct observation where 'I my self, and other persons of good note and quality have at the same time together been ear witnesses and eye witnesses upon the places'. For such sources – the 'relations' of 'godly Ministers, and understanding conscientious Christians' – circumstantial evidence had to suffice for legitimation. Edwards appealed to the 'many circumstances of names, places, conditions, time, and confident asseverations of the certainty of them, the relations coming to me by providence, and occasionally spoken of in the hearing of others as well as my self . . . and so delivered as there can be no reason in the world to thinke they should be false, but much every way to beleeve them true'.[28]

In both his original accounts, and still more when forced to defend his stories against critics, Edwards validated his material through juxtaposing different forms of evidence – spoken, written, and printed. There is no clear hierarchy of authorisation – printed evidence is not necessarily preferred to oral or manuscript testimony; the truth is told in *Gangraena* through processes of complex mutual reinforcement. The willingness of informants to back up conversation through written testimony or going into print, or the vouching for a manuscript or printed account through a direct oral encounter are mobilised to support crucial stories. One elaborate example reveals how oral communication was confirmed by writing and further oral approval. In part II Edwards explained how he had received startling information included at the last minute in part I: 'On the 9. Day of this present February, I was informed for certain that one Cosens of Rochester in Kent said, that Jesus Christ was a Bastard, and that if he were upon

---

[27] *Gangraena*, part I, pp. 4–5. [28] *Gangraena*, part I, pp. 4–6.

the earth again, he would be ashamed of many things he then did.' When
this accusation was questioned by John Goodwin, Edwards explained it
had come from a godly Rochester preacher whom he had encountered
'accidentally' when 'going in London upon my occasions'. 'I writ it from
this Ministers mouth that I might neither forget nor mistake it, and read it
to him after I had done, and upon reading, he approved it as his sense, and
that which he had related'. Edwards did not consistently privilege print,
talk or writing. The probity of his informants had as much weight as the
media through which their testimony came to him. Cosens' denouncer
was 'a reverend godly Minister well known, living also upon the place, who
could upon no reason be judged to do it out of partiality or for sinister
ends'.[29]

In *Gangraena* print is praised for its openness, for accepting a publicity which, if from orthodox sources, implied veracity.[30] On the other
hand, manuscript evidence suggested the certainty or commitment of legal depositions – talk fixed in an authoritative written record. Sometimes
oral communication had a direct authenticity lacking in written material.
Nonetheless Edwards seems to have presented written (manuscript and
printed) evidence in preference to his own direct knowledge. He was an
old acquaintance, for example, of the recently dead exiled minister John
Archer, whose unorthodox views on God as the author of sin had been
well known to London Puritans since the 1630s. But Archer's errors were
included in *Gangraena* as they appeared in his posthumous printed work
Comfort for Beleevers – or more precisely as they had been highlighted
and condemned in a declaration by the Assembly of Divines, presented in
manuscript to the parliament and then printed by Edwards' own bookseller,
Ralph Smith.[31]

'Hearsay' – uncorroborated talk – was clearly dubious evidence, so
Edwards took pains to 'acquaint the Reader with the course and way I
have taken to come to the truth of things, and not to go upon hearsay'. He
would interrogate his informants, enquiring

[29] *Gangraena,* part I, p. 180 for the original story; part II, pp. 127, 114 for the validation. The London
Presbyterian clergy had greater access to the 'mysteries' of the Stationers' Company than is implied
by A. Johns, *The Nature of the Book: Print and Knowledge in the Making* (Chicago, 1998).
[30] Conversely print was also linked to the shameless propagandising of the sectaries.
[31] The Bishop of London had questioned Archer in 1630 for catechising that God was the author
of sin 'in some respects'. Edwards succeeded Archer in a living in Hertford, by which time the
latter was in exile in Holland; correspondence between the two men was included in *Antapologia*:
Guildhall Library, London; GL MS 9531/15, fos. 22r, 23v–24r; *Gangraena,* part I, p. 20; *Comfort for
Beleevers about their Sinnes and Troubles* (1645); *A Short Declaration of the Assembly of Divines by way
of Detestation of this Abominable and Blasphemous Opinion* (1645).

whether they were ear witnesses or no; if not ear witnesses, who they had the reports from, and how they came to know them, and where, and by whom, and upon what occasion these points were delivered? if they said they were ear and eye witnesses, yet if there was but one single witnesse, I have used to question, who else was present? and to enquire after circumstances and occasions, and accordingly have gone to other persons named, from one to another, to finde out the bottome and truth both of opinions held, and practises used.[32]

Although talk was a source of useful information, writing was obviously essential to the systematic reproduction and dissemination of material as the Cosens example showed. Edwards was thus a careful record keeper:

that I might be the more faithful relator of the opinions and wayes of the sectaries of this time, and know when and where to put more or lesse waight of credit upon informations and relations, I have a long time used to write down daily the same day, yea the same hour (when I could get opportunity of privacie) the occurrences both of opinions and practises that concern our sectaries, and that in such a manner and way, that looking upon my papers a year after I can judge of what authority the relations are. . . .

This methodology was still praised within the circle of the radical reformer Samuel Hartlib a decade later when an associate recommended to Hartlib: 'Out of Mr Edwards *Gangraena* much may be applied to Intelligence and Communication'.[33]

Two other important categories of manuscript source dominate *Gangraena*, besides Edwards' own written records: the formal records of legal and administrative institutions, and the complex genre of letters. The blasphemies of Robert Cosens at Rochester, originally communicated in conversation in a London street, were further proved through orders of parliamentary committees and depositions taken before JPs and 'set down . . . to a tittle' in print. Similar remarks by 'one Coleburne of Watford . . . a great Anabaptist and Sectarie . . . that our saviour Christ was a bastard, and the first time that he taught was in a tub upon the sea' were based on Kings Bench records.[34] In the methodological preface already quoted Edwards insisted that the willingness of letter-writers to allow their private manuscript communications into a public realm of print was a guarantee of their truthfulness:

---

[32] *Gangraena*, part I, pp. 6–7.
[33] *Gangraena*, part I, p. 7; Sheffield University Library, Hartlib Manuscripts, 29/5/51b, Ephemerides 1655, part IV. The recommendation came from a Mr Tong.
[34] *Gangraena*, part II, pp. 115–20, 116.

Some errors, were proved and made manifest in the narration of the stories and Letters . . . wherein the naming of some persons, places, occasions of writing, the persons writ unto, their writing in a publike way, and not a private manner; the willingness to have them published, with many other concurrent circumstances, do declare they are not feigned nor counterfeited, but reall and certain.[35]

These two straightforward contrasts between public and private, print and manuscript, break down on further examination of the role of letters in *Gangraena*, and in early modern culture generally. Letters had complex and slippery generic associations lying between the public and the private, the factual and the fictional.[36] They had connotations of intimacy and friendship, so that the very common genre of the printed letter has been seen as a way of echoing the directness of oral or manuscript communication in the more abstract and novel medium of print: 802 anonymous items in Wing's Short Title Catalogue of works published from 1641–1700, are described as 'Letters to', and there are many hundreds more printed letters by named authors. On the other hand many manuscript letters had a public role: the letters of Erasmus, Samuel Rutherford, John Cotton and George Fox, first written to individuals, are well-known examples of correspondence collected and circulated for pastoral or polemical purposes.[37]

The letters printed in *Gangraena* thus recollected material familiar to many readers. The variety of contexts for these letters – the contrasts in how Edwards obtained them, and in the reactions to them, provide excellent illustrations of the complex, often circular ways in which different forms of encounter and communication interacted within religious polemic. In part I, Edwards printed some fifteen letters, mostly from Robert Harmar, a Colchester minister who had contacted Edwards after reading his earlier attack on 'Independency', *Antapologia* (London, 1644). Here, Edwards' fame had spread through print, creating a relationship conducted through writing, which was in turn reproduced in print. Another letter 'written to me by a Person Religious, and cordially affected to the Parliament', was identified in part II as from a long-standing friend and neighbour of Edwards,

[35] *Gangraena*, part I, p. 6. In fact the authors of letters printed in part I of *Gangraena* were only given in part II so that John Goodwin was able to denounce them as 'Apocryphall' and to allege that Edwards 'feareth lest the contents of the letters being evicted of forgery and untruth', the writers would be dishonoured: Goodwin, *Cretensis*, pp. 7–8.

[36] A. Patterson, *Censorship and Interpretation: The Conditions of Writing and Reading in early Modern England* (Madison, WI, 1984), pp. 204–19; Johns, *Nature of the Book*, p. 459.

[37] D. F. McKenzie, 'Speech-Manuscript-Print', in D. Oliphant and R. Bradford (eds.), *New Directions in Textual Studies* (Austin, TX, 1990), p. 103; C. Guillen, 'Notes Towards the Study of the Renaissance Letter', in B. K. Lewalski (ed.), *Renaissance Genres. Essays on Theory, History and Interpretation* (Cambridge, MA and London, 1986), pp. 70–101.

Josiah Ricraft.[38] This extended denunciation of William Kiffin and Thomas Webb was likely written at Edwards' request expressly for publication. Here a pre-existing personal relationship prompted the production of script for printing.

In his first part, Edwards appealed to readers for further information and consequently more letters were included in the later volumes of *Gangraena*.[39] About a third of these letters had been sent to Edwards directly, some again from people who knew him only as an author of a printed attack on sectarianism: 'A Copie of a Letter lately written to me from a godly Minister in the West of England', began, 'Whom (though unknown to me by sight) I love and honor for your love to truth, and for your zeale against the spreading infectious Errours of these times.' Others came from personal acquaintances such as the Yarmouth preacher John Brinsley, whom Edwards knew through his bookseller Ralph Smith, or zealous London Presbyterians such as Ricraft and Henry Roborough, a veteran harrier of sectarianism in the city.[40] Half of the letters were passed on to Edwards by their original recipients; again these men knew through personal acquaintance, or through reading Edwards' books, that their material would interest him. Many of these men were Londoners or London-based: nine ministers, including three members of the Westminster Assembly, six MPs or Peers and six citizens. Finally Edwards printed fourteen letters intercepted from sectaries, such as the four letters concerning the activities of Thomas Collier, the baptist evangelist in Somerset.[41]

The letters put into print by Edwards might be prompted by conversation. The first two letters in part I were an account of a conference with the general baptist Henry Denne written to Edwards by William Strong, and a letter from Richard Baxter to Strong on 'anabaptism' passed on to Edwards. In part II, Edwards outlined his discussions with Strong 'who after he had told me by word of mouth the contents of this Letter, promised to send it me in a Letter, and I acquainted him then what use it was for, and he said he would justifie what he writ, and named others in whose presence Master Denne maintained these points.'[42] Other letters reported

---

[38] The letters in part I are concentrated in pp. 49–70 (second sequence). Names of writers were not given there but Edwards identified them in part II, pp. 53–4.

[39] The texts of twenty-four letters are included throughout *Gangraena*, part II, of sixty-two in part III, while it is clear that in other sections letters have been paraphrased within passages of Edwards' own prose. Letters that are just mentioned in passing or in margins, where no text is given, have not been counted.

[40] *Gangraena*, part II, pp. 161, 170, 166–8.

[41] *Gangraena*, part III, pp. 51–4; it is not clear how Edwards obtained this material.

[42] *Gangraena*, part I, pp. 49–50; part II, p. 54.

on conversations, including conversations about his own books, as when a 'Reverend and Learned Minister in the Northerne parts' explained to 'a worthy friend' in London:

An eminent Parliament man of our Country came downe lately, with whom I had some conference about Master Edwards, and about the Schismes and Blasphemies that are broached and connived at amongst you; He said he thought that Master Edwards was a very wicked man, and did as much as was in him to embroyle the Kingdome in a new Warre.[43]

Finally, printed letters might inaugurate direct and troubled personal relationships, particularly between Edwards and the subjects of *Gangraena*. As he explained in the Preface to part III: 'some who having beene mentioned in Letters written up to friends, and printed by me, have come to my house, denying peremptorily those things spoken of them in the Letters, desiring to know who writ them that they might have reparations'. This passage referred to John Mascall, a Dover Independent, but John Lanseter also visited Edwards to complain about the account given of his preaching in a letter from a group of Suffolk ministers.[44]

The impact of his book, according to Edwards, was evident in both manuscript testimony and approving talk. He exulted that *Gangraena* was 'doing much good, as I can prove by plentifull testimonies of letters written from many parts, as also by speeches expressed of it', adding in the margin: 'I received a Letter last week out of the Countrey subscribed with 20 hands of godly Ministers testifying to my Work, and earnestly intreating my constant pursuance . . . A Letter from a godly Minister out of Warwickshire writes thus, M Ed. book does much good here'.[45] Edwards' judgement was, of course, widely challenged by his subjects and other radical critics. As *Gangraena*'s narratives were based on books, writings, and talk often promiscuously intermingled so his critics mobilised conversations, manuscripts and printed books against him. Religious rivalries spawned a complex web of polemical communication strategies. John Goodwin's *Cretensis* mounted a sustained defence of Robert Cosens, the Rochester blasphemer, using a range of manuscript material and direct testimony much as Edwards himself had done. The county committee papers, according to Goodwin, did not record Cosens' calling Christ a bastard: 'as appeares by the said Examination under the hand of the Clerk of the said Committee which I saw and read'. Cosens himself contradicted Edwards'

---

[43] See, e.g., *Gangraena*, part III, p. 65.
[44] *Gangraena*, part III, sig. *4r–v is quoted. For examples of direct encounters see Hughes, 'Approaches to Presbyterian Print Culture', p. 107.
[45] *Gangraena*, part II, p. 135.

accusation that he had troubled orthodox ministers: 'though he confes-
seth that he went to Mr Clare upon the preaching of a Sermon, and told
him that he had not delivered the Truth, yet that he any wayes threatned
Mr Clare, he absolutely denieth'. 'This Counter-Information I had from
the mouth of the said Cosens himselfe and have the particulars under his
hand.' The methods, if not the conclusions, are shared with Edwards.[46] In
other echoes of Edwards, Goodwin also solicited a written denial by the
Stepney Independent Jeremiah Burroughs of a story in *Gangraena* that he
was anxious about the spread of heresy in his neighbourhood, and printed
extracts from the letters of John Ellis, a Colchester Independent preacher
denounced by Edwards' regular correspondent Robert Harmar. Goodwin
drew also on printed books, quoting the Presbyterian John Ball in support
of his own orthodoxy on justification.[47]

Goodwin's attempt to turn the tables on Edwards with the dark threat, 'I
my self have a Manuscript by me', helps us identify more precisely the role
of print in religious competition in the 1640s. For Goodwin, as for Edwards,
print was a means by which opponents could be publicly discredited – often
through the dissemination of manuscript or oral evidence acquired through
local, personal connections. Goodwin's 'manuscript' concerned Edwards'
apparently irregular attempts to obtain a pastoral living. It 'came to my
hands above a yeare since' and 'discourseth his jugling and indirect walking
between the two Townes of Godalmin in Surrey, and Dunmow in Essex.
The writing will be attested by good hands, and if there be no remedy, will
be content to submit it selfe to the Presse.'[48] That this written evidence
spoke – 'discourseth' – of Edwards' misdeeds and that it might somehow
passively 'submit itself' to print is again suggestive of the intermingling of
speech, manuscript and print.

In the London of the 1640s religious and political rivals often combined
polemical publication with direct confrontation. Indeed printed books,
or the threat of books – might themselves be the weapons for personal
attack as well as more general campaigning. The threat to print material
discreditable to an opponent is revealed again in an exchange with the
Independent activist John Price (a member of Goodwin's congregation)
reported by the Presbyterian stationer and author John Bellamy (an associate
of Edwards). During arguments over the Presbyterian City Remonstrance
in May 1646, Bellamy, its probable author, offered to give Price, a leading
opponent of its call for Presbyterian church government and a speedy
peace with the royalists, 'all the faire quarter that possibly I could in this

---

[46] Goodwin, *Cretensis*, pp. 39–40.   [47] *Ibid.*, pp. 42–4, 20–1 respectively.   [48] *Ibid.*, p. 34.

our Conflict'. Bellamy showed Price 'in Writing this my Justification of the City Remonstrance and its Vindication, before ever I tendered it to be licensed, or Printed, and desired you to peruse it'. Bellamy offered to remove any 'matters of fact' Price objected to, but Price rejected his overtures. In less conciliatory mode Price in turn informed Bellamy 'there is a Booke of the History of my [Bellamy's] Life already drawn up and fitted for the Presse, wherein are many heavie charges laid against me'. In the company of mutual acquaintances, including the minister Samuel Clarke and the bookseller Henry Overton, Bellamy nonetheless read extracts from his own Epistle, in 'which I told you, that in my apprehension, they were things which most nearly concerned your Person'.[49]

The intimate conflicts of Bellamy and Price, Edwards and Goodwin, combining bitter personal attacks with profound differences of religious and political principle, were made known to contemporaries, as they are known to us, through the medium of print. Specific, personal attacks were transmitted to Eisenstein's 'invisible public' as part of general campaigns to determine the nature of the settlement that would follow parliament's victory in the first Civil War. Print, as Eisenstein argued, did indeed serve as a generalising and abstracting force. But it also *and at the same time* remained embedded in relationships founded on personal ties and neighbourhood links, with conversations and manuscript records. Indeed arguments over the veracity and propriety of printed books were a prominent element in religious and political conflicts on the streets of London. There is no need to make some artificial, exclusive choice between printed, written and spoken forms of communication.

In the last analysis, for the religious and political rivals of the 1640s, print does seem to have overtaken preaching, oral debate or manuscript circulation as a means of spreading authoritative information and appealing for support. As we have seen, it was not necessarily the case that print was more authoritative than oral or written forms of communication, but it was clearly a more efficient means of disseminating positions to a broad and engaged reading public at a time of national crisis. Partisan publication worked to define allegiance – Presbyterian or sectarian – amongst people unacquainted with the leading combatants. The *de facto* absence of censorship meant that objectionable views were spread widely through print and called out for public refutation. The issues at stake for competing

---

[49] John Bellamie, *A Justification of the City Remonstrance and its Vindication* (1646), pp. 47–8, 32. Clarke and Overton were brothers-in-law, although they disagreed fundamentally on city religion and politics.

factions on the parliamentary side by the mid-1640s drew Presbyterians and their opponents to print in order to mobilise support in London and in provincial England for particular visions of the parliamentary cause. Parliament was on the verge of gaining the power to achieve its ends, but was fatefully divided within itself over what these ends should be – in this unprecedented situation, orthodox and sectary, Presbyterian and Independent resorted rapidly and frequently to print. Edwards, Goodwin, Vines, Bellamy and Price were competing for the highest possible stakes, for the reformation of the Church according to God's word and the settlement of the state. Print was essential to this competition.

For Edwards, printed books were a main, but not the only vehicle for mobilisation – petitioning was at least as important (although it was assumed petitions would become printed texts as well as signed, attested manuscripts and practical activities):

it were good to set forth some Books against the errours of our times, with joynt consent in the name of all the Ministers, to send out some grave Admonition to the people, in the name of the City-Ministers subscribed by all, to warn the people, in the name of God to beware of the errours of these times, and to withdraw from sectaries, and to return again into the bosome of the Church; and lastly, for the Ministers to make a Remonstrance of all the Errours, Heresies, Blasphemies, Schisms, Insolencies, Tumults, that have been in England these last five yeers, out of all the Printed Books, publike Sermons, preachings in private Houses, discourses of the sectaries; and with a Petition humbly to present it to both Houses, with hands subscribed of all the Orthodox godly Ministers in this Kingdom.

Error too was spread by public and private preaching as well as books, but in urging fellow defenders of Presbyterian orthodoxy into action, Edwards clearly gave priority to the press: 'Lets therefore fill all Presses, cause all Pulpits to ring, and so possesse Parliament, City and whole Kingdom against the sects, and of the evil of schism, and a Toleration, that we may no more hear of a Toleration, nor of separated Churches.'[50]

It has usually been assumed that the enemies of Presbyterianism – the radical separatists, the Levellers and parliament's politicised army – were the most committed to spreading their views in print amongst a wide readership, encouraged to think for themselves.[51] There may be two, connected,

---

[50] *Gangraena*, part 1, pp. 164–6.
[51] Amongst a vast literature, W. Haller, *Liberty and Reformation in the Puritan Revolution* (New York, 1955) and C. Hill, *The World Turned Upside Down* (Harmondsworth, 1972) are representative. For an extended version of the argument presented here see my '"Popular" Presbyterianism in the 1640s and 1650s: The Cases of Thomas Edwards and Thomas Hall', in N. Tyacke (ed.), *England's Long Reformation 1500–1800* (1998).

misunderstandings here – both about the nature of radicalism and the uses of print.[52] The traditional narrative of parliamentarian factionalism in the 1640s links radicalism with anti-authoritarianism and with emancipation through print. Yet Presbyterians too sought a radical transformation, albeit an authoritarian one – a godly reformation of Church and people through tightly ordered ecclesiastical government. To achieve these ends Presbyterians, particularly in Edwards' London, mobilised significant sections of the city's people to push reluctant parliamentarians into a more thoroughgoing Presbyterian settlement.[53] Books like *Gangraena* were central to this rousing public campaign; print was a crucial means by which Presbyterian zeal was rallied against sectarian excess.

Edwards' hostility to Independent use of the press, and his acute sensitivity to the dangers of radical books, meant that his preference was for the suppression of unlicensed printing, and the burning of 'wicked books' (whether licensed or not): 'The wicked books, printed of late years, (some whereof licensed, dispersed, cryed up) should be openly burnt by the hand of the hangman.' A convenient list of such books was given.[54] But wicked books continued to spread, and so orthodox books like *Gangraena* were needed to convert people from error and schism. Edwards thus hoped for a wide readership: he had written for all ranks and opinions, 'for all sorts of men, Magistrates, Ministers, people, both those that stand, and those that are fallen, yea the very sectaries themselves'.[55] He invoked also an active, judicious readership, qualified to decide between his defence of orthodoxy, and the wicked books written against him: 'every indifferent Reader' was to weigh Edwards' evidence, using it to 'ballance, yea to weigh down *Cretensis*'.[56] Edwards was in effect encouraging the reading of sectarian print as well as of orthodox books – even though he confidently expected a judicious reader to be convinced by his own books. Hence his detailed commentaries guiding readers through the wicked books of Goodwin, Peter and Lilburne.

Edwards' worst fear was that his books would not be read. He was bitterly conscious of the danger that his defence of the truth would be marginalised or suppressed. *Gangraena* was a vital, endangered book:

---

[52] For cautions about the nature of 1640s radicalism, see J. C. Davis, 'Religion and the Struggle for Freedom in the English Revolution', *HJ*, 35 (1992), 507–30; for pioneering discussion of Presbyterian use of print in the 1640s see S. Achinstein, *Milton and the Revolutionary Reader* (Princeton, 1994).

[53] For London Presbyterianism see K. Lindley, *Popular Politics and Religion in Civil War London* (Aldershot, 1997); E. Vernon, 'The Sion College Conclave and London Presbyterianism during the English Revolution', Ph.D. thesis, University of Cambridge (1999).

[54] *Gangraena*, part I, p. 171.   [55] *Gangraena*, part I, sig. 4r.   [56] *Gangraena*, part II, p. 48.

I have been told also from good hands, that my books are so hated among the Sectaries in the Army, that no Commanders nor Officers dare be knowne to have them, or to read them: and some Presbyterians (whose names I shall conceale) getting the books, have been forced to read them by stealth in the night in their beds, when they have been sure none should carry tales of them. The Presbyterians and Orthodox have been glad to deale with my books in the Army, as the Protestants are glad to doe with Bibles, Mr Perkins Works etc in Countries, as Spain, where the Inquisition is in force.[57]

To modern liberal sensibilities, *Gangraena* is a call for persecution. We would now be most likely to associate the authoritarian self-righteous Presbyterian Edwards with the Spanish Inquisition, yet he located himself amongst its victims. For Edwards, the capacity – the freedom – to attack his opponents in print was crucial to the defence of religious truth against error and schism. Refuting sectarianism in print was only possible because of networks of letter writers and other manuscript circulation, and because of innumerable oral conversations, sermons and debates. Yet print – in a period of fundamental religious and political cleavage – was the ultimate weapon wielded on all sides. As with other chapters in this volume, an exploration of *Gangraena* Edwards' attitudes to print suggests that simple contrasts between radical and orthodox Protestant, or Protestant and Catholic do not survive analysis of the polemical constructions that originally inspired them.

[57] *Gangraena*, part III, p. 106.

14
Epilogue
Margaret Aston

'The uses of script and print' is a timely topic for a world in which the handwritten letter seems as rare as a carrier pigeon, and printing has become part of the ordinary equipment of a desk. Reflecting, in the usual way, our contemporary concerns back into the angle of our vision of the past, such changes in the means of communication have become of pressing interest, and as the papers in this collection show, they can shed new light on old questions. Revisionism is not a word that appears in these pages, but at a number of points existing assumptions are subjected to critical scrutiny. The complex interrelationships of script and print, the communications of ear and page, suggest not so much a Gutenberg watershed as a lasting permeability affecting different media and modes of discourse throughout the period. 'Interaction' rather than 'impact' is the word that perhaps best describes the dynamism of texts, their makers, owners, readers, users and hearers through the centuries here under discussion, in which printing opened up new possibilities of so many kinds.

If print like writing is the continuation of speech by other means, there is much to be learned here about the interweaving of words on the page with words in the air. As Ann Hughes puts it, 'talk generated manuscripts which in turn were given renewed oral confirmation'[1] – which in turn might result in publication. Publication could mean many different things, and to have reached the page in whatever form by no means insulated a discourse from future oral intervention. Getting a work into circulation was different in the day of Julian of Norwich from what it was in the days of William Perkins or Thomas Edwards, but it still remained at least in part the case that, in Felicity Riddy's words, '"publication" is short for public conversation'.[2] Sermons in the sixteenth century, like *A Revelation of Love* in the fourteenth or *Gangraena* in the seventeenth, 'came out of the sea of talk' and were 'cast back into it'.[3] But to what extent did publication

---

[1] Above p. 263.   [2] Above p. 43.   [3] *Eadem*, above p. 48..

become different with print and was it already in this period associated with a feeling that authors and books could by this means reach out to the future for some kind of immortality? Are there any signs of conscious inhibition about moving from script to print?

Pages and people were caught up in a process of continuous interplay, only parts of which may leave still perceptible marks. Do even the seemingly most 'pragmatic' of scripts, a town's administrative records, reflect oral communications and personal viewpoints? We may need decipherment of a special kind to extract, as Andrew Butcher suggests we can, understanding of an urban 'speech community' from the records of a medieval town clerk. In the case of particularly controversial sermons we may gather some idea of the relationship of oral fireworks and the passage of texts onto pages. William Taylor's inflammatory preaching against clerical possessions at Paul's Cross in 1406, like Dean Richard Thompson's provocative sermon in Bristol Cathedral in the 1680s, claiming that there had been no Popish Plot, only a Presbyterian one, resulted in notable furores that in both cases fed public interest with widespread textual transmission in records of their respective addresses.[4] Such occasions are suggestive of the ways in which talk and gossip nurtured and were themselves nourished by script and print in ways comparable in kind if not in scale to modern newsprint. It may well be, as Jonathan Barry suggests, that the circumstances of their reception as well as the character of their authors tended always to play a significant role in determining which sermons were multiplied for wide reading in script or print.

Countless sermons, besides those which still exist in huge numbers in manuscript as well as print, were lost with the words in the air, and while the numbers that survive in manuscript are only a small proportion of those that once existed, so the numbers that were printed when that became a possibility, are only a fraction of those committed to paper. And of course all sermons on the page were related in a wide variety of ways to the sermon heard and delivered. The preacher who jotted down some outline or summary of his address might have left it at that. Or, working up later a full version of his delivered sermon, he might elaborate and extend, even taking account of the reactions of his congregation. Repeating, taking to heart and memorising the recollected essentials of heard sermons were

---

[4] A. Hudson (ed.), *Two Wycliffe Texts: The Sermon of William Taylor 1406; The Testimony of William Thorpe 1407*, EETS, OS 301 (Oxford, 1993), pp. xiii–xvii; above p. 202.

aspects of domestic religion long before the Reformation.[5] Sermon texts in manuscript, as well as print, could serve this kind of pious recapitulation, and oral recovery and repetition were capable of feeding back into the textual record, as well as extending and extrapolating from the heard words.

Perhaps sermons were a special case when it came to the relationship of the spoken and recorded word. In the world of sixteenth-century reformers, the great emphasis on St Paul's *fides ex auditu* (Romans 10:17), acted as a powerful lever to keep printed divinity in constant communion with the inspiration of the spoken word. It became an elementary commonplace among believers that this was the means by which faith was 'wrought'. 'By what meanes doth God begin or beget Faith in his Children? 'Ordinarily, by hearing the Word preached'; that was the unambiguous answer in William Crashaw's *Meate for Men* in 1629.[6] Nothing must trammel the pure vitality of the gospel in the mouth, converting, consoling and congregating believers through the all-powerful word in the ear. Prophesying, as currently understood and practised, was a proof of this commitment in action. And Alexandra Walsham shows us here how it was the voices of the page that – substituting for that the irreplaceable advent of faith by direct speech – kept those debarred from pulpits at work preaching, as a second best alternative, through the medium of the pen. It might have seemed almost a contradiction in terms.[7]

Erasmus' translation of St John's Gospel as *In principio erat sermo* may have shocked some, but to others it represented a very present reality, the voice of the living word.[8] The sense that the message was only intact in speech and ear might deter transmission to the pages of unmediated print. Did the divine aura of the oral prompt hesitation about transferring the preached message into printed texts? Calvin's reluctance to put his sermons into print reflects (as Jean-François Gilmont has suggested) a sense of the

---

[5] For Anne Hudson's example of a Lollard preacher who left his text behind with his audience so that 'whoso likith mai overse it' (cited above p. 213) see A. Hudson, *Lollards and their Books* (1985), p. 9; M. Aston, *Lollards and Reformers* (1984), p. 204.

[6] William Crashaw, *Meate for Men. Or, a Principall Service of the Sacraments* (1629), sig. A4v. Crashaw's companion-piece catechism, *Milke for Babes. Or, a North-countrie Catechism*, is on Ian Green's list of 'best and steady sellers' in *Print and Protestantism in Early Modern England* (Oxford, 2000), Appendix 1 (unpaginated).

[7] Above ch. 11. Also on preaching and printing, with examples of Protestant preachers who had misgivings about going into print see A. Walsham, *Providence in Early Modern England* (Oxford, 1999), pp. 51–64.

[8] Subsequently retreating from some of the daring of his *Novum Instrumentum* of 1516 Erasmus still registered a protest on this score. '*Miror autem cur verbum, magis placuerit latinis quam sermo*', given the element of the spoken in the Greek *logos*; *In Annotationes novi testamenti praefatio* (Basel, 1518), p. 162; C. de Hamel, *The Book: A History of the Bible* (London and New York, 2001), pp. 225–6.

separation between the preacher's delivery and the printed page. The word in the mouth was one thing – and Calvin had no objection to notes being taken at his sermons. But to give them to posterity with the considered formality of edited versions was another matter, and he only produced one such volume in 1552. When in 1546 for the first time two of Calvin's sermons appeared in print (in response to such demand that it would have been 'too much trouble to write so many times') the preface was revealing. Readers were advised that the author 'was not accustomed to having his sermons printed', and 'he had not written them' nor composed them 'to be published through the world'. This small simple book contained the words delivered uniquely on each occasion, 'gathered from his mouth, as he spoke in the pulpit'.[9] How could any text replicate or replace the electric one-off charge of the preacher's voice? The bulk of sermons that has come down to us in manuscript may in part be a residue of that awareness, reflecting the combined assurance and nervousness of Protestant preachers, trying to relate the primacy of speech to alternative media of discourse.

We have learnt a lot about silent reading, but what about noisy reading? Surely more remains to be said about the sound of the page, as articulated by individual or group, declaratory or explanatory, mouthed loudly or softly, said or sung.[10] Group reading and hearing in many contexts was not inherently altered by the difference in format of script or print. The methods of publicising legal and official government information changed little when printed paper texts took the place of scribal parchment ones. Voices remained important. Proclamations, which throughout the period were a central means of publishing the law and conveying the royal will, reflect the interdependence of oral and textual communication. In the thirteenth century copies of Magna Carta were displayed in cathedral churches, and it became common practice for important texts to be posted on church doors or public places such as town or village crosses. Oral explication (including impromptu translation of Latin documents) was part of this process, and essential for the communication of legislation. At the same time the entire process was open to misunderstanding, if not abuse, given the likely gaps in understanding between readers and hearers – witness what Anthony

---

[9] *Deux sermons de M. Iean Calvin* (Geneva, 1546), 'L'imprimeur aux lecteurs', sig. A4v; J.-F. Gilmont, 'Protestant Reformations and Reading', in G. Cavallo and R. Chartier (eds.), *A History of Reading in the West*, trans. L.G. Cochrane (Cambridge, 1999), pp. 213–37, at 234–6.

[10] One might distinguish noisy reading from reading aloud, on which the literature is growing; see e.g., R. Chartier, 'Reading Matter and "Popular" Reading: From the Renaissance to the Seventeenth Century', in Cavallo and Chartier (eds.), *History of Reading*, pp. 269–83.

Musson has to say about limitations to 'the accessibility of statutes in a real sense'.[11] Those who could participate in such information services (or initiate their own publicity) increased in number as literacy extended through these centuries. They might indeed choose silent admonitory pages as a means of advertising causes with the advantage of anonymity. The Lollards' posting and scattering of bills in 1395, 1414 and 1431 was a kind of voiceless proclaiming of dangerously inflammatory appeals.

Print certainly affected the impact of such sharing of the page. If by the seventeenth century it came to seem in some quarters that greater knowledge of letters brought more dissidence and disobedience, which printing 'divulged' against the government,[12] the disruptive reverberations of the printed page remained constrained in practice by the limitations of individual reading skills. Printed service books and Bibles placed in churches provoked those of conservative temperament. The churchwarden (aptly named Vigorouse) who rudely ejected from his church of Langham in Essex, two girls whom he found on Ascension Day 1534, sitting in their pew saying matins together 'upon an English Primer', clearly felt that such behaviour marked the beginning of a fateful heretical upheaval.[13] The girls were probably only murmuring quietly in their pew. Ten years later, when the English Bible arrived for the first time officially in churches, the authorities became deeply worried about group readings of the book 'aloud and with noise'.[14] There seemed to be a freshly dangerous dimension to loud corporate reading when it conflicted with traditional orthodoxy. It has to be borne in mind, however, that those who could thus give voices to pages, whether for their own or others' benefit, could be as baffled by the appearance of the page in print as they were by the page of script. The inability to read handwriting continued through the period and those who could manage the Gothic black letter of ballads and Bibles might have had difficulties with a page in Roman typeface. The fact that as late as 1757 the 'antiquated type of an act of parliament' was for some the equivalent of Chinese characters, is a reminder of the varying degrees of

---

[11] For Elizabethan proclamations ordered to be read aloud by parish clergy see K. Thomas, 'The Meaning of Literacy in Early Modern England', in G. Baumann (ed.), *The Written Word: Literacy in Transition* (Oxford, 1986), pp. 97–131, at 106.

[12] Thomas, 'Meaning of Literacy', pp. 117–18.

[13] J. Oxley, *The Reformation in Essex to the Death of Mary* (Manchester, 1965), pp. 85–6; *L&P*, vol. VII, p. 45 (no. 145).

[14] D. S. Kastan, '"The Noyse of the New Bible": Reform and Reaction in Henrician England', in C. McEachern and D. Shuger (eds.), *Religion and Culture in Renaissance England* (Cambridge, 1997), pp. 46–68; M. Aston, 'Lap Books and Lectern Books: The Revelatory Book in the Reformation', in R. N. Swanson (ed.), *The Church and the Book*, SCH 38 (Woodbridge, forthcoming).

accessibility of printed pages, and limitations on the numbers of their mediators.[15]

The link between text and voice was transformed when it came with melody. Words that are sung (and repeatedly sung), particularly in shared unison, have their own unique way of implanting themselves in heads, and tunes can affect the meaning and reception of words. Christopher Marsh shows how much ballads have to tell us here. Although they were increasingly absorbed by contemporaries in the way that most of us do today – by reading – the musical content that made ballads vital to hearers and singers (non-readers as well as readers) in the sixteenth and seventeenth centuries, was itself a constituent element in how they were received and perceived. Marsh's demonstration of the satire and innuendo that well-known tunes could lend to ballad texts (through politically acceptable or sexually suggestive associations) is an eye (or ear)-opener that we all – textually focused as we are – ignore at our peril. Recovery of the sounds of the past may be something that requires particular skills, but to lose the oral dimension of the text may, as we learn here, lead to serious misunderstanding.

And there was another important sphere in which the alliance of tune and metrical verse informed the use and reception of print for a vast number of contemporaries. Are we yet anywhere near gauging the importance of the metrical psalms for the development of the Reformation? Those who scored reforming points in Exeter and London at the start of Elizabeth's reign by hearty psalm-singing, 'Geneva fashion', made the most of intoxicating group-voicing of word and tune. Psalm-singing, which took off initially with popular tunes and remained predominantly unison rather than part-song, was officially attached to sermons as well as morning and evening prayer. This form of worship was fully endorsed in 1645 by the Directory of Worship, which stated it to be a Christian duty 'to praise God publicly, by singing of psalms together in the congregation, and also privately in the family'.[16] Music, like learning by heart (which singing could facilitate by almost indirect means), was important for the appropriation of texts: the habitual familiarity with sets of words that become ineradicably part of an individual's memory. The half-literate Thomas Highway, deemed

---

[15] A. Fox, *Oral and Literate Culture in England 1500–1700* (Oxford, 2000), pp. 43, 44–5 (cited), 91–2, 312–13; Thomas, 'Meaning of Literacy', pp. 99–100.

[16] J. G. Nichols (ed.), *Diary of Henry Machyn*, Camden Society 42 (1848), pp. 212, 228, 247; S. E. Lehmberg, *The Reformation of Cathedrals* (Princeton, NJ, 1988), pp. 154–5; N. Temperley, *The Music of the English Parish Church* (Cambridge, 1979), vol. I, pp. 42–3, 53–83 (cited at 78); R. A. Leaver, *'Goostly Psalmes and Spirituall Songes': English and Dutch Metrical Psalmes from Coverdale to Utenhove 1535–1566* (Oxford, 1991), pp. 240–1, 267, 314–15.

so unsuitable a candidate for the position of parish clerk at Myddle in Shropshire in the reign of Charles II, could 'sing but one tune of the psalmes' – though he might have had the metrical words of several lodged in his head.[17] The process of personal incorporation of the word can take place in many ways and by people of different kinds and ages. It is likely to be promoted by the set forms and formulae of print, including Psalm books and the Book of Common Prayer, whose phraseology became part of England's inherited verbal repertoire for centuries, thanks to constant hearing and repeating. Printed formularies helped the development of a shared vocabulary of public discourse.

But clearly it would be a mistake to make opposing categories of script and the private as against print and the public. Books in print as much as books in manuscript were treasured private possessions. The Nuremberg humanist and book collector Hieronymus Münzer (1437–1508) went to the great length of making his own copy of Terence's comedies when he was a student at Leipzig in 1470.[18] James Clark shows us how, at the same time that the sponsorship of printing by the Benedictine order enabled some English monasteries to improve their conventual libraries before the Dissolution, bibliophile monks were building up in their own private book collections independently of their community's advantage.[19] Print and script crossed and conjoined public and private arenas. It was possible for a text that was inherently a deeply personal statement of faith to be given to the reading public in print, whence it could be arrogated and taken back into the sphere of private religious affirmation, and the domain of an individual's script. An example of this is the testament of William Tracy, who became famous among early English Protestants as a martyr cruelly exhumed and posthumously burned as a heretic in 1532 on account of the expressions of faith in his will. This will, regarded as an exemplary document of Protestant faith, circulated in manuscript and was then printed in 1535 with commentaries by William Tyndale and John Frith, with reprints in the 1540s. These publications in turn allowed other testators of several counties in the following decades to model the preambles of their own testaments (still in manuscript) on that of Tracy. Then, a generation later, in 1563 the inclusion of Tracy's testament in John Foxe's 'Book of Martyrs' in a sense established it as an authoritative Protestant text. The interplay between

---

[17] R. Gough, *The History of Myddle*, ed. D. Hey (Harmondsworth, 1981), p. 45.

[18] E. P. Goldschmidt, *Hieronymus Münzer und seine Bibliothek* (1938), pp. 16–17, 133–4. The *editio princeps* of Terence appeared the following year.

[19] Above chapter 4, including pp. 81–2 on monks' personal collections of printed books which they retained at the Dissolution, when conventual manuscripts were confiscated by the crown.

printed text, scattered manuscript testaments, and the end-product of the famous work of history, allowed for interludes of oral manipulation and textual reconstruction. Public print and personal script mutually reinforced each other.[20] The oral interface was not thereby excluded, though it is as invisible as inaudible.

In the seventeenth century we still have to take account of 'the power of the unprinted'.[21] Julia Crick demonstrates the actuality of this statement by looking at the transcription carried out by antiquarian scholars who, in addition to the publications for which they are famous, also copied and collected a great bulk of documentary material. Charters in particular show that this process of accumulation by transcription, serving ends that reached beyond antiquarian research, wove to and fro between script and print, gathering material of either kind and setting the results in manuscript volumes as well as printed works. This pool of scribal culture constituted a huge library of unknown dimensions within private walls that could seem publicly threatening when the censors of state had cause to think and worry about it.

By no means all writers of private thoughts and experiences wanted their 'self-textualisation' to include publication of the remote control kind effected by print.[22] Manuscript held advantages that made it a preferred option for some unstoppable pen-pushers long after the advent of printing. The handwritten page provided opportunities for circulating works among known groups, communication between friends, or for self-examination, confession, or reflection, talking to yourself and others on paper with a freedom and degree of control that kept writer in touch with reader. Publication in such cases was not a matter of finalising a text, going public in the hard form and chosen numbers of printed copy – reaching the maximum number of readers which is the criterion of modern success – but of communicating with a known readership. Shakespeare's 'sugared sonnets among his private friends' first circulated in this way, and it was through the security of such 'coterie literature', as it has been called, that other poets (Sidney, Marlowe and Donne, who printed very little of his verse) initially reached known audiences with some of their best known works.[23] It was only on his deathbed that George Herbert provided for the manuscript of 'The Temple'

---

[20] J. Craig and C. Litzenberger, 'Wills as Religious Propaganda: The Testament of William Tracy', *JEH*, 44 (1993), 415–31; John Foxe, *Actes and Monumentes* (1563), pp. 510–11, (1570); vol. II, p. 1186.
[21] Above p. 116; H. Love, *Scribal Publication in Seventeenth-Century England* (Oxford, 1993), pp. 85–9.
[22] Felicity Riddy's phrase; above p. 43 and n. 60.
[23] S. Orgel, 'Mr Who He?', *London Review of Books* 24/15 (8 August 2002), 7; Love, *Scribal Publication*, ch. 2, and for Donne's misgivings about printing pp. 4, 39–40, 51, 145–7, 170.

to be given to Nicholas Ferrar with a view to publication: the only verses he published during his lifetime were in Latin.[24] Sir William Drake (1609–69), whose copious notebooks can tell us so much about what a well-educated gentleman read and reflected on, is also very revealing of the intellectual undergrowth of script in seventeenth-century England.[25] Self-edification on paper in a diary, commonplace collections and notebook, sometimes seems obsessive. It was a phenomenon that existed in its own right, unrelated to the ambitions and perils of print. Drake was not a man for print.[26] In an earlier generation John Bruen esquire (who died in 1629), exercised such 'conscionable diligence' and industry, noting and then rewriting 'in a more legible hand' the teaching and preaching of ministers, that over thirty-five years he accumulated a huge manuscript collection. This entire holograph library was created for the benefit of his family and friends. It was to them, not the wider readership of the printed page that he left it, in the earnest hope that his heirs would 'read over, if were but once in all their life, the bookes that he hath thus written'.[27] Beside the growing numbers of those who resorted to print to control or convert the world, or in hopes of making it their oyster, there was always a stream of writers and readers whose textual output remained in manuscript.

Some communications of the page were obviously closer to talk than others. Throughout this period (as is still, just, the case today) the handwritten letter amounted to personal converse on the page. Almost by definition, such paper-talk normally belonged to a private world of mutual exchange that was far removed from the public property of the printing shop. To put pen to paper in this way (even for those in official or semi-official capacities, who docketed their in-tray with annotations of sender and date of reception), was to assume a degree of privacy that required subterfuge and official networks of spies seriously to upset. Most letter-writers no more expected a risk of being published than (the days of Thomas Cromwell aside) they feared a spy to be lurking behind the hedge or in the alehouse when they talked to their neighbours. Lord Conway might well have spluttered with outrage when in 1636 he opened a letter from George Garrard, the earl of Northumberland's chaplain. It started with a request. 'My Lord. I am much

[24] The 1623 congratulatory *Oratio* on Prince Charles' return from Spain; *STC* 13181 and 4488.
[25] K. Sharpe, *Reading Revolutions: The Politics of Reading in Early Modern England* (New Haven and London, 2000), pp. 69–75, 341–3.
[26] See Wing 2136–2138 for *Sir William Drake his Speech in Parliament* (1641) and *The Long Parliament Revived* (1661), the latter of which is by another of his name. Sharpe, *Reading Revolutions*, pp. 152–4, 253–4.
[27] William Hinde, *A Faithfull Remonstrance of the Holy Life and Happy Death of John Bruen* (1641), p. 102; Thomas, 'Meaning of Literacy', p. 122, n. 8.

beholding to you for your letters. They are of soe excellent a strayne, for stile and singular expressions, that I am much tempted to crave your pardon, for my serious purpose to print them.' Conway wrote back in no uncertain terms. 'My letters to you are privat assurances of my love and to you onely particular, not epistles generall.'[28]

'Epistles general' have an almost apostolic sound, as if there was a category of letter properly belonging to the world at large. Such appears to have been the understanding of Thomas Edwards, for whom letters, when entrusted to the public sphere of print, were *ipso facto* to be regarded as trustworthy; 'the willingness to have them published, with many other concurrent circumstances, do declare they are not feigned nor counterfeited, but reall and certain'.[29] That seems to betray a trust in both human nature and the press that few of us would subscribe to. And Edwards, who printed contemporary letters in *Gangraena*, some sent to him spontaneously, others apparently at his request, knew all too well about allegations of untruthfulness in these sources.

Did the letters of Protestants smuggled in and out of Marian prisons have something of the character of epistles general? Their transition from script to print, as described here by Thomas Freeman, is revealing of the process of combing and grooming that might be deemed necessary to make private assurances into general reading. These prisoners (John Bradford, John Careless, John Philpot and others), who managed to carry out so much writing or copying during their incarceration, sought supporters outside to see that their treatises and accounts of their examinations were disseminated among their followers. The textual exchanges acted as a mutual support system in time of persecution, in which the letter or exhortation could be thought of in terms of the early Church. But the prison writings that did so much to hold the movement together were deliberately withheld from printing while the dangers of reprisals remained. When the martyrs' letters were published in 1564[30] they were carefully edited to remove any potentially embarrassing or damaging passages that might detract from the character of their writers or diminish the apostolic analogy of their circumstance.[31] Talk

[28] A. J. Taylor, 'The Royal Visit to Oxford in 1636: A Contemporary Narrative', Oxoniensia 1 (1936), 151–8, at 152–3 (punctuation altered).

[29] Cited by Ann Hughes, above p. 266.

[30] *Certain most Godly, Fruitful, and Comfortable Letters of such True Saintes and Holy Martyrs of God* (1564), STC 5886.

[31] S. Wabuda, 'Henry Bull, Miles Coverdale, and the Making of Foxe's *Book of Martyrs*', in D. Wood (ed.), *Martyrs and Martyrologies*, SCH 30 (Oxford, 1993), pp. 245–58; T. Freeman, '"The Good Ministrye of Godlye and Vertuouse Women": The Elizabethan Martyrologists and the Female Supporters of the Marian Martyrs', *JBS*, 39 (2000), 8–33.

is slippery – things come out which one may regret, or which the recipient may disapprove of. The same goes for letters. The fact that the letters of the martyrs were both treasured and only printed after careful editing and indeed censoring out of errors and embarrassments reflects the differing effects and advantages of script and print. The written texts which still survive were themselves silent witnesses to the Marian persecution. But they had to be made ready before being sent into the reading world of printed books. Statements that could flow freely within known circles of friends in the discourse of mouth and pen seemed to be fixed with dangerous immutability once they were mechanically reproduced on the printed page. So editors sieved and authors might hesitate.

The history of the successive editions of John Foxe's *Actes and Monuments* might be taken as the paradigm of an author struggling with the fixity of print. Foxe, writing as both author and editor, was in a sense working to prove that print is not immutable. Further work brought in more material and the process was not only one of expansion, but of correction, some of which derived from contemporary sources. The printed text existed in a mart of exchange with its readers and critics, alongside the researches of its author and his helpers. It had to take account of the talk, correspondence, correction and controversy that surrounded it (not unlike Thomas Edwards' work on *Gangraena*). Continuing revision was to bring up to date – or nearer to the truth as the author saw it. This process only works as long as readers forget as well as read, publishers are prepared to republish, and owners (like churches, whose books used to wear out more quickly than those of private readers) are prepared to throw out old editions and buy new ones. Foxe succeeded triumphantly in one sense, keeping up with the towering volumes of script and print that lay behind his work through the four successive editions published in his lifetime. In another (longer term) sense he failed, leaving behind a work that was a lasting monument to the mutable text in its successive printed forms. The complexity of the 'Book of Martyrs' in its various editions proved too much for the capacity of subsequent editors and the discernment of readers.[32] This intractable, if not insoluble problem of displaying and understanding the mutating text is only beginning to be resolved today by electronic means. It is interesting that in the eighteenth century the Academy Lectures of Philip Doddridge (1702–51) circulated for about seventy years after his death in both printed

---

[32] T. Freeman, 'Texts, Lies, and Microfilm: Reading and Misreading Foxe's "Book of Martyrs"', *Sixteenth Century Journal*, 30 (1999), 23–46.

and manuscript form, so that they should remain amenable to change and not be regarded as set in stone.[33]

That brings us to the critical question of whether print *per se* had trans-formative power. Did the Reformation succeed, where medieval heretical movements had not, through the ability of the printing press to dissem-inate texts in numbers and ways not possible for scribal copyists? Or is Luther's success, as contrasted with that of Waldo, Wycliffe or Hus, to be attributed not so much to the power of movable type against pen, as to the ineffectiveness of repression and persecution? If multiplication is the heart of the matter, 'print, like manuscript' as Scott Mandelbrote reminds us, 'preserved only by multiplication', and in both cases the process entailed error.[34] But when it came to the balance of authority, the reiterations of print could weigh against respect for ancient manuscript sources, so critical for scriptural translation. It buttressed the Authorised Version, with its in-corporation of words made venerable through generations of publication, against the need for further resort '*ad fontes*'.

It is refreshing to have clearly set out for our inspection the enormous scribal capacity of the Franciscan and Dominican orders in the thirteenth and fourteenth centuries, and the impressive potential numbers both of mendicant copyists and manuscripts extant in 1500. It is healthy to be forced to reappraise (and here Alexandra Walsham joins David d'Avray in such prompting) the retrospective confidence of John Foxe and others in the providential invention of the art of printing to accomplish changes in the Church. Given the need to take proper account of so many factors, including the differing doctrinal challenges and ecclesiastical and political scenes, this is clearly not a question that can be confined to a few pages. We have to consider the content as well as format of texts circulated in different heretical circles, and the explanations for the Nicodemism that in the fifteenth century enabled Lollards as well as Waldensians to combine outward conformity with domestic continuity of their beliefs.[35] The text-exchanges between old and new heretics are revealing. On one hand there is the well-known case of the hopeful Lollards of 1526 offering 'old bookes' of gospels and epistles to new-style reformers who rebuffed them with the comparison of the newly printed New Testament 'of more cleyner

---

[33] I. Rivers, *The Defence of Truth through the Knowledge of Error: Philip Doddridge's Academy Lectures*, Friends of Dr Williams's Library Fifty-Sixth Lecture (Dr Williams's Trust, 2003), p. 17. I am most grateful to the author for sending information before publication.
[34] Above p. 139.
[35] On Reformation Nicodemism, see Freeman, above p. 245, n. 54.

Englishe'.[36] On the other hand we have the meeting of 1530 at which Waldensians from the Alps interrogated Oecolampadius in Basel, resulting in the former reporting essential agreement on matters of faith; the only difference being that 'we have not grasped the sense of Scripture as correctly as you'.[37]

When comparing script and print it is essential to bear in mind questions of speed as well as numbers. If nothing could match or overtake the spread of speech or letter rushed on the galloping horse, the message that the courier carried in his pouch was obviously going to be put on paper or parchment by the racing pen many times faster than could ever be equalled by a team of typesetters. Bills or single-sheet posters (like those of sixteenth-century Protestants as well as earlier Lollards) could be prepared and distributed to several places at once much more quickly by dictating to a team of scribes than resorting to the typesetter's office.[38] But the numbers that could be simultaneously produced against the clock depended on length of text and the incalculable ability to collect a group of scribes together. To be sure, printing offered the opportunity to produce multiple copies of exact messages, but it by no means followed that as a result more copies of particular texts rapidly reached more hands. If we are usually left guessing the exact numbers of any edition, printers themselves had to guess the likely take-up of their product.[39] So we are also left guessing the potential capacity of scribes to have done for Luther what they did for medieval sermon production – or for heretics. If in the fifteenth century Vespasiano da Bisticci accomplished the feat of getting forty-five scribes to produce 200 volumes for Cosimo de' Medici in twenty-two months, how many scribes would it have taken to produce the estimated 300,000 copies of Luther's thirty publications printed between 1517 and 1520? Whatever we make of that, it still leaves open the other historical 'if' in this hypothetical equation of what might have happened had (for example) Frederick the Wise stifled Luther in the Wartburg or Mary Tudor succeeded Henry VIII instead of Edward VI.

That printing could and did play a critical role in politics, to the extent of promoting and profoundly affecting revolutionary causes was proved in

---

[36] J. Strype, *Ecclesiastical Memorials*, vol. i. ii (Oxford, 1822), pp. 54–5; Aston, *Lollards and Reformers*, p. 231.

[37] M. Lambert, *Medieval Heresy: Popular Movements from the Gregorian Reform to the Reformation*, 3rd edn (Oxford, 2002), pp. 384, 389, 396–7.

[38] A point made at the conference by Elisabeth Leedham-Green. See Walsham above p. 215 for sixteenth-century handwritten bills.

[39] Above pp. 112, 195.

the English Civil War. Popular use of print reached unparalleled levels in the 1640s, and the textuality of a dividing nation was manifested in numerous forms from the petitions presented to Parliament or the Protestations displayed in the hats and girdles of Kentishmen riding into London, to the king's printed declaration distributed among his followers at a gathering in Yorkshire in 1642.[40] Most important of all was what happened in parliament. When the Long Parliament met, Parliament had no access to the printing press. In the course of one year that changed dramatically. In 1641 the course of events was transformed by a series of publications, starting with the order of the House of Commons on 5 May for printing the Preamble and Protestation they had made two days before. This document, with its oath of support for 'the true reformed Protestant religion', and opposition to 'popish innovation', was printed in 11,000 copies for members to send into the country. In 1642 Parliamentarians regarded it as effectively justifying the resort to arms, and the square paper of this text was displayed, banner-like, spiked on the pikes of the armed men escorting the Commons to Westminster.[41] On more than one occasion the country was moved a step further towards Civil War by the unilateral action of the House of Commons, ordering the printing of documents that took their challenging policies directly into local parishes. On 8 September the *Order by the Commons against innovations in religion*, which directly challenged the policy of the upper House, and the validity of which proved contentious among the Commons themselves, was printed in 4,275 copies, despite the protest of some members. Both these publications (copies of which were to be sent by knights and burgesses into their localities) seem to have advanced parliament's case in dangerously destructive ways, and the former, publicised and binding individuals to a printed oath, has been seen as playing a major role in forging popular support for parliament. The latter measure was itself deeply divisive and enough to cause some people seriously to reconsider

[40] N. Wallington, *Historical Notices of Events Occurring Chiefly in the Reign of Charles I*, 2 vols. (1869), vol. II, pp. 9, 71–2.

[41] S. Lambert (ed.), *Printing for Parliament, 1641–1700*, List and Index Society 20 (1984), pp. i, 1, 7: F. S. Siebert, *Freedom of the Press in England 1476–1776* (Urbana, 1965), pp. 180–91; C. Russell, *The Fall of the British Monarchies 1637–1642* (Oxford, 1991), pp. 294–5, 452. The text of the *Preamble with the Protestation* (BL 112 f. 43/2), the two parts clearly defined with separate headings (not shown in S. R. Gardiner's *Constitutional Documents of the Puritan Revolution* (Oxford, 1951), pp. 155–6) measures about 10 × 7$\frac{1}{2}$ inches, fitting the description of its being 'like a little square banner' (Russell, *Fall of British Monarchies*, p. 452). I am indebted to John Walter's insights on the importance of the Protestation; see his *Understanding Popular Violence in the English Revolution* (Cambridge, 1999), p. 292 ff.

their position.[42] By mid-December 1641 Parliament's hold on the plenitude of print, grasped by some as the readiest means to 'satisfie the whole kingdom', kept the House in session into the hours of darkness, vehemently debating whether or not the Grand Remonstrance should be printed. The majority, urging 'order it, order it' won, resulting in the printing of at least eleven editions of this massive list of grievances.[43] The medium of print enabled the House of Commons to overrule the wishes of the Lords and to implement in parish and shire policies that led to iconoclasm and the resort to arms.

Perusing the chapters in this book should stimulate readers to rethink some accepted assumptions. If we all suffer from the prejudices (and imbalanced perceptions) of half a millennium of print culture, today's incipient emergence from ancient intellectual deference to the primacy of print offers new opportunities for reassessment. The linked arguments encountered in these chapters must make us more conscious of the mutuality of exchange that operated in the early modern period between the spoken, handwritten and printed, something that existed in the learned Latin world as well as in the sphere of popular print and the vernacular. Speaking and singing, reading, writing and reciting, looking at texts on walls and in books, half hearing, half understanding, rereading and rewriting, set the scripts and books of the seventeenth century, like those of the fourteenth, in multi-layered communications of eyes and ears. Drawing dividing lines seems as difficult as drawing a perfect circle. But there is undoubtedly satisfaction in a collation that becomes more whole even as we digest its parts.

---

[42] Lambert, *Printing for Parliament*, pp. 2, 7; W. A. Shaw, *A History of the English Church . . . 1640–1660*, 2 vols. (1900), vol. I, pp. 107–9; W. H. Coates (ed.), *The Journal of Sir Simonds D'Ewes* (New Haven, 1942), pp. 66, 78, 79, 81, 187; *Journals of the House of Commons*, II, pp. 132–3, 135, 279, 280, 283, 389; T. Cooper (ed.), *The Journal of William Dowsing* (Woodbridge, 2001), pp. 340–41, M. Aston, *England's Iconoclasts* (Oxford, 1988), pp. 75–6, n. 32.

[43] Coates (ed.), *D'Ewes Journal*, pp. 294–5, describing this tense debate, shows that there was a substantial opposition of over a third of those voting; Lambert, *Printing for Parliament*, p. 4; Gardiner, *Constitutional Documents*, pp. 202–32 (lacking the peroration as Lambert points out); Thomason Tracts E 181/2. *A Remonstrance of the State of the Kingdom* proclaims on its title-page the Commons' resolution of 15 December 1641 that it should be printed: 'It is this day Resolv'd upon the Question, By the House of Commons, That Order shall now be given for the Printing of the Remonstrance'.

Index